GLENCOE

Grammar
AND
Composition
Handbook

HIGH SCHOOL 1

 Glencoe
McGraw-Hill

New York, New York
Columbus, Ohio
Woodland Hills, California
Peoria, Illinois

Printed in the United States of America.

Send all inquiries to:
Glencoe/McGraw-Hill
8787 Orion Place
Columbus, Ohio 43240

ISBN 0-02-817551-4 (Student Edition)
Language Arts Grammar and Composition Handbook, High School 1

4 5 6 7 8 9 10   026   04 03 02 01 00

Table of Contents at a Glance

Table of Contents

Chapter 20   Accessing Electronic Resources

Table of Contents

Part One

● ● ● ● ● ● ● ● ● ● ● ● ● ● ●

Ready Reference

The **Ready Reference** consists of three parts. The **Glossary of Terms** is a quick reference to language arts terms, defined and cross-referenced to relevant lessons. The **Usage Glossary** lists pairs of words that are easily confused and provides explanation for the correct usage of each word. The third part is **Abbreviations,** which consists of lists of many commonly used abbreviations.

GLOSSARY OF TERMS

abbreviation An abbreviation is a shortened form of a word. Most abbreviations have periods. If you are unsure of how to write an abbreviation, consult a dictionary (pages 82, 353).

EXAMPLE Gerry left at 8:00 A.M.

EXAMPLE Did she really leave at 8:00 A.M.?

abstract noun An abstract noun names an idea, a quality, or a characteristic (page 95). *See concrete noun.*

EXAMPLES attitude dignity loyalty sadness temperature

action verb An action verb tells what someone or something does. Some action verbs express physical action. Others express mental action (page 106).

EXAMPLE Ted **waved** the signal flag. **[physical action]**

EXAMPLE He **hoped** for success. **[mental action]**

active voice An action verb is in the active voice when the subject of the sentence performs the action (page 208). *See passive voice.*

EXAMPLE The brown bear **caught** a salmon.

adjective An adjective is a word that modifies a noun or a pronoun by limiting its meaning. An adjective tells *what kind, which one, how many,* or *how much* (page 110).

EXAMPLES

interesting poem	**romantic** story	**many** novels
these ideas	**Irish** ballad	**cracked** pitcher
enough plates	**second** time	**no** excuse
afternoon class	**cheese** sandwich	**football** game

adjective clause An adjective clause is a subordinate clause that modifies a noun or a pronoun. An adjective clause may begin with a relative pronoun *(who, whom, whose, that,* or *which)* or the word *where* or *when.* An adjective clause normally follows the word it modifies (page 167).

EXAMPLE   Magazines **that inform and entertain** are my favorites. [The adjective clause tells *what kind* and modifies *Magazines.*]

adjective phrase An adjective phrase is a prepositional phrase that modifies a noun or a pronoun (page 147).

EXAMPLE   Tim chose the sandwich **with cheese.** [adjective phrase modifying a noun]

adverb An adverb is a word that modifies a verb, an adjective, or another adverb (page 114).

EXAMPLES

modifying verbs   **Never** swim alone.
                       verb

                       He has **seldom** complained.
                       verb   verb

modifying adjectives   The movie was **very** scary and **too** long.
                       adjective   adjective

modifying adverbs   She **almost** always waited **quite** patiently.
                       adverb   adverb

EXAMPLES   When?   It should arrive **Saturday.**
            Where?   Leave your coat **there.**
            How?   He stacked the books **neatly.**
            To what degree?   We were **very** sorry.

Glossary of Terms   **5**

adverb clause An adverb clause is a subordinate clause that modifies a verb, an adjective, or another adverb in the main clause. It tells *when, where, how, why, to what extent,* or *under what conditions* (page 168).

EXAMPLE **Before I took the test,** I studied for hours. **[The adverb clause tells *when* and modifies the verb *studied*.]**

adverb phrase An adverb phrase is a prepositional phrase that modifies a verb, an adjective, or another adverb (page 148).

EXAMPLE Andy works well **under pressure. [adverb phrase modifying the adverb *well*.]**

agreement Agreement is the match between grammatical forms. A verb must agree with its subject (page 215). A pronoun must agree with its antecedent (page 242).

EXAMPLE The **freshmen** and **sophomores are debating** today. **[subject-verb agreement]**

EXAMPLE **Lissa** thanked **her** brother for driving **her** to the dance. **[pronoun-antecedent agreement]**

antecedent An antecedent is the word or group of words to which a pronoun refers or that a pronoun replaces. All pronouns must agree with their antecedents in number, gender, and person (page 242).

EXAMPLE *Octavio Paz* is one of the greatest poets of **his** era. **[singular masculine pronoun]**

EXAMPLE *Emily Dickinson* wrote **her** poems on scrap paper. **[singular feminine pronoun]**

EXAMPLE *Walt Whitman* and *Emily Dickinson* are famous for **their** poetry. **[plural pronoun]**

apostrophe An apostrophe (') is a punctuation mark used in possessive nouns, possessive indefinite pronouns, and contractions. In contractions it shows that one or more letters have been left out (page 346).

EXAMPLE Leon didn't bring Celia's book, so she needs to borrow someone's.

appositive An appositive is a noun or a pronoun that is placed next to another noun or pronoun to identify it or give additional information about it (page 149).

EXAMPLE My friend **Ethan** works at a bookstore after school. **[The appositive *Ethan* identifies the noun *friend*.]**

appositive phrase An appositive phrase is an appositive plus any words that modify the appositive (page 149).

EXAMPLE He is saving money to travel to Bogotá, **the capital of Colombia. [The appositive phrase, in blue type, identifies *Bogotá*.]**

article Articles are the adjectives *a, an,* and *the. A* and *an* are called **indefinite articles**. They can refer to any one of a kind of person, place, or thing. *A* is used before consonant sounds, and *an* is used before vowel sounds. *The* is the **definite article**. It refers to a specific person, place, or thing (page 113).

EXAMPLES

indefinite **a** ring, **a** used computer, **an** egg, **an** hour

definite **the** ring, **the** used computer, **the** egg, **the** hour

auxiliary verb The most common auxiliary verbs are forms of *be* and *have*. They help the main verb express time by forming the various tenses (page 108).

EXAMPLE We **will** weed the vegetable garden this morning.

EXAMPLE Sandra **has** already weeded the peppers and the tomatoes.

EXAMPLE We **were** weeding the flower beds when the rain started.

The other auxiliary verbs are not used primarily to express time. They are often used to emphasize meaning.

EXAMPLE I **should be** leaving.

EXAMPLE **Could** he **have** forgotten?

EXAMPLE Marisa **may** already **be** finished.

case Personal pronouns have three cases, or forms. The three cases are called **nominative, objective,** and **possessive.** The case of a personal pronoun depends on the pronoun's function in a sentence—that is, whether it's a subject, a complement, an object of a preposition, or a replacement for a possessive noun (page 233).

| | **PERSONAL PRONOUNS** | | |
CASE	**SINGULAR PRONOUNS**	**PLURAL PRONOUNS**	**FUNCTION IN SENTENCE**
nominative	I, you, she, he, it	we, you, they	subject or predicate nominative
objective	me, you, her, him, it	us, you, them	direct object, indirect object, or object of preposition
possessive	my, mine, your, yours, her, hers, his, its	our, ours, your, yours, their, theirs	replacement for possessive noun(s)

clause A clause is a group of words that has a subject and a predicate (verb). A clause can function as a sentence by itself or as part of a sentence (page 164).

EXAMPLE The curtain rose.

closing A closing is a way to end a letter. It begins with a capital letter and is followed by a comma (pages 295, 331).

EXAMPLES Yours truly,   Sincerely,
          Affectionately,   Your friend,

collective noun A collective noun is singular in form but names a group (pages 97, 220).

EXAMPLES family   herd   company   band   team
          audience troop   committee   jury   flock

colon A colon (:) is a punctuation mark. It's used to introduce a list and to separate the hour and the minutes when you write the time of day. It's also used after the salutation of a business letter (page 316).

EXAMPLE We need these ingredients: milk, eggs, and raisins.

EXAMPLE The race will start at exactly 2:15 P.M.

EXAMPLE Dear Senator Mathers:

comma A comma (,) is a punctuation mark that's used to separate items or to set them off from the rest of a sentence (page 320).

EXAMPLE You'll find spoons, forks, and knives in that drawer.

EXAMPLE The clowns, who had crammed themselves into the tiny car, all jumped out at once.

comma splice One type of run-on sentence, a comma splice, occurs when two main clauses are joined by a comma only (page 178).

EXAMPLES

comma splice	It rained the entire time the boys were on vacation, they still enjoyed the trip.
correct	It rained the entire time the boys were on vacation. They still enjoyed the trip.
correct	It rained the entire time the boys were on vacation, but they still enjoyed the trip.
correct	It rained the entire time the boys were on vacation; they still enjoyed the trip.

common noun A common noun is the general—not the particular—name of a person, place, thing, or idea (page 96). *See proper noun.*

EXAMPLES

person	artist, uncle, poet
place	country, lake, park
thing	shuttle, vehicle, play
idea	era, religion, movement

comparative degree The comparative degree of an adjective or adverb is the form that shows two things being compared (page 256).

EXAMPLE Kim's dog is **smaller** than my dog. **[adjective]**

EXAMPLE My dog ran **more swiftly** than the cat. **[adverb]**

complement A complement is a word or a group of words that completes the meaning of a verb (page 137). *See also direct objects, indirect objects,* and *subject complements (predicate nominatives* and *predicate adjectives).*

EXAMPLE Carlos served **dinner.**

EXAMPLE Maria admires **him** deeply.

complete predicate The complete predicate consists of the simple predicate, or verb, and all the words that modify it or complete its meaning (page 132).

EXAMPLE The team **will be going from Illinois to Rhode Island by way of Cedar Point in Sandusky, Ohio.**

complete subject The complete subject consists of the simple subject and all the words that modify it (page 132).

EXAMPLE **The small black kitten in the top cage** is the one for me.

complex sentence A complex sentence has one main clause and one or more subordinate clauses (page 174).

Main Clause

EXAMPLE I like Toni Cade Bambara's stories
S V

Subordinate Clause

Subordinate
Clause

because they have characters I can believe in.
S V S V V

Subordinate Clause　　Main Clause

EXAMPLE When I read her stories, I enjoy them
S V S V

Subordinate Clause

because they are realistic.
S V

compound-complex sentence A compound-complex sentence has two or more main clauses and at least one subordinate clause (page 175).

Main Clause　　　　Subordinate Clause

EXAMPLE I read *Frankenstein,* which Mary Shelley wrote,
S V S S V

Main Clause

and I reported on it.
S V

compound predicate A compound predicate (or compound verb) is made up of two or more verbs or verb phrases that are joined by a conjunction and have the same subject (page 134).

EXAMPLE Maria **opened** her book, **grabbed** a pencil, and **started** her homework.

EXAMPLE Seagulls **will glide** or **swoop** down to the ocean.

compound preposition A compound preposition is a preposition that is made up of more than one word (page 119).

EXAMPLES

according to	because of	next to
ahead of	by means of	instead of
along with	except for	on account of

compound sentence A compound sentence contains two or more main clauses (page 173).

EXAMPLE
Main Clause
Stories about the Old West are entertaining, **and**
S   V   V

Main Clause
stories set in foreign countries are interesting.
S   V   V

EXAMPLE
Main Clause   Main Clause
Stories entertain me, **and** riddles amuse me, **but**
S   V   S   V

Main Clause
poems are my favorite.
S   V

EXAMPLE
Main Clause   Main Clause
Comedies delight us; tragedies often teach us something.
S   V   S   V

compound subject A compound subject is made up of two or more simple subjects that are joined by a conjunction and have the same verb (page 133).

EXAMPLE **Tomatoes** and **carrots** are colorful vegetables.

EXAMPLE **Tomatoes** or **carrots** would add color to the salad.

EXAMPLE **Tomatoes, carrots,** and **peppers** are healthful.

compound verb *See compound predicate.*

concrete noun A concrete noun names an object that occupies space or can be recognized by any of the senses (sight, smell, hearing, taste, and touch) (page 95). *See abstract noun.*

EXAMPLES air melody stone aroma heat

conjunction A conjunction is a word that joins single words or groups of words (page 120). *See coordinating conjunction, correlative conjunction, and subordinating conjunction.*

conjunctive adverb A conjunctive adverb is used to clarify the relationship between clauses of equal weight in a sentence. Conjunctive adverbs are preceded by semicolons and followed by commas (page 123).

EXAMPLES

to replace *and*	also, besides, furthermore, moreover
to replace *but*	however, nevertheless, nonetheless, still, though
to state a result	accordingly, consequently, then, therefore, thus
to state equality	equally, indeed, likewise, similarly

EXAMPLE Janine is not very organized**; accordingly,** she carries a day planner and consults it often.

contraction A contraction is a single word made up of two words that have been combined by omitting letters. Common contractions combine a subject and a verb or a verb and the word *not* (page 348).

EXAMPLES	you'd	*is formed from*	you had, you would
	you're		you are
	who's		who is, who has

coordinating conjunction A coordinating conjunction joins words or groups of words that have equal grammatical weight in a sentence (page 120).

and   but   or   so   nor   yet   for

EXAMPLE   One **and** six are seven. **[two nouns]**

EXAMPLE   Merlin was smart **but** irresponsible. **[two adjectives]**

EXAMPLE   Let's put the note on the TV **or** on the refrigerator.
[two prepositional phrases]

EXAMPLE   I wanted a new sun hat, **so** I bought one.
[two complete thoughts]

EXAMPLE   He did not complain, **nor** did he object to our plan.
[two complete thoughts]

EXAMPLE   Lightning struck the barn, **yet** no fire started.
[two complete thoughts]

EXAMPLE   We didn't explore the summit that night, **for** the climb
had exhausted us. **[two complete thoughts]**

correlative conjunction Correlative conjunctions work in pairs to join words and groups of words of equal grammatical weight in a sentence (page 121).

both . . . and   just as . . . so   not only . . . but (also)
either . . . or   neither . . . nor   whether . . . or

EXAMPLE   **Both** he **and** I were there.

EXAMPLE   **Either** she will sew new curtains, **or** I will put up
the old blinds.

EXAMPLE   I **not only** scrubbed **but also** waxed the floor.

dangling modifier Dangling modifiers seem logically to modify no word at all. To correct a sentence that has a dangling modifier, you must supply a word that the dangling modifier can sensibly modify (page 269).

EXAMPLES

dangling   **Working all night long,** the fire was extinguished. **[participial phrase logically modifying no word in the sentence]**

clear   **Working all night long,** the firefighters extinguished the fire. **[participial phrase modifying *firefighters*]**

dangling   **Sleeping soundly,** my dream was interrupted by the alarm. **[participial phrase logically modifying no word in the sentence]**

clear   **Sleeping soundly,** I had my dream interrupted by the alarm. **[participial phrase modifying *I*]**

dash A dash (—) is a punctuation mark. It's usually used in pairs to set off a sudden break or change in thought or speech (page 334).

EXAMPLE   Lionel Washington—he was my Boy Scout troop leader—is running for city council.

declarative sentence A declarative sentence makes a statement. A declarative sentence usually ends with a period but can end with an exclamation mark. This type of sentence is the most frequently used in speaking and writing (page 171).

EXAMPLE   I have four pets.

EXAMPLE   Two of my pets are dogs.

EXAMPLE   That's the cutest puppy I've ever seen!

demonstrative adjective A demonstrative adjective modifies a noun and points out something by answering the question *which one?* or *which ones? This, that, these,* and *those* are demonstrative adjectives when they modify nouns (page 110).

EXAMPLE   Bring **this** ticket with you; give **that** ticket to a friend.

EXAMPLE   We need **these** props; **those** props can be stored.

demonstrative pronoun A demonstrative pronoun points out specific persons, places, things, or ideas (page 102).

DEMONSTRATIVE PRONOUNS

singular	This	That
plural	These	Those

EXAMPLE   Bring **this** with you.

EXAMPLE   Give **that** to a friend.

EXAMPLE   We'll need **these** for the show.

EXAMPLE   The director wrote **those.**

dependent clause *See subordinate clause.*

direct address Direct address is a name, a word, or a phrase used in speaking directly to a person. Words used in direct address are set off by commas (page 330).

EXAMPLE   **Christie,** do you like my haircut?

EXAMPLE   You can't park here, **buddy.**

EXAMPLE   I am very proud of you, **Daughter,** and I want you to know it.

direct object A direct object answers the question *what?* or *whom?* after an action verb (page 138).

EXAMPLE   Carlos served **dinner.**

Carlos served a Japanese **dinner** and a fabulous **dessert.**

EXAMPLE Paula called **Carlos** on the telephone.

direct quotation A direct quotation gives the speaker's exact words. It is preceded and followed by quotation marks (page 294).

EXAMPLE My little brother asked, **"Why can't I go too?"**

double comparison Don't use both *-er* and *more*. Don't use both *-est* and *most*. To do so would be an error called a double comparison (page 260).

EXAMPLES

incorrect A redwood grows more taller than an oak.

correct A redwood grows **taller** than an oak.

incorrect Aunt Ellie is my most kindest aunt.

correct Aunt Ellie is my **kindest** aunt.

double negative A double negative is the use of two or more negative words to express the same idea. Use only one negative word to express a negative idea (page 266).

EXAMPLES

incorrect I don't have no stereo equipment.

correct I do**n't** have **any** stereo equipment.

correct I have **no** stereo equipment.

incorrect We haven't seen no concerts this year.

correct We have**n't** seen **any** concerts this year.

correct We have seen **no** concerts this year.

emphatic forms of a verb The present tense and the past tense have additional forms, called emphatic forms, that

Glossary of Terms **17**

add special force, or emphasis, to the verb. You make the emphatic forms by using *do, does,* or *did* with the base form of the verb (page 205).

EXAMPLES

present emphatic	I **do hope** the train is on time.
	Tom **does have** a plane to catch.
past emphatic	He **did miss** his plane the last time because of a late train.

end mark An end mark is a punctuation mark used at the end of a sentence. Periods, question marks, and exclamation points are end marks (pages 314–315).

EXAMPLE   Here is your clean laundry.

EXAMPLE   Did you forget your jacket?

EXAMPLE   What a gorgeous salad that is!

essential clause Some adjective clauses are necessary to make the meaning of a sentence clear. Such an adjective clause is called an *essential clause,* or a *restrictive clause.* Do not set off an essential clause with commas (page 167).

EXAMPLE   Magazines **that have no substance** bore me.

EXAMPLE   Many writers **whose works have become famous** began their writing careers at the *New Yorker* magazine.

exclamation point An exclamation point (!) is a punctuation mark used to end a sentence that shows strong feeling (exclamatory). It's also used after strong interjections (page 314).

EXAMPLE   Yikes! We'll be late!

exclamatory sentence An exclamatory sentence expresses strong emotion and ends with an exclamation point. Note that exclamatory sentences can be declarative (first example), imperative (second example), or interrogative (third example) while expressing strong emotion. In writing, exclamatory sentences should be used sparingly so as not to detract from their effectiveness (page 171).

EXAMPLE   She is such a beautiful dog!

EXAMPLE   Don't chew on that!

EXAMPLE   What do you think you are doing!

future perfect tense Use the future perfect tense to express one future action or condition that will begin *and* end before another future event starts.

You form the future perfect tense by using *will have* or *shall have* with the past participle of a verb: *will have practiced, shall have flown* (page 202).

EXAMPLE   By September I **will have saved** fifty dollars.
           [The money will be saved by the time another future event, the arrival of September, occurs.]

future tense Use the future tense to express an action or a condition that will occur in the future (pages 198–199).

EXAMPLE   Robby **will order** the supplies.

EXAMPLE   I **will pack** the car in the morning.

gender The gender of a noun may be masculine (male), feminine (female), or neuter (referring to things) (page 242).

EXAMPLES **man** (masculine)   **aunt** (feminine)   **notebook** (neuter)

gender-neutral language Language that does not assume the gender of a noun is called gender-neutral language. Use gender-neutral language when the gender is unknown or could be either masculine or feminine (pages 243, 444).

EXAMPLE   An *author* must capture **his or her** readers' interest.

EXAMPLE   *Authors* must capture **their** readers' interest.

EXAMPLE   *Authors* must capture readers' interest.

gerund   A gerund is a verb form that ends in *-ing* and is used in the same ways a noun is used (page 153).

EXAMPLE   **Cooking** is an enjoyable activity. **[gerund as subject]**

EXAMPLE   My younger sister likes **swimming.** **[gerund as direct object]**

gerund phrase   A gerund phrase contains a gerund plus any complements and modifiers (page 153).

EXAMPLE   **Cross-country skiing** is good exercise.

EXAMPLE   **Billie Holiday's soulful singing** delighted many audiences.

helping verb   *See auxiliary verb.*

hyphen   A hyphen (-) is a punctuation mark that's used in compound words (page 349).

EXAMPLE   Luis's great-grandfather hung twenty-one bird feeders.

By permission of Mell Lazarus and Creators Syndicate.

imperative sentence An imperative sentence gives a command or makes a request. An imperative sentence usually ends with a period but can end with an exclamation mark. In imperative sentences, the subject *you* is understood (page 171).

EXAMPLE Get off the table.

EXAMPLE Duck!

indefinite pronoun An indefinite pronoun refers to persons, places, things, or ideas in a more general way than a noun does (page 104).

INDEFINITE PRONOUNS

always singular	another	either	neither	other
	anybody	everybody	no one	somebody
	anyone	everyone	nobody	someone
	anything	everything	nothing	something
	each	much	one	
always plural	both	few	many	
	others	several		
singular or plural	all	any	enough	most
	none	some		

EXAMPLE **Everybody** needs food. [The indefinite pronoun *everybody* refers to people in general.]

EXAMPLE Did you get **enough** to eat? [The indefinite pronoun *enough* refers to a general, not a specific, amount.]

EXAMPLE After two bowls of chili, I did not want **another.** [The indefinite pronoun *another* has the antecedent *bowls (of chili)*.]

independent clause An independent clause has a subject and a predicate and expresses a complete thought. It is the only type of clause that can stand alone as a sentence. An independent clause is also called a main clause (page 164).

EXAMPLE   **The curtain rose.**

EXAMPLE   **The cast bowed,** and **the audience applauded.**

indirect object   An indirect object answers the question *to whom? for whom? to what?* or *for what?* after an action verb (page 138).

EXAMPLE   Tyrone served his **sisters** dinner.

indirect quotation   An indirect quotation paraphrases a speaker's words and should not be capitalized or enclosed in quotation marks (page 294). *See direct quotation.*

EXAMPLE   My brother asked why he couldn't go.

infinitive   An infinitive is a verb form that is usually preceded by the word *to* and is used as a noun, an adjective, or an adverb (page 154).

EXAMPLE   His goal is **to graduate.** [infinitive as predicate nominative]

EXAMPLE   They have the desire **to win.** [infinitive as adjective]

infinitive phrase   An infinitive phrase contains an infinitive plus any complements and modifiers (page 155).

EXAMPLE   We stopped **to look at the beautiful scenery.**

EXAMPLE   **To be a good friend** is my goal.

intensive pronoun   An intensive pronoun ends with *-self* or *-selves* and is used to draw special attention to a noun or a pronoun already named (pages 102, 239).

EXAMPLE   He **himself** delivered the flowers.

EXAMPLE   You must sign the application **yourself.**

interjection   An interjection is a word or phrase that expresses emotion or exclamation. An interjection has no grammatical connection to other words (page 125).

EXAMPLE **Oh, my!** What is that?

EXAMPLE **Ouch,** it's hot!

interrogative pronoun An interrogative pronoun is used to form questions (page 103).

who	whom	what	which	whose
whoever	whomever	whatever	whichever	

EXAMPLE **Who** is at the door?

EXAMPLE **Whom** would you prefer?

EXAMPLE **Whose** is this plaid coat?

EXAMPLE **Whatever** is that odd noise?

interrogative sentence An interrogative sentence asks a question. It usually ends with a question mark but can end with an exclamation point if it expresses strong emotion (page 171).

EXAMPLE How many pets do you have**?**

EXAMPLE What in the world were you thinking**!**

intransitive verb An intransitive verb is *not* followed by a word that answers the question *what?* or *whom?* (page 106). *See transitive verb.*

EXAMPLE The batter **swung** wildly. **[The verb is followed by a word that tells *how*.]**

inverted order A sentence written in inverted order, in which the predicate comes before the subject, serves to add emphasis to the subject (pages 136, 225).

EXAMPLES

PREDICATE	SUBJECT
Across the field **galloped**	the three **horses.**
In the distance **flowed**	a **river.**

Glossary of Terms   **23**

irregular verb An irregular verb forms its past and past participle in some way other than by adding *-ed* or *-d* to the base form (page 189).

EXAMPLES

BASE FORM	PAST FORM	PAST PARTICIPLE
be, am, are, is	was, were	been
swim	swam	swum
put	put	put
write	wrote	written
lie	lay	lain

italics Italics are printed letters that slant to the right. *This sentence is printed in italic type.* Italics are used for the titles of certain kinds of published works, works of art, foreign terms, and other situations. In handwriting, underlining is a substitute for italics (page 343).

EXAMPLE   This ***Newsweek*** magazine has an article about Picasso's painting ***Guernica.***

EXAMPLE   Cicero's saying ***Omnia praeclara rara*** can be translated as "All excellent things are scarce."

linking verb A linking verb links, or joins, the subject of a sentence (often a noun or a pronoun) with a noun, a pronoun, or an adjective that identifies or describes the subject. A linking verb does not show action. *Be* in all its forms—*am, is, are, was, were*—is the most commonly used linking verb (page 108).

EXAMPLE   The person behind the mask **was** you.

EXAMPLE   The players **are** ready.

EXAMPLE   Archery **is** an outdoor sport.

EXAMPLE   They **were** sports fans.

Several other verbs besides *be* can act as linking verbs.

OTHER VERBS THAT CAN BE LINKING VERBS

appear	grow	seem	stay
become	look	sound	taste
feel	remain	smell	turn

EXAMPLE   This salad **tastes** good.

EXAMPLE   The sun **feels** warm on my shoulders.

EXAMPLE   You **look** comfortable.

EXAMPLE   The leaves **turned** brown.

main clause A main clause has a subject and a predicate and expresses a complete thought. It is the only type of clause that can stand alone as a sentence. A main clause is also called an **independent clause** (page 164).

EXAMPLE   **The curtain rose.**

EXAMPLE   **The cast bowed,** and **the audience applauded.**

EXAMPLE   **The curtains closed for several minutes,** but **the applause continued.**

main verb A main verb is the last word in a verb phrase. If a verb stands alone, it's a main verb (page 108).

EXAMPLE   The band members have been **selling** light bulbs for a month.

EXAMPLE   One band member **sold** two cases of light bulbs.

misplaced modifier Misplaced modifiers modify the wrong word, or they seem to modify more than one word in a sentence. To correct a sentence that has a misplaced modifier, move the modifier as close as possible to the word it modifies (page 267).

misplaced	**Soaring over the edge of the cliff,** the photographer captured an image of the eagle. **[participial phrase incorrectly modifying *photographer*]**
clear	The photographer captured an image of the eagle **soaring over the edge of the cliff. [participial phrase correctly modifying *eagle*]**

nominative case Use the nominative case for a pronoun that is a subject or a predicate nominative (page 233).

EXAMPLE **We** have raised enough money.

EXAMPLE The lead soprano will be **she.**

nonessential clause An adjective clause that adds information to a sentence but is not necessary to make the meaning of the sentence clear is called a *nonessential clause* or a *nonrestrictive clause.* Always use commas to set off a nonessential clause (pages 168, 324).

EXAMPLE James Thurber, **who was a famous humorist,** wrote for the *New Yorker.*

EXAMPLE His stories, **which include humorous incidents from his childhood in Ohio,** make funny and interesting reading.

nonrestrictive clause *See nonessential clause.*

noun A noun is a word that names a person, a place, a thing, or an idea (page 93).

EXAMPLES

person	uncle, doctor, baby, Luisa, son-in-law
place	kitchen, mountain, website, West Virginia

thing	apple, tulip, continent, seagull, amplifier
idea	respect, pride, love, appreciation, century

noun clause A noun clause is a subordinate clause that is used as a noun within the main clause of a sentence. You can use a noun clause as a subject, a direct object, an indirect object, an object of a preposition, or a predicate nominative (page 169).

EXAMPLE **Whoever wins the election** will speak. **[noun clause as subject]**

number Number refers to the form of a word that indicates whether it is singular or plural. A verb must agree with its subject in number (page 215).

	SINGULAR	PLURAL
EXAMPLE	The **athlete exercises.**	The **athletes exercise.**
EXAMPLE	The **cat scratches.**	The **cats scratch.**

object complement An object complement answers the question *what?* after a direct object. That is, it *completes* the meaning of the direct object by identifying or describing it (page 139).

EXAMPLE Residents find the park **peaceful.** **[adjective]**

EXAMPLE Maya appointed me **spokesperson** and **treasurer.** **[nouns]**

EXAMPLE My grandmother considers the property **hers.** **[pronoun]**

object of a preposition An object of a preposition is the noun or pronoun that ends a prepositional phrase (page 118).

EXAMPLE The diamonds in the **vault** are priceless. **[*In* shows the relationship between the diamonds and the object of the preposition, *vault*.]**

objective case Use the objective case for a pronoun that is a direct object, an indirect object, or an object of a preposition (pages 233–234).

EXAMPLE   The coach trained **her.** **[direct object]**

EXAMPLE   The prompter gave **me** my cues. **[indirect object]**

EXAMPLE   Third prize was split between **me** and **him.** **[object of preposition]**

parentheses Parentheses ( ) are punctuation marks used to set off words that define or explain another word (page 335).

EXAMPLE   Myanmar **(**formerly Burma**)** is on the Bay of Bengal.

parenthetical expression Parenthetical expressions are side thoughts that add information. Parenthetical expressions should be set off by commas, dashes, or parentheses (pages 326, 335–337).

EXAMPLES   in fact   on the other hand   on the contrary
           by the way   to be exact   after all

EXAMPLE   **By the way,** did Mom call today?

EXAMPLE   I'm responsible for about a hundred tickets—**to be exact,** 106.

participial phrase A participial phrase contains a participle plus any complements and modifiers (page 151).

EXAMPLE   The dog saw many ducks **swimming in the lake.**

EXAMPLE   **Barking loudly,** the dog approached the water.

participle A participle is a verb form that can function as an adjective (pages 111, 151).

EXAMPLE   A **moving** van is parked on our street. **[present participle]**

EXAMPLE   The dogs watched the **striped** cat. **[past participle]**

passive voice An action verb is in the passive voice when its action is performed on the subject (page 208). *See active voice.*

EXAMPLE   A salmon **was caught** by the brown bear.

past perfect tense Use the past perfect tense to indicate that one past action or condition began *and* ended before another past action or condition started. You form the past perfect tense by using the auxiliary verb *had* with the past participle of a verb: *had praised, had written* (page 201).

EXAMPLE

PAST   **PAST PERFECT**
Pat **dedicated** her play to the drama teacher who **had encouraged** her long ago. **[First the drama teacher encouraged Pat; then years later Patricia acknowledged her teacher's support.]**

past tense Use the past tense to express an action or a condition that was started and completed in the past (page 198).

EXAMPLE   The track meet **went** well.

EXAMPLE   Nan **set** a new school record for the shot put.

period A period (.) is a punctuation mark used to end a sentence that makes a statement (declarative) or gives a command (imperative). It's also used at the end of many abbreviations (pages 314, 353).

EXAMPLE   I can't tell whether this recipe specifies "1 tsp." or "1 tbsp." of cinnamon. **[declarative]**

EXAMPLE   Please mail a check to Dr. Benson. **[imperative]**

personal pronoun A personal pronoun refers to a specific person, place, thing, or idea by indicating the person speaking (the first person), the person being spoken to (the second person), or any other person, place, thing, or idea being discussed (the third person). Like a noun, a personal pronoun expresses number; that is, it can be singular or plural (pages 99, 233).

PERSONAL PRONOUNS

	SINGULAR	PLURAL
first person	I, me	we, us
second person	you	you
third person	he, him, she, her, it	they, them

EXAMPLES

first person	The song was dedicated to **me.** [*Me* refers to the person speaking.]
second person	Sam will copy the document for **you.** [*You* refers to the person being spoken to.]
third person	**She** gave **him** the good news. [*She* and *him* refer to the people being talked about.]

phrase A phrase is a group of words that acts in a sentence as a single part of speech (page 147).

positive degree The positive degree of an adjective or adverb is the form that cannot be used to make a comparison. This form appears as the entry word in a dictionary (page 256).

EXAMPLE My dog is **small.**

EXAMPLE The cat ran **swiftly.**

possessive pronoun A possessive pronoun takes the place of the possessive form of a noun (page 100).

POSSESSIVE PRONOUNS

	SINGULAR	PLURAL
first person	my, mine	our, ours
second person	your, yours	your, yours
third person	his, her, hers, its	their, theirs

predicate The predicate is the part of the sentence that says something about the subject (page 131).

EXAMPLE Garth Brooks **will perform.**

predicate adjective A predicate adjective follows a linking verb and points back to the subject and further describes it (page 140).

EXAMPLE   Firefighters are **brave.**

EXAMPLE   Firefighters must be extremely **careful.**

predicate nominative A predicate nominative is a noun or a pronoun that follows a linking verb and points back to the subject to rename it or to identify it further (page 140).

EXAMPLE   Sopranos are **singers.**

EXAMPLE   Many current opera stars are **Italians** or **Spaniards.**

EXAMPLE   Fiona became both a **musician** and an **architect.**

preposition A preposition is a word that shows the relation-ship of a noun or a pronoun to another word in a sentence (page 118).

| aboard | beneath | in | regarding |
| about | beside | inside | respecting |

EXAMPLE   I read **to** Carlito **from** the new book.

prepositional phrase A prepositional phrase is a group of words that begins with a preposition and ends with a noun or a pronoun that is called the object of the preposition (page 147).

EXAMPLE   The diamonds **in the vault** are priceless. **[*In* shows the relationship between the diamonds and the object of the preposition, *vault*.]**

EXAMPLE   The telephone rang four times **during dinner. [*During* shows the relationship between *rang* and the object of the preposition, *dinner*.]**

EXAMPLE   Here is a gift **for you. [*For* relates *gift* to the object of the preposition, *you*.]**

present perfect tense Use the present perfect tense to express an action or a condition that occurred at some *indefinite* *time* in the past. You form the present perfect tense by using *has* or *have* with the past participle of a verb: *has permitted, have cut* (page 200).

EXAMPLE The living-room clock **has stopped.**

EXAMPLE They **have brought** the new couch a day early.

present tense The present tense expresses a constant, repeated, or habitual action or condition. It can also express a general truth or an action or a condition that exists only now. It is sometimes used in historical writing to express past events and, more often, in poetry, fiction, and journalism (especially in sports writing) to convey to the reader a sense of being there. This usage is sometimes called the *historical present tense* (page 195).

EXAMPLE Isaac **likes** the taste of tea with honey in it. **[not just this cup of tea but every cup of tea; a repeated action]**

EXAMPLE Emily **bakes** wonderful spice cookies. **[always; a habitual action]**

EXAMPLE Gold **is** valuable. **[a general truth]**

EXAMPLE I **see** a hummingbird at the feeder. **[at this very moment]**

EXAMPLE The goalie **throws** her body across the opening and **blocks** the shot in the final seconds of the game. **[historical present]**

principal parts of verbs All verbs have four principal parts: a *base form*, a *present participle*, a *simple past form*, and a *past participle*. All the verb tenses are formed from these principal parts (page 187).

EXAMPLES

PRINCIPAL PARTS OF VERBS

BASE FORM	PRESENT PARTICIPLE	PAST FORM	PAST PARTICIPLE
play	playing	played	played
carry	carrying	carried	carried
sing	singing	sang	sung

progressive forms of a verb Each of the six tenses has a progressive form that expresses a continuing action. You make the progressive forms by using the appropriate tense of the verb *be* with the present participle of the main verb (page 204).

READY REFERENCE

EXAMPLE

present progressive	They *are* traveling.
past progressive	They *were* traveling.
future progressive	They *will be* traveling.
present perfect progressive	They *have been* traveling.
past perfect progressive	They *had been* traveling.
future perfect progressive	They *will have been* traveling.

pronoun A pronoun is a word that takes the place of a noun, a group of words acting as a noun, or another pronoun. The word or group of words to which a pronoun refers is called its antecedent (page 98).

EXAMPLE Though Georgia O'Keeffe was born in Wisconsin, **she** grew to love the landscape of the American Southwest. **[The pronoun *she* takes the place of its proper noun antecedent, *Georgia O'Keeffe*.]**

EXAMPLE When Georgia O'Keeffe and Alfred Stieglitz were married in 1924, **both** were famous artists. **[The pronoun *both* takes the place of the nouns *Georgia O'Keeffe* and *Alfred Stieglitz*.]**

EXAMPLE Though O'Keeffe **herself** was a painter, **her** husband was a photographer. **[The pronouns *herself* and *her* take the place of the nouns *O'Keeffe* and *O'Keeffe's*.]**

proper adjective A proper adjective is formed from a proper noun. It begins with a capital letter (page 113).

EXAMPLE Vancouver is a **Canadian** city.

EXAMPLE We visited the **London** Zoo.

proper noun A proper noun is the name of a particular person, place, thing, or idea (page 96). *See common noun.*

EXAMPLES

PROPER NOUNS

person	Michelangelo, Uncle Louis, Maya Angelou
place	Mexico, Lake Superior, Yellowstone National Park
thing	*Challenger*, Jeep, *Romeo and Juliet*
idea	Industrial Age, Judaism, Romanticism

question mark A question mark (**?**) is a punctuation mark used to end a sentence that asks a question (interrogative) (page 315).

EXAMPLE   Can you imagine what life would be like without television**?**

quotation marks Quotation marks (" ") are punctuation marks used to enclose the exact words of a speaker. They're also used for titles of certain published works (page 338).

EXAMPLE   "Let's record ourselves reading aloud," said Lou, "and give the tape to the children's hospital."

EXAMPLE   They decided on something a bit more cheerful than "The Pit and the Pendulum."

reflexive pronoun A reflexive pronoun always ends with *-self* or *-selves* and refers, or reflects back, to the subject of the sentence, indicating that the same person or thing is involved. A reflexive pronoun always adds information to a sentence (pages 101–102, 239).

EXAMPLE Jim uses a stopwatch to time **himself** on the track.

EXAMPLE She taught **herself** to play the piano.

EXAMPLE We imagined **ourselves** dancing in a forest glade.

regular verb A regular verb forms its past and past participle by adding *-ed* or *-d* to the base form (page 189).

EXAMPLES

REGULAR VERBS

BASE FORM	PAST FORM	PAST PARTICIPLE
climb	climbed	climbed
skate	skated	skated
trot	trotted	trotted

relative pronoun A relative pronoun is used to begin a subordinate clause (pages 103–104).

RELATIVE PRONOUNS

who	whoever	which	that
whom	whomever	whichever	what
whose	whatever		

EXAMPLE The driver **who** arrived last parked over there. [**The relative pronoun *who* begins the subordinate clause *who arrived last*.**]

EXAMPLE The meal **that** you prepared was delicious. [**The relative pronoun *that* begins the subordinate clause *that you prepared*.**]

restrictive clause *See essential clause.*

run-on sentence A run-on sentence is two or more complete sentences written as though they were one sentence (page 178). *See comma splice.*

EXAMPLE	**run-on**	It rained the entire time the boys were on vacation they still enjoyed the trip.
	run-on	It rained the entire time the boys were on vacation but they still enjoyed the trip.
	run-on	It rained the entire time the boys were on vacation, they still enjoyed the trip.
	correct	It rained the entire time the boys were on vacation. They still enjoyed the trip.
	correct	It rained the entire time the boys were on vacation, but they still enjoyed the trip.
	correct	It rained the entire time the boys were on vacation; they still enjoyed the trip.

salutation A salutation is the greeting in a letter. The first word and any proper nouns in a salutation should be capitalized. In a friendly letter, the salutation ends with a comma; in a business letter, the salutation ends with a colon (pages 295, 317, 331).

EXAMPLE My dear cousin Nancy,

Dear Councilwoman Ramos:

semicolon A semicolon (;) is a punctuation mark used to join the main clauses of a compound sentence (page 318).

EXAMPLE Juliana will sing the melody; Maurice and Lee will harmonize.

sentence A sentence is a group of words that expresses a complete thought (page 130).

EXAMPLE Hector Hugh Munro wrote stories using the pseudonym Saki.

sentence fragment A sentence fragment is an error that occurs when an incomplete sentence is punctuated as though it were complete (page 177).

EXAMPLE

fragment	**The two weary hikers walking for hours.** **[lacks complete predicate]**
complete sentence	The two weary hikers had been walking for hours.

simple predicate The simple predicate is the verb or verb phrase that expresses an action or a state of being about the subject of the sentence (page 131).

EXAMPLE   The team **will be going** from Illinois to Rhode Island by way of Cedar Point in Sandusky, Ohio.

simple sentence A simple sentence contains only one main clause and no subordinate clauses (page 172).

EXAMPLE   Stories entertain.

EXAMPLE   Long, complicated, fantastic stories with aliens, space travelers, and happy endings entertain and educate men, women, and children all over the world.

simple subject The simple subject is the key noun or pronoun (or word or word group acting as a noun) that tells what the sentence is about (page 131).

EXAMPLE   The black **kitten** in the top cage is the one for me.

subject The subject is the part of the sentence that names whom or what the sentence is about (page 131).

EXAMPLE   **Dogs** were barking.

subject complement A subject complement follows a subject and a linking verb and identifies or describes the subject (page 139). *See predicate nominative and predicate adjective.*

EXAMPLE   Sopranos are **singers.**

EXAMPLE   The star of the opera was **she.**

EXAMPLE   The singer grew **hoarse.**

subordinate clause A subordinate clause, also called a dependent clause, has a subject and a predicate but does not express a complete thought, so it cannot stand alone as a sentence (page 164).

EXAMPLE   **When the dog barked,** the baby cried.

EXAMPLE   Dogs **that obey** are a joy.

EXAMPLE   **Whoever joins the circus** will travel across the country.

subordinating conjunction A subordinating conjunction joins two clauses, or ideas, in such a way as to make one grammatically dependent on the other. The idea, or clause, that a subordinating conjunction introduces is said to be "subordinate," or dependent, because it cannot stand by itself as a complete sentence (page 122).

after	as though	since	until
although	because	so long as	when
as	before	so (that)	whenever

EXAMPLE   We can skate on the pond **when** the ice is thicker.

EXAMPLE   We can't skate **until** the ice is thicker.

superlative degree The superlative degree of an adjective or adverb is the form that shows three or more things being compared (page 256).

EXAMPLE   Of the three dogs, Ray's dog is the **smallest** one.

EXAMPLE   The squirrel ran **most swiftly** of all.

syllable When a word must be divided at the end of a line, it is generally divided between syllables or pronounceable parts. Because it is often difficult to decide where a word should be divided, consult a dictionary. In general, if a word contains two consonants occurring between two vowels or if it contains double consonants, divide the word between the two consonants (page 352).

EXAMPLES   profes-sor   foun-tain   struc-ture

                 tomor-row   lin-ger   sup-per

tense Tenses are the forms of a verb that help to show time. There are six tenses in English: *present, past, future, present perfect, past perfect,* and *future perfect* (page 195).

EXAMPLE

present tense	I sing.
past tense	I sang.
future tense	I shall (*or* will) sing.
present perfect tense	I have sung.
past perfect tense	I had sung.
future perfect tense	I shall (*or* will) have sung.

FRANK & ERNEST® by Bob Thaves

FRANK AND ERNEST reprinted by permission of Newspaper Enterprise Association, Inc.

transitive verb A transitive verb is an action verb followed by a word or words that answer the question *what?* or *whom?* (page 106). *See intransitive verb.*

EXAMPLE   The batter **swung** the bat confidently. **[The action verb *swung* is followed by the noun *bat*, which answers the question *swung what?*]**

verb A verb is a word that expresses action or a state of being and is necessary to make a statement (page 105).

EXAMPLE   The bicyclist **grinned.**

EXAMPLE   The riders **seem** enthusiastic.

verbal A verbal is a verb form that functions in a sentence as a noun, an adjective, or an adverb. Verbals are *participles, gerunds,* and *infinitives.* Each of these can be expanded into phrases (page 151).

EXAMPLE   **Exhausted,** the team headed for the locker room. **[past participle]**

EXAMPLE   **Swimming** is my sport. **[gerund]**

EXAMPLE   I want **to win. [infinitive]**

verb phrase A verb phrase consists of a main verb and all its auxiliary, or helping, verbs (page 108). The most common auxiliary verbs are forms of *be* and *have.* They help the main verb express time by forming the various tenses.

EXAMPLE   We **will weed** the vegetable garden this morning.

EXAMPLE   We **were weeding** the flowerbeds when the rain started.

The other auxiliary verbs are not used primarily to express time. They are often used to emphasize meaning.

EXAMPLE   I **should be leaving.**

EXAMPLE   **Could** he **have forgotten?**

verbal phrase A verbal phrase is a verbal plus any complements and modifiers (page 151).

EXAMPLE   **Frightened by the barking dogs,** the kittens ran to their mother. **[participial phrase]**

EXAMPLE   **Swimming twenty laps a day** is my goal. **[gerund phrase]**

EXAMPLE   I like **to sing the fight song. [infinitive phrase]**

voice Voice is the form a verb takes to explain whether the subject performs the action or the action is performed upon the subject. An action verb is in the active voice when the subject of the sentence performs the action. An action verb is in the passive voice when its action is performed on the subject (page 208).

EXAMPLE   The brown bear **caught** a salmon. **[active voice]**

EXAMPLE   A salmon **was caught** by the brown bear. **[passive voice]**

USAGE GLOSSARY

This glossary presents some particularly troublesome matters of usage. The glossary will guide you in choosing between words that are often confused. It will also alert you to certain words and expressions you should avoid when you speak or write for school or business.

a, an Use *a* before words that begin with a consonant sound. Use *an* before words that begin with a vowel sound.

EXAMPLES **a** poem, **a** house, **a** yacht, **a** union, **a** one-track mind

EXAMPLES **an** apple, **an** icicle, **an** honor, **an** umbrella, **an** only child

accede, exceed *Accede* means "to agree." *Exceed* means "to go beyond."

EXAMPLE I **acceded** to Mom's wishes.

EXAMPLE Don't **exceed** the speed limit.

accept, except *Accept* is a verb that means "to receive" or "to agree to." *Except* is usually a preposition meaning "but." *Except* may also be a verb that means "to leave out or exclude."

EXAMPLE Will you **accept** our thanks?

EXAMPLE The president **accepted** the terms of the treaty.

EXAMPLE Everyone will be there **except** you. **[preposition]**

EXAMPLE The government **excepts** people with very low incomes from paying taxes. **[verb]**

access, excess *Access* means "admittance." An *excess* is a surplus.

EXAMPLE The thief gained **access** to the building with a stolen key.

EXAMPLE We have an **excess** of musical talent in our class.

adapt, adopt *Adapt* means "to change to meet new requirements" or "to adjust." *Adopt* means "to accept and take as one's own."

EXAMPLE   I can **adapt** to new surroundings easily.

EXAMPLE   We can **adapt** this old bathrobe for a Roman senator's costume.

EXAMPLE   I think that dog has **adopted** you.

advice, advise *Advice*, a noun, means "an opinion offered as guidance." *Advise*, a verb, means "to give advice" or "to counsel."

EXAMPLE   Why should I **advise** you when you never accept my **advice**?

affect, effect *Affect* is a verb that means "to cause a change in" or "to influence the emotions of." *Effect* may be a noun or a verb. As a noun, it means "result." As a verb, it means "to bring about or accomplish."

EXAMPLE   The mayor's policies have **affected** every city agency.

EXAMPLE   The mayor's policies have had a positive **effect** on every city agency. **[noun]**

EXAMPLE   The mayor has **effected** positive changes in every city agency. **[verb]**

ain't *Ain't* is unacceptable in speaking and writing unless you're quoting someone's exact words or writing dialogue. Use *I'm not; you, we,* or *they aren't; he, she,* or *it isn't.*

all ready, already *All ready* means "completely ready." *Already* is an adverb that means "before" or "by this time."

EXAMPLE   The band was **all ready** to play its last number, but the fans were **already** leaving the stadium.

all right, alright The spelling *alright* is not acceptable in formal writing. Use *all right.*

EXAMPLE   Don't worry; everything will be **all right**.

all the farther, all the faster These expressions are not acceptable in formal speech and writing. Use *as far as* and *as fast as.*

EXAMPLE   Five hundred miles was **as far as** [*not* all the farther] we could drive in a single day.

EXAMPLE   This is **as fast as** [*not* all the faster] I can pedal.

all together, altogether Use *all together* to mean "in a group." Use *altogether* to mean "completely" or "in all."

EXAMPLE   Let's cheer **all together**.

EXAMPLE   You are being **altogether** silly.

EXAMPLE   I have three dollars in quarters and two dollars in dimes; that's five dollars **altogether**.

allusion, illusion An *allusion* is an indirect reference. An *illusion* is a false idea or appearance.

EXAMPLE   Her speech included an **allusion** to one of Robert Frost's poems.

EXAMPLE   The shimmering heat produced an **illusion** of water on the road.

almost, most Don't use *most* in place of *almost.*

EXAMPLE   Marty **almost** [*not* most] always makes the honor roll.

a lot, alot, allot *A lot* should always be written as two words. It means "a large number or amount." Avoid using *a lot* in formal writing; be specific. The verb *allot* means "to assign or set aside" or "to distribute."

EXAMPLE **A lot** [*not* **Alot**] of snow fell last night.
Better: A great deal of snow fell last night.

EXAMPLE The legislature will **allot** funds for a new capitol.

altar, alter An *altar* is a raised structure at which religious ceremonies are performed. *Alter* means "to change."

EXAMPLE The bride and groom approached the **altar**.

EXAMPLE The wardrobe manager **altered** some of the costumes to fit the new cast members.

among, between In general use *among* to show a relationship in which more than two persons or things are considered as a group.

EXAMPLE The committee will distribute the used clothing **among** the poor families in the community.

EXAMPLE There was confusion **among** the players on the field.

In general, use *between* to show a relationship involving two persons or things, to compare one person or thing with an entire group, or to compare more than two items within a group.

EXAMPLE Mr. and Mrs. Ito live halfway **between** Seattle and Portland. **[relationship involving two places]**

EXAMPLE What was the difference **between** Frank Sinatra and other vocalists of the twentieth century? **[one person compared with a group]**

EXAMPLE Emilio could not decide **between** the collie, the cocker spaniel, and the beagle. **[items within a group]**

amount, number *Amount* and *number* both refer to quantity. Use *amount* for things that can't be counted. Use *number* for things that can be counted.

EXAMPLE Fort Knox contains a vast **amount** of gold.

EXAMPLE Fort Knox contains a large **number** of gold bars.

and/or This expression, once common in legal language, should be avoided in general writing. Change *and/or* to "this *or* that *or both*."

EXAMPLE We'll go hiking **or** skiing **or both**. [*not* We'll go hiking **and/or** skiing.]

anxious, eager *Anxious* comes from *anxiety;* therefore, it implies uneasiness or apprehension. It is not a synonym for *eager,* which means "filled with enthusiasm."

EXAMPLE Jean was **anxious** about her test results.

EXAMPLE She was **eager** [*not* anxious] to begin college.

anyways, anywheres, everywheres, nowheres, somewheres Write and speak these words without the final *s: anyway, anywhere, everywhere, nowhere, somewhere.*

ascent, assent An *ascent* is a rise or an act of climbing. *Assent* as a verb means "to agree or consent"; as a noun, it means "agreement" or "consent."

EXAMPLE We watched the **ascent** of the balloon.

EXAMPLE Will your parents **assent** to our plans? [verb]

EXAMPLE They were happy to give their **assent** to the plans. [noun]

a while, awhile Use *a while* after a preposition. Use *awhile* as an adverb.

EXAMPLE She read for **a while**.

EXAMPLE She read **awhile**.

bad, badly *Bad* is an adjective; use it before nouns and after linking verbs to modify the subject. *Badly* is an adverb; use it to modify action verbs.

EXAMPLE   Clara felt **bad** about the broken vase.

EXAMPLE   The team performed **badly** in the first half.

bare, bear   *Bare* means "naked." A *bear* is an animal.

EXAMPLE   Don't expose your **bare** skin to the sun.

EXAMPLE   There are many **bears** in Yellowstone National Park.

base, bass   One meaning of *base* is "a part on which something rests or stands." *Bass* pronounced to rhyme with *face* is a type of voice. When *bass* is pronounced to rhyme with *glass*, it's a kind of fish.

EXAMPLE   Who is playing first **base**?

EXAMPLE   We need a **bass** singer for the part.

EXAMPLE   We caught several **bass** on our fishing trip.

because of, due to   Use *because of* with action verbs. Use *due to* with linking verbs.

EXAMPLE   The game was canceled **because of** rain.

EXAMPLE   The cancellation was **due to** rain.

being as, being that   Some people use these expressions instead of *because* in informal conversation. In formal speaking and writing, use *because*.

EXAMPLE   **Because [*not* Being as]** their car broke down, they were late.

EXAMPLE   They were late **because [*not* being that]** their car broke down.

beside, besides   *Beside* means "at the side of" or "next to." *Besides* means "in addition to."

EXAMPLE   Katrina sat **beside** her brother at the table.

EXAMPLE   **Besides** yogurt and fruit, the lunchroom serves muffins and bagels.

blew, blue *Blue* is the color of a clear sky. *Blew* is the past tense of *blow*.

EXAMPLE   She wore a **blue** shirt.

EXAMPLE   The dead leaves **blew** along the driveway.

boar, bore A *boar* is a male pig. *Bore* means "to tire out with dullness"; it can also mean "a dull person."

EXAMPLE   Wild **boars** are common in parts of Africa.

EXAMPLE   Please don't **bore** me with your silly jokes.

born, borne *Born* means "given life." *Borne* means "carried" or "endured."

EXAMPLE   The baby was **born** at three o'clock in the morning.

EXAMPLE   Migrant workers have **borne** many hardships over the years.

borrow, lend, loan *Borrow* means "to take something with the understanding that it will be returned." *Lend* means "to give something with the understanding it will be returned." *Borrow* and *lend* are verbs. *Loan* is a noun. Some people use *loan* as a verb, but most authorities prefer *lend*.

EXAMPLE   May I **borrow** your bicycle for an hour?

EXAMPLE   Will you **lend** me five dollars? [verb]

EXAMPLE   I'll repay the **loan** on Friday. [noun]

bow When *bow* is pronounced to rhyme with *low*, it means "a knot with two loops." When *bow* rhymes with *how*, it means "to bend at the waist."

EXAMPLE   Can you tie a good **bow**?

EXAMPLE   Actors **bow** at the end of a play.

brake, break As a noun, a *brake* is a device for stopping something or slowing it down. As a verb, *brake* means "to stop or slow down"; its principal parts are *brake, braking, braked,* and *braked.* The noun *break* has several meanings: "the result of breaking," "a fortunate chance," or "a short rest." The verb *break* also has many meanings. A few are "to smash or shatter," "to destroy or disrupt," "to force a way through or into," or "to surpass or excel." Its principal parts are *break, breaking, broke,* and *broken.*

EXAMPLE Rachel, please put a **brake** on your enthusiasm.
[noun]

EXAMPLE He couldn't **brake** the car in time to avoid the accident.
[verb]

EXAMPLE To fix the **break** in the drainpipe will cost a great deal of money. **[noun]**

EXAMPLE Don't **break** my concentration while I'm studying.
[verb]

bring, take *Bring* means "to carry from a distant place to a closer one." *Take* means "to carry from a nearby place to a more distant one."

EXAMPLE Will you **bring** me some perfume when you return from Paris?

EXAMPLE Remember to **take** your passport when you go to Europe.

bust, busted Don't use these words in place of *break, broke, broken,* or *burst.*

EXAMPLE Don't **break** [*not* bust] that vase!

EXAMPLE Who **broke** [*not* busted] this vase?

EXAMPLE Someone has **broken** [*not* busted] this vase.

EXAMPLE The balloon **burst** [*not* busted] with a loud pop.

EXAMPLE The child **burst** [*not* busted] into tears.

buy, by *Buy* is a verb. *By* is a preposition.

EXAMPLE   I'll **buy** the gift tomorrow.

EXAMPLE   Stand **by** me.

can, may *Can* indicates ability. *May* expresses permission or possibility.

EXAMPLE   I **can** tie six kinds of knots.

EXAMPLE   "You **may** be excused," said Dad. **[permission]**

EXAMPLE   Luanna **may** take some college classes during her senior year. **[possibility]**

can't hardly, can't scarcely These phrases are considered double negatives. Don't use *hardly* or *scarcely* with *not* or the contraction *n't.*

EXAMPLE   I **can [*not* can't] hardly** lift this box.

EXAMPLE   The driver **can [*not* can't] scarcely** see through the thick fog.

capital, capitol A *capital* is a city that is the seat of a government. *Capital* can also mean "money or property." As an adjective, capital can mean "involving execution" or "referring to an uppercase letter." *Capitol,* on the other hand, refers only to a building in which a legislature meets.

EXAMPLE   What is the **capital** of Vermont?

EXAMPLE   Anyone starting a business needs **capital**.

EXAMPLE   **Capital** punishment is not used in this state.

EXAMPLE   Hester Prynne embroidered a **capital** *A* on her dress.

EXAMPLE   The **capitol** has a gold dome.

carat, caret, carrot, karat A *carat* is a unit of weight for measuring gems. (A similar word, *karat*, is a measure for expressing the fineness of gold.) A *caret* is a proofreader's mark indicating an insertion. A *carrot* is a vegetable.

EXAMPLE   She was wearing a one-**carat** diamond set in a ring of eighteen-**karat** gold.

EXAMPLE   Draw a **caret** at the point where you want to insert a word.

EXAMPLE   Lottie fed her horse a **carrot**.

cent, scent, sent A *cent* is a penny. A *scent* is an odor. *Sent* is the past and past participle of *send*.

EXAMPLE   I haven't got one **cent** in my pocket.

EXAMPLE   The **scent** of a skunk is unpleasant.

EXAMPLE   I **sent** my grandma a birthday card.

choose, chose *Choose* is the base form; *chose* is the past tense. The principal parts are *choose, choosing, chose,* and *chosen*.

EXAMPLE   Please **choose** a poem to recite in class.

EXAMPLE   Brian **chose** to recite "The Charge of the Light Brigade."

cite, sight, site To *cite* is to quote or refer to. *Cite* can also mean "to summon to appear in a court of law." As a noun, *sight* means "vision." As a verb, *sight* means "to see." As a noun, a *site* is a place or a location; as a verb, *site* means "to place or locate."

EXAMPLE   Consuela **cited** three sources of information in her report.

EXAMPLE   The officer **cited** the driver for speeding.

EXAMPLE   My **sight** is perfect. **[noun]**

EXAMPLE   We **sighted** a scarlet tanager on our hike. **[verb]**

EXAMPLE   The board of education has chosen a **site** for the new high school. **[noun]**

EXAMPLE   The school will be **sited** on Meadow Boulevard. **[verb]**

clothes, cloths   *Clothes* are what you wear. *Cloths* are pieces of fabric.

EXAMPLE   Please hang all your **clothes** in your closet.

EXAMPLE   Use these **cloths** to wash the car.

coarse, course   *Coarse* means "rough," "crude," "not fine," "of poor quality." *Course* can mean "a school subject," "a path or way," "order or development," or "part of a meal." *Course* is also used in the phrase *of course.*

EXAMPLE   To begin, I will need some **coarse** sandpaper.

EXAMPLE   Mrs. Baldwin won't tolerate **coarse** language.

EXAMPLE   Are you taking any math **courses** this year?

EXAMPLE   The hikers chose a difficult **course** through the mountains.

complement, complementary; compliment, complimentary
As a noun, *complement* means "something that completes"; as a verb, it means "to complete." As a noun, *compliment* means "a flattering remark"; as a verb, it means "to praise." *Complementary* and *complimentary* are the adjective forms of the words.

EXAMPLE   This flowered scarf will be the perfect **complement** for your outfit. **[noun]**

EXAMPLE   This flowered scarf **complements** your outfit perfectly. **[verb]**

EXAMPLE   Phyllis received many **compliments** on her speech. **[noun]**

EXAMPLE   Many people **complimented** Phyllis on her speech.
          [verb]

EXAMPLE   Either hat would be **complementary** to that outfit.
          [adjective]

EXAMPLE   The hostess was especially **complimentary** to Phyllis.
          [adjective]

compose, comprise   *Compose* means "to make up." *Comprise*
means "to include."

EXAMPLE   The mayor, the superintendent of schools, and the
          police chief **compose** the committee.

EXAMPLE   The committee **comprises** the mayor, the
          superintendent of schools, and the police chief.

consul; council, councilor; counsel, counselor   A *consul* is a
government official living in a foreign city to protect his or
her country's interests and citizens. A *council* is a group of
people gathered for the purpose of giving advice. A
councilor is one who serves on a council. As a noun, *counsel*
means "advice" or "an attorney." As a verb, *counsel* means
"to give advice." A *counselor* is one who gives counsel.

EXAMPLE   The **consul** protested to the foreign government about
          the treatment of her fellow citizens.

EXAMPLE   The city **council** met to discuss the lack of parking
          facilities at the sports field.

EXAMPLE   The defendant received **counsel** from his **counsel**.
          [nouns]

EXAMPLE   The attorney **counseled** his client to plead innocent.
          [verb]

continual, continually; continuous, continuously   *Continual*
describes action that occurs over and over but with pauses
between occurrences. *Continuous* describes an action that

continues with no interruption. *Continually* and *continuously* are the adverb forms of the adjectives.

EXAMPLE   I could not concentrate because of the **continual** banging of the screen door and the **continuous** blare of the radio.

EXAMPLE   This television ad is aired **continually**; I've seen it six times tonight.

EXAMPLE   The rain fell **continuously**.

could of, might of, must of, should of, would of After the words *could, might, must, should,* and *would,* use the helping verb *have* or its contraction, *'ve,* not the word *of.*

EXAMPLE   **Could** you **have** prevented the accident?

EXAMPLE   You **might have** swerved to avoid the other car.

EXAMPLE   You **must have** seen it coming.

EXAMPLE   I **should've** warned you.

dear, deer *Dear* is a word of affection and is used to begin a letter. It can also mean "expensive." A *deer* is an animal.

EXAMPLE   Talia is my **dear** friend.

EXAMPLE   We saw a **deer** at the edge of the woods.

desert, dessert *Desert* has two meanings. As a noun, it means "dry, arid land" and is accented on the first syllable. As a verb, it means "to leave" or "to abandon" and is accented on the second syllable. A *dessert* is something sweet eaten after a meal.

EXAMPLE   This photograph shows a sandstorm in the **desert**. **[noun]**

EXAMPLE   I won't **desert** you in your time of need. **[verb]**

EXAMPLE   Strawberry shortcake was served for **dessert**.

different from, different than In most cases, *different from* is the correct choice. Use *different than* only if *than* introduces a subordinate clause.

EXAMPLE   Square dancing is **different from** ballroom dancing.

EXAMPLE   I felt **different than** I had felt before.

diner, dinner A *diner* is someone who dines or a place to eat. A *dinner* is a meal.

EXAMPLE   The **diners** at the corner **diner** enjoy the corned beef hash.

EXAMPLE   **Dinner** will be served at eight.

discover, invent *Discover* means "to come upon something for the first time." *Invent* means "to produce something original."

EXAMPLE   Marie Curie **discovered** radium.

EXAMPLE   Eli Whitney **invented** the cotton gin.

doe, dough A *doe* is a female deer. *Dough* is a mixture of flour and a liquid.

EXAMPLE   A **doe** and a stag were visible among the trees.

EXAMPLE   Knead the **dough** for three minutes.

doesn't, don't *Doesn't* is a contraction of *does not.* It is used with *he, she, it,* and all singular nouns. *Don't* is a contraction of *do not.* It is used with *I, you, we, they,* and all plural nouns.

EXAMPLE   She **doesn't** know the answer to your question.

EXAMPLE   The twins **don't** like broccoli.

emigrate, immigrate Use *emigrate* to mean "to leave one country and go to another to live." Use *immigrate* to mean "to come to a country to settle there." Use the preposition *from* with *emigrate.* Use *to* or *into* with *immigrate.*

EXAMPLE   Karl **emigrated** from Germany.

EXAMPLE   He **immigrated** to the United States.

eye, I An *eye* is what you see with; it's also a small opening in a needle. *I* is a personal pronoun.

EXAMPLE   **I** have something in my **eye**.

farther, further Use *farther* in referring to physical distance. Use *further* in all other situations.

EXAMPLE   San Antonio is **farther** south than Dallas.

EXAMPLE   We have nothing **further** to discuss.

fewer, less Use *fewer* with nouns that can be counted. Use *less* with nouns that can't be counted. *Less* may also be used with numbers that are considered as single amounts or single quantities.

EXAMPLE   There are **fewer** students in my math class than in my physics class.

EXAMPLE   I used **less** sugar than the recipe recommended.

EXAMPLE   David had **less** than two dollars in his pocket.
           [**Two dollars** is treated as a single sum, not as individual dollars.]

EXAMPLE   I can be there in **less** than thirty minutes. [**Thirty minutes** is treated as a single period of time, not as individual minutes.]

figuratively, literally *Figuratively* means "not truly or actually but in a symbolic way." *Literally* means "truly" or "actually."

EXAMPLE   Dad hit the ceiling, **figuratively** speaking.

EXAMPLE   You can't take him **literally** when he talks about the
          fish he's caught.

flaunt, flout   *Flaunt* means "to make a showy display." *Flout*
means "to defy."

EXAMPLE   Enrique **flaunted** his knowledge of computer science
          at every opportunity.

EXAMPLE   Darla **flouted** the law by jaywalking.

flour, flower   *Flour* is used to bake bread. A *flower* grows in
a garden.

EXAMPLE   Sift two cups of **flour** into a bowl.

EXAMPLE   A daisy is a **flower**.

for, four   *For* is a preposition. *Four* is a number.

EXAMPLE   Wait **for** me.

EXAMPLE   I have **four** grandparents.

formally, formerly   *Formally* is the adverb form of *formal,*
which has several meanings: "according to custom, rule, or
etiquette"; "requiring special ceremony or fancy clothing";
or "official." *Formerly* means "previously."

EXAMPLE   The class officers will be **formally** installed on
          Thursday.

EXAMPLE   Ed was **formerly** employed by Kwik Kar Kleen.

go, say   Don't use forms of *go* in place of forms of *say.*

EXAMPLE   I tell her the answer, and she **says** [*not* goes], "I don't
          believe you."

EXAMPLE   I told her the news, and she **said** [*not* went], "Are you
          serious?"

good, well *Good* is an adjective; use it before nouns and after linking verbs to modify the subject. *Well* is an adverb; use it to modify action verbs. *Well* may also be an adjective meaning "in good health."

EXAMPLE You look **good** in that costume.

EXAMPLE Joby plays the piano **well**.

EXAMPLE You're looking **well** in spite of your cold.

grate, great A *grate* is a framework of bars set over an opening. *Grate* also means "to shred by rubbing against a rough surface." *Great* means "wonderful" or "large."

EXAMPLE The little girl dropped her lollipop through the **grate**.

EXAMPLE Will you **grate** this cheese for me?

EXAMPLE You did a **great** job!

had of Don't use *of* between *had* and a past participle.

EXAMPLE I wish I **had known** [*not* had of known] about this sooner.

had ought, hadn't ought, shouldn't ought *Ought* never needs an auxiliary verb. Use *ought* by itself.

EXAMPLE You **ought** to win the match easily.

EXAMPLE You **ought** not to blame yourself. *or* You **shouldn't** blame yourself.

hanged, hung Use *hanged* when you mean "put to death by hanging." Use *hung* in all other instances.

EXAMPLE This state **hanged** three convicts between 1900 and 1950.

EXAMPLE We **hung** Yoko's painting over the fireplace.

healthful, healthy *Healthful* means "favorable to one's health," or "wholesome." *Healthy* means "in good health."

EXAMPLE   We chose **healthful** picnic foods: whole-grain breads, juices, cheese, and fresh fruits.

EXAMPLE   A **healthy** person is likely to live longer than an unhealthy one.

hear, here   *Hear* is a verb meaning "to be aware of sound by means of the ear." *Here* is an adverb meaning "in or at this place."

EXAMPLE   I can **hear** you perfectly well.

EXAMPLE   Please put your books **here**.

he, she, it, they   Don't use a pronoun subject immediately after a noun subject, as in *The girls they baked the cookies.* Omit the unnecessary pronoun: *The girls baked the cookies.*

holey, holy, wholly   *Holey* means "having holes." *Holy* means "sacred." *Wholly* means "completely."

EXAMPLE   I hate wearing **holey** socks.

EXAMPLE   Religious travelers make pilgrimages to **holy** places.

EXAMPLE   That dog is **wholly** devoted to you.

how come   In formal speech and writing, use *why* instead of *how come.*

EXAMPLE   **Why** weren't you at the meeting? [*not* **How come you weren't at the meeting?**]

imply, infer   *Imply* means "to suggest." *Infer* means "to draw a conclusion from something."

EXAMPLE   The baby's crying **implied** that he was hungry.

EXAMPLE   I **inferred** from the baby's crying that he was hungry.

in, into, in to Use *in* to mean "inside" or "within." Use *into* to show movement from the outside to a point within. Don't write *into* when you mean *in to.*

EXAMPLE   Jeanine was sitting outdoors **in** a lawn chair.

EXAMPLE   When it got too hot, she went **into** the house.

EXAMPLE   She went **in to** get out of the heat.

ingenious, ingenuous *Ingenious* means "clever," "inventive," "imaginative." *Ingenuous* means "innocent," "childlike," "sincere."

EXAMPLE   What an **ingenious** plan you have dreamed up!

EXAMPLE   Her **ingenuous** enthusiasm for the cafeteria food made us smile.

inside of Don't use *of* after the preposition *inside.*

EXAMPLE   **Inside** [*not* **inside of**] the cupboard were several old photograph albums.

irregardless, regardless Use *regardless.* Both the prefix *ir-* and the suffix *–less* have negative meanings; therefore, *irregardless* is a double negative, which is incorrect.

EXAMPLE   **Regardless** [*not* **Irregardless**] of what the critics said, I liked that movie.

its, it's *Its* is the possessive form of *it. It's* is a contraction of *it is* or *it has.*

EXAMPLE   The dishwasher has finished **its** cycle.

EXAMPLE   **It's** [**It is**] raining again.

EXAMPLE   **It's** [**It has**] been a pleasure to meet you, Ms. Donatello.

kind of, sort of Don't use these expressions as adverbs. Use *somewhat* or *rather* instead.

EXAMPLE   We were **rather** sorry to see him go. [*not* We were kind of sorry to see him go.]

kind of a, sort of a, type of a Omit the word *a*.

EXAMPLE   What **kind of** dog is that? [*not* What kind of a dog is that?]

knead, need *Knead* means "to mix or work into a uniform mass." As a noun, a *need* is a requirement. As a verb, *need* means "to require."

EXAMPLE   **Knead** the clay to make it soft.

EXAMPLE   I **need** a new jacket.

knight, night A *knight* was a warrior of the Middle Ages. *Night* is the time of day during which it is dark.

EXAMPLE   A handsome **knight** rescued the fair maiden.

EXAMPLE   **Night** fell, and the moon rose.

later, latter *Later* is the comparative form of *late*. *Latter* means "the second of two."

EXAMPLE   They will arrive on a **later** flight.

EXAMPLE   He arrived **later** than usual.

EXAMPLE   Both Scott and Sabrina are running for class president; I'm voting for the **latter**.

lay, lie *Lay* means "to put" or "to place." Its principal parts are *lay, laying, laid,* and *laid.* Forms of *lay* are usually followed by a direct object. *Lie* means "to rest or recline" or "to be positioned." Its principal parts are *lie, lying, lay,* and *lain.* Forms of *lie* are never followed by a direct object.

EXAMPLE   **Lay** your coat on the bed.

EXAMPLE   The children are **laying** their beach towels in the sun to dry.

Usage Glossary   **61**

EXAMPLE   Dad **laid** the baby in her crib.

EXAMPLE   Myrna had **laid** the book beside her purse.

EXAMPLE   **Lie** down for a few minutes.

EXAMPLE   The lake **lies** to the north.

EXAMPLE   The dog is **lying** on the back porch.

EXAMPLE   This morning I **lay** in bed listening to the birds.

EXAMPLE   You have **lain** on the couch for an hour.

lead, led As a noun, *lead* has two pronunciations and several meanings. When it's pronounced to rhyme with *head,* it means "a metallic element." When it's pronounced to rhyme with *bead,* it can mean "position of being in first place in a race or contest," "example," "clue," "leash," or "the main role in a play."

EXAMPLE   **Lead** is no longer allowed as an ingredient in paint.

EXAMPLE   Jason took the **lead** as the runners entered the stadium.

EXAMPLE   Follow my **lead**.

EXAMPLE   The detective had no **leads** in the case.

EXAMPLE   Only dogs on **leads** are permitted in the park.

EXAMPLE   Who will win the **lead** in this year's musical production?

As a verb, *lead* means "to show the way," "to guide or conduct," "to be first." Its principal parts are *lead, leading, led,* and *led.*

EXAMPLE   Ms. Bachman **leads** the orchestra.

EXAMPLE   The trainer was **leading** the horse around the track.

EXAMPLE   An usher **led** us to our seats.

EXAMPLE   Gray has **led** the league in hitting for two years.

learn, teach *Learn* means "to receive knowledge." *Teach* means "to give knowledge."

EXAMPLE   Manny began to **learn** to play the piano at the age of six.

EXAMPLE   Ms. Guerrero **teaches** American history.

leave, let *Leave* means "to go away." *Let* means "to allow to."

EXAMPLE   I'll miss you when you **leave**.

EXAMPLE   **Let** me help you with those heavy bags.

like, as, as if, as though *Like* can be a verb or a preposition. It should not be used as a subordinating conjunction. Use *as, as if*, or *as though* to introduce a subordinate clause.

EXAMPLE   I **like** piano music. **[verb]**

EXAMPLE   Teresa plays the piano **like** a professional. **[preposition]**

EXAMPLE   Moira plays **as** [*not* like] her teacher taught her to play.

EXAMPLE   He looked at me **as if** [*not* like] he'd never seen me before.

EXAMPLE   You sound **as though** [*not* like] you disagree.

like, say Don't use the word *like* in place of forms of *say*.

EXAMPLE   I tell him to scroll down, and **he says** [*not* he's like], "What's scrolling down?"

EXAMPLE   I told her to turn left, and **she said** [*not* she was like], "Left!"

loath, loathe *Loath* means "reluctant or unwilling." *Loathe* means "to hate."

EXAMPLE   Jeanine was **loath** to accept the responsibility.

EXAMPLE   Leonardo **loathes** sports.

loose, lose The adjective *loose* means "free," "not firmly attached," or "not fitting tightly." The verb *lose* means "to misplace" or "to fail to win."

EXAMPLE   Don't **lose** that **loose** button on your shirt.

EXAMPLE   If we **lose** this game, we'll be out of the tournament.

mail, male   *Mail* is what turns up in your mailbox. A *male* is a man.

EXAMPLE   We received four pieces of **mail** today.

EXAMPLE   The **males** in the chorus wore red ties.

main, mane   *Main* means "most important." A *mane* is the long hair on a horse's neck.

EXAMPLE   What is your **main** job around the house?

EXAMPLE   The horse's **mane** was braided with colorful ribbons.

mean, medium, average   The *mean* of a set of numbers is a middle point. To get the arithmetic mean, you add up all the items in the set and divide by the number of items. The *medium* is the middle number when the items are arranged in order of size. The *average*, a noun, is the same as the arithmetic mean; as an adjective, *average* is "usual" or "typical."

EXAMPLE   The **mean** value of houses in a neighborhood is found by adding together all their selling prices and dividing the sum by the number of houses.

EXAMPLE   We lined up all the ponies from smallest to biggest, and Taminka chose the **medium** one, the one in the center of the row.

EXAMPLE   Let's figure out the **average** of all our test scores; then we can tell whether as a class we've improved.

EXAMPLE   This crop of tomatoes is nothing unusual; it's pretty **average**.

meat, meet *Meat* is food from an animal. Some meanings of *meet* are "to come face to face with," "to make the acquaintance of," and "to keep an appointment."

EXAMPLE   Some people don't eat **meat**.

EXAMPLE   **Meet** me at the library at three o'clock.

miner, minor *Miner* is a noun that means "one who works in a mine." *Minor* can be a noun or an adjective. As a noun, it means "a person under legal age." As an adjective, it means "small in importance."

EXAMPLE   Coal **miners** often suffer from a disease known as black lung.

EXAMPLE   **Minors** are restricted by law from certain activities.

EXAMPLE   Several well-known actors had **minor** roles in the film.

minute When *minute* is pronounced min′it, it means "sixty seconds" or "a short period of time." When *minute* is pronounced mī noot′, it means "very small."

EXAMPLE   I'll be with you in a **minute**.

EXAMPLE   Don't bother me with **minute** details.

moral, morale As a noun, a *moral* is a lesson taught by a fable or a story. As an adjective, *moral* means "decent," "right," "proper." *Morale* means "mental attitude."

EXAMPLE   Did you understand the **moral** of that story?

EXAMPLE   Jackson has strong **moral** principles.

EXAMPLE   The team's **morale** would be improved by a win.

nauseated, nauseous *Nauseated* means "feeling nausea," or "experiencing nausea, as in sea-sickness." *Nauseous*, on the other hand, means "causing nausea," or "sickening."

EXAMPLE   My **nauseated** family could not stand to look any
           longer at the **nauseous** dish of scrambled eggs and
           leftovers I had placed in front of them.

object *Object* is stressed on the first syllable when it means
"a thing." *Object* is stressed on the second syllable when it
means "oppose."

EXAMPLE   Have you ever seen an unidentified flying **object**?

EXAMPLE   Mom **objected** to the proposal.

off Don't use *off* in place of *from*.

EXAMPLE   I'll borrow some money **from** [*not* **off**] my brother.

off of Don't use *of* after the preposition *off*.

EXAMPLE   He fell **off** [*not* **off of**] the ladder, but he didn't hurt
           himself.

ordinance, ordnance An *ordinance* is a law. *Ordnance* is a
word for military weapons and equipment.

EXAMPLE   Our town has an **ordinance** against lying on the
           sidewalk.

EXAMPLE   Private Malloy was assigned to guard the **ordnance**.

ought to of Don't use *of* in place of *have* after *ought to*.

EXAMPLE   You **ought to have** [*not* **ought to of**] known better.

outside of Don't use *of* after the preposition *outside*.

EXAMPLE   I'll meet you **outside** [*not* **outside of**] the library.

overlook, oversee Overlook can mean "to look past or
miss," and "to look down at from above." *Oversee* means
"to supervise workers or work."

EXAMPLE Lynn calculated the net profit we made from the car wash, but she had **overlooked** the cost of the lemonade and snacks provided for the workers.

EXAMPLE The ridgetop cabin **overlooks** the whole valley.

EXAMPLE Part of the caretaker's job is to **oversee** the garden staff, the groundskeeping staff, and the security staff.

pair, pare, pear A *pair* is two. *Pare* means "to peel." A *pear* is a fruit.

EXAMPLE I bought a new **pair** of socks.

EXAMPLE **Pare** the potatoes and cut them in quarters.

EXAMPLE Would you like a **pear** or a banana?

passed, past *Passed* is the past form and the past participle of the verb *pass*. *Past* can be an adjective, a preposition, an adverb, or a noun.

EXAMPLE We **passed** your house on the way to school. **[verb]**

EXAMPLE The **past** week has been a busy one for me. **[adjective]**

EXAMPLE We drove **past** your house. **[preposition]**

EXAMPLE At what time did you drive **past**? **[adverb]**

EXAMPLE I love Great-grandma's stories about the **past**. **[noun]**

pause, paws A *pause* is a short space of time. *Pause* also means "to wait for a short time." *Paws* are animal feet.

EXAMPLE We **pause** now for station identification.

EXAMPLE I wiped the dog's muddy **paws**.

peace, piece *Peace* means "calmness" or "the absence of conflict." A *piece* is a part of something.

EXAMPLE We enjoy the **peace** of the countryside.

EXAMPLE   The two nations have finally made **peace**.

EXAMPLE   May I have another **piece** of pie?

persecute, prosecute *Persecute* means "to torment." *Prosecute* means "to bring legal action against."

EXAMPLE   Bullies sometimes **persecute** younger, weaker children.

EXAMPLE   The government **prosecuted** Al Capone for tax evasion.

personal, personnel *Personal* means "private" or "individual." *Personnel* are employees.

EXAMPLE   Employees should not make **personal** telephone calls during working hours.

EXAMPLE   All **personnel** will receive a bonus in July.

plain, plane *Plain* means "not fancy," "clear," or "a large area of flat land." A *plane* is an airplane or a device for smoothing wood; it can also mean "a flat surface."

EXAMPLE   He wore a **plain** blue tie.

EXAMPLE   The solution is perfectly **plain** to me.

EXAMPLE   Buffalo once roamed the **plains**.

EXAMPLE   We took a **plane** to Chicago.

EXAMPLE   Jeff used a **plane** to smooth the rough wood.

EXAMPLE   The two metal surfaces of this machine must be perfect **planes**.

precede, proceed *Precede* means "to go before" or "to come before." *Proceed* means "to continue" or "to move along."

EXAMPLE   Our band **preceded** the homecoming floats as the parade **proceeded** through town.

precedence, precedents *Precedence* means "superiority of rank or position." *Precedents* are previous events that serve as examples for future actions or decisions.

EXAMPLE   Doing your schoolwork has **precedence** over playing computer games.

EXAMPLE   The legal **precedents** for the decision were clear and numerous.

principal, principle As a noun, *principal* means "head of a school"; it can also mean "a sum of money borrowed or invested." As an adjective, *principal* means "main" or "chief." *Principle* is a noun meaning "basic truth or belief" or "rule of conduct."

EXAMPLE   Mr. Washington, our **principal**, will speak at the morning assembly. **[noun]**

EXAMPLE   What was your **principal** reason for joining the club? **[adjective]**

EXAMPLE   The **principle** of fair play is important in sports.

quiet, quit, quite The adjective *quiet* means "silent" or "motionless." The verb *quit* means "to stop" or "to give up or resign." The adverb *quite* means "very" or "completely."

EXAMPLE   Please be **quiet** so I can think.

EXAMPLE   Shirelle has **quit** the swim team.

EXAMPLE   We were **quite** sorry to lose her.

raise, rise *Raise* means "to cause to move upward." It can also mean "to breed or grow" and "to bring up or rear." Its principal parts are *raise, raising, raised,* and *raised.*

Forms of *raise* are usually followed by a direct object. *Rise* means "to move upward." Its principal parts are *rise, rising, rose,* and *risen.* Forms of *rise* are never followed by a direct object.

EXAMPLE **Raise** your hand if you know the answer.

EXAMPLE My uncle is **raising** chickens.

EXAMPLE Grandma and Grandpa Schwartz **raised** nine children.

EXAMPLE Steam **rises** from boiling water.

EXAMPLE The sun is **rising**.

EXAMPLE The children **rose** from their seats when the principal entered the room.

EXAMPLE In a short time, Loretta **had risen** to the rank of captain.

rap, wrap *Rap* means "to knock." *Wrap* means "to cover."

EXAMPLE **Rap** on the door.

EXAMPLE **Wrap** the presents.

rational, rationale *Rational,* an adjective, means "sensible," "sane." A *rationale* is a reason for doing something. *Rationale* is a noun.

EXAMPLE Melody always behaves in a **rational** manner.

EXAMPLE I didn't understand Clive's **rationale** for quitting his job.

read, reed *Read* means "to understand the meaning of something written." A *reed* is a stalk of tall grass.

EXAMPLE Will you **read** Jimmy a story?

EXAMPLE We found a frog in the **reeds** beside the lake.

real, really *Real* is an adjective; use it before nouns and after linking verbs to modify the subject. *Really* is an adverb; use it to modify action verbs, adjectives, and other adverbs.

EXAMPLE   Winona has **real** musical talent.

EXAMPLE   She is **really** talented.

real, reel *Real* means "actual." A *reel* is a spool to wind something on, such as a fishing line.

EXAMPLE   I have a **real** four-leaf clover.

EXAMPLE   My dad bought me a new fishing **reel**.

reason is because Don't use *because* after *reason is*. Use *that* after *reason is*, or use *because* alone.

EXAMPLE   The **reason** I'm tired **is that** I didn't sleep well last night.

EXAMPLE   I'm tired **because** I didn't sleep well last night.

respectfully, respectively *Respectfully* means "with respect." *Respectively* means "in the order named."

EXAMPLE   The audience listened **respectfully** as the poet read his latest work.

EXAMPLE   Sue, Jerry, and Chad will be president, secretary, and treasurer, **respectively**.

root, rout, route, en route A *root* is a part of a plant. As a verb, *rout* means "to defeat"; as a noun, it means "a defeat." A *route* is a road or way for travel. *En route* means "on the way."

EXAMPLE   A carrot is a **root**.

EXAMPLE   The Tigers **routed** the Bears in last week's game. **[verb]**

EXAMPLE   The game ended in a **rout** for the Bears. **[noun]**

EXAMPLE   Let's take the **route** that runs along the river.

EXAMPLE   We stopped for lunch **en route**.

row When *row* is pronounced to rhyme with *low,* it means "a series of things arranged in a line" or "to move a boat by using oars." When *row* is pronounced to rhyme with *how,* it means "a noisy quarrel."

EXAMPLE   We sat in the last **row** of the theater.

EXAMPLE   Let's **row** across the lake.

EXAMPLE   My sister and I had a serious **row** yesterday, but today we've forgotten about it.

said, says *Said* is the past form and the past participle of *say. Says* is used in the present tense with *he, she, it,* and all singular nouns. Don't use *says* when you should use *said.*

EXAMPLE   At dinner last night, Neil **said** he wasn't hungry.

EXAMPLE   He always **says** that, but he eats everything anyway.

sail, sale A *sail* is part of a boat. It also means "to travel in a boat." A *sale* is a transfer of ownership in exchange for money.

EXAMPLE   As the boat **sails** away, the crew raise the **sail.**

EXAMPLE   The **sale** of the house was completed on Friday.

sea, see A *sea* is a body of water. *See* means "to be aware of with the eyes."

EXAMPLE   The **sea** is rough today.

EXAMPLE   I can **see** you.

set, sit *Set* means "to place" or "to put." Its principal parts are *set, setting, set,* and *set.* Forms of *set* are usually followed by a direct object. *Sit* means "to place oneself in a seated position" or "to be in a seated position." Its principal parts are *sit, sitting, sat,* and *sat.* Forms of *sit* are not followed by a direct object.

Set is an intransitive verb when it's used with *sun* to mean "the sun is going down" or "the sun is sinking below the horizon." When *set* is used in this way, it is not followed by a direct object.

EXAMPLE   Lani **set** the pots on the stove after the sun **set**.

EXAMPLE   The children **sit** quietly at the table.

sew, sow *Sew* means "to work with needle and thread." When *sow* is pronounced to rhyme with *how*, it means "a female pig." When *sow* is pronounced to rhyme with *low*, it means "to plant."

EXAMPLE   Can you **sew** a button on a shirt?

EXAMPLE   The **sow** has five piglets.

EXAMPLE   Some farmers **sow** corn in their fields.

shear, sheer *Shear* has to do with cutting or breaking off. *Sheer* can mean "thin and fine," "utter or complete," or "steep."

EXAMPLE   It's time to **shear** the sheep.

EXAMPLE   He decided to **shear** off his beard.

EXAMPLE   The bride's veil was made of a **sheer** fabric.

EXAMPLE   You are talking **sheer** nonsense.

EXAMPLE   It was a **sheer** drop from the top of the cliff.

shined, shone, shown Both *shined* and *shone* are past tense forms and past participles of *shine*. Use *shined* when you mean "polished"; use *shone* in all other instances.

EXAMPLE   Clete **shined** his shoes.

EXAMPLE   The sun **shone** brightly.

EXAMPLE   Her face **shone** with happiness.

Shown is the past participle of *show;* its principal parts are *show, showing, showed,* and *shown*.

EXAMPLE   You **showed** me these photographs yesterday.

EXAMPLE   You have **shown** me these photographs before.

slow, slowly *Slow* may be used as an adverb only in such expressions as *Go slow* or *Drive slow.* In other instances where an adverb is needed, *slowly* should be used. You can't go wrong if you always use *slow* as an adjective and *slowly* as an adverb.

EXAMPLE   We took a **slow** ferry to the island.

EXAMPLE   The ferry moved **slowly** through the water.

some, somewhat Don't use *some* as an adverb in place of *somewhat.*

EXAMPLE   The team has improved **somewhat** [*not* some] since last season.

son, sun A *son* is a male child. A *sun* is a star.

EXAMPLE   Kino is Mr. and Mrs. Akawa's **son**.

EXAMPLE   We watched as the **sun** rose [over the horizon].

stationary, stationery *Stationary* means "fixed" or "unmoving." *Stationery* is writing paper.

EXAMPLE   This classroom has **stationary** desks.

EXAMPLE   Rhonda likes to write letters on pretty **stationery**.

straight, strait *Straight* means "not crooked or curved"; it can also mean "direct" or "directly." A *strait* is a narrow waterway connecting two larger bodies of water. In the plural, it can also mean "difficulties" or "distress."

EXAMPLE   Can you draw a **straight** line without a ruler?

EXAMPLE   We drove **straight** to the airport.

EXAMPLE   The **Strait** of Gibraltar connects the Mediterranean Sea and the Atlantic Ocean.

EXAMPLE   People who don't control their spending often find themselves in financial **straits**.

sure, surely *Sure* is an adjective; use it before nouns and after linking verbs to modify the subject. *Surely* is an adverb; use it to modify action verbs, adjectives, and other adverbs.

EXAMPLE   Are you **sure** about that answer?

EXAMPLE   You are **surely** smart.

tail, tale A *tail* is what a dog wags. A *tale* is a story.

EXAMPLE   The dog's **tail** curled over its back.

EXAMPLE   Everyone knows the **tale** of Goldilocks and the three bears.

tear When *tear* is pronounced to rhyme with *ear*, it's a drop of fluid from the eye. When *tear* is pronounced to rhyme with *bear*, it means "a rip" or "to rip."

EXAMPLE   A **tear** fell from the child's eye.

EXAMPLE   **Tear** this rag in half.

than, then *Than* is a conjunction used to introduce the second part of a comparison.

EXAMPLE   LaTrisha is taller **than** LaToya.

EXAMPLE   Ted ordered more food **than** he could eat.

Then has several related meanings that have to do with time: "at that time," "soon afterward," "the time mentioned," "at another time." *Then* can also mean "for that reason" or "in that case."

EXAMPLE   My grandmother was a young girl **then**.

EXAMPLE   We ate lunch and **then** washed the dishes.

EXAMPLE   I look forward to seeing you **then**.

EXAMPLE   Sometimes I feel completely confident; **then** I feel totally incompetent.

EXAMPLE   "It's raining," said Joy.

"**Then** we can't go," wailed her brother.

that there, this here   Don't use *there* or *here* after *that, this, those,* or *these.*

EXAMPLE   I can't decide whether to read **this** [*not* **this here**] magazine or **that** [*not* **that there**] book.

EXAMPLE   Fold **these** [*not* **these here**] towels and hang **those** [*not* **those there**] shirts in the closet.

that, which, who   *That* may refer to people or things. *Which* refers only to things. *Who* refers only to people.

EXAMPLE   The poet **that** wrote *Leaves of Grass* is Walt Whitman.

EXAMPLE   I have already seen the movie **that** is playing at the Bijou.

EXAMPLE   The new play, **which** closed after a week, received poor reviews.

EXAMPLE   Students **who** do well on the test will receive scholarships.

their, there, they're   *Their* is a possessive form of *they;* it's used to modify nouns. *There* means "in or at that place." *They're* is a contraction of *they are.*

EXAMPLE   A hurricane damaged **their** house.

EXAMPLE   Put your books **there**.

EXAMPLE   **They're** our next-door neighbors.

theirs, there's   *Theirs* is a possessive form of *they* used as a pronoun. *There's* is a contraction of *there is.*

EXAMPLE   **Theirs** is the white house with the green shutters.

EXAMPLE   **There's** your friend Chad.

them   Don't use *them* as an adjective in place of *those.*

EXAMPLE   I'll take one of **those** [*not* **them**] hamburgers.

this kind, these kinds Use the singular forms *this* and *that* with the singular nouns *kind*, *sort*, and *type*. Use the plural forms *these* and *those* with the plural nouns *kinds*, *sorts*, and *types*.

EXAMPLE   Use **this kind** of lightbulb in your lamp.

EXAMPLE   Do you like **these kinds** of lamps?

EXAMPLE   Many Pakistani restaurants serve **that sort** of food.

EXAMPLE   **Those sorts** of foods are nutritious.

EXAMPLE   **This type** of dog makes a good pet.

EXAMPLE   **These types** of dogs are good with children.

thorough, through, threw *Thorough* means "complete." *Through* is a preposition meaning "into at one side and out at another." *Through* can also mean "finished." *Threw* is the past tense of *throw*.

EXAMPLE   We gave the bedrooms a **thorough** cleaning.

EXAMPLE   A breeze blew **through** the house.

EXAMPLE   At last I'm **through** with my homework.

EXAMPLE   Lacey **threw** the ball.

to, too, two *To* means "in the direction of"; it is also part of the infinitive form of a verb. *Too* means "very" or "also." *Two* is the number after *one*.

EXAMPLE   Jaleela walks **to** school.

EXAMPLE   She likes **to** study.

EXAMPLE   The soup is **too** salty.

EXAMPLE   May I go, **too**?

EXAMPLE   We have **two** kittens.

toward, towards People in Great Britain use *towards*, but the preferred form in the United States is *toward*.

EXAMPLE   Smiling, she walked **toward** me.

try and Use *try to.*

EXAMPLE   Please **try to** [*not* **try and**] be on time.

type, type of Don't use *type* as an adjective.

EXAMPLE   What **type of** music [*not* **what type music**] do you like?

uninterested, disinterested *Uninterested* means "not interested," "unenthusiastic," and "indifferent." *Disinterested* means "impartial," "unbiased, not favoring either side in a dispute."

EXAMPLE   I threw the collie a biscuit, but, supremely **uninterested**, he let it lie where it fell.

EXAMPLE   The judge listened carefully to all the witnesses in that tangled case before handing down her **disinterested** and even-handed decision.

unless, without Don't use *without* in place of *unless.*

EXAMPLE   **Unless** [*not* **Without**] I earn some money, I can't go to camp.

used to, use to The correct form is *used to.*

EXAMPLE   We **used to** [*not* **use to**] live in Cleveland, Ohio.

waist, waste Your *waist* is where you wear your belt. As a noun, *waste* means "careless or unnecessary spending" or "trash." As a verb, it means "to spend or use carelessly or unnecessarily."

EXAMPLE   She tied a colorful scarf around her **waist**.

EXAMPLE   Buying those skis was a **waste** of money.

EXAMPLE   Put your **waste** in the dumpster.

EXAMPLE   Don't **waste** time worrying.

wait, weight *Wait* means "to stay or remain." *Weight* is a measurement.

EXAMPLE   **Wait** right here.

EXAMPLE   Her **weight** is 110 pounds.

wait for, wait on *Wait for* means "to remain in a place in anticipation of something expected." *Wait on* means "to act as a server."

EXAMPLE   **Wait for** me at the bus stop.

EXAMPLE   Nat and Tammy **wait on** diners at The Golden Griddle.

way, ways Use *way*, not *ways*, in referring to distance.

EXAMPLE   It's a long **way** [*not* **ways**] to Tipperary.

weak, week *Weak* means "feeble" or "not strong." A *week* is seven days.

EXAMPLE   She felt **weak** for a **week** after the operation.

weather, whether *Weather* is the condition of the atmosphere. *Whether* means "if"; it is also used to introduce the first of two choices.

EXAMPLE   The **weather** in Portland is mild and rainy.

EXAMPLE   Tell me **whether** you can go.

EXAMPLE   I can't decide **whether** to fly or drive.

when, where Don't use *when* or *where* incorrectly in writing a definition.

EXAMPLE   A simile is a comparison using *like* or *as*. [*not* **A simile is when you compare two things using** *like* **or** *as*.]

EXAMPLE   A watercolor wash is a thin coat of paint applied to paper that has been dampened with water. [*not* **A watercolor wash is where you dampen the paper before applying paint.**]

where Don't use *where* in place of *that.*

EXAMPLE   I see **that** [*not* **where**] the Cubs are in the basement again.

where . . . at Don't use *at* after *where.*

EXAMPLE   **Where** is your mother? [*not* **Where is your mother at?**]

who, whom *Who* is the nominative case. Use it for subjects and predicate nominatives. *Whom* is the objective case. Use it for direct objects, indirect objects, and objects of prepositions.

EXAMPLE   **Who** is that woman with the red umbrella?

EXAMPLE   **Whom** did you see at the mall?

who's, whose *Who's* is a contraction of *who is* or *who has. Whose* is the possessive form of *who.*

EXAMPLE   **Who's [Who is]** conducting the orchestra?

EXAMPLE   **Who's [Who has]** read this book?

EXAMPLE   **Whose** umbrella is this?

wind When *wind* rhymes with *finned*, it means "moving air." When *wind* rhymes with *find*, it means "to wrap around."

EXAMPLE   The **wind** is strong today.

EXAMPLE   **Wind** the bandage around your ankle.

wood, would *Wood* comes from trees. *Would* is an auxiliary verb.

EXAMPLE **Would** you prefer a **wood** bookcase or a metal one?

wound When *wound* is pronounced to rhyme with *sound,* it is the past tense of *wind.* When *wound* is pronounced wo͞ond, it means "an injury in which the skin is broken."

EXAMPLE I **wound** the bandage around my ankle to cover the **wound**.

your, you're *Your* is the possessive form of *you. You're* is a contraction of *you are.*

EXAMPLE **Your** arguments are convincing.

EXAMPLE **You're** doing a fine job.

ABBREVIATIONS

An abbreviation is a short way to write a word or a group of words. Abbreviations should be used sparingly in formal writing except for a few that are actually more appropriate than their longer forms. These are *Mr., Mrs.,* and *Dr.* (*doctor*) before names, *A.M.* and *P.M.,* and *B.C.* and *A.D.*

Some abbreviations are written with capital letters and periods, and some with capital letters and no periods; some are written with lowercase letters and periods, and some with lowercase letters and no periods. A few may be written in any one of these four ways and still be acceptable. For example, to abbreviate *miles per hour,* you may write *MPH, M.P.H., mph,* or *m.p.h.*

Some abbreviations may be spelled in more than one way. For example, *Tuesday* may be abbreviated *Tues.* or *Tue. Thursday* may be written *Thurs.* or *Thu.* In the following lists, only the most common way of writing each abbreviation is given.

When you need information about an abbreviation, consult a dictionary. Some dictionaries list abbreviations in a special section in the back. Others list them in the main part of the book.

MONTHS

Jan.	January	none	July
Feb.	February	Aug.	August
Mar.	March	Sept.	September
Apr.	April	Oct.	October
none	May	Nov.	November
none	June	Dec.	December

DAYS

Sun.	Sunday	Thurs.	Thursday
Mon.	Monday	Fri.	Friday
Tues.	Tuesday	Sat.	Saturday
Wed.	Wednesday		

TIME AND DIRECTION

CDT	central daylight time	MST	mountain standard time
CST	central standard time	PDT	Pacific daylight time
DST	daylight saving time	PST	Pacific standard time
EDT	eastern daylight time	ST	standard time
		NE	northeast
EST	eastern standard time	NW	northwest
		SE	southeast
MDT	mountain daylight time	SW	southwest

A.D.	in the year of the Lord (Latin *anno Domini*)
B.C.	before Christ
B.C.E.	before the common era
C.E.	common era
A.M.	before noon (Latin *ante meridiem*)
P.M.	after noon (Latin *post meridiem*)

MEASUREMENT

The same abbreviation is used for both the singular and the plural meaning of measurements. Therefore, *ft.* stands for both *foot* and *feet,* and *in.* stands for both *inch* and *inches.* Note that abbreviations of metric measurements are commonly written without periods. U.S. measurements, on the other hand, are usually written with periods.

Metric System

Mass and Weight

t	metric ton
kg	kilogram
g	gram
cg	centigram
mg	milligram

Capacity

kl	kiloliter
l	liter
cl	centiliter
ml	milliliter

Length

km	kilometer
m	meter
cm	centimeter
mm	millimeter

U.S. Weights and Measures

Weight

wt.	weight
lb.	pound
oz.	ounce

Capacity

gal.	gallon
qt.	quart
pt.	pint
c.	cup
tbsp.	tablespoon
tsp.	teaspoon
fl. oz.	fluid ounce

Length

mi.	mile
rd.	rod
yd.	yard
ft.	foot
in.	inch

MISCELLANEOUS MEASUREMENTS

p.s.i.	pounds per square inch
MPH	miles per hour
MPG	miles per gallon
d.p.i.	dots per inch
rpm	revolutions per minute
C	Celsius, centigrade
F	Fahrenheit
K	kelvin
kn	knot
kW	kilowatt

COMPUTER AND INTERNET

CPU	central processing unit
CRT	cathode ray tube
DOS	disk operating system
e-mail	electronic mail
K	kilobyte
URL	uniform resource locator
DVD	digital video disc
d.p.i	dots per inch
WWW	World Wide Web
ISP	internet service provider
DNS	domain name system

UNITED STATES (U.S.)

In most cases, state names and street addresses should be spelled out. The postal abbreviations in the following lists should be used with ZIP codes in addressing envelopes. They may also be used with ZIP codes for return addresses and inside addresses in business letters. The traditional state abbreviations are seldom used nowadays, but occasionally it's helpful to know them.

State	Traditional	Postal
Alabama	Ala.	AL
Alaska	none	AK
Arizona	Ariz.	AZ
Arkansas	Ark.	AR
California	Calif.	CA
Colorado	Colo.	CO
Connecticut	Conn.	CT
Delaware	Del.	DE
District of Columbia	D.C.	DC
Florida	Fla.	FL
Georgia	Ga.	GA
Hawaii	none	HI
Idaho	none	ID
Illinois	Ill.	IL
Indiana	Ind.	IN
Iowa	none	IA
Kansas	Kans.	KS
Kentucky	Ky.	KY
Louisiana	La.	LA
Maine	none	ME
Maryland	Md.	MD
Massachusetts	Mass.	MA
Michigan	Mich.	MI
Minnesota	Minn.	MN
Mississippi	Miss.	MS

Missouri	Mo.	MO
Montana	Mont.	MT
Nebraska	Nebr.	NE
Nevada	Nev.	NV
New Hampshire	N.H.	NH
New Jersey	N.J.	NJ
New Mexico	N. Mex.	NM
New York	N.Y.	NY
North Carolina	N.C.	NC
North Dakota	N. Dak.	ND
Ohio	none	OH
Oklahoma	Okla.	OK
Oregon	Oreg.	OR
Pennsylvania	Pa.	PA
Rhode Island	R.I.	RI
South Carolina	S.C.	SC
South Dakota	S. Dak.	SD
Tennessee	Tenn.	TN
Texas	Tex.	TX
Utah	none	UT
Vermont	Vt.	VT
Virginia	Va.	VA
Washington	Wash.	WA
West Virginia	W. Va.	WV
Wisconsin	Wis.	WI
Wyoming	Wyo.	WY

POSTAL ADDRESS ABBREVIATIONS

The following address abbreviations are recommended by the U.S. Postal Service to speed mailing. In most writing, these words should be spelled out.

Alley	ALY	North	N
Annex	ANX	Parkway	PKY
Avenue	AVE	Place	PL
Boulevard	BLVD	Plaza	PLZ
Center	CTR	River	RIV
Circle	CIR	Road	RD
Court	CT	South	S
Drive	DR	Square	SQ
East	E	Station	STA
Estates	EST	Street	ST
Expressway	EXPY	Terrace	TER
Heights	HTS	Trace	TRCE
Highway	HWY	Trail	TRL
Island	IS	Turnpike	TPKE
Lake	LK	Viaduct	VIA
Lane	LN	Village	VLG
Lodge	LDG	West	W
Mount	MT		

ADDITIONAL ABBREVIATIONS

ac	alternating current
dc	direct current
AM	amplitude modulation
FM	frequency modulation
RF	radio frequency
ASAP	as soon as possible

e.g.	for example (Latin *exempli gratia*)
etc.	and others, and so forth (Latin *et cetera*)
i.e.	that is (Latin *id est*)
Inc.	incorporated
ISBN	International Standard Book Number
lc	lowercase
misc.	miscellaneous
p.	page
pp.	pages
re	with regard to
R.S.V.P.	please reply (French *répondez s'il vous plaît*)
SOS	international distress signal
TM	trademark
uc	uppercase
vs.	versus
w/o	without

TEST FRIDAY!

© 1997 Randy Glasbergen

GLASBERGEN

"Class, I've got a lot of material to cover, so to save time I won't be using vowels today. Nw lts bgn, pls pn t pg 122."

Part Two

● ● ● ● ● ● ● ● ● ● ● ● ●

Grammar, Usage, and Mechanics

Chapter 1

Parts of
Speech

•••••••••••••••••

PRETEST   **Identifying Parts of Speech**

For each numbered word in the paragraph below, write one of these words to identify its part of speech: noun, pronoun, verb, adjective, adverb, preposition, conjunction, interjection.

   Something odd happened[1] yesterday[2] when Mom was next door at a neighbor's[3] house. I[4] was alone,[5] calmly[6] doing my homework,[7] when I smelled oatmeal[8] cookies baking. "Whoa!"[9] I said[10] to myself.[11] I checked[12] the kitchen, but[13] the oven[14] was off. "Either this is a[15] delusion," I muttered, "or[16] there are oatmeal cookies nearby."[17] After looking into the empty oven[18] once more, I went back[19] to my homework. When[20] Mom returned, the first[21] thing she[22] did was call to[23] me upstairs.[24] "Golly,[25] Chris, why didn't you[26] eat these cookies? I put them[27] in the toaster oven and set[28] the timer on[29] automatic so they'd be warm!"[30]

1.1 NOUNS

A **noun** is a word that names a person, a place, a thing, or an idea.

EXAMPLES	PERSON	uncle, doctor, baby, Luisa, son-in-law
	PLACE	kitchen, mountain, website, West Virginia
	THING	apple, tulip, continent, seagull, amplifier
	IDEA	respect, pride, love, appreciation, century

SINGULAR AND PLURAL NOUNS

Nouns can be singular or plural, depending on whether they name *one* person, place, thing, or idea or *more than one*.

To form the plural of most nouns, simply add –*s*. Other plural nouns are formed in different ways. For nouns ending in *s*, *ch*, *sh*, *x*, or *z*, add –*es* to form the plural. For nouns ending in *y* preceded by a consonant, change the *y* to *i* and add –*es*. For most nouns ending in *f* or *fe*, change the *f* to *v* and add –*s* or –*es*. Other nouns have irregular plurals (for example, *man/men*, *child/children*, *woman/women*). Some nouns do not change form from singular to plural (for example, *sheep/sheep*).

EXAMPLES	SINGULAR	girl, switch, hobby, life, goose, fish
	PLURAL	girls, switches, hobbies, lives, geese, fish

PRACTICE Plural Nouns

Write the plural form of each noun. Consult a dictionary if you need help.

1. star   **5.** waltz   **9.** box

2. trout   **6.** mystery   **10.** onion

3. half   **7.** flash

4. joy   **8.** tooth

POSSESSIVE NOUNS

The possessive form of a noun can show possession, ownership, or the general relationship between two nouns. Add an apostrophe and –*s* to form the possessive of any singular noun, even one that already ends in *s*. Use an apostrophe alone to form the possessive of a plural noun that ends in *s*.

EXAMPLES

SINGULAR POSSESSIVE	PLURAL POSSESSIVE
the **kitten's** tail	the **kittens'** tails
her **dress's** collar	her **dresses'** collars
the **wife's** speech	the **wives'** speeches
the **cookie's** decoration	the **cookies'** decorations
the **story's** villain	the **stories'** villains
the **watch's** battery	the **watches'** batteries

Add an apostrophe and –*s* to form the possessive of a plural noun that does not end in *s*.

EXAMPLES the **oxen's** stalls

the **children's** books

the **women's** trophies

Rewrite each phrase below using the possessive form of the noun in parentheses.

1. the (women) banquet
2. (Shawna) talent
3. Chef (Lorenson) recipe
4. the (building) location
5. the (books) titles

6. Mr. (Sims) accident
7. (Congress) schedule
8. the (children) fever
9. (Alfonso) job
10. the (orange) seeds

COMPOUND NOUNS

A **compound noun** is a noun made of two or more words. Compound nouns may be open, hyphenated, or closed.

EXAMPLES	OPEN	gray fox, press secretary, line of sight
	HYPHENATED	mother-in-law, tenth-grader, good-bye
	CLOSED	folksinger, headlight, postmaster

CONCRETE AND ABSTRACT NOUNS

A **concrete noun** names an object that occupies space or can be recognized by any of the senses (sight, smell, hearing, taste, touch).

EXAMPLES air   melody   stone   aroma   heat

An **abstract noun** names an idea, a quality, or a characteristic.

EXAMPLES attitude   dignity   loyalty   sadness   temperature

GRAMMAR/USAGE/MECHANICS

COMMON AND PROPER NOUNS

A **common noun** is the general—not the particular—
name of a person, place, thing, or idea.

EXAMPLES		COMMON NOUNS
	PERSON	artist, uncle, poet
	PLACE	country, lake, park
	THING	shuttle, vehicle, play
	IDEA	era, religion, movement

A **proper noun** is the name of a particular person,
place, thing, or idea.

EXAMPLES		PROPER NOUNS
	PERSON	Michelangelo, Uncle Louis, Maya Angelou
	PLACE	Mexico, Yellowstone National Park, Lake Superior
	THING	*Challenger*, Jeep, *Romeo and Juliet*
	IDEA	Industrial Age, Judaism, Romanticism

A **proper noun** is capitalized. A common noun is
usually not capitalized unless it is the first word of a
sentence.

PRACTICE Common, Proper, Concrete, and Abstract
Nouns

Identify each noun by writing common *or* proper. *If a
noun is common, also write* concrete *or* abstract *to further
identify it.*

1. Homer's *Odyssey* is an epic poem.
2. Who is the Steelers' new quarterback?

3. Victoria saw Mrs. Ramos fall and helped her up.
4. Honesty is one of Andy's best qualities.
5. One goal for good health is to drink eight glasses of water every day.
6. Bessie Coleman was the first African American female pilot.
7. Like any explorer, astronauts cherish the hope of discovering a new world.
8. Has Michiko ever written a song?
9. The vision of Chief Wilma Mankiller is to lead the Cherokee Nation to self-reliance.
10. The language we call Old English was spoken during the Middle Ages.

Collective Nouns

A **collective noun** is singular in form but names a group.

| EXAMPLES | family | herd | company | band | team |
| | audience | troop | committee | jury | flock |

A collective noun is sometimes considered singular and sometimes considered plural. If you are talking about a group as a whole acting together, consider the collective noun singular. (Sometimes the word *its* will refer to the collective noun used as a singular noun.) If you are talking about the individual members of a group, consider the collective noun plural. (Sometimes the word *their* will refer to the collective noun used as a plural noun.)

| EXAMPLES | SINGULAR | The **jury** *is* ready with *its* verdict. |
| | PLURAL | The **jury** *are* comparing *their* interpretations of the evidence. |

PRACTICE **Collective Nouns**

Write each collective noun. Label it S *if it's singular and* P *if it's plural.*

1. The audience rise to their feet and cheer.

2. Each class is expected to complete the voting process by 11:00 A.M.

3. Today the auto workers' union ends its strike.

4. The homeowners' association plans to hold a summer picnic next month.

5. The corporation acquires its new subsidiary next week.

6. In India, the Congress Party express their hopes for a majority in the next election.

7. Our family usually chooses a vacation destination a year in advance.

8. The orchestra play their instruments with warmth.

9. The new Jefferson football team hosts its traditional rival in just one month.

10. The anxious herd watch nearby hills for the first sign of a predator.

1.2 PRONOUNS

A **pronoun** is a word that takes the place of a noun, a group of words acting as a noun, or another pronoun. The word or group of words to which a pronoun refers is called its **antecedent**.

EXAMPLE   Though Georgia O'Keeffe was born in Wisconsin, **she** grew to love the landscape of the American Southwest. **[The pronoun *she* takes the place of its proper noun antecedent, *Georgia O'Keeffe*.]**

EXAMPLE   When Georgia O'Keeffe and Alfred Stieglitz were married in 1924, **both** were famous artists. **[The pronoun *both* takes the place of the nouns *Georgia O'Keeffe* and *Alfred Stieglitz*.]**

Though O'Keeffe **herself** was a painter, **her** husband was a photographer. [**The pronouns** *herself* **and** *her* **take the place of** *O'Keeffe* **and** *O'Keeffe's*.]

All pronouns in English can be put into these categories: personal and possessive pronouns, reflexive and intensive pronouns, demonstrative pronouns, interrogative pronouns, relative pronouns, and indefinite pronouns.

PERSONAL AND POSSESSIVE PRONOUNS

A **personal pronoun** refers to a specific person, place, thing, or idea by indicating the person speaking (the first person), the person or people being spoken to (the second person), or any other person, place, thing, or idea being discussed (the third person).

Like a noun, a personal pronoun expresses number; that is, it can be singular or plural.

PERSONAL PRONOUNS		
	SINGULAR	**PLURAL**
FIRST PERSON	I, me	we, us
SECOND PERSON	you	you
THIRD PERSON	he, him, she, her, it	they, them

EXAMPLE **FIRST PERSON**   The song was dedicated to **me**.
[*Me* **refers to the person speaking.**]

SECOND PERSON   Sam will copy the document for **you**.
[*You* **refers to the person being spoken to.**]

THIRD PERSON   **She** gave **him** the news. [*She* **and** *him* **refer to the people being talked about.**]

GRAMMAR/USAGE/MECHANICS

Third-person singular pronouns also express **gender**. *He* and *him* are masculine; *she* and *her* are feminine; *it* is neither masculine nor feminine but neuter.

A **possessive pronoun** takes the place of the possessive form of a noun.

POSSESSIVE PRONOUNS

	SINGULAR	PLURAL
FIRST PERSON	my, mine	our, ours
SECOND PERSON	your, yours	your, yours
THIRD PERSON	his, her, hers, its	their, theirs

Notice that no possessive personal pronoun contains an apostrophe. Take particular note that the possessive pronoun *its* in the preceding chart has no apostrophe. It is a serious but common error to mistake *its* and *it's*.

EXAMPLE   The pup is chasing **its** tail. [**possessive pronoun**]

EXAMPLE   **It's** a pity we have no camera. [**contraction for *It is***]

Some possessive pronouns must be used before nouns. Others can stand alone.

EXAMPLE   **USED BEFORE A NOUN**   This is **your** keyboard.

EXAMPLE   **USED ALONE**   This keyboard is **yours**.

PRACTICE Personal Pronouns

Write each pronoun. Identify it by writing first person, second person, *or* third person. *Then write* singular *or* plural. *If the pronoun is possessive, write* possessive.

1. Mike hit a home run today; it is his first at this school.
2. Lupe and Lisa took their books to lunch.

3. Loren and her brother Patrick are taking a course in CPR; they would like to make medicine their career.
4. A lizard tastes and smells with its tongue.
5. "You probably won't believe us," said Ross, "but Sam and I saw a UFO last night as we were on our way home."
6. Alanna cut her finger, now it is bandaged.
7. When Tran Chu left for the Math Olympiad, his entire class showed up to wish him luck.
8. Sipra forgot her lunch, but two classmates shared theirs with her.
9. How quickly we forget past favors; the big question today is "What have you done for me lately?"
10. "This knapsack is mine," said Sherif. "You must have left yours back at the campsite, Frank."

FRANK & ERNEST® by Bob Thaves

FRANK AND ERNEST reprinted by permission of Newspaper Enterprise Association, Inc.

REFLEXIVE AND INTENSIVE PRONOUNS

Reflexive and intensive pronouns are formed by adding –*self* or –*selves* to certain personal and possessive pronouns.

REFLEXIVE AND INTENSIVE PRONOUNS

	SINGULAR	PLURAL
FIRST PERSON	myself	ourselves
SECOND PERSON	yourself	yourselves
THIRD PERSON	himself, herself, itself	themselves

Notice that there is no such word as *hisself*, *theirself*, or *theirselves*.

A **reflexive pronoun** refers, or reflects back, to the subject of the sentence, indicating that the same person or thing is involved. A reflexive pronoun always adds information to a sentence.

EXAMPLE   Jim uses a stopwatch to time **himself** on the track.

EXAMPLE   She taught **herself** to play the piano.

EXAMPLE   We imagined **ourselves** dancing in a forest glade.

An **intensive pronoun** adds emphasis to another noun or pronoun in the same sentence.

EXAMPLE   He **himself** delivered the flowers.

EXAMPLE   You must sign the application **yourself**.

EXAMPLE   Mariko **herself** made the bridesmaids' dresses.

EXAMPLE   Pepe, Jaime, and César designed the float **themselves**.

An intensive pronoun does not add information to a sentence. If the intensive pronoun is left out, the sentence still has the same meaning. Often, but not always, an intensive pronoun comes immediately after its antecedent.

DEMONSTRATIVE PRONOUNS

A **demonstrative pronoun** points out specific persons, places, things, or ideas.

DEMONSTRATIVE PRONOUNS

SINGULAR	this	that
PLURAL	these	those

EXAMPLE **This** is your locker.

EXAMPLE **That** is your assignment.

EXAMPLE **These** are the shrubs to be trimmed.

EXAMPLE My uniform is cleaner than **those**.

INTERROGATIVE AND RELATIVE PRONOUNS

An **interrogative pronoun** is used to form questions.

INTERROGATIVE PRONOUNS

who	whom	whose
what	which	whoever
whomever	whatever	whichever

EXAMPLE **Who** is at the door?

EXAMPLE **Whom** would you prefer?

EXAMPLE **Whose** is this plaid coat?

EXAMPLE **What** is for lunch?

EXAMPLE **Which** of these books is your favorite?

EXAMPLE **Whatever** were you thinking of?

A **relative pronoun** is used to begin a special subject-verb word group called a subordinate clause. (See Chapter 4.)

RELATIVE PRONOUNS

who	whoever	which	that
whom	whomever	whichever	what
	whose	whatever	

EXAMPLE The driver **who** arrived last parked over there. [**The relative pronoun *who* begins the subordinate clause *who arrived last*.**]

EXAMPLE The meal **that** you prepared was delicious. [**The relative pronoun *that* begins the subordinate clause *that you prepared*.**]

INDEFINITE PRONOUNS

An **indefinite pronoun** refers to persons, places, things, or ideas in a more general way than a noun does.

EXAMPLE **Everybody** needs food. [**The indefinite pronoun *everybody* refers to people in general.**]

EXAMPLE Did you get **enough** to eat? [**The indefinite pronoun *enough* refers to a general, not a specific, amount.**]

EXAMPLE After two bowls of chili, I did not want **another**. [**The indefinite pronoun *another* has the antecedent *bowls (of chili)*.**]

SOME INDEFINITE PRONOUNS

all	both	everything	nobody	others
another	each	few	none	several
any	either	many	no one	some
anybody	enough	most	nothing	somebody
anyone	everybody	much	one	someone
anything	everyone	neither	other	something

Write each pronoun. Identify it by writing reflexive, intensive, demonstrative, interrogative, relative, *or* indefinite.

1. None of the soldiers who left camp this morning have returned.

2. Pointing to the stacked cases, Ariel whispered, "Whoever wins those will never have to buy canned corn again!"

3. Much of the conference involved archaeology, and as a result, few attended.

4. The ninth-graders themselves planted the garden, and no one else has cared for the growing plants.

5. Mother taught herself to ski and now teaches the skill to anyone who wants to learn.

6. Whatever happened to the survivors of the avalanche, a topic that most refuse to discuss?

7. "Whose is this?" asked Ingrid, holding up the half-eaten sandwich that had appeared under the bed.

8. Those whom Mr. Simmons has excused from the test may leave now.

9. Sean and Jaime arrived late from Tampa, and as a result, neither got much sleep last night.

10. The president gave himself a month to find a new media expert, but so far no candidates whom he has interviewed have been hired.

1.3 VERBS

A **verb** is a word that expresses action or a state of being and is necessary to make a statement.

| EXAMPLES | The bicyclist **grinned**. | The right gear **is** important. |
| EXAMPLES | A spectator **cheered** loudly. | The riders **seem** enthusiastic. |

The primary characteristic of a verb is its ability to express time—present, past, and future. Verbs express time by means of *tense* forms.

EXAMPLE	**PRESENT TENSE**	They **watch** the race together.
EXAMPLE	**PAST TENSE**	They **watched** the race together.
EXAMPLE	**FUTURE TENSE**	They **will watch** the race together.

ACTION VERBS

An **action verb** tells what someone or something does.

Some action verbs express physical action. Others express mental action.

| EXAMPLE | **PHYSICAL ACTION** | Ted **waved** the signal flag. |
| EXAMPLE | **MENTAL ACTION** | He **hoped** for success. |

A **transitive verb** is followed by a direct object—that is, a word or words that answer the question *what?* or *whom?*

| EXAMPLE | The batter **swung** the bat confidently. [The action verb *swung* is followed by the noun *bat,* which answers the question *swung what?*] |

An **intransitive verb** is *not* followed by a direct object.

| EXAMPLE | The batter **swung** wildly. [The verb is followed by a word that tells *how*.] |

To decide whether a verb in a sentence is transitive or intransitive, ask *what?* or *whom?* after the verb. If the answer is given in the sentence, the verb is transitive. If the answer is not given in the sentence, the verb is intransitive.

PRACTICE **Transitive and Intransitive Verbs**

Write each verb. Identify it by writing transitive *or* intransitive. *If it is transitive, write the word or words that answer the questions* what? *or* whom?

1. Robert "Tree" Cody, a member of the Dakota Sioux, speaks on Native American history throughout the United States.

2. A six-year-old boy in New Haven once saved a three-year-old child.

3. Hilda hid Jonny's gift until his birthday.

4. The Dixwell Dragons win the basketball tournament almost every year.

5. Zambia's flag features three stripes: the red stripe symbolizes freedom, the black stripe represents the people, and the orange stripe signifies its mineral wealth.

6. The senator spoke to the press from the platform of a caboose.

7. The United States Holocaust Memorial Museum opened in Washington, D.C., in 1993.

8. The Christmas in April program recruits volunteers who repair homes for low-income, elderly, and developmentally challenged people.

9. Maria recognized her little brother by his Halloween costume.

10. The town of Mystic, Connecticut, preserves for citizens and visitors alike its colorful two-hundred-year-old history.

LINKING VERBS

A **linking verb** links, or joins, the subject of a sentence (often a noun or a pronoun) with a noun, a pronoun, or an adjective that identifies or describes the subject. A linking verb does not show action.

Be in all its forms—*am, is, are, was, were*—is the most commonly used linking verb.

EXAMPLES The person behind the mask **was** you.

The players **are** ready.

EXAMPLES Archery **is** an outdoor sport.

They **were** sports fans.

Several other verbs besides *be* can act as linking verbs.

OTHER VERBS THAT CAN BE LINKING VERBS

look	remain	seem	become
stay	grow	appear	sound
taste	smell	feel	turn

EXAMPLES This salad **tastes** good.

The sun **feels** warm on my shoulders.

EXAMPLES You **look** comfortable.

The leaves **turned** brown.

VERB PHRASES

The verb in a sentence may consist of more than one word. The words that accompany the main verb are called **auxiliary**, or helping, **verbs**.

A **verb phrase** consists of a main verb and all its auxiliary, or helping, verbs.

AUXILIARY VERBS			
FORMS OF *BE*	am, is, are, was, were, being, been		
FORMS OF *HAVE*	has, have, had, having		
OTHER AUXILIARIES	can, could	may, might	must
	do, does, did	shall, should	will, would

The most common auxiliary verbs are forms of *be* and *have*. They help the main verb express time by forming the various tenses.

EXAMPLE   We **will weed** the vegetable garden this morning.

EXAMPLE   Sandra **has** already **weeded** the peppers and the tomatoes.

EXAMPLE   We **were weeding** the flower beds when the rain started.

The other auxiliary verbs are not used primarily to express time. They are often used to emphasize meaning.

EXAMPLE   I **should be leaving**.

EXAMPLE   **Could** he **have forgotten**?

EXAMPLE   Marisa **may** already **be finished**.

PRACTICE   Verbs and Verb Phrases: Transitive, Intransitive, and Linking

Write each verb and verb phrase. Identify it by writing transitive, intransitive, *or* linking.

1. The crowd grew quiet. The president stepped up to the podium.
2. Yes, sir, Juan has been here all morning.
3. Ginger, I will leave your lunch in the refrigerator.
4. André fell in gym class last period.
5. Marisa may have forgotten her keys this morning.
6. What are you cooking, Ron?

7. The light show is spectacular.

8. The ugly duckling became a beautiful swan.

9. Which of you have been absent from school this week?

10. The Appalachian Trail stretches from Maine to Georgia.

1.4 ADJECTIVES

An **adjective** is a word that modifies a noun or a pronoun by limiting its meaning. An adjective tells *what kind, which one, how many,* or *how much.*

EXAMPLES

red barn	**that** notebook	**seven** apples
interesting poem	**romantic** story	**many** novels
these ideas	**Irish** ballad	**cracked** pitcher
enough plates	**second** time	**no** excuse
afternoon class	**cheese** sandwich	**football** game

Pronouns can also serve as adjectives. For example, possessive pronouns (*my, our, your, his, her, its,* and *their*) act as adjectives when they modify nouns. Demonstrative pronouns (*this, that, these,* and *those*) can also be considered demonstrative adjectives when they modify nouns. Similarly, nouns can serve as adjectives. Possessive nouns, like possessive pronouns, can be used as adjectives. In fact, any noun that modifies another noun can be considered an adjective.

EXAMPLES   **my** kitten **[possessive adjective]**

those bicycles **[demonstrative adjective]**

Lucy's report **[possessive noun acting as adjective]**

leather shoes **[noun acting as adjective]**

Two verb forms can also act as adjectives: the present participle, which ends in *–ing*, and the past participle, which either ends in *–ed* or is irregularly formed.

EXAMPLES a **spinning** top   some **burned** toast   a **fallen** tree

Adjectives may appear in various positions in relation to the words they modify.

EXAMPLE How **suspenseful** this *movie* is!

EXAMPLE That **suspenseful** *movie* was very popular.

EXAMPLE The *movie* is **suspenseful**.

EXAMPLE The critics considered the *movie* **suspenseful**.

EXAMPLE The *movie*, relentlessly **suspenseful**, ended suddenly.

PRACTICE **Adjectives and the Words They Modify**

Write each adjective and the word it modifies. Don't write articles.

1. Five hundred tired fans waited in line for four hours.
2. No one in our class had ever heard of the Buffalo Soldiers.
3. Mrs. Angelini requests an aisle seat at concerts.
4. Who ate that peanut butter sandwich? I was saving it for my lunch!
5. The Argus Clearinghouse (http://www.clearinghouse.net) is a useful collection of four hundred or more guides to the Internet.
6. Yes, the new PTA president is George's mother.
7. Who would make this long trip just to see some petrified wood?
8. When Dad returned from his Paris trip, he brought me some wonderful French perfume.
9. Do we have enough orange juice for Kia's friends?
10. Television networks air a dizzying variety of drama and comedy programs.

FORMS OF ADJECTIVES

Many adjectives have different forms to indicate their degree of comparison. The **positive form** indicates no comparison. The **comparative form** compares two nouns or pronouns. The **superlative form** compares more than two nouns or pronouns.

EXAMPLES	POSITIVE	COMPARATIVE	SUPERLATIVE
	smooth	smoother	smoothest
	happy	happier	happiest
	thin	thinner	thinnest
	beautiful	more beautiful	most beautiful
	good, well	better	best
	bad	worse	worst
	many, much	more	most
	little	less	least

PRACTICE Comparative and Superlative Adjectives

Write the correct comparative or superlative form of the adjective in parentheses. Consult a dictionary if necessary.

1. Sliding downhill was (smooth) than I expected.
2. This is the (snowy) winter we have had in years.
3. California is a large state. Texas, however, is (large) than California, and Alaska is the (large) state in the United States.
4. Sofia's goal is to become the (good) doctor in Missouri.
5. The next time I suggest hiking up Millis Hill, please remind me that today's trip was the (unpleasant) one I've ever taken.
6. In my opinion, no one is (qualified) than Kecia to lead our class next year.

7. Few are (happy) than my brothers when vacation starts, but Mom is always (happy) of all when they start school again.

8. How much (long) will it be before all the grass is cut?

9. The 630-foot Gateway Arch in St. Louis is the (tall) monument in the United States.

10. Saint Louis University now stands on reclaimed land that once housed some of the (bad) slums in Missouri.

ARTICLES

Articles are the adjectives *a, an,* and *the. A* and *an* are called **indefinite articles**. They can refer to any one of a kind of person, place, thing, or idea. *A* is used before consonant sounds, and *an* is used before vowel sounds. *The* is the **definite article**. It refers to a specific person, place, thing, or idea.

EXAMPLES

INDEFINITE	He found **a** ring.	I ate **an** egg.
	I have **a** used computer.	It's almost **an** hour since he left.
DEFINITE	He found **the** ring.	I ate **the** egg.
	I have **the** used computer.	It's almost **the** hour for lunch.

PROPER ADJECTIVES

A **proper adjective** is formed from a proper noun. It begins with a capital letter.

EXAMPLE   Vancouver is a **Canadian** city.

EXAMPLE   We visited the **London** Zoo.

The following suffixes, along with others, are often used to form proper adjectives: *-n, -ian, -an, -ese, -ic,* and *-ish.* Sometimes there are other changes as well. Check the spelling in a dictionary if necessary.

EXAMPLES	PROPER NOUNS	PROPER ADJECTIVES
	Queen Victoria	Victorian
	Egypt	Egyptian
	Mexico	Mexican
	Lebanon	Lebanese
	Celt	Celtic
	Ireland	Irish

PRACTICE Proper Adjectives

Rewrite each phrase, changing the noun in boldfaced type into a proper adjective. Consult a dictionary if necessary.

1. the embassy of **Japan**
2. mythology of **Greece** and **Rome**
3. the Alps of **Switzerland**
4. the people of **Wales**
5. the Vikings of **Denmark**
6. the canals of **Holland**
7. the veldt of **Africa**
8. the language of **China**
9. winters in **Iceland**
10. hot spices of **Thailand**

1.5 ADVERBS

An **adverb** is a word that modifies a verb, an adjective, or another adverb by making its meaning more specific.

The following sentences illustrate the use of adverbs to modify verbs, adjectives, and adverbs.

EXAMPLES

MODIFYING VERBS   **Never** swim alone.
                        verb

                        He has **seldom** complained.
                        verb   verb

MODIFYING ADJECTIVES   The movie was **very** scary and **too** long.
                             adjective   adjective

MODIFYING ADVERBS   She **almost** always waited **quite** patiently.
                          adverb   adverb

Adverbs modify by answering these questions: *When? Where? How? To what degree?*

EXAMPLES **WHEN?**   It should arrive **Saturday**.
                                     I changed the schedule **again**.

              WHERE?   Leave your coat **there**.
                                     He drove **south**.

              HOW?   He stacked the books **quickly** and **neatly**.
                                     Carefully I counted them.

              TO WHAT DEGREE?   We were **very** sorry.
                                     We had arrived **quite** late.

When an adverb modifies a verb or a verb phrase, it may sometimes be placed in various positions relative to the verb or verb phrase. When an adverb modifies an adjective or another adverb, it usually comes directly before the modified word.

EXAMPLES **MODIFYING A VERB**   **Now** the room *is* ready.
                                      The room **now** *is* ready.
                                      The room *is* **now** ready.
                                      The room *is* ready **now**.

MODIFYING AN ADJECTIVE	The ice *is* **dangerously** *soft*.
	You look **terribly** *tired*.
MODIFYING AN ADVERB	I answered **too** *slowly*.
	It **almost** *never* rains this hard.

NEGATIVE WORDS AS ADVERBS

The word *not* and the contraction *n't* (as in *don't* and *won't*) are adverbs. Other negative words can function as adverbs of time and place.

EXAMPLES The bell has **not** rung.   The toy is **nowhere** to be seen.

She is **scarcely** awake.   I have **never** danced with her.

PRACTICE Adverbs

Write each adverb and the word it modifies. Then tell whether the modified word is a verb, *an* adjective, *or another* adverb.

1. Jessica jumped up and ran from the table.
2. I have never seen a more glorious sunset!
3. To drive from Hartford to New Haven, go south on I-91.
4. Luke is suspiciously sick before a math test.
5. The boys ran down the hill too fast. One of them fell and hurt his ankle badly.
6. Beowulf grasped the monster's arm, wrenched it mightily, and pulled it out of its socket.
7. Soon afterward, Marcus lay the book on the table again.
8. The cinnamon cat padded quietly into the kitchen and sat down contentedly by the window.
9. Mia's sculpture is particularly smooth.
10. Mauritza quickly keyed in the URL for the Internet Public Library, <http://www.ipl.org/>. She easily found some quite useful articles and almost too many books.

ADVERBS THAT COMPARE

Like adjectives, some adverbs have different forms to indicate their degree of comparison. The comparative form of an adverb compares two actions. The superlative form of an adverb compares more than two actions.

For most adverbs of only one syllable, add *–er* to make the comparative form and *–est* to make the superlative form.

EXAMPLES

POSITIVE	COMPARATIVE	SUPERLATIVE
runs **fast**	runs **faster**	runs **fastest**
pays **soon**	pays **sooner**	pays **soonest**
works **hard**	works **harder**	works **hardest**

Most adverbs that end in *–ly* or have more than one syllable use the word *more* to form the comparative and *most* to form the superlative.

EXAMPLES

POSITIVE	COMPARATIVE	SUPERLATIVE
eats **healthfully**	eats **more healthfully**	eats **most healthfully**
checks **often**	checks **more often**	checks **most often**
snores **loudly**	snores **more loudly**	snores **most loudly**

Some adverbs form the comparative and superlative irregularly.

EXAMPLES

POSITIVE	COMPARATIVE	SUPERLATIVE
swims **well**	swims **better**	swims **best**
dives **badly**	dives **worse**	dives **worst**
cares **little**	cares **less**	cares **least**
sees **far**	sees **farther**	sees **farthest**
researches **far**	researches **further**	researches **furthest**

Write the comparative and superlative forms of each adverb. Consult a dictionary if necessary.

1. heartily
2. soon
3. sadly
4. badly

5. little
6. clearly
7. well
8. quickly

9. secretly
10. fast

1.6 PREPOSITIONS

A **preposition** is a word that shows the relationship of a noun or a pronoun to another word in a sentence.

A **prepositional phrase** is a group of words that begins with a preposition and ends with a noun or a pronoun that is called the **object of the preposition**.

EXAMPLE   The diamonds **in** the vault are priceless. [*In* shows the relationship between the diamonds and the object of the preposition, *vault*.]

EXAMPLE   The telephone rang four times **during** dinner. [*During* shows the relationship between *rang* and the object of the preposition, *dinner*.]

EXAMPLE   Here is a gift **for** you. [*For* relates *gift* to the object of the preposition, *you*.]

COMMONLY USED PREPOSITIONS

aboard	beneath	in	regarding
about	beside	inside	respecting
above	besides	into	since
across	between	like	through
after	beyond	near	throughout
against	but (except)	of	to

GRAMMAR/USAGE/MECHANICS

along	by	off	toward
amid	concerning	on	under
among	despite	onto	underneath
around	down	opposite	until
as	during	out	up
at	except	outside	upon
before	excepting	over	with
behind	for	past	within
below	from	pending	without

A **compound preposition** is a preposition that is made up of more than one word.

COMPOUND PREPOSITIONS		
according to	because of	instead of
ahead of	by means of	next to
along with	except for	on account of
apart from	in addition to	on top of
aside from	in front of	out of
as to	in spite of	owing to

Some words may be used as either prepositions or adverbs. A word is used as a preposition if it has a noun or a pronoun as its object. A word is used as an adverb if it does not have an object.

EXAMPLES

WORD USED AS PREPOSITION
I left my boots **outside** the back door.
The speech was **over** my head.
Everyone came **aboard** the boat.

WORD USED AS ADVERB
I left my boots **outside**.
The speech was **over**.
Everyone came **aboard**.

Write each prepositional phrase. Underline the preposition and draw a circle around the object of the preposition.

1. The paramedics responded to the emergency call.
2. How many sandwiches shall we make for the picnic?
3. From the porch I could see all the way to the river.
4. Everyone at the twins' party received a prize except Anjelica.
5. We stayed up until midnight. The UFO never reappeared.
6. In spite of Emilio's objections, the immigration officer refused him entry to Mexico.
7. Prior to Jorge's arrival, geometry was boring. Now, however, we look forward to every class.
8. Alicia stood before the huge audience and gave her speech with confidence.
9. Is Helena the capital of Washington or of Montana?
10. The rabbit squeezed under the fence, hopped out of the yard, and stopped for a moment by the brook.

1.7 CONJUNCTIONS

A **conjunction** is a word that joins single words or groups of words.

COORDINATING CONJUNCTIONS

A **coordinating conjunction** joins words or groups of words that have equal grammatical weight in a sentence.

COORDINATING CONJUNCTIONS						
and	but	or	so	nor	yet	for

EXAMPLE One **and** six are seven. **[two nouns]**

EXAMPLE Merlin was smart **but** irresponsible. **[two adjectives]**

EXAMPLE Let's put the note on the TV **or** on the refrigerator. **[two prepositional phrases]**

EXAMPLE I wanted a new sun hat, **so** I bought one. **[two complete thoughts]**

EXAMPLE He did not complain, **nor** did he object to our plan. **[two complete thoughts]**

EXAMPLE Lightning struck the barn, **yet** no fire started. **[two complete thoughts]**

When used as a coordinating conjunction, *for* means "for the reason that" or "because."

EXAMPLE We didn't explore the summit that night, **for** the climb had exhausted us.

CORRELATIVE CONJUNCTIONS

Correlative conjunctions work in pairs to join words and groups of words of equal grammatical weight in a sentence.

CORRELATIVE CONJUNCTIONS		
both . . . and	just as . . . so	not only . . . but (also)
either . . . or	neither . . . nor	whether . . . or

Correlative conjunctions make the relationship between words or groups of words a little clearer than do coordinating conjunctions.

EXAMPLES

COORDINATING CONJUNCTIONS	CORRELATIVE CONJUNCTIONS
He **and** I were there.	**Both** he **and** I were there.
She will sew new curtains, **or** I will put up the old blinds.	**Either** she will sew new curtains, **or** I will put up the old blinds.
I scrubbed **and** waxed the floor.	I **not only** scrubbed **but also** waxed the floor.

Write all conjunctions. Then identify them as either coordinating *or* correlative.

1. At the shore, you'll see seagulls both on the sand and in the water.
2. Neither Luis nor I voted for the amendment.
3. In 1500 the cities now known as Cahokia, Illinois, and Albuquerque, New Mexico, were already large.
4. Either come to the party or stay away.
5. Apparently Ron found nothing on the counter or under the table.
6. Mr. Palumbo ordered the pasta primavera, and he ate it with gusto.
7. Not only has the Antietam battlefield been restored, but parts of Fort Sumter have also been completely rebuilt.
8. The weather has grown very cold today, yet it has not snowed.
9. Just as the days grow longer in springtime, so the nights grow longer in fall.
10. Ebenezer Scrooge was rich but not happy.

SUBORDINATING CONJUNCTIONS

A **subordinating conjunction** joins two clauses, or thoughts, in such a way as to make one grammatically dependent on the other.

The thought, or clause, that a subordinating conjunction introduces is said to be "subordinate," or dependent, because it cannot stand by itself as a complete sentence.

EXAMPLE We can skate on the pond **when** the ice is thicker.

EXAMPLE We can't skate **until** the ice is thicker.

EXAMPLE **Because** the ice is still too thin, we must wait for a hard freeze.

COMMON SUBORDINATING CONJUNCTIONS

after	as though	since	until
although	because	so long as	when
as	before	so (that)	whenever
as far as	considering (that)	than	where
as if	if	though	whereas
as long as	inasmuch as	till	wherever
as soon as	in order that	unless	while

PRACTICE Subordinating Conjunctions

Write each subordinating conjunction.

1. I'll go with you wherever you go.
2. You may as well eat dinner as long as you're here.
3. Since Peppermint may be upset by our move, I'll keep her inside for now.
4. No one may leave until the exam is over.
5. Although it was cold that morning, Knut wore only a light jacket over his school clothes.
6. New England's climate is cool and humid, whereas the Southwest's is hot and dry.
7. After his stay on the Mir space station, the astronaut headed back to Earth.
8. Please come to visit us if you're ever in Topeka.
9. While you finish your homework, I'll scrub the floor.
10. Don't expect lunch unless you're home by noon.

CONJUNCTIVE ADVERBS

A **conjunctive adverb** is used to clarify the relationship between clauses of equal weight in a sentence.

Conjunctive adverbs are usually stronger, more precise, and more formal than coordinating conjunctions. Notice that only a comma is used with a coordinating conjunction to separate the clauses. When a conjunctive adverb is used between clauses, a semicolon precedes the conjunctive adverb and a comma follows it.

GRAMMAR/USAGE/MECHANICS

EXAMPLES

COORDINATING CONJUNCTION   The civilization of the Incas was advanced, **but** they never invented the wheel.

CONJUNCTIVE ADVERB   The civilization of the Incas was advanced; **however,** they never invented the wheel.

There are many conjunctive adverbs, and they have many uses, as the following examples show.

EXAMPLES

TO REPLACE *AND*   also, besides, furthermore, moreover

TO REPLACE *BUT*   however, nevertheless, nonetheless, still

TO STATE A RESULT   accordingly, consequently, then, therefore, thus

TO STATE EQUALITY   equally, indeed, likewise, similarly

PRACTICE **Conjunctive Adverbs**

Write each underlined word. If it's a coordinating conjunction, label it CC. *If it's a conjunctive adverb, label it* CA.

1. It's my turn to fix dinner; <u>therefore</u>, I can't go to the mall with you after school.
2. Ceil didn't buy any peaches, <u>but</u> she got a melon.
3. Luke's new tennis racket lies forgotten in his closet, <u>and</u> his new skates are in a dark corner; <u>similarly</u>, these new skis will probably be abandoned soon.

4. Of course you may come along on our trip to the park; <u>indeed</u>, I'll be glad of your help with the dogs.

5. Bela didn't want a new coat, <u>nor</u> did he think new boots were necessary.

6. Robbinette's recipe for hot cider is my favorite, <u>for</u> she stirs it with a cinnamon stick.

7. Leeza has become better organized lately; <u>consequently</u>, she found her summer-school application form after only a short search.

8. The vandals were evidently wearing gloves; we did find one long blonde hair stuck to a graffito, <u>however</u>.

9. Going to that movie would keep you out too late on a school night; <u>also</u>, the subject matter isn't suitable for a person your age.

10. This applicant lacks experience; she has, <u>nonetheless</u>, demonstrated the ability to manage a big project.

1.8 INTERJECTIONS

An **interjection** is a word or a phrase that expresses emotion or exclamation. An interjection has no grammatical connection to other words.

EXAMPLES **Oh, my!** What is that?   **Yikes**, I'll be late!

Ouch! It's hot!   **Ah**, that's better.

PRACTICE Interjections

Identify each interjection.

1. "Oh, my goodness!" cried Mrs. Wallace, the head librarian. "We've got mites in the atlas again!"

2. "No kidding!" chuckled Len, her assistant. "Tell them to enjoy their trip."

3. Sanchita rounded the corner at the bottom of the hill. "Uh-oh!" she gasped. "I forgot to have the brakes fixed on this bike!"

4. "Hee, hee!" chortled the villainous banker. "I finally own the mortgage on the widow's little cabin!"

5. "Ha!" laughed the widow. "Keep it. *I* own the mortgage on your penthouse!"

6. "Say, Charlie," called his teacher. "I noticed that you didn't hand in your homework this morning."

7. "Well, Mr. Anderson," Charlie answered, "I was going to tell you that our canary ate it, but we only have a dog."

8. Six-year-old Ignatius woke up late with a start. "Oh, rats!" he grumbled. "If today's not Saturday, I'm going to be tardy!"

9. Janine looked down into the cereal bowl and gagged. "Eeew, what *is* that stuff? It looks just awful!"

10. "Yuck!" exclaimed Cindy. "You're right, but I don't know what it is. That's *your* bowl."

PRACTICE Parts of Speech

Use each word below in two sentences as two different parts of speech. You will write a total of twenty sentences. In each sentence, circle the word. After each sentence, give the word's part of speech.

EXAMPLE block

ANSWER Walk the dog around the (block.) noun

(Block) that play! verb

1. rash	**5.** down	**9.** which
2. circle	**6.** around	**10.** art
3. bow	**7.** find	
4. back	**8.** goodness	

Rewrite the following passage, correcting errors in spelling, capitalization, grammar, and usage. Add any missing punctuation. There are ten errors. Some sentences are correct.

Nikki Giovanni

¹You may think of Nikki Giovanni as a writer of wonderful children's poetry. ²Thats true, but she is also much more. ³As well as poetry, she writes essays and short storys about individual growth, personal struggles for independence and fulfillment, and her concern for humanity as a global community. ⁴She has published her conversations with James Baldwin and with Margaret Walker, two high-profile African american writers. ⁵She has contributed to books such as "The 100 Best Colleges for African American Students" and *African American Literature: An Anthology of Nonfiction, Fiction, Poetry, and Drama.*

⁶Giovanni gives lectures and poetry readings all over the United States, speaking about the past, the present and the future of African Americans. ⁷She teaches coarses at many universities, and she have accepted a permanent position as Professor of English at Virginia Polytechnic Institute and State University. ⁸She has been Woman of the Year three times: for *Ebony, Mademoiselle,* and *Ladies Home Journal.* ⁹She has recorded at least seven albums and CDs, including 1997's *In Philadelphia.* ¹⁰A 1987 PBS film *Spirit to Spirit: The Poetry of Nikki Giovanni,* winned the Oakland Museum Film Festival's Silver Apple Award and is now available on videotape. ¹¹Her nineteen ninety-seven book *Love Poems* contains twenty original poems along with many of her best-known love poems from previous books.

For each numbered word in the paragraph below, write one of these words to identify its part of speech: noun, pronoun, verb, adjective, adverb, preposition, conjunction, interjection.

What[1] caused[2] such a great[3] empire as Rome[4] to fall? It[5] wasn't just the fierce[6] northern[7] and[8] eastern tribes. Instead, it was[9] the Roman Empire's[10] tremendous[11] wealth, power, pride, and position.[12] Once,[13] early in[14] its history, Rome had been justly[15] proud of its[16] virtues, its heroes, and its civilized[17] way of life. While[18] the empire[19] grew, however, Romans[20] began to value honor less[21] and wealth and[22] power more. When[23] personal[24] pride, courage, and honesty died,[25] Rome began to fall. By[26] the early fourth century after Christ, nothing[27] could keep the barbarians from pouring in.[28] Rome had crumbled[29] from the[30] inside.

Chapter 2

Parts of the Sentence

• • • • • • • • • • • • • • • •

PRETEST   **Simple and Complete Subjects
and Predicates**

*Identify each underlined word or group of words in the
paragraph by writing one of these labels:* simple subject,
complete subject, simple predicate, *or* complete predicate.

[1]Everyone in the car pool this morning griped and complained about the
weather. [2]Lanna found the Boston days much too cold. [3]She wanted a home
in Florida. [4]The skiers, Haji and Stan, had their own ideas. [5]They required
snow and lots of it. [6]Jerol is a cross-country runner. [7]He wished for perpetu-
ally mild days and nights. [8]Sarcastic as usual, I grinned and voted for rain.
[9]Only Mr. Johansson, today's chauffeur, expressed another point of view.
"[10]Here you are, in a heated car, on the way to a heated school building.
[11]How can you complain about the weather? [12]Appreciate your
opportunities." [13]Down the Massachusetts Pike rolled one silent car.

129

Identify each underlined word or group of words by writing one of these labels: direct object, indirect object, object complement, predicate nominative, predicate adjective.

14. Architecture has always been an <u>interest</u> of mine.

15. In the spring, Guillermo gives his <u>garden</u> a good cleaning.

16. Carson McCullers wrote <u>*The Heart Is a Lonely Hunter*</u>.

17. Mrs. Garanzini found the music <u>dreadful</u>.

18. That brief visit remains my mom's favorite <u>memory</u>.

19. The Tivoli Gardens is a vast <u>array</u> of shops, restaurants, rides, and galleries.

20. Seafood lovers love <u>Scandinavia</u>.

21. Arte found that the newest chorus member was <u>she</u>.

22. Of all colleges, my brother considers Notre Dame his <u>favorite</u>.

23. Cary, North Carolina, is <u>charming</u>.

24. At five o'clock, Linda feeds her <u>cats</u> their evening meal.

25. Cinnamon, Peppermint, and Rosemary are not <u>pets</u> but members of the family.

26. Both the Nile and the Mississippi form <u>deltas</u>.

27. This costume is much too <u>big</u> for me.

28. Age has taken its <u>toll</u> on Copenhagen, Denmark.

2.1 SIMPLE SUBJECTS AND SIMPLE PREDICATES

A **sentence** is a group of words that expresses a complete thought.

Every sentence has two basic parts, a *subject* and a *predicate*.

The **subject** is the part of the sentence that names whom or what the sentence is about.

The **predicate** is the part of the sentence that says something about the subject.

Both the subject and the predicate can consist of more than one word.

The **simple subject** is the key noun or pronoun that tells what the sentence is about.

The **simple predicate** is the verb or verb phrase that expresses an action or a state of being about the subject of the sentence.

Remember, a simple predicate that is a verb phrase consists of a verb and any auxiliary, or helping, verbs.

EXAMPLES	SIMPLE SUBJECT	SIMPLE PREDICATE
	Garth Brooks	will perform.
	Dogs	were barking.
	Michael Jordan	jumped.
	Things	change.

You find the simple subject by asking *who?* or *what?* about the verb. For example, in the first sentence above, the proper noun *Garth Brooks* answers the question *Who will perform?*

PRACTICE **Simple Subjects and Simple Predicates**

Write each simple subject and simple predicate. Underline the simple predicate.

1. Two days of rain and fog can make a whole week dreary and disagreeable.

2. Charles Dickens used his father as a model for Wilkins Micawber in *David Copperfield.*

3. In the first row, Tandra Sen will stand next to Chris Johnson.

4. The 8:15 train goes to Baltimore on weekdays but not weekends.

5. Nobody told me about the new class schedule.

6. Nina listened carefully to the symphony's first movement.

7. You will sing solo today.

8. In spite of the bad weather, everyone is here on time today.

9. The squirrel is one of nature's best acrobats.

10. That last concert deserved its special mention in today's newspaper.

2.2 COMPLETE SUBJECTS AND COMPLETE PREDICATES

In most sentences, the addition of other words and phrases to the simple subject and the simple predicate expands or modifies the meaning of the sentence.

The **complete subject** consists of the simple subject and all the words that modify it.

The **complete predicate** consists of the simple predicate, or verb, and all the words that modify it or complete its meaning.

EXAMPLES	COMPLETE SUBJECT	COMPLETE PREDICATE
	Talented Garth Brooks	will perform his biggest hits.
	Large dogs	were barking at strangers on the sidewalk.
	The athletic Michael Jordan	jumped above the rim.
	Many things	change daily.

Complete Subjects and Complete Predicates

Identify each underlined complete subject or complete predicate by writing CS *or* CP.

1. <u>The rafters of the opera house</u> shook with the tremendous crescendos of Wagner's *The Twilight of the Gods.*
2. Lily and Tamiko <u>are very much concerned about the gap in the ozone layer</u>.
3. <u>Henri and Marquise</u> have spoken to the coach about this year's soccer team.
4. The first baseball of spring <u>crashed through the window</u>.
5. The magnificent Bayeux Tapestry <u>tells the story of the victory of William the Conqueror over the Anglo-Saxons in A.D. 1066</u>.
6. <u>The character with the dusty hat, the tattered coat, and the ill-fitting pants</u> is usually played by Charlie Chaplin.
7. Robin <u>has the attendance reports for the first semester</u>.
8. <u>Charli</u> likes scarlet tanagers better than blue jays.
9. My friend Robert <u>has never missed a class or failed a test</u>.
10. <u>Jaime's new red balloon</u> sailed through the window, past the trees, and into the clouds.

2.3 COMPOUND SUBJECTS AND COMPOUND PREDICATES

A **compound subject** is made up of two or more simple subjects that are joined by a conjunction and have the same verb.

The conjunctions most commonly used to join the subjects in a compound subject are *and* and *or.*

EXAMPLE **Tomatoes** and **carrots** are colorful vegetables.

EXAMPLE **Tomatoes** or **carrots** would add color to the salad.

Correlative conjunctions may also be used to join compound subjects.

EXAMPLE   Neither the **tomato** nor the **pepper** grows underground.

EXAMPLE   Both the **tomato** and the **pepper** are rich in vitamin C.

When there are more than two subjects, the conjunction is usually used only between the last two subjects, and the subjects are separated by commas.

EXAMPLE   **Tomatoes, carrots,** and **peppers** are healthful.

Some sentences have more than one simple predicate.

A **compound predicate** (or **compound verb**) is made up of two or more verbs or verb phrases that are joined by a conjunction and have the same subject.

EXAMPLE   Horses **gallop** and **charge**.

EXAMPLE   Maria **opened** her book, **grabbed** a pencil, and **started** her homework.

In compound verbs that contain verb phrases, the auxiliary verb may or may not be repeated before the second verb.

EXAMPLE   Seagulls **will glide** or **swoop** down to the ocean.

EXAMPLE   We **have tested** these procedures and **have found** them good.

A sentence may have both a compound subject and a compound predicate.

EXAMPLE   **Butterflies** and **hummingbirds dart** and **dip** in the air.

Simple and Compound Subjects and Predicates

Write CS *if a sentence has a compound subject. Write* CP *if there is a compound predicate. Then write the simple subjects and the simple predicates.*

1. Wheat and apples are two of Washington state's most important crops.
2. Its clear glacial lakes and deep forests make Washington a breathtaking stop on a western trip.
3. Noah Webster wrote the first truly American dictionary, simplified the spelling of many words, and campaigned for the first American copyright laws.
4. Matthew Arnold and William Butler Yeats are both famous for the echoing sound effects in their poetry.
5. You or Mai will go to the mall with your father.
6. Waterfalls in Yosemite National Park plunge over tall cliffs and merge with the waters below.
7. The Zambezi River rises in Zambia and follows a winding course across Mozambique.
8. Bill, Connie, and Adam sing very well.
9. You have read or memorized plenty of poetry in the last week.
10. We remember and honor Washington, Jefferson, and Lincoln as visionary leaders.

2.4 ORDER OF SUBJECT AND PREDICATE

In English the subject comes before the verb in most sentences. Some exceptions to this normal word order are discussed on the next page.

In **commands** and **requests,** the subject is usually not stated. The predicate is the entire sentence. The pronoun *you* is understood to be the subject.

EXAMPLES   [You] **Run!**   [You] **Give** it to me.   [You] Please **be** careful.

Questions frequently begin with a verb or a helping verb or the words *who, whom, what, when, where, why,* or *how.*

EXAMPLE   **Was** she correct?

EXAMPLE   **Have** you **read** Gary Soto's stories?

EXAMPLE   **Whom** did he invite?

In these cases, the subject generally follows the verb or helping verb. To find the subject of a question, rearrange the words to form a statement.

EXAMPLES

SUBJECT	PREDICATE
She	was correct.
You	have read Gary Soto's stories.
He	did invite whom.

A sentence written in **inverted order,** in which the predicate comes before the subject, serves to add emphasis to the subject.

EXAMPLES

PREDICATE	SUBJECT
Across the field **galloped**	the three **horses.**
In the distance **flowed**	a **river.**

Remember, a word in a prepositional phrase is never the subject.

When the word *there* or *here* begins a sentence and is followed by a form of the verb *to be,* the subject follows the verb. The word *there* or *here* is never the subject.

PREDICATE   **SUBJECT**

There **is**   a **chill** in the air.

Here **are**   my **thoughts** on the matter.

You can find the subject in an inverted sentence by asking *who?* or *what?* about the predicate.

EXAMPLES What galloped across the field? The three horses did.

What is in the air? A chill is.

PRACTICE **Identifying Simple Subjects and Predicates in Sentences With Unusual Order**

Write each simple subject and simple predicate. If a subject is understood, write [You].

1. Have a good time at the game!

2. Has anyone seen my red corduroy blazer?

3. Downwind from the paper mill drifted the unpleasant odor of sulfur.

4. Here is the list of drama club members.

5. Where is Pittsburgh on this map?

6. Over the hurdles bounded the Cricco twins.

7. Does Marjorie consider my ideas odd?

8. Please park on the street, not on the lawn.

9. There were some grapes on the table a minute ago.

10. Now, tell me all about your vacation.

2.5 COMPLEMENTS

A **complement** is a word or a group of words that completes the meaning of a verb.

There are four kinds of complements: *direct objects, indirect objects, object complements,* and *subject complements.*

DIRECT OBJECTS

A **direct object** answers the question *what?* or *whom?* after an action verb.

The subject of a sentence usually performs the action indicated by the verb. That action may be directed toward or received by someone or something—the direct object. Direct objects are nouns, pronouns, or words acting as nouns, and they may be compound. Only transitive verbs have direct objects.

EXAMPLE   Carlos served **dinner.** [Carlos served *what?*]

EXAMPLE   Maria admires **him** deeply. [Maria admires *whom?*]

EXAMPLE   Carlos served a Mexican **dinner** and a fabulous **dessert.** [Carlos served *what?*]

INDIRECT OBJECTS

An **indirect object** answers the question *to whom? for whom? to what?* or *for what?* after an action verb.

A sentence can have an indirect object only if it has a direct object. Two clues can help you identify indirect objects. First, an indirect object always comes between the verb and the direct object.

EXAMPLE   Tyrone sent **me** a letter. [Tyrone sent a letter *to whom?*]

EXAMPLE   Kim saved **Rosa** and **Manuel** seats. [Kim saved seats *for whom?*]

Second, if you add the word *to* or *for* in front of an indirect object, you haven't changed the meaning of the sentence.

Debra sent Todd a postcard.

Debra sent a postcard to Todd.

Notice that in the second sentence, the proper noun *Todd* is no longer an indirect object. It has become the object of a preposition (see p. 118).

OBJECT COMPLEMENTS

An **object complement** answers the question *what?* after a direct object. That is, it *completes* the meaning of the direct object by identifying or describing it.

Object complements occur only in sentences with direct objects and only in those sentences with the following action verbs or with similar verbs that have the general meaning of "make" or "consider":

appoint	make	consider	think
choose	render	find	vote
elect	call	name	prove

An object complement usually follows a direct object. It may be an adjective, a noun, or a pronoun.

EXAMPLE   Residents find the park **peaceful.** [adjective]

EXAMPLE   Maya appointed me **spokesperson** and **treasurer.** [nouns]

EXAMPLE   My grandmother considers the property **hers.** [pronoun]

SUBJECT COMPLEMENTS (PREDICATE NOMINATIVES, PREDICATE ADJECTIVES)

A **subject complement** follows a subject and a linking verb and identifies or describes the subject.

There are two kinds of subject complements: *predicate nominatives* and *predicate adjectives*.

A **predicate nominative** is a noun or a pronoun that follows a linking verb and points back to the subject to rename it or to identify it further.

EXAMPLE   Sopranos are **singers.**

EXAMPLE   The star of the opera was **she.**

EXAMPLE   Many current opera stars are **Italians** or **Spaniards.**

Predicate nominatives are usually found in sentences that contain forms of the linking verb *be*. A few other linking verbs (for example, *become* and *remain*) can also be followed by predicate nominatives.

EXAMPLE   Fiona became both a **musician** and an **actress.**

EXAMPLE   That experience remains a cherished **memory** for me.

A **predicate adjective** follows a linking verb and points back to the subject and further describes it.

EXAMPLE   Firefighters are **brave.**

EXAMPLE   Firefighters must be extremely **careful.**

EXAMPLE   Most firefighters are **dedicated** and **hardworking.**

Predicate adjectives may follow any linking verb.

EXAMPLE   I feel very **confident.**

EXAMPLE   My sister appeared **angry.**

EXAMPLE   The spoiled milk smelled **bad.**

EXAMPLE   Heidi seemed **intelligent** and **efficient.**

EXAMPLE   The trumpet sounded **sour.**

EXAMPLE   The soup tasted **salty**.

EXAMPLE   Overnight the maple leaves all turned **red.**

PRACTICE   Complements

Write each complement and identify it by writing DO *for a direct object,* IO *for an indirect object,* OC *for an object complement,* PN *for a predicate nominative, and* PA *for a predicate adjective.*

1. This new broccoli dish tastes delicious!
2. Iñigo sent me a card from Seville!
3. Ms. DiGiulio appointed Tamara captain.
4. People call Philadelphia "the city of brotherly love."
5. Deborah seems very sure of herself.
6. Damaged tankers usually cause oil spills.
7. A forest of pine trees is a place of unusual beauty.
8. The air often becomes still just before a storm.
9. On Saint Lucia's Day in Sweden, the oldest daughter serves her family breakfast in bed.
10. In 1960 voters elected John F. Kennedy president.
11. Fruit and vegetables are important sources of vitamins and minerals.
12. Does this spider look dead to you?
13. Ralph and Antwan will silk-screen the posters for the school play.
14. Kamala is a volunteer at the neighborhood soup kitchen.
15. Alex offered me two free tickets to Friday's concert.
16. The Talbots always remained close to their family in Quebec.

17. Was Paris or Helen of Troy the cause of the Trojan War?
18. After ten years of fierce battles, the Greeks won the war.
19. Luciano Pavarotti is one of the world's best tenors.
20. The city of Hamden has opened a new shelter for the homeless on Center Street.

PRACTICE Proofreading

Rewrite the following passage, correcting errors in spelling, capitalization, grammar, and usage. Add any missing punctuation. There are ten errors. Some sentences are correct.

The Epic

¹an epic is a long narrative poem or story about a hero who belongs to a noble or royal family. ²In many epics, there is someting supernatural or magical about the hero's birth and death? ³The hero's central motivation is to perform brave deeds that will protect his people. ⁴Many of these brave deeds involve quests, or long, difficult journeys hunting for a rare treasure, a magical sword, ore a kidnapped princess. ⁵Epic heroes sometimes fight other human beings they also battle monsters and spirits. ⁶An epick hero can win the day by fighting hard, behaving honorably, and protecting the innocent. ⁷Often the hero's enemy will suggest a trade and then try to cheat. ⁸That means the enemys downfall is the enemy's own fault. ⁹Some epic heroes of ancient literature is King Arthur of the Round Table, the Babylonian Gilgamesh, hercules, and Beowulf. ¹⁰In more recent times, Superman, Batman, and other superheroes from comic books has many qualities of an epic hero. ¹¹Modern science fiction stories and movies often use for their main characters a man or woman who possesses many traits of the classical epic hero.

Identify each underlined word or group of words in the paragraph by writing one of these labels: simple subject, complete subject, simple predicate, complete predicate.

How did <u>the constellations</u>[1] get their names? To ancient peoples, <u>arrangements</u>[2] of stars <u>formed</u>[3] pictures in the sky. <u>Pegasus, with its square body, long neck, and oustretched legs,</u>[4] reminded the Greeks of their mythological winged horse. <u>Perseus and Orion</u>[5] reminded them of two of their heroes. <u>Across the night sky with outstretched wings flies</u>[6] Cygnus. This constellation <u>gets its name from the Greek word *kyknos*,</u> "swan."[7] Renaissance astronomers <u>gave</u>[8] other constellations less poetic names. Here in the northern hemisphere is <u>Triangulum, "triangle."</u>[9] In the southern hemisphere you can look up and locate Telescopium and Microscopium. <u>Are</u>[10] there any guesses about these names?

POSTTEST **Complements**

Identify each underlined word or group of words by writing one of these labels: direct object, indirect object, object complement, predicate nominative, predicate adjective.

11. <u>What</u> did Maria say?
12. Ducks and geese have very strong <u>wings</u>.
13. Did you give the <u>baby</u> the cereal in the small jar?
14. Who elected <u>Norman</u> <u>chairman</u>?
15. Sasha's family are nearly all <u>musicians</u>.
16. "Oh, my!" said Grandmother. "This soup smells <u>terrible</u>!"
17. Tracy showed <u>Armando</u> her <u>photos</u> of Yosemite National Park.

18. Unrefrigerated dairy products become <u>bad</u> very quickly.
19. <u>Whom</u> did the class choose for president?
20. A female fox is called a <u>vixen</u>.
21. Joe told <u>Carlos</u> a true story.
22. I don't feel very <u>well</u>.
23. That's a lovely <u>picture</u> of your brother.
24. <u>Which</u> of the kittens have you chosen?
25. Please help <u>me</u>!
26. Send this <u>message</u> to the meeting coordinator.
27. My violin solo sounded <u>sour</u> to me.
28. The president appointed an <u>accountant</u> <u>treasurer</u>.
29. Kami and Jonas wrote <u>us</u> a <u>play</u> over the summer.
30. Does something in this cabin smell <u>rotten</u> to anyone but me?

Chapter 3

Phrases

● ● ● ● ● ● ● ● ● ● ● ● ● ● ● ●

PRETEST **Prepositional Phrases**

Write the prepositional phrases. For each, write the word or words modified by the phrase. Then write ADJ *for adjective or* ADV *for adverb to identify the type of phrase.*

1. Nobody in the room heard me enter except the old dog in the corner behind the stove.
2. Under the table hid the tiniest kitten.
3. A group of students left on a picnic.
4. A member of the wedding party spilled gravy on the bride's gown.
5. One child nearly fell off the steps.
6. Everyone near me must have heard my hungry stomach growl.
7. The children stood inside the barn and watched the cows with their calves.
8. Beyond the field, a river flowed to the sea.
9. The men's chorus entertained their guests throughout the day.
10. Seven passengers aboard the ship became seasick during the storm.

Identify each italicized word or words by writing one of these labels: appositive, participle, gerund, infinitive.

11. A left-fielder *playing* for our team was hit by a high fly.
12. *Playing* softball is Marla's favorite hobby.
13. Ezra stopped at the hospital *to see* his brother.
14. Three *talented* boys, *students* at Chambers Junior High, wanted *to meet* the Cardinals' star pitcher.
15. Lucia had *to wait* for her *bowling* partner.
16. The neighbors, all close *friends,* came to our party.
17. Mr. Alessandro enjoyed his hobby of *growing* roses.
18. I left the meeting early *to get* my *certified* letter.
19. *Smiling* warmly, the mayor greeted us each in turn.
20. Five students, all *members* of Mr. Grossman's class, won trophies for *diving.*

Identify each italicized group of words by writing one of these labels: prepositional phrase, appositive phrase, participial phrase, gerund phrase, infinitive phrase.

21. Atlanta, *the capital of Georgia,* is a large and busy city.
22. *Remaining at home* was the best thing John could do.
23. *Hoping for a mild winter,* Julie decided *to cut her hair very, very short.*
24. The food *left on the plate* had been Tony's.
25. *By keeping the child busy,* Ruth helped her *to stay out of trouble.*
26. Computers *used in millions of homes* are expected *to be both better and cheaper* by the end *of the next five years.*
27. *To revisit the land of her birth* was Mrs. Campbell's fondest wish.

28. The ranchers prevented their horses *from wandering away by keeping them in the barn.*

29. *Made in Switzerland,* this cheese is both mild and sweet.

30. Rhonda, *an excellent swimmer,* participates *in at least ten competitions a year.*

3.1 PREPOSITIONAL PHRASES

A **phrase** is a group of words that acts in a sentence as a single part of speech.

A **prepositional phrase** is a group of words that begins with a preposition and ends with a noun or a pronoun, which is called the **object of the preposition.**

EXAMPLE   The staircase leads **to the attic.**
[***Attic*** is the object of the preposition *to.*]

EXAMPLE   The staircase is too steep **for her.**
[***Her*** is the object of the preposition *for.*]

For a list of common prepositions, see page 118.

Be careful to distinguish between the preposition *to* (*to the store*, *to Detroit*) and the *to* that marks an infinitive (*to see*, *to revise*). See page 154 for more about infinitives.

Adjectives and other modifiers may be placed between a preposition and its object. Also, a preposition may have more than one object.

EXAMPLE   The staircase leads **to the crowded, dusty attic and the roof. [adjectives added, two objects]**

A prepositional phrase usually functions as an adjective or an adverb. When it is used as an adjective, it modifies a noun or a pronoun and is called an *adjective phrase.* An adjective phrase usually follows the word it modifies.

EXAMPLE They used the staircase **on the left.**
[adjective phrase modifying the noun *staircase*]

EXAMPLE Which **of the staircases** leads downstairs?
[adjective phrase modifying the pronoun *which*]

When a prepositional phrase is used as an adverb, it modifies a verb, an adjective, or an adverb and is called an *adverb phrase*.

EXAMPLE **At midnight** I went downstairs **to the kitchen.**
[adverb phrases modifying the verb *went*]

EXAMPLE My grandfather explained that a daily walk

is healthful **for him.** [adverb phrase modifying the adjective *healthful*]

EXAMPLE She skis very well **for a beginner.**
[adverb phrase modifying the adverb *well*]

An adverb phrase that modifies a verb may appear in different positions in a sentence.

EXAMPLE She wore a beautiful diamond ring **on her finger.**
[adverb phrase modifying *wore*]

EXAMPLE **On her finger,** she wore a beautiful diamond ring.
[adverb phrase modifying *wore*]

EXAMPLE She wore **on her finger** a beautiful diamond ring.
[adverb phrase modifying *wore*]

Writing Tip

Place adjective and adverb phrases exactly where they belong. A misplaced phrase can be confusing. See pages 267–268 for more about misplaced modifiers.

Write the prepositional phrases. For each, write the word or words modified by the phrase. Then write ADJ *for adjective or* ADV *for adverb to identify the type of phrase.*

1. The legs of that chair aren't very strong.
2. It was the most beautiful day of summer.
3. The furniture in the attic has been stored for many years.
4. Please take the cake out of the oven.
5. We went to the supermarket for party supplies.
6. The members of Mia's sorority work at the neighborhood soup kitchen on Saturdays.
7. Sondra always writes with fluency.
8. Five of Mr. Rasmussen's paintings have been sold to buyers across the country.
9. Tina borrowed my map of Chicago.
10. The streets in many Nantucket neighborhoods are paved with clamshells.

3.2 APPOSITIVES AND APPOSITIVE PHRASES

An **appositive** is a noun or a pronoun that is placed next to another noun or pronoun to identify it or give additional information about it.

EXAMPLE My friend **Ethan** works at a bookstore after school. **[The appositive *Ethan* identifies the noun *friend*.]**

An **appositive phrase** is an appositive plus any words that modify the appositive.

EXAMPLE He is saving money to travel to Bogotá, **the capital of Colombia. [The appositive phrase, in blue type, identifies Bogotá.]**

Use commas to set off any appositive or appositive phrase that is not essential to the meaning of the sentence.

EXAMPLE   Ethan's friend **Julie** also works at the bookstore. **[The appositive *Julie* is essential because Ethan has more than one friend.]**

EXAMPLE   Eric, **Ethan's twin brother,** does not work. **[The appositive phrase is not essential because Ethan has only one twin brother.]**

Usually an appositive or an appositive phrase follows the noun or pronoun it identifies or explains. Occasionally an appositive phrase precedes the noun or pronoun.

EXAMPLE   **A hard worker,** Ethan will save money quickly.

PRACTICE   Appositives and Appositive Phrases

Write each appositive or appositive phrase and the noun or pronoun that is identified or explained by the appositive.

1. Our class's most accomplished musician, Minta has won several awards.

2. Diane's cousin Jeanne will visit her next week.

3. Fred memorized a sonnet, a poem of fourteen lines.

4. The citizens of Saskatchewan, a Canadian province, are used to cold weather.

5. Charity and Joseph announced their engagement in Des Moines, a city in Iowa.

6. My brother's car, a battered Ford sedan, runs well for its age.

7. A relief pitcher, Amedeo waited hopefully in the dugout.

8. Rita expects no party on Valentine's Day, her birthday.

9. Mom packed my favorite sandwich, tuna salad on wheat bread, in my lunch today.

10. A valuable vitamin, riboflavin belongs to the B group.

3.3 VERBALS AND VERBAL PHRASES

A **verbal** is a verb form that functions in a sentence as a noun, an adjective, or an adverb.

A **verbal phrase** is a verbal plus any complements and modifiers.

Verbals are *participles, gerunds,* and *infinitives.* Each of these can be expanded into phrases.

PARTICIPLES AND PARTICIPIAL PHRASES

A **participle** is a verb form that can function as an adjective.

Present participles always end in *–ing* (*moving*). *Past participles* often end in *–ed* (*striped*), but some are irregularly formed (*broken*). Many commonly used adjectives are actually participles.

EXAMPLE   A **moving** van is parked on our street.

EXAMPLE   The dogs barked at the **striped** cat.

EXAMPLE   The **broken** window suggested **frightening** possibilities.

When a participle is part of a verb phrase, the participle is not functioning as an adjective.

EXAMPLES

| PARTICIPLE AS AN ADJECTIVE | The **confused** child was afraid. |
| PARTICIPLE IN A VERB PHRASE | The teacher **has confused** our names. |

A **participial phrase** contains a participle plus any complements and modifiers.

Participial phrases can be placed in various positions in a sentence. They always act as adjectives.

EXAMPLE   The dog saw many ducks **swimming in the lake.**

EXAMPLE   **Barking loudly,** the dog approached the water.

EXAMPLE   The ducks, **startled by the noise,** rose and flew away quickly.

EXAMPLE   The **sorely disappointed** dog returned to the campsite.

A participial phrase at the beginning of a sentence is usually followed by a comma.

PRACTICE **Participles and Participial Phrases**

Write the participles and participial phrases. Then write the word or words each participle or participial phrase modifies.

1. Purring loudly, the kitten curled up in my lap and fell asleep.
2. The plane, flying low, practically skimmed the tops of the trees.
3. The emergency call, reported at 5:00, was answered immediately.
4. Completed a week early, Sonia's report had been well researched.
5. The music blasting from the parked car was most annoying.
6. The exhausted girls looked forward to a good night's sleep.
7. Realizing her luck, Yolanda clasped the winning lottery ticket in her hand and smiled.
8. Relieved, Deirdre answered the phone.
9. In tears, Larry hugged his recovered pet and thanked the rescuer.
10. The band, pleased by the enthusiastic applause, played splendidly.

GERUNDS AND GERUND PHRASES

A **gerund** is a verb form that ends in *–ing* and is used in the same ways a noun is used.

EXAMPLE **Cooking** is an enjoyable activity. **[gerund as subject]**

EXAMPLE My younger sister likes **swimming.**
[gerund as direct object]

EXAMPLE Tony gives **baking** his best effort.
[gerund as indirect object]

EXAMPLE How much money have you saved for **shopping?**
[gerund as object of preposition]

EXAMPLE Dustin's favorite sport is **skiing.**
[gerund as predicate nominative]

EXAMPLE My hobbies, **drawing** and **painting,** require patience.
[gerunds as appositives]

A **gerund phrase** contains a gerund plus any complements and modifiers.

EXAMPLE **Cross-country skiing** is good exercise.

EXAMPLE **Billie Holiday's soulful singing** delighted many audiences.

Although both a gerund and a present participle end in *-ing*, they function as different parts of speech. A gerund is used as a noun, whereas a present participle is used as part of a verb phrase or as an adjective.

EXAMPLES

PARTICIPLE AS AN ADJECTIVE	**Reading her new book,** Isabella became sleepy.
PARTICIPLE IN A VERB PHRASE	Isabella **was reading** in the window seat.
GERUND	**Reading** is Isabella's favorite pastime.

Write the gerunds and gerund phrases. Identify the way each is used by writing one of these labels: subject, direct object, indirect object, object of a preposition, predicate nominative, appositive.

1. Finding a good parking space is very important to Mom.
2. I'd give Anderson's *Handling the Pain* a good review.
3. By working hard, Jeremy brought up his math grade.
4. Michiko's favorite activity is playing her flute.
5. Dad's job involved keeping the babies in sight.
6. The musician's goal, playing flawlessly, was naive.
7. Fighting back tears was difficult for me just then.
8. The headmaster was not good at giving praise.
9. The twins enjoy skating.
10. Good luck can come from losing one's keys.
11. Skipping rope is a good exercise.
12. The second alternative, fighting bravely, was Aza's choice.
13. Hiking seemed a good idea at the time.
14. Mr. Kaseler finally finished reading.
15. In forgiving Ryan, Pete had triumphed over his anger.

INFINITIVES AND INFINITIVE PHRASES

An **infinitive** is a verb form that is usually preceded by the word *to* and is used as a noun, an adjective, or an adverb.

When you use the word *to* before the base form of a verb, *to* is not a preposition but part of the infinitive form of the verb.

EXAMPLE   **To stand** can be uncomfortable. **[infinitive as subject]**

EXAMPLE   Infants first learn **to creep. [infinitive as direct object]**

EXAMPLE   His goal is **to graduate. [infinitive as predicate nominative]**

They have the desire **to win. [infinitive as adjective]**

I was ready **to leave. [infinitive as adverb]**

An **infinitive phrase** contains an infinitive plus any complements and modifiers.

EXAMPLE We stopped **to look at the beautiful scenery.**

EXAMPLE **To be a good friend** is my goal.

EXAMPLE Obedience school teaches dogs **to behave well.**

PRACTICE **Infinitives and Infinitive Phrases**

Write the infinitives and infinitive phrases. For each, write noun, adjective, *or* adverb *to tell how the infinitive or infinitive phrase is being used.*

1. Jim liked to sing in the shower.
2. Taree left to buy groceries.
3. Kurt managed to disregard his fears.
4. I must make an effort to work faster.
5. To have his artwork in the show was enough for Ken.
6. We played to win.
7. Franz is the person to choose in the election.
8. The bodyguard's job is to protect Mr. Williamson from harm.
9. My father gave me the will to live.
10. The guide urged the travelers to continue their trip.

PRACTICE **Appositives and Verbals**

Identify each italicized term by writing one of these labels: appositive, participle, gerund, infinitive.

1. *Rejoicing* in his friend's victory made Raul happy.
2. The team's urge *to win* was overwhelming.
3. Our *swimming* instructor taught us the scissors kick.

4. We hopped into the *waiting* cab.

5. Alyssa's houseguest, *her cousin Molly,* will stay for a week.

6. *Driving* from the mountain cabin to the airport was the only logical choice.

7. Suddenly Mrs. Gaspar was a *changed* woman.

8. Wayne is the only sensible person *to select* for this difficult job.

9. The guests enjoyed *singing* under the stars.

10. Our *defeated* players slowly dragged themselves off the field.

PRACTICE **Phrases**

Identify each italicized group of words by writing one of these labels: prepositional phrase, appositive phrase, participial phrase, gerund phrase, infinitive phrase.

1. The desire *to do a good job* was strong *in Jake.*

2. The foghorn *moaning in the distance* made Janna feel sad.

3. *Making silk-screen prints* was one of Iona's hobbies.

4. *Entering the room,* Monica startled Mrs. Albertson.

5. My sister's Girl Scout troop, *exhausted by their trip,* slept all the way home.

6. We went *to the tourist office* and got help *to plan our next vacation.*

7. Mr. and Mrs. Fibonacci hosted the twins, *Dorothy's cousins.*

8. Michael finally stopped *writing his letter* and looked up *at the clock.*

9. Stockholm, *the peaceful city on the lake,* was the next stop.

10. After much effort, Stanley finally learned *to play the trumpet.*

Rewrite the following passage, correcting errors in spelling, capitalization, grammar, and usage. Add any missing punctuation. There are ten errors. Some sentences are correct.

Mohandas Gandhi

[1]Mohandas Gandhi was one of India's most popular leaders. [2]A Lawyer by trade, he left the law to fight personally for his peoples' rites against their British rulers. [3]Deep comitted to nonviolence Gandhi was determined to win India's freedom by avoiding confrontation. [4]Over the years he developed a code of action knowed today as passive resistance or civil disobedience. [5]Gandhi's code called for nonviolent noncooperation to achieve independence. [6]Whenever armed British solders came to enforce the ocupation government's laws, Gandhi urged his people not to fight. [7]Instead, they stood still, refusing to move back or forward, and refusing to give into the soldiers. [8]Unwilling to shoot the unarmed crowd, the British usually retreated. [9]However, in the massacre of Amritsar, British soldiers killed almost four hundred of Gandhi's followers. [10]Both Gandhi and his followers knew that nonviolent protests can lead to imprisonment and even death, but they remained loyal to the independence movement until Great Britain granted the independence of India and Pakistan in 1947.

Write the prepositional phrases. For each, write the word or words modified by the phrase. Then write ADJ *for adjective or* ADV *for adverb to identify the phrase.*

1. The man in the ticket booth was Mr. Cramer.
2. We moved to Rhode Island in 1960.
3. Melinda faithfully wrote to her pen pal for years.
4. The child across from me had a bad cold.
5. My mother is the woman in the bright red coat.

6. The difficulty of chess makes it a game for serious players.
7. The soccer team practiced without a pause for three hours.
8. I asked my aunt for a ride to the mall.
9. The blue sedan with the white top is Mom's.
10. That trunk in the attic holds a wealth of memories.

POSTTEST Appositives and Verbals

Identify each italicized word or words by writing one of these labels: appositive, participle, gerund, infinitive.

11. The *frightened* people ran for their lives.
12. Rani learned not *to ride* fast over cobbled streets.
13. The *wailing* of the bagpipes frightened the baby.
14. For tomorrow I plan *to learn* a poem by heart.
15. Helen promoted the practice of *making* contributions to good causes.
16. Stamford, *a city in Connecticut,* houses many New York workers.
17. *Reaching* the Big Apple by nine o'clock, they begin work.
18. By evening, *returning* to Connecticut is a relief.
19. Which of Melville's works is our *assigned* book?
20. My fondest wish, *to see Frank Sinatra,* never came true.

POSTTEST Phrases

Identify each italicized group of words by writing one of these labels: prepositional phrase, appositive phrase, participial phrase, gerund phrase, infinitive phrase.

21. *Learning math* has always been one *of my most serious challenges*.
22. The trout, *exhausted by its struggle,* finally stopped fighting.

23. Raleigh's daily newspaper, the *News and Observer,* reaches several cities *in North Carolina.*

24. *To find his way home* would be a difficult task.

25. Bruce calmed Aimee's fears *by offering to take her home.*

26. *An inland sea,* the Mediterranean separates Europe from Africa.

27. My little sister learned the name of my book *by reading the title upside down.*

28. Who is the passenger *riding in the red car?*

29. The situation *covered in tonight's news* is a tragedy.

30. Hartford, *the capital of Connecticut,* is also the headquarters *of many large insurance companies.*

Chapter 4

Clauses and Sentence Structure

• • • • • • • • • • • • • •

PRETEST   **Main and Subordinate Clauses**

Write each boldfaced clause and label it M *for main or* S *for subordinate. Then identify each subordinate clause as adjective* (ADJ), *adverb* (ADV), *or noun* (N).

1. **Because he has a doctor's appointment,** Stan won't be at practice this afternoon.
2. The teacher **that I respect most** is Mrs. Price.

3. **Tessa won't be in homeroom today,** but **she'll return in time for geometry class.**

4. He will probably ask us **who the president was in 1968.**

5. **Mr. Rodriquez will give the chapter test this Tuesday;** he will give the midterm exam next Friday.

6. Did Luke tell you **when he will leave on Saturday morning?**

7. **When the other bands arrive for the competition,** we will greet them.

8. Gino and Aaron have the flu; **consequently, they won't start in the game Friday night.**

9. The Sweetheart Dance committee met last night; **they discussed hiring a disc jockey instead of a band.**

10. **Erin will be responsible for the tickets,** and **Nick will take care of the refreshments.**

11. **Mr. Canini asked for volunteers in the stadium,** but **we were tutoring at the elementary school.**

12. I didn't hurry **because Sarah and Juan were late.**

13. My father will speak to our history class **because he was in Vietnam during the Tet Offensive.**

14. Rachel's brother, **who is also a college student,** works forty hours a week in the factory.

15. I can go to the movies with you and Anthony Friday night; **however, I must be home early.**

16. The people **who designed the poster** are Angel and Jennifer.

17. **As he walked through the cafeteria,** Les felt everyone's eyes on him.

18. **Suzanne worked at the pool last summer,** and **she saved her money for a new stereo.**

19. **Whoever goes to the game** is invited to the dance afterwards.

20. **Lisa and Nathan didn't come to the party together;** they're mad at each other.

Identify each sentence by writing S for simple, C for compound, CX for complex, or CC for compound-complex.

21. Jake has been saving his money for six months to go to Washington, D.C.

22. Next semester Rita is taking home economics, and Louisa is taking photography.

23. Because photography students need cameras, Louisa is looking for someone who will lend her one.

24. Other students will use the cameras that the school provides, but these cameras may not leave the school grounds.

25. One school camera shoots only black-and-white film; I prefer that film since it makes crisper shadows than color film.

26. The main goal of our group is to finish this project before spring break.

27. Aunt Sarah was one of the first women managers in the company; the company dedicated its new building to her.

28. When summer comes, Renée will learn to swim and dive at the summer camp in the next county.

29. Please come to the play next week.

30. Ben is playing the piano for the program; consequently, he won't sit with the orchestra.

PRETEST Kinds of Sentences

Identify each sentence by writing D for declarative, IT for interrogative, IM for imperative, or E for exclamatory.

31. Have you ever made a vegetarian pizza?

32. It's easy and delicious!

33. First, make a bread dough and spread it out on an oiled pizza pan.

34. Rub a little olive oil on top of the dough, as well.

35. My dad likes to roast jalapeño peppers, remove the skins, and add them to the dough.

36. Jalapeño peppers are too hot for me!

37. Spread tomato sauce over the dough.

38. What chopped raw vegetables do you like— mushrooms, onions, olives, green peppers?

39. Mom always puts a great deal of grated provolone or mozzarella cheese on last.

40. Bake at 400 degrees until the cheese turns golden brown, and enjoy.

PRETEST **Fragments and Run-ons**

Identify each numbered item by writing F *for fragment,* R *for run-on sentence, or* S *for sentence.*

41. Interested in taking photos of sporting events.

42. Mrs. Stone canceled the general meeting of the Latin Club but the executive committee will meet to discuss the festival.

43. Antonio will run in the track meet this weekend, Cara will help the officials with statistics.

44. Letter to the group that will be going on the field trip to the zoo.

45. The Parent-Teacher Association will supply drivers and chaperones; my parents, however, will not be helping out this time.

46. On the day before the field trip.

47. Students will discuss the subjects of their field-trip reports with their teachers.

48. I will prepare an oral report, I hate to type.

49. I want to talk about zoo animals that are not from this climate and how the zoo keeps them comfortable.

50. It sounds like a huge subject perhaps I should limit myself to the tropical birds.

4.1 MAIN CLAUSES

A **clause** is a group of words that has a subject and a predicate (verb). A clause can function as a sentence by itself or as part of a sentence.

A **main clause** has a subject and a predicate and expresses a complete thought. It is the only type of clause that can stand alone as a sentence. A main clause is also called an **independent clause.**

Every sentence must have at least one main clause. In the following examples, the clauses express complete thoughts, so they are main clauses. Note that a coordinating conjunction is not part of a main clause.

Main Clause

EXAMPLE   **The curtain rose.**
            Subject   Verb

Main Clause   Main Clause

EXAMPLE   **The cast bowed,** and **the audience applauded.**
            Subject   Verb   Subject   Verb

Both the subject and the predicate of a main clause may be compound.

Main Clause

EXAMPLE   **The actors and crew smiled and bowed,** and
                Subject   Subject   Verb   Verb

Main Clause

            the audience cheered and clapped.
            Subject   Verb   Verb

4.2 SUBORDINATE CLAUSES

A **subordinate clause,** also called a **dependent clause,** has a subject and a predicate but does not express a complete thought, so it cannot stand alone as a sentence.

There are three types of subordinate clauses: *adjective clauses,* which modify nouns or pronouns; *adverb clauses,* which modify verbs, adjectives, or adverbs; and *noun clauses,* which function as nouns.

A subordinate clause is dependent on the rest of the sentence because a subordinate clause does not make sense by itself. A subordinating conjunction or a relative pronoun usually introduces a subordinate clause. (See Lesson 1.2 on page 104 for a list of relative pronouns. See Lesson 1.7 on page 123 for a list of subordinating conjunctions.)

EXAMPLE

In some cases, a relative pronoun can also function as the subject or some other part of a subordinate clause.

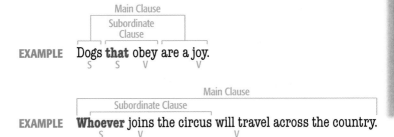

EXAMPLE

In the first example, the subordinating conjunction *when* placed before *the dog barked* creates a word group—*when the dog barked*—that cannot stand alone as a main clause. Although the clause has a subject and a predicate, it does not express a complete thought.

In the second example, the relative pronoun *that* begins a subordinate clause that comes between the subject and the verb of the main clause. *That* also serves as the subject of the subordinate clause, and *obey* is its verb. *That obey* cannot, however, stand alone.

Chapter 4 Clauses and Sentence Structure   **165**

In the third example, the subordinate clause functions as the subject of the sentence. *Whoever* functions as the subject of the subordinate clause, *whoever joins the circus. Joins* is the verb, and *the circus* is the direct object. *Whoever joins the circus* cannot, however, stand alone.

PRACTICE **Subordinate Clauses**

Write the subordinate clause from each sentence.

1. Because she was late, she skipped breakfast.
2. Maggie read the book while Seth looked for more information on the Internet.
3. Julio and his friends went to a movie that they had already seen.
4. Louisa is someone who knows what she wants from life.
5. If you aren't too busy, we can fix your bike tire now.
6. Whatever you decide will be fine with me.
7. Jerry, whose speech was very short, graciously accepted the award.
8. Please explain to me where the new shopping mall will be.
9. Sean will baby-sit unless someone will take his place.
10. Dr. García, who has an office on the next street, lives not far from us.

PRACTICE **Main and Subordinate Clauses**

Copy the sentences. Underline the main clauses once and the subordinate clauses twice.

1. Unless Rachel goes with us, we won't know how to get there.
2. Whenever it snows, Alfonso and Max head for the slopes.
3. Alicia knows when the new merchandise arrives at the mall.

4. The band, which comes from England, will play at a local club Friday night.

5. We observed while the teacher dissected the frog.

6. Although Mai Ling later joined in, she did not begin singing with the rest of the choir.

7. Doing well in English is what is most important right now.

8. Anyone who is going to the movie should be at my house at seven o'clock.

9. Clare cleaned her room before she left for the party.

10. Alex's project, which was a demonstration of centrifugal force, won first prize.

4.3 ADJECTIVE CLAUSES

An **adjective clause** is a subordinate clause that modifies a noun or a pronoun.

An adjective clause may begin with a relative pronoun (*who, whom, whose, that,* or *which*) or the word *where* or *when.* An adjective clause normally follows the word it modifies.

EXAMPLE Magazines **that inform and entertain** are my favorites.

EXAMPLE Several writers **whom I admire** contribute to magazines.

EXAMPLE The store **where I buy magazines** sponsors readings by contributors.

Sometimes the relative pronoun is dropped from the beginning of an adjective clause.

EXAMPLE *National Geographic* is the magazine **I like best.**
[The relative pronoun *that* has been omitted.]

Some adjective clauses are necessary to make the meaning of a sentence clear. Such an adjective clause is called an *essential clause,* or a *restrictive clause.* It must not be set off with commas.

EXAMPLE   Magazines **that have no substance** bore me.

EXAMPLE   Many writers **whose works have become famous**
           began their writing careers at the *New Yorker*
           magazine.

An adjective clause that is not necessary to make the
meaning of the sentence clear, even though it may add
information to a sentence, is called a *nonessential clause*
or a *nonrestrictive clause.* Always use commas to set off a
nonessential clause.

EXAMPLE   James Thurber**, who was a famous humorist,** wrote
           for the *New Yorker.*

EXAMPLE   His stories**, which include humorous incidents from
           his childhood in Ohio,** make funny and interesting
           reading.

When choosing between *that* and *which* to introduce
an adjective clause, use *that* to begin an essential clause
and *which* to begin a nonessential clause.

EXAMPLE   Magazines **that include art and literature** are
           interesting and educational.

EXAMPLE   The *New Yorker*, **which includes fiction and poetry,**
           competes with *Vanity Fair.*

4.4 ADVERB CLAUSES

An **adverb clause** is a subordinate clause that modifies
a verb, an adjective, or an adverb. It tells *when, where,
how, why, to what extent,* or *under what conditions.*

Adverb clauses begin with subordinating conjunctions
(page 122). An adverb clause can come either before or
after the main clause. When an adverb clause comes first,
separate it from the main clause with a comma. (See
Lesson 11.6.)

EXAMPLE **Before I took the test,** I studied for hours. **[The adverb clause tells _when_ and modifies the verb _studied_.]**

EXAMPLE I studied longer **than I had ever studied before.** **[The adverb clause tells _to what_ extent and modifies the adverb _longer_.]**

EXAMPLE I was happy **because I passed the test.** **[The adverb clause tells _why_ and modifies the adjective _happy_.]**

Elliptical adverb clauses have words left out of them. You can easily supply the omitted words because they are understood or implied.

EXAMPLE She can swim faster **than I. [_Can swim_ has been omitted.]**

EXAMPLE **While walking,** she listens to the radio. **[_She is_ has been omitted.]**

4.5 NOUN CLAUSES

A **noun clause** is a subordinate clause that is used as a noun within the main clause of a sentence.

You can use a noun clause as a subject, a direct object, an indirect object, an object of a preposition, or a predicate nominative.

EXAMPLE **Whoever wins the election** will speak. **[noun clause as subject]**

EXAMPLE The reporter will do **whatever is required** to get an interview. **[noun clause as direct object]**

EXAMPLE The senator will give **whoever asks** an interview. **[noun clause as indirect object]**

EXAMPLE A news story should begin with **whatever gets the reader's attention.** **[noun clause as object of a preposition]**

EXAMPLE That is **why she included specific data in the article.** **[noun clause as predicate nominative]**

The following are some words that can be used to introduce noun clauses.

how	whatever	which	whose
however	when	whichever	why
if	where	who, whom	
that	wherever	whoever	
what	whether	whomever	

Sometimes the introductory word is dropped from a noun clause.

EXAMPLE   I believe **most readers will be entertained by this article. [*That* has been omitted from the beginning of the clause.]**

PRACTICE   Kinds of Subordinate Clauses

Write the subordinate clause from each sentence. Then write ADJ *if it's an adjective clause,* ADV *if it's an adverb clause, or* N *if it's a noun clause.*

1. We can go to the game as long as we get home by eleven o'clock.
2. This week's *Newsweek* magazine, which should arrive today, might be a good source of information.
3. Whichever dress you choose will be fine for the banquet.
4. Heather can take the test when she is ready.
5. Franco's main concern is why the error occurred in the first place.
6. Joanne will show you the watch that she wants for her birthday.
7. Whoever gets there first must build the fire.
8. Whenever Luis prepares dinner, I get home on time.
9. Deidre will never forget the time when she lost her dog.
10. The people who were most helpful were the Red Cross volunteers.

4.6 FOUR KINDS OF SENTENCES

Sentences are often classified according to their purpose. There are four purposes that sentences may have: to make a statement, to give an order or make a request, to ask a question, and to express strong emotion.

A **declarative sentence** makes a statement.

EXAMPLE   I have four pets.

EXAMPLE   Two of my pets are dogs.

A declarative sentence usually ends with a period but can end with an exclamation mark. This type of sentence is the most frequently used in speaking and writing.

An **imperative sentence** gives a command or makes a request.

EXAMPLE   Get off the table.

EXAMPLE   Zelda, please leave the cats alone.

An imperative sentence usually ends with a period but can end with an exclamation mark. In imperative sentences, the subject *you* is understood.

An **interrogative sentence** asks a question.

EXAMPLE   How many pets do you have?

EXAMPLE   Do you like rottweilers?

An interrogative sentence usually ends with a question mark but can end with an exclamation mark if it expresses strong emotion.

An **exclamatory sentence** expresses strong emotion.

EXAMPLE   She is such a beautiful dog!

EXAMPLE   Don't chew on that!

EXAMPLE   What do you think you're doing!

An exclamatory sentence ends with an exclamation point. Note that sentences are not only exclamatory but can be declarative (first example on the previous page), imperative (second example), or interrogative (third example) while expressing strong emotion. In writing, exclamatory sentences should be used sparingly so as not to detract from their effectiveness.

PRACTICE **Kinds of Sentences**

Identify each sentence by writing D *for declarative,* IT *for interrogative,* IM *for imperative, or* E *for exclamatory.*

1. What time does the next plane leave?
2. Randy will go on vacation with his parents.
3. Please check your work more carefully next time.
4. That was the best movie I've seen in a long time!
5. Josh and Suzanne have been next-door neighbors since first grade.
6. Leave the room quietly when the bell rings.
7. Have you seen Will Smith's new movie?
8. This salsa is so hot it makes my eyes water!
9. I hope to catch up on my reading during spring break.
10. Don't forget to bring your literature books tomorrow.

4.7 SIMPLE AND COMPOUND SENTENCES

Sentences are sometimes classified by their structure. The four sentence structures are *simple, compound, complex,* and *compound-complex.*

A **simple sentence** contains only one main clause and no subordinate clauses.

A simple sentence may contain a compound subject, a compound predicate, or both. The subject and the predicate can be expanded with adjectives, adverbs, prepositional phrases, appositives, and verbal phrases.

EXAMPLE Stories entertain. **[simple sentence]**

EXAMPLE Stories and riddles entertain and amuse. **[simple sentence with compound subject and compound predicate]**

EXAMPLE Stories about the Old West entertain adults and children alike. **[simple sentence including a prepositional phrase, a direct object, and an adverb]**

A **compound sentence** contains two or more main clauses.

The main clauses in a compound sentence may be joined in any of four ways.

1. Usually they are joined by a comma and a coordinating conjunction (*and, but, or, so, nor, yet, for*).

EXAMPLE Stories about the Old West are entertaining**, and** stories set in foreign countries are interesting.

EXAMPLE Stories entertain me**, and** riddles amuse me**, but** poems are my favorite.

2. Main clauses in a compound sentence may be joined by a semicolon used alone.

EXAMPLE Talented oral storytellers are rare**;** Spalding Gray is exceptional.

3. Main clauses in a compound sentence may be joined by a semicolon and a conjunctive adverb (such as *however, therefore, nevertheless*).

EXAMPLE Stories entertain and amuse**; however,** poems are delightful.

4. Main clauses in a compound sentence may be joined by a semicolon and an expression such as *for example*.

EXAMPLE Many authors write stories and poems**; for example,** Sherman Alexie is known for both his stories and his poems.

Identify each sentence by writing S *for a simple sentence or* C *for a compound sentence.*

1. Gina and Rick will conduct the experiment in chemistry class today.
2. Sara worked last summer and saved enough money for a computer.
3. The entire crowd waited quietly, and Niki walked to the line and made the free throw.
4. The delivery person arrived late, but the pizza was still warm.
5. The people in the home stands threw paper onto the floor; consequently, the referee called a foul on the home team.
6. The dance committee and the freshman class will decorate the gym and sell tickets.
7. David washed and dried the uniforms, and Ingrid filled the water bottles.
8. José is on the yearbook staff this year; he won't be writing for the newspaper.
9. Mrs. Levinson assigned us a paper and a project.
10. Li-Cheng ran the fastest mile, but Keri won the five-kilometer run.

4.8 COMPLEX AND COMPOUND-COMPLEX SENTENCES

A **complex sentence** has one main clause and one or more subordinate clauses.

Main Clause

EXAMPLE I like Toni Cade Bambara's stories
S V

Subordinate Clause

because they have good characters.
S   V

Subordinate Clause

EXAMPLE When I read her stories, I enjoy them
      S V   S V

Subordinate Clause

because they are believable.
       S   V

A **compound-complex sentence** has two or more main clauses and at least one subordinate clause.

Main Clause   Subordinate Clause

EXAMPLE I read *Frankenstein*, which Mary Shelley wrote,
      S V   S   V

Main Clause

and I reported on it.
    S   V

PRACTICE **Complex and Compound-Complex Sentences**

Identify each sentence by writing CX *for complex sentence or* CC *for compound-complex sentence. Then write the subordinate clause from each sentence.*

1. The runners who completed the marathon celebrated at the finish line.
2. Because she arrived first, Kristin unlocked the door, but she left the key in the lock.
3. Lee didn't know when we would return, but we went with him anyway.
4. Tonight we'll just eat whatever is left from lunch, and tomorrow we'll order pizza.
5. Although the lead actor had the flu, we presented the play.
6. The pool where we usually swim is too small for swim team practice.
7. Because he is a member of the school board, Mr. Williams spoke in favor of the bond issue, but he didn't give it his complete support.

8. Leonardo DiCaprio is the actor who starred in *Titanic*.

9. The assembly, which will be in the gym, won't last very long; however, everyone must attend.

10. Although Joey and Dawson are good friends, they often argue, and sometimes they stay angry for days.

"WHAT'S THE BIG SURPRISE? ALL THE LATEST THEORIES OF LINGUISTICS SAY WE'RE BORN WITH THE INNATE CAPACITY FOR GENERATING SENTENCES."

PRACTICE **Simple, Compound, Complex, and Compound-Complex Sentences**

Copy the following sentences. Identify each sentence by writing S for simple, C for compound, CX for complex, and CC for compound-complex. Underline each main clause once and each subordinate clause twice.

1. Lauren and Jerome will set up for the meeting, and the rest of us will clean up later.

2. Because our history class will be at the museum, I'll miss the Spanish quiz, but I'll take it after school.

3. In history class, our group is writing and presenting a report about the culture and history of Australia.

4. Mr. Tananka helped us identify the person who could answer the questions correctly.

5. James's injury was why the coach took him out of the game, but he was able to play during the fourth quarter.

6. Anna and Luis will buy the tickets, which go on sale tomorrow.

7. Joe's brother has the lead in the musical because his voice best fits the part.

8. Will you read your report to the class?

9. My dad taped *Silas Marner* last week; we can watch it in English class tomorrow.

10. After we paint the scenery Saturday, we will set it up on the stage, but the cast won't rehearse onstage until Monday.

4.9 SENTENCE FRAGMENTS

A **sentence fragment** is an error that occurs when an incomplete sentence is punctuated as though it were complete.

There are three things you should look for when you review your work for sentence fragments. First look for a group of words without a subject. Then look for a group of words without a complete predicate, especially a group that contains a verbal or a verbal phrase. Finally, be sure you haven't punctuated a subordinate clause as if it were a complete sentence.

Many times you can correct a sentence fragment by attaching it to a main clause. Other times you may need to add words to make the sentence complete.

FRAGMENT	COMPLETE SENTENCE
Beck and Ally started the hike on the main trail. **Wanted to explore a remote area of the park.** [lacks subject]	Beck and Ally started the hike on the main trail, but they wanted to explore a remote area of the park.
The two weary hikers walking for hours. [lacks complete predicate]	The two weary hikers had been walking for hours.
The concerned and tired hikers. [lacks complete predicate and contains verbal]	The concerned and tired hikers found a faint trail.
When they stopped to rest. They checked their compass and trail guide. [subordinate clause]	When they stopped to rest, they checked their compass and trail guide.

Sentence fragments can be used to produce special effects, such as adding emphasis or showing realistic dialogue. Remember that professional writers use sentence fragments carefully and intentionally. In most of the writing you do, including your writing for school, you should avoid sentence fragments.

4.10 RUN-ON SENTENCES

A **run-on sentence** is two or more complete sentences written as though they were one sentence.

There are two types of run-on sentences. The first occurs when two main clauses are joined by a comma only. This is an error called a *comma splice.*

EXAMPLE

RUN-ON It rained the entire time Gabriel and Jeffrey were on vacation, they still enjoyed the trip.

The second type of run-on sentence occurs when two main clauses have no punctuation separating them. This can occur with or without a conjunction.

RUN-ON   It rained the entire time Gabriel and Jeffrey were on vacation they still enjoyed the trip.

RUN-ON   It rained the entire time Gabriel and Jeffrey were on vacation but they still enjoyed the trip.

You can correct a run-on sentence in several ways. The method you choose in correcting your writing will depend on the relationship you want to show between the two clauses.

EXAMPLES

METHOD OF CORRECTING RUN-ON	COMPLETE SENTENCE
Add end punctuation between the clauses and make two sentences.	It rained the entire time Gabriel and Jeffrey were on vacation. **T**hey still enjoyed the trip.
Separate the clauses with a comma and a coordinating conjunction.	It rained the entire time Gabriel and Jeffrey were on vacation, **but** they still enjoyed the trip.
Separate the clauses with a semicolon.	It rained the entire time Gabriel and Jeffrey were on vacation; they still enjoyed the trip.
Add a semicolon and a conjunctive adverb between the clauses.	It rained the entire time Gabriel and Jeffrey were on vacation; **however,** they still enjoyed the trip.
Change one of the main clauses to a subordinate clause. Add a comma if the subordinate clause comes first.	**Although** it rained the entire time Gabriel and Jeffrey were on vacation, they still enjoyed the trip.

GRAMMAR/USAGE/MECHANICS

Identify each numbered item by writing F *for fragment or* R *for run-on sentence. Then rewrite each item, correcting the error.*

1. Luis will play with the symphony orchestra next month, his parents will be at the performance.
2. Angela and Su Lin didn't bring the poster board and they went back for it.
3. Want to see a movie Friday night.
4. The main concern of the committee.
5. Erica took the Scholastic Aptitude Test this spring she will take it again in the fall.
6. The team before the play-offs.
7. Tina was on the all-conference team last year she was on the all-district team this year.
8. The Spanish Club meets once a month and the Key Club meets every other week.
9. Because Ms. Jameson postponed the test until Wednesday.
10. Ran her fastest time in the citywide trials.

PRACTICE Proofreading

Rewrite the following passage, correcting errors in spelling, capitalization, grammar, and usage. Add any missing punctuation. There are ten errors. Some sentences are correct.

Alice Walker

[1]Alice Walker, was born in Eatonville Georgia, in 1944. [2]She has been a social worker, a teacher a lecturer, a novelist, and a poet. [3]Her very popular novel *The Color Purple,* which was publish in 1982, won a Pulitzer Prize and was later the basis for a successful movie? [4]In *The Color Purple,* two sisters right letters to try to stay in touch during thirty years of hardships and challenges. [5]It has been called a feminist novel.

GRAMMAR/USAGE/MECHANICS

[6]Certainly it is one what celebrates black women's fight for empowerment and recognition. [7]Other book's of Walker's include *You Can't Keep a Good Woman Down* and *In Search of Our Mothers' Gardens.* [8]In 1998 she published *Langston Hughes, American Poet.* [9]This is an illustrated biography of won of the famousest members of the Harlem Renaissance. [10]Whichever of Walker's books you choose, you'll be sure to find a powerful story that will stay with you for a long time.

POSTTEST   Main and Subordinate Clauses

Identify each boldfaced, numbered clause as M *for main or* S *for subordinate. Then identify each subordinate clause as adjective* (ADJ), *adverb* (ADV), *or noun* (N).

Although Guy de Maupassant also wrote novels, plays, and travel sketches,[1] short stories were **what he most often wrote.**[2] **That he was a master of the short story**[3] is obvious in some of his most famous stories, **which include "Tallow Ball," "The Necklace," "The Piece of String," and "Two Friends."**[4]

Maupassant was born in 1850 near Dieppe, France.[5] He had a younger brother, Hervé, **who was born in 1856.**[6] **In 1869 Maupassant began to study law in Paris,**[7] but he left his studies and fought in the Franco-German War. In many of his stories, he wrote about **what he experienced in the war.**[8]

Author Gustave Flaubert, **who was Maupassant's good friend,**[9] strongly influenced **how Maupassant wrote.**[10] Flaubert once called Maupassant a disciple **whom he loved as a son.**[11]

That he could row[12] was one of Maupassant's talents. **He was an oarsman**[13] who could row up to fifty miles in a single day.[14] He loved the water and, **whenever he could,**[15] he included nautical imagery in his writing. **As he grew older,**[16] Maupassant was very concerned with his health, and **he often complained of eye problems and migraine headaches.**[17] **His brother's death in 1888 deeply affected him.**[18] He grieved so severely **that he was placed in an institution,**[19] where he died one month before his forty-third birthday.[20]

Chapter 4 Clauses and Sentence Structure   **181**

Identify each sentence by writing S *for simple,* C *for compound,* CX *for complex, or* CC *for compound-complex.*

21. Guy de Maupassant wrote approximately three hundred short stories during his career.

22. He often wrote about characters who struggled against their fate.

23. Greed or ambition often lead to the downfall of his characters.

24. "The Necklace" is about a woman who borrowed a diamond necklace from a friend.

25. She lost the borrowed necklace, and she bought another one.

26. She returned the new necklace to the woman who had loaned the other necklace to her, and she kept the loss secret.

27. After ten years of hard work, she paid for the necklace, but the work robbed her of her youth and beauty.

28. She learned that the borrowed necklace had not been made of real diamonds.

29. Knowing that she had worked so hard made her angry, but she realized that she had learned a great deal from the experience.

30. What was the lesson she had learned?

POSTTEST Kinds of Sentences

Identify each sentence by writing D *for declarative,* IT *for interrogative,* IM *for imperative, or* E *for exclamatory.*

31. Brianna, please help Hiroshi put the chairs around the table.

32. What time will Lee and Joel start the meeting?

33. If we start the meeting by seven-thirty, can you serve the refreshments at nine o'clock?

34. This is the most important meeting of the year!

35. After we elect next year's officers, we will discuss the spring dance.

36. I can hardly believe that the dance is only two months away!

37. Come into the room and sit down so we can start the meeting.

38. Who is willing to be the chairperson for the dance committee?

39. Isabel, Lee, Steve, and Hiroshi could be responsible for the decorations because they're all very imaginative.

40. The dance will be a success only if we all do our very best.

POSTTEST **Fragments and Run-ons**

Identify each numbered item by writing F for fragment, R for run-on sentence, or S for sentence.

41. Hiking for fun and exercise.

42. Before you go hiking, make sure that you have comfortable shoes with good support.

43. A wonderful hobby.

44. You should dress appropriately for the weather and you should always be prepared for rain.

45. Pack your backpack carefully don't include anything that's not necessary.

46. Sunscreen, insect repellent, sunglasses, bottled water, and small snacks.

47. You shouldn't hike alone you shouldn't hike after dark.

48. Wear heavy socks to help prevent blisters.

49. Feet dry and comfortable.

50. Tiring if you don't rest from time to time.

Chapter 5

Verb Tenses and Voice

● ● ● ● ● ● ● ● ● ● ● ● ● ● ●

PRETEST **Verb Forms**

Write the correct form of the verb in parentheses.

1. The package (burst) open with a pop.
2. Whom has the class (choose) as president?
3. Suddenly one gray seal (dive) into the icy water.
4. What has the child (draw) on her homemade card?
5. No one had ever (become) so graceful so quickly.
6. Has Jeremy (leave) his coat at home?
7. At eight o'clock last night, Pamela (sit) down and (begin) to write.
8. I have (know) about your plans for three months.
9. It (be) Mrs. McGuire who always used to sit on that bench.
10. My dad has (sell) computer equipment for three years now.
11. Who (pay) for my theater ticket last night?
12. Susan (lie) down for an hour and got up feeling better.

13. As a surprise, Matthew (shine) Bobbi's shoes yesterday.

14. Last year Ignacio (see) a polar bear up close.

15. So far Arnold has (sleep) in that chair for an hour.

16. Yes, Mr. Mullins, I (read) the notice on the bulletin board last week.

17. Myron (have) his tonsils out when he was in the second grade.

18. Last summer, without warning, the dock suddenly (break) loose and (sink).

19. Igasho accidentally (throw) away his collection of baseball cards.

20. The wind (blow) fiercely all night and all the next day.

PRETEST Verb Tenses

Identify the italicized verb tense by writing one of these labels: present, past, future, present perfect, past perfect, future perfect.

21. By nightfall, Jon *had packed* all our camping gear in the truck.

22. The boys *washed* the dishes, *dried* them, and *put* them away.

23. That view of Mount Shasta *is* magnificent!

24. *Have* you ever *eaten* squid?

25. *Will* you *come* with us, Marianne?

26. In A.D. 79, Mount Vesuvius *erupted* and *destroyed* the towns of Pompeii and Herculaneum.

27. By dawn, the storm *will have raged* for forty-eight hours.

28. Who *lost* a snowshoe on the trail yesterday?

29. Who *wants* some warm carrot cake?

30. *Has* anyone *seen* Ching in the past two days?

Identify the italicized verb form by writing one of these labels: present progressive, past progressive, future progressive, present perfect progressive, past perfect progressive, future perfect progressive, present emphatic, past emphatic.

31. *Will* you *be coming* with us to the concert tonight, Eric?

32. At two o'clock, how many hours *will* we *have been traveling?*

33. Yes, Marilyn *does keep* her hair dryer downstairs.

34. Mateo *has been driving* for four hours already.

35. By the next ice age, we *will* still *be waiting* for Adela.

36. *Had* you *been watching* the gray whales for long when the rain started?

37. Keith and Chim *do have* to leave tonight.

38. Yolanda *is typing* your letter right now.

39. Yes, Keiko, Kimiko *did receive* the role of Juliet.

40. In April our midtown office *was* still *processing* your mail.

Rewrite each sentence, correcting verbs in the wrong tense and verbs in passive voice that should be in active voice.

41. After the stove had been cleaned by the boys, five dirty cake pans were found in the oven by the girls.

42. The terrier that was bathed by Anna earlier should now be brushed by her.

43. Murals had been painted by the Etruscans long before any were ever painted by the Romans.

44. No, Winston, the last ice age is ending long before the Renaissance began.

45. The children at MacGregor Day Care Center were being entertained by two volunteers in clown suits.

46. As seven of his classmates watched, Calvin will cook a delicious meal.

47. Dr. Hanamoto gave me this prescription before he moves his practice to Newark.

48. Once the new tile had been put in place by the tile setters, instructions in caring for it were given to us by them.

49. The painters will have been out of the house before the decorators deliver our new furniture.

50. Deena may be considered cold by visitors, but she is known to be warm and caring by her friends.

5.1 PRINCIPAL PARTS OF VERBS

All verbs have four **principal parts:** a *base form,* a *present participle,* a *simple past form,* and a *past participle.* All the verb tenses are formed from these principal parts.

EXAMPLES

PRINCIPAL PARTS OF VERBS

BASE FORM	PRESENT PARTICIPLE	PAST FORM	PAST PARTICIPLE
play	playing	played	played
watch	watching	watched	watched
break	breaking	broke	broken
hire	hiring	hired	hired
be	being	was, were	been

You can use the base form (except the base form of *be*) and the past form by themselves as main verbs. To function as the simple predicate in a sentence, the present participle and the past participle must always be used with one or more auxiliary verbs.

EXAMPLE   Monkeys **climb.** [base or present form]

EXAMPLE   Monkeys **climbed.** [past form]

EXAMPLE   Monkeys **are climbing.** [present participle with the auxiliary verb *are*]

EXAMPLE   Monkeys **have climbed.** [past participle with the auxiliary verb *have*]

PRACTICE Principal Parts of Verbs

Write the correct form of the principal part of the verb in parentheses.

1. The Egyptians have (past participle of *cultivate*) dates for centuries.
2. Today, more Egyptians than ever are (present participle of *grow*) cotton.
3. The eagle (past form of *swoop*) down to capture its prey.
4. Shawnee, is that your poster (present participle of *hang*) at the visitors' entrance?
5. Who (past form of *paint*) *American Gothic?*
6. That famous painter must surely (base form of *be*) Grant Wood.
7. In about an hour we will be (present participle of *taste*) freshly (past participle of *bake*) bread.
8. Mr. Hathaway (past form of *suggest*) that Shirley try out for the drama club comedy.
9. Poet Robert Frost is well (past participle of *regard*) for his poem "Birches."
10. What has Mrs. Shigeta (past participle of *report*) to the school board?

5.2 REGULAR AND IRREGULAR VERBS

A **regular verb** forms its past and past participle by adding *-ed* or *-d* to the base form.

EXAMPLES

REGULAR VERBS		
BASE FORM	**PAST FORM**	**PAST PARTICIPLE**
climb	climbed	climbed
skate	skated	skated
learn	learned	learned

Some regular verbs undergo spelling changes when *-ed* is added.

EXAMPLES spy + **-ed** = spied

trot + **-ed** = trotted

refer + **-ed** = referred

An **irregular verb** forms its past and past participle in some way other than by adding *-ed* or *-d* to the base form.

EXAMPLES

COMMON IRREGULAR VERBS		
BASE FORM	**PAST FORM**	**PAST PARTICIPLE**
be, am, are, is	was, were	been
bear	bore	borne
beat	beat	beaten *or* beat
become	became	become

Common Irregular Verbs, *continued*

BASE FORM	PAST FORM	PAST PARTICIPLE
begin	began	begun
bite	bit	bitten *or* bit
blow	blew	blown
break	broke	broken
bring	brought	brought
burst	burst	burst
buy	bought	bought
cast	cast	cast
catch	caught	caught
choose	chose	chosen
come	came	come
creep	crept	crept
cut	cut	cut
dive	dived *or* dove	dived
do	did	done
draw	drew	drawn
drink	drank	drunk
drive	drove	driven
eat	ate	eaten
fall	fell	fallen
feel	felt	felt
find	found	found
fling	flung	flung
fly	flew	flown

Common Irregular Verbs, continued

BASE FORM	PAST FORM	PAST PARTICIPLE
freeze	froze	frozen
get	got	got *or* gotten
give	gave	given
go	went	gone
grow	grew	grown
hang*	hung *or* hanged	hung *or* hanged
have	had	had
hit	hit	hit
hold	held	held
keep	kept	kept
know	knew	known
lay**	laid	laid
lead	led	led
leave	left	left
lend	lent	lent
let	let	let
lie**	lay	lain
lose	lost	lost
make	made	made
pay	paid	paid
put	put	put
read	read	read
ride	rode	ridden
ring	rang	rung

Common Irregular Verbs, continued

BASE FORM	PAST FORM	PAST PARTICIPLE
rise**	rose	risen
run	ran	run
say	said	said
see	saw	seen
seek	sought	sought
sell	sold	sold
set***	set	set
shake	shook	shaken
shine****	shone *or* shined	shone *or* shined
shrink	shrank *or* shrunk	shrunk *or* shrunken
sing	sang	sung
sink	sank	sunk
sit***	sat	sat
sleep	slept	slept
speak	spoke	spoken
spend	spent	spent
spring	sprang *or* sprung	sprung
steal	stole	stolen
sting	stung	stung
swear	swore	sworn
swim	swam	swum
swing	swung	swung
take	took	taken
teach	taught	taught

Common Irregular Verbs, continued

BASE FORM	PAST FORM	PAST PARTICIPLE
tear	tore	torn
tell	told	told
think	thought	thought
throw	threw	thrown
wear	wore	worn
weave	wove	woven
win	won	won
write	wrote	written

*Use *hanged* to refer to death by hanging. For all other uses, *hung* is correct.

**For more detailed instruction on *lay* versus *lie* and *rise* versus *raise*, see the Usage Glossary pages 61 and 69.

***For more detailed instruction on *sit* versus *set*, see the Usage Glossary page 72.

****Shone* is intransitive. (The sun *shone*.) *Shined* is transitive. (I *shined* my shoes.)

PRACTICE Past Forms and Past Participles

Copy and complete the chart. Make sure that you have spelled each form correctly.

BASE FORM	PAST FORM	PAST PARTICIPLE
1. see		
2. fly		
3. gather		

Practice, Past Forms and Past Participles, continued

BASE FORM	PAST FORM	PAST PARTICIPLE
4. bear		
5. choose		
6. grow		
7. keep		
8. remember		
9. lie		
10. ring		
11. put		
12. climb		
13. write		
14. become		
15. tell		
16. let		
17. seek		
18. carry		
19. sit		
20. throw		
21. rise		
22. believe		
23. hurry		
24. wear		
25. begin		

Write the correct form of the verb in parentheses.

1. Juan has (draw) a striking likeness of his mother.

2. Yesterday the ocean (be) a beautiful, clear blue green.

3. Lim Sing has (hang) paper lanterns from the trees for our summer picnic.

4. In India, Gandhi's assassin was (hang) for his crime.

5. Last night the midwinter full moon (shine) brilliantly on the snow.

6. How many altos will be (choose) for the chorus?

7. Melanie had (shine) the flashlight right in my face!

8. A few weeks ago, Latrice (break) a tooth on a piece of peanut brittle.

9. By this evening, everyone will have (write) a personal anecdote for English class.

10. Last night Guadalupe (see) the constellation Orion for the first time.

5.3 TENSE OF VERBS

The **tenses** of a verb are the forms that help to show time.

There are six tenses in English: *present, past, future, present perfect, past perfect,* and *future perfect.*

PRESENT TENSE

The present-tense form of a verb is the same as the verb's base form, except for the third-person singular, which adds *-s* or *-es.* The exceptions are the verb *have* (which has the third-person singular form *has*) and the verb *be.*

PRESENT TENSE OF THE VERB *STAY*

	SINGULAR	PLURAL
FIRST PERSON	I **stay.**	We **stay.**
SECOND PERSON	You **stay.**	You **stay.**
THIRD PERSON	She, he, or it **stays.** Joanie **stays.**	They **stay.** The dogs **stay.**

PRESENT TENSE OF THE VERB *BE*

	SINGULAR	PLURAL
FIRST PERSON	I **am** sure.	We **are** sure.
SECOND PERSON	You **are** sure.	You **are** sure.
THIRD PERSON	She, he, or it **is** sure. Henry **is** sure.	They **are** sure. The children **are** sure.

The **present tense** expresses a constant, repeated, or habitual action or condition. It can also express a general truth.

EXAMPLE   Isaac **likes** the taste of tea with honey in it. [**not just this cup of tea but every cup of tea; a repeated action**]

EXAMPLE   Emily **bakes** wonderful spice cookies. [**always; a habitual action**]

EXAMPLE   Gold **is** valuable. [**a general truth**]

The **present tense** can also express an action or a condition that exists only now.

EXAMPLE   Krista **feels** good about her score on the science test. **[not always but just now]**

EXAMPLE   I **see** a hummingbird at the feeder. **[at this very moment]**

The **present tense** is sometimes used in historical writing to express past events and, more often, in poetry, fiction, and journalism (especially in sports writing) to convey to the reader a sense of being there. This usage is sometimes called the *historical present tense.*

EXAMPLE   Washington **continues** to beg the Continental Congress for supplies.

EXAMPLE   The goalie **throws** her body across the opening and **blocks** the shot in the final seconds of the game.

PRACTICE Present Tense

Write a sentence using each of the following verb forms. The content of your sentence should express the kind of present tense indicated in parentheses.

1. does (a repeated action)
2. brings (a repeated action)
3. rings (a constant action)
4. are (a general truth)
5. carries (a repeated action)
6. hears (at this moment)
7. decides (a habitual action)
8. rises (a constant action)
9. is (a general truth)
10. studies (a repeated action)

PAST TENSE

Use the **past tense** to express an action or a condition that was started and completed in the past.

EXAMPLE The track meet **went** well.

EXAMPLE Nan **set** a new school record for the shot put.

EXAMPLE The sprinters **ran** like antelopes.

EXAMPLE The coach **praised** the hurdlers.

Nearly all regular and irregular verbs (except *be*) have just one past-tense form, such as *climbed* or *ran*. The verb *be* has two past-tense forms, *was* and *were*.

EXAMPLES

PAST TENSE OF THE VERB *BE*		
	SINGULAR	**PLURAL**
FIRST PERSON	I **was** sure.	We **were** sure.
SECOND PERSON	You **were** sure.	You **were** sure.
THIRD PERSON	She, he, or it **was** sure. Maude **was** sure.	They **were** sure. The dancers **were** sure.

FUTURE TENSE

Use the **future tense** to express an action or a condition that will occur in the future.

You form the future tense of any verb by using the auxiliary verb *shall* or *will* with the base form: *I shall study; you will go.* Note: In modern American English, *shall* is very seldom used except for questions in which *I* or *we* is the subject: *Shall I call you? Shall we go now?*

EXAMPLE Robby **will order** the supplies.

EXAMPLE I **will pack** the car in the morning.

There are three other ways to express future time besides using the future tense. They are as follows:

1. Use *going to* with the present tense of *be* and the base form of a verb.

EXAMPLE Robby **is *going to* order** the supplies.

2. Use *about to* with the present tense of *be* and the base form of a verb.

EXAMPLE Robby **is *about to* order** the supplies.

3. Use the present tense with an adverb or an adverb phrase that shows future time.

EXAMPLE Robby **leaves *tomorrow.***

EXAMPLE Robby **arrives *on tomorrow's train.***

PRACTICE **Future Tense**

Rewrite each sentence so that the verb expresses the future tense in the four ways taught in this lesson. For each sentence given here, be sure you have four different responses.

1. Seamus ran for the office of class president.
2. Alison congratulated Nancy Anderson on her award.
3. Mrs. Patterson spoke to Kenesha's teacher.
4. The sophomores found out who won the election.
5. Emilio and Vicente showed the film to the class.

PRACTICE **Present, Past, and Future Tenses**

Identify the italicized verb tense by writing one of these labels: present, past, future.

1. At the ceremony, Nate *will present* a tribute to Mrs. Westin.
2. Marcia *struggled* up the snowy hill with her sled.
3. How long *shall* I *wait* for you, Amanda?

4. The pastry chef *makes* ten different desserts each morning.

5. The news story *aired* on five major channels.

6. Our local weather station *predicts* sunny weather for today.

7. Who *will take* my place on Friday?

8. We *gave* our old comic books to the after-school program.

9. To distinguish a frog from a toad, biologists *examine* these characteristics.

10. Willem *measured* the angle with his protractor.

5.4 PERFECT TENSES

PRESENT PERFECT TENSE

> Use the **present perfect tense** to express an action or a condition that occurred at some *indefinite time* in the past.

You form the present perfect tense by using *has* or *have* with the past participle of a verb: *has permitted, have cut.*

Do not be confused by the word *present* in the name of the present perfect tense. This tense expresses past time. The word *present* refers to the tense of the auxiliary verb *has* or *have.*

EXAMPLE   The living-room clock **has stopped.**

EXAMPLE   They **have brought** the new couch a day early.

The present perfect tense can refer to completed action in past time only in an indefinite way. Adverbs such as *yesterday* cannot be added to make the time more specific.

EXAMPLE   Chandra **has completed** her project.

EXAMPLE   Jack **has** always **wanted** to visit Mexico.

To be specific about completed past time, you would normally use the simple past tense.

EXAMPLE Chandra **completed** her project yesterday.

EXAMPLE Jack **wanted** to visit Mexico last summer.

The present perfect tense can also be used to express the idea that an action or a condition *began in the past and is still happening.* To communicate this idea, you would normally add adverbs (or adverb phrases or clauses) of time.

EXAMPLE The mall **has displayed** our artwork for two weeks.

EXAMPLE We **have kept** a spare house key under this rock ever since I left my key at school.

PAST PERFECT TENSE

Use the **past perfect tense** to indicate that one past action or condition began *and* ended before another past action or condition started.

You form the past perfect tense by using the auxiliary verb *had* with the past participle of a verb: *had praised, had written.*

Past

EXAMPLE Patricia **dedicated** her play to the drama teacher who

Past Perfect

had encouraged her long ago. [**First the drama teacher encouraged Patricia; then years later Patricia acknowledged her teacher's support.**]

Past Perfect

EXAMPLE The meat loaf **had dried** to shoe leather by the time I

Past

remembered to check it. [**First the meat loaf dried up; then I remembered to check it.**]

FUTURE PERFECT TENSE

Use the **future perfect tense** to express one future action or condition that will begin *and* end before another future event starts.

You form the future perfect tense by using *will have* or *shall have* with the past participle of a verb: *will have practiced, shall have flown.*

EXAMPLE   By September I **will have saved** fifty dollars. [**The money will be saved by the time another future event, the arrival of September, occurs.**]

EXAMPLE   Before Maggie's baby is born, I **will have made** a quilt for the child's crib. [**The quilt will be made before another future event, the baby's birth, occurs.**]

PRACTICE   Perfect Tenses

Read the verb in parentheses. Then write it in the tense indicated in brackets.

1. Ty (varnish) the steps before I left. [past perfect]
2. For years they (enjoy) this view. [present perfect]
3. Ric (work) there for a year. [present perfect]
4. By the end of this month, Nancy (work) for the parks division for nine years. [future perfect]
5. Before today's victory, Ms. Kostas already (win) three international tennis tournaments. [past perfect]
6. The board (explore) the intriguing possibilities. [present perfect]
7. He (agree) not to press charges. [present perfect]
8. By ten o'clock, one of these three artists (claim) the esteemed Statler award. [future perfect]
9. Luke and Austin Bailey not (expect) to come face to face with a grizzly bear. [past perfect]
10. Sara already (mention) her plans. [present perfect]

VERB TENSE TIME LINE

FUTURE PERFECT
- future action or condition will begin *and* end before another starts

I **will have finished** my work before I leave.

FUTURE
- action or condition will occur in the future

I **will finish** my work tonight.

FUTURE

NOW

PRESENT
- action or condition exists only now
- constant, repeated, or habitual action or condition
- a general truth

I **finish** my work on time.

PAST

PRESENT PERFECT
- action or condition that occurred at an *indefinite* past time
- action began in the past and still occurs now

I **have finished** my work.

PAST PERFECT
- past action or condition began *and* ended before another past action or condition started

I **had finished** my work before I left.

PAST
- action or condition was started and completed in the past

I **finished** my work.

GRAMMAR/USAGE/MECHANICS

PRACTICE **All Six Tenses**

Identify the italicized verb tense by writing one of these labels: present, past, future, present perfect, past perfect, future perfect.

1. *Has* Mrs. Kim *seen* the decorations in the dining room yet?
2. *Will* you *have arranged* for the transportation by tomorrow morning?
3. Earlier this morning I *felt* a little feverish.
4. Who *eats* all the caramels every time we have a box of chocolates?
5. *Had* Alan ever *ridden* a horse before today?
6. The "Star-Spangled Banner" *had* just *begun,* and the fans *had risen* to their feet, when the thunderstorm *started.*
7. Derek *tears* his shirt during almost every football game.
8. Esperanza *ran* out of toothpaste this morning.
9. *Has* anyone here ever *flown* over an ocean?
10. *Will* you *put* everything away by five o'clock?

5.5 PROGRESSIVE AND EMPHATIC FORMS

Each of the six tenses has a **progressive** form that expresses a continuing action.

You make the progressive forms by using the appropriate tense of the verb *be* with the present participle of the main verb.

EXAMPLES

PRESENT PROGRESSIVE	They *are* traveling.
PAST PROGRESSIVE	They *were* traveling.
FUTURE PROGRESSIVE	They *will be* traveling.
PRESENT PERFECT PROGRESSIVE	They *have been* traveling.
PAST PERFECT PROGRESSIVE	They *had been* traveling.
FUTURE PERFECT PROGRESSIVE	They *will have been* traveling.

The present tense and the past tense have additional forms, called **emphatic forms,** that add special force, or emphasis, to the verb.

You make the emphatic forms by using *do, does,* or *did* with the base form of the verb.

PRESENT EMPHATIC   I **do hope** the train is on time.

Tom **does have** a plane to catch.

PAST EMPHATIC   He **did miss** his plane the last time because of a late train.

PRACTICE Progressive and Emphatic Forms

Identify the italicized verb form by writing one of these labels: present progressive, past progressive, future progressive, present perfect progressive, past perfect progressive, future perfect progressive, present emphatic, past emphatic.

1. *Will* you *be participating* in this year's run for freedom?
2. By midnight, how long *will* we *have been waiting?*
3. Yes, Odessa *does like* summer squash.
4. The Johnson twins *have been volunteering* at the hospital for three years.
5. On Friday I *will* still *be working* part time at the post office.
6. By eight o'clock, Leo *had* already *been swimming* too long.
7. Yes, I think we *do have* another shirt in your size.
8. Marisa *is waiting* in front of your house now, Ms. Delaney.
9. You're right, ma'am, we *did forget* to mail your water bill this month.
10. We *were traveling* in Canada when we heard the news.

5.6 CONSISTENCY OF TENSES

Don't shift, or change, tenses when two or more events occur at the same time.

EXAMPLES **INCORRECT** The soloist **stopped** suddenly and **coughs** loudly. **[The tense needlessly shifts from the past to the present.]**

CORRECT The soloist **stopped** suddenly and **coughed** loudly. **[Now it is clear that both events happened at nearly the same time.]**

INCORRECT The radio operator **removes** his headphones. He **rushed** to the captain with the message. **[The tense needlessly shifts from the present to the past.]**

CORRECT The radio operator **removes** his headphones. He **rushes** to the captain with the message. **[It is clear that both events happened at nearly the same time.]**

Do shift tenses to show that one event precedes or follows another.

EXAMPLES **INCORRECT** By the time we **found** the campsite, the others **ate** all the hot dogs. **[The two past-tense verbs give the mistaken impression that both events—the finding of the campsite and the eating of the hot dogs—happened at the same time.]**

CORRECT By the time we **found** the campsite, the others **had eaten** all the hot dogs. **[The shift from the past tense *(found)* to the past perfect tense *(had eaten)* clearly shows that the others ate the hot dogs before we found the campsite.]**

Keep a statement about a general truth in the present tense even if other verbs are in the past tense.

EXAMPLE   We **remembered** that the freezing point of water **is** thirty-two degrees Fahrenheit.

PRACTICE   Consistency of Tenses

Find the first verb that appears in each sentence. Then write the consistent tense of the verb in parentheses.

1. Bobbi saved twenty dollars, but now she (had not found, cannot find) the money.
2. In times past, chickens were kept in cages; today, though, many farmers (allowed, allow) them to roam in enclosed areas.
3. Alexandra watched the clouds as they (floated, float) in the sky.
4. Many Algonquian tribes befriended the Pilgrims and (teach, taught) them to grow corn and pumpkins.
5. The Lorensons, now in their sixties, have saved fifty dollars a month since they (were married, had been married) in 1960.
6. Franklin learned in the fourth grade that Earth (has revolved, revolves) around the sun.
7. I will be home by six o'clock, and we (shall have, have had) dinner at seven.
8. Because of compound interest, Amelia has $255.00 in her account instead of the $240.00 that she (deposited, will deposit).
9. When Aunt Marcia gave me this dress, I (am, was) only three years old.
10. Grandpa showed us that watering a transplanted sapling every day (results, has resulted) in a healthy tree.

5.7 VOICE OF VERBS

An action verb is in the **active voice** when the subject of the sentence performs the action.

EXAMPLE The brown bear **caught** a salmon.

An action verb is in the **passive voice** when its action is performed on the subject.

EXAMPLE A salmon **was caught** by the brown bear.

Generally the active voice is stronger, but at times the passive voice is preferable or even necessary. If you don't want to call attention to the performer of the action or don't know who the performer is, use the passive voice.

EXAMPLE All the costumes **were ruined.** [You may not want to identify the culprit.]

EXAMPLE The bank **was robbed.** [You may not know who the culprit is.]

You form the passive voice by using a form of the auxiliary verb *be* with the past participle of the verb. The tense of a passive verb is determined by the tense of the auxiliary verb.

EXAMPLE The song **is sung** by the choir. [present tense, passive voice]

EXAMPLE The song **was sung** by the choir. [past tense, passive voice]

EXAMPLE The song **will be sung** by the choir. [future tense, passive voice]

PRACTICE Active and Passive Voice

Rewrite each sentence, changing active verbs to passive and passive verbs to active.

1. Up to 130 pounds of vegetable matter are eaten daily by each hippopotamus in the preserve.
2. Ginger ate the last piece of cornbread.

3. The last piece of the puzzle was added by Leroy.
4. The mail carrier heard the child's frantic cries.
5. The river had been crossed by the hippopotamus in about five minutes.
6. Mr. Harris's entire stock of seed corn was eaten by the birds.
7. Among other things, corn, soybeans, and cotton are raised by North Carolina farmers.
8. Sir Caraway and his servants guarded the gate.
9. The luggage had already been packed by the Petrillo family.
10. The semifinal match had been won by the Charleston Chargers.

PRACTICE Proofreading

Rewrite the following passage, correcting errors in spelling, capitalization, grammar, and usage. Add any missing punctuation. There are ten errors. Some sentences are correct.

Chitra Banerjee Divakaruni

[1]This poet, short story writer and novelist was borned in India but now lives with her husband and too children in both San Francisco and Houston. [2]She often write about characters with traditional Indian backgrounds who are having trouble adapting to the more open Western culture. [3]Many of her main characters are immigrant Indian woman, as is she herself. [4]Divakarunis experiences, including her work with victims of domestic violence, helps her write stories with great emotional intensity. [5]in an interview published in *Atlantic Unbound,* she said, "I would very much like women of all backgrounds to pick up my books, because women's experiences are much more similar than we ordinarily think. [6]We can learn so much from one another." [7]Many readers find that Divakaruni's works immerse them in Indian culture. [8]"But I write just as much about America, about what coming to America does to people and

for people, and what immigrant people do to America and for America," Divakaruni said in the interview cited above. [9]The themes that push her to write—tradition, individuality, freedom, and loyalty—leave her explore how people turn back to their roots to work out their own responses to life's challenges. [10]The thoughts and hearts of new friends are shown to us by her.

POSTTEST Verb Forms

Write the correct form of the verb in parentheses.

1. Have you ever (drived, driven) on any of the Hawaiian islands?
2. I (seen, saw) Mount Waialeale, often called "the wettest spot on earth."
3. When I left the mountain, I (feel, felt) decidedly clammy.
4. How did Miyoko (broken, break) her arm?
5. The kitten (creeped, crept) into Lucy's bed and snuggled under the covers.
6. Rana watched Bob at the table and asked, "How long has it (be, been) since you have (eaten, ate)?"
7. Monica (sat, set) the vase on the table and walked away.
8. "That's a good book, Odelie," (say, said) Tamara. "When I (taken, took) it out at the library, I enjoyed it very much."
9. Paul had (rose, risen) at nine o'clock but was still sleepy.
10. Caroline's note said "I have (gone, went) to the bakery, but I'll be home soon."
11. Hong Kong is a group of islands that seem to have (springed, sprung) out of the South China Sea.
12. Britain (held, holds) it as a dependency for many years, but now it belongs to China.
13. Many businesspeople are (drew, drawn) to Hong Kong because of its bustling economic climate.

14. "Why have you (chose, chosen) this film, Evelyn?" asked Carol.

15. "I'm thirsty," said Lio, "but I have already (drunk, drank) three glasses of water."

16. Is it possible that my dresses (shrink, shrunken) a little every time I (wear, worn) them?

17. Entering the tent, Geralyn (shone, shined) her flashlight everywhere checking for snakes.

18. Sanskrit is an ancient language that is (spoke, spoken) by only a few people today.

19. Polar bears seldom (frozen, freeze) in the far north because a layer of fat under their skin (keeps, kept) them warm.

20. Jeannine, what have you (teached, taught) the first graders today?

POSTTEST Verb Tenses

Identify the italicized verb tense by writing one of these labels: present, past, future, present perfect, past perfect, future perfect.

21. Marie *asked* the waiter for more salad dressing.

22. *Have* all the homework assignments *been completed?*

23. Chen *had* already *painted* the room when Albert *arrived.*

24. What *will happen* to Luigi in the hospital?

25. Mrs. Cambridge *felt* much better after her tooth had been fixed.

26. The Crenshaws *had forgotten* all of their luggage.

27. By next week, these Air Force cadets *will have finished* basic training.

28. Our English teacher *makes* poetry fun.

29. What *shall* we *do* about Rahul's sick parakeet?

30. By Friday, each student *will have completed* a questionnaire.

Identify the italicized verb form by writing one of these labels: present progressive, past progressive, future progressive, present perfect progressive, past perfect progressive, future perfect progressive, present emphatic, past emphatic.

31. I *am going* to the park to find my lost football.

32. How many of you *have been studying* for longer than two hours?

33. I *do think* Lani is a very intelligent girl.

34. The people who *had been journeying* across the frozen plains were known as Sami.

35. These hardy people *have been living* north of the Arctic Circle for more than six hundred years.

36. Before we reach home, we *will have been traveling* for many hours.

37. The meadowlark that *was singing* outside your window is not a lark at all but a member of the blackbird family.

38. Yes, Jeremy *did miss* class this morning because of a loose filling.

39. At ten o'clock, I *will have been correcting* exam papers for five straight hours!

40. This is the third year that Keisha *will be singing* in the school chorus.

POSTTEST **Consistency of Verb Tense and Voice**

Rewrite each sentence, correcting verbs in the wrong tense and verbs in passive voice that should be in active voice.

41. I learned that three teaspoons equalled one tablespoon.

42. Charles Dickens will be writing his stories in the nineteenth century—about the same time Edgar Allan Poe was writing his.

43. The kettle of corn and beans was cooked by the chef.

44. The audience was being entertained by the actors in the drama.

45. After the car was washed by Amanda, Simon had vacuumed the interior.

46. As Lianne looked on, the painting was completed by Bob.

47. Dr. Hansen filled the cavity in Leroy's molar after he drills it.

48. When the computer had been installed by the technician, a lesson in using it was given to me by him.

49. The road was repaired by the construction workers during rush hour.

50. Her space suit will be put on by the astronaut before the countdown begins.

Chapter 6

Subject-Verb Agreement

● ● ● ● ● ● ● ● ● ● ● ● ● ● ●

PRETEST   **Subject-Verb Agreement**

Write the main word or words from the subject of each sentence. Then write the correct verb from the choice in parentheses.

  1. The barges on the canal (transport, transports) wheat.
  2. The headlights of the oncoming cars (dazzle, dazzles) a driver at night.
  3. This vase of flowers (make, makes) a lovely display.
  4. The thunder (sound, sounds) like fireworks.
  5. Either the Andersons' children or their dog (has, have) dug this hole.
  6. The orchestra (is, are) tuning their instruments.
  7. Politics (is, are) one of my dad's greatest interests.

8. Many a senator (has, have) introduced legislation.
9. Every student in this classroom (is, are) important.
10. Each of the children (receives, receive) a balloon.
11. Five dollars (is, are) the price of this picture frame.
12. Half of this melon (is, are) yours.
13. Seventy-five percent of my classmates (agrees, agree).
14. Twenty-five millimeters (equals, equal) one inch.
15. Linda's "Sequoias" (is, are) her best work so far.
16. Honduras (is, are) a country in Central America.
17. The colors in this photo (is, are) surprisingly lifelike.
18. Pain, in addition to tiredness, (causes, cause) many accidents.
19. Lions and tigers (is, are) cats.
20. Across the grasslands (sounds, sound) the roars of lions.
21. Of all the students in Carlson High, few (goes, go) to the opera.
22. Several of my friends (likes, like) broccoli.
23. Every child (has, have) his or her own unique qualities.
24. Here (is, are) the boxes for your project.
25. (Does, Do) Mandy enjoy country music?

6.1 AGREEMENT OF SUBJECTS AND VERBS

A verb must agree with its subject in number.

Number refers to the form of a word that indicates whether it is singular or plural. A singular subject indicates *one* and requires a singular verb. Plural subjects indicate *more than one* and require plural verbs. With most regular verbs, add *-s* or *-es* to form the singular.

EXAMPLES

SINGULAR
The **athlete exercises.**

PLURAL
The **athletes exercise.**

An exception to the rule occurs with the pronouns *I* and *you*. Both require the form of a verb without -*s* or -*es*, even when *you* refers to one person. The only exception is *be*—when *I* is the subject, the verb form is *am*.

EXAMPLE **I love** animals.

EXAMPLE **You are** my best friend.

Whether functioning as main verbs or auxiliary verbs, *be, have,* and *do* change in form to show agreement.

EXAMPLES

SINGULAR	PLURAL
I **am** happy.	We **are** happy.
The dog **has** food.	The dogs **have** food.
I **do** trust you.	He **does** trust you.

When *be, have,* and *do* are used as auxiliary verbs, they indicate the number of a verb phrase. Notice that the following main verbs do not change form.

EXAMPLES

SINGULAR	PLURAL
He **has seen** the movie.	They **have seen** the movie.
She **is going** to work.	They **are going** to work.
Does she **stay** here?	**Do** they **stay** here?

Note that *were* is plural except in two cases: first, when its subject is the second-person singular personal pronoun, *you;* and second, when it is the verb in a statement that is contrary to fact.

EXAMPLES **You were** the skateboard king. **[singular subject]**

If I were a lottery winner, I would buy you that car.
[The subordinate clause containing *were* is contrary to fact.]

Write the correct verb from the choices in parentheses.

1. Lonnie, you (is, are) my very best friend.
2. I (am, are) only one voice among billions.
3. We (attends, attend) class regularly.
4. These cherries (is, are) delicious.
5. Reynaldo (has, have) seen this week's hit movie.
6. The girls' softball team (has, have) won all its games.
7. You (is, are) nervous, of course, but you will do well.
8. Freighters still (carries, carry) Midwestern grain.
9. (Does, Do) the nurses take breaks on schedule?
10. My cats (watches, watch) the birds for hours.

6.2 INTERVENING PHRASES

Don't mistake a word in an intervening phrase for the subject of a sentence.

The simple subject is never in a prepositional phrase.

EXAMPLE   The **foliage** on the trees **provides** shade. [The singular verb *provides* agrees with the singular subject, *foliage,* not with the plural object of the preposition, *trees.*]

EXAMPLE   The **spices** in the food **are** tasty. [The plural verb *are* agrees with the plural subject, *spices,* not with the object of the preposition, *food.*]

If a singular subject is linked to another noun by a phrase, the subject is still considered singular. Expressions such as *accompanied by, as well as, in addition to, plus,* and *together with* introduce phrases that modify the subject without changing its number.

EXAMPLE   **Sleet,** in addition to snow, **is** a driver's nightmare.

EXAMPLE   **Paula,** along with her friends, **goes** to the mall.

Most of the following sentences contain an error in Subject-Verb Agreement. For each sentence, write the subject and the corrected verb. If a sentence is already correct, write C.

1. The snow in the Pyrenees often become alarmingly deep.
2. Snowstorms as well as strong winds often keeps people away from the mountain passes.
3. In North America, snow, together with ice and wind, causes problems in the upper Midwest.
4. The birds, as well as the frogs and the crickets, lulls me to sleep tonight.
5. The silt in the Tigris and Euphrates rivers made Mesopotamia one of the most fertile areas of the ancient world.
6. The most dangerous weather feature of the eastern United States are hurricanes.
7. Hurricanes, as well as tropical storms, batter the area from Florida to Massachusetts.
8. Cool water, accompanied by cool winds, probably sound like bliss to those in hot desert areas.
9. My hunger, as well as the time of day, suggest a question.
10. Hard rain, in addition to strong winds, hampers the game in Three Rivers Stadium tonight.

6.3 AGREEMENT WITH COMPOUND SUBJECTS

A compound subject that is joined by *and* or *both … and* is plural unless its parts belong to one unit or they both refer to the same person or thing.

| PLURAL | The **lion** and the **tiger are roaring.** |
| | Both **skiing** and **skating are** fun. |

SINGULAR	**Peanut butter** and **jelly is** my favorite type of
	sandwich. **[one unit]**
	His best **friend** and **companion is** George. **[one person]**

With compound subjects joined by *or* or *nor* (or by *either…or* or *neither…nor*), the verb agrees with the subject closer to it.

EXAMPLES

| SINGULAR | My **dog** or my **cat is** responsible for this mess. |
| | Neither the **cows** nor the **goat eats** bananas. |

| PLURAL | Either the **dog** or the **cats are** responsible for this mess. |
| | Neither the **cows** nor the **goats eat** bananas. |

PRACTICE Agreement with Compound Subjects

Write the complete subject of each sentence. Then write the correct verb from the choice in parentheses.

1. The *Iliad* and the *Odyssey* (was composed, were composed) between 800 and 700 B.C.
2. Both Athena and Poseidon (has played, have played) important parts in these great epics.
3. Writers and literature students often (prefers, prefer) the works of authors closer to their own time.
4. *The Old Man and the Sea* and *The Secret Sharer* (is, are) favorites of Leslie and Grace.
5. Both politics and the weather (has influenced, have influenced) the writers of many novels.
6. Neither George nor the twins (appreciates, appreciate) ancient literature.
7. Good looks and bad tempers (is, are) qualities of many literary characters today.

GRAMMAR/USAGE/MECHANICS

8. Either Mr. Echevarria or Ms. Olivero (is teaching, are teaching) a course in Spanish literature next year.

9. (Does, Do) the juniors or the seniors read *The Return of the Native?*

10. Debra Johnson or Lillian and Tom Nash (is scheduled, are scheduled) to read aloud in class today.

6.4 AGREEMENT WITH SPECIAL SUBJECTS

COLLECTIVE NOUNS

A **collective noun** names a group of persons, things, or animals.

When a collective noun subject refers to a group as a whole, it requires a singular verb. When a collective noun subject refers to each member of a group individually, it requires a plural verb.

EXAMPLES

SINGULAR His **family is** from Italy.

PLURAL His **family are getting** haircuts today.

When deciding the number of the verb needed for a collective noun subject, look for the pronouns *its* and *their.* When a collective noun is referred to by *its,* the collective noun requires a singular verb. When a collective noun is referred to by *their,* the collective noun needs a plural verb.

EXAMPLES

SINGULAR The **committee submits** *its* report.

PLURAL The **committee sign** *their* names.

SPECIAL NOUNS

Certain nouns that end in *s,* such as *mathematics, molasses,* and *news,* require singular verbs.

EXAMPLES **Mathematics is** my favorite subject.

The news was good.

Certain other nouns that end in *s,* such as *scissors, pants, binoculars,* and *eyeglasses,* require plural verbs.

EXAMPLES **The scissors were** sharp.

Your **eyeglasses need** cleaning.

Many other nouns that end in *s,* such as *mumps, measles, ethics, statistics,* and *politics,* depending on the meaning, may require either a singular or a plural verb. In general, if the noun refers to a whole, such as a disease or a science, it requires a singular verb. If it refers to qualities, activities, or individual items, it requires a plural verb.

EXAMPLES

SINGULAR **Measles is** a childhood disease.

PLURAL **Measles cover** the sick child's body.

SINGULAR **Statistics is** an interesting subject.

PLURAL **Statistics show** that women live longer than men.

MANY A, EVERY, AND *EACH*

When *many a, every,* or *each* precedes a subject, whether simple or compound, the subject is considered singular.

EXAMPLE *Many a* **student lives** in this dorm.

EXAMPLE *Many a* **giraffe** and **elephant inhabits** this nature preserve.

EXAMPLE *Every* **player has won** at least one game.

EXAMPLE *Every* **chair, bench,** and **table was taken.**

EXAMPLE *Each* **poem was studied.**

EXAMPLE *Each* **story** and **novel was read.**

NOUNS OF AMOUNT

When a plural noun of amount refers to one unit, it acts as a singular subject. When it refers to individual units, it acts as a plural subject.

EXAMPLES   **SINGULAR   Three dollars is** not too much.

PLURAL   Three dollars are on the table.

When a fraction or a percentage refers to a singular word, it requires a singular verb. When it refers to a plural word, it requires a plural verb.

EXAMPLES

SINGULAR   One-fourth of the cookie dough **is** in the bowl.

PLURAL   One-fourth of the cookies **are** in this box.

Units of measurement usually require singular verbs.

EXAMPLE   **Ten kilometers works** out to one myriameter.

TITLES

A title of a creative work always acts as a singular subject, even if a noun within the title is plural.

EXAMPLE   **"Glory Days" describes** high school experiences.

COUNTRIES AND CITIES

The names of countries and cities require singular verbs.

EXAMPLE   **New Orleans hosts** Mardi Gras every spring.

PRACTICE   **Agreement with Special Subjects**

Write the correct verb form from the choice in parentheses.

1. The football team (is having, are having) their physicals.
2. Our local teamsters' union (was deciding, were deciding) which of its two offers to accept.

3. Physics (is, are) an intriguing subject.

4. The hedge clippers (seems, seem) to work now.

5. Family genetics (was, were) an important consideration in choosing Jerol's therapy.

6. Many a town in the Wild West (was abandoned, were abandoned) when gold or silver mines were depleted.

7. Several dollars per barrel (was, were) often spent for clean water in the mining camps.

8. On the frontier, fifty percent of the workers' food (was, were) made from flour.

9. Five thousand six hundred eighty feet (equals, equal) one mile.

10. Seychelles (is, are) an African country.

6.5 INDEFINITE PRONOUNS AS SUBJECTS

Some indefinite pronouns are always singular, some are always plural, and others may be singular or plural.

INDEFINITE PRONOUNS	
SINGULAR	another, anybody, anyone, anything, each, either, everybody, everyone, everything, neither, nobody, no one, nothing, one, somebody, someone, something
PLURAL	both, few, many, others, several
SINGULAR OR PLURAL	all, any, enough, most, much, none, some

Singular indefinite pronouns require singular verbs. Plural indefinite pronouns require plural verbs.

EXAMPLES   **SINGULAR** **Everybody is** going to the concert.

                   PLURAL   **Few have** the patience she has.

The number of the pronouns in the last group depends on the words to which they refer. If the pronoun refers to a singular word, then it requires a singular verb. If the pronoun refers to a plural word, it requires a plural verb.

SINGULAR **Most** of the pie **was eaten.** [*Most* refers to *pie*, a singular noun]

PLURAL **Most** of the cookies **were** still there. [*Most* refers to *cookies,* a plural noun]

The indefinite pronouns *any* and *none* can be singular subjects even when they refer to a plural word. It depends on whether you are thinking of each thing separately or of several things acting as one group.

EXAMPLES

Any of these bikes **is** ready. [**Any one bike is ready.**]
Any of these bikes **are** ready. [**All these bikes are ready.**]
None of these pens **has** a cap. [**Not one pen has a cap.**]
None of these pens **have** caps. [**No pens have caps.**]

COMMITTED reprinted by permission of United Feature Syndicate, Inc.

Write the correct verb from the choice in parentheses for each sentence.

1. Everyone (seems, seem) to be flying kites these days.
2. Someone (has, have) a kite with a giant flower on it.
3. Many kites are flying, but few (is, are) so decorative.
4. (Has, Have) anyone seen Ramona today?
5. A good-sized piece of watermelon is left, but (is, are) there enough for four people?
6. I have some pencils, but there (is, are) not enough for all of you.
7. Tranh found five books, and some of them (is, are) on our reading list.
8. Either of the McIntyre twins (is, are) available for tutoring.
9. Accidents happen, but nobody ever (seems, seem) to know anything about them.
10. Where are all the prizes? Most (has, have) already been won.

PRACTICE Indefinite Pronouns as Subjects

From the chart in this lesson, choose five indefinite pronouns that are always singular, and write sentences using each as a subject. Then do the same for five that are always plural and five that can be either singular or plural. Underline the verb in each sentence.

6.6 AGREEMENT IN INVERTED SENTENCES

In an **inverted sentence,** the subject follows the verb.

Inverted sentences often begin with prepositional phrases. Don't mistake the object of the preposition for the subject.

SINGULAR Across the seas **sails** the young **immigrant.**

PLURAL In the jungle **roar** the **lions.**

In sentences beginning with *there* or *here,* the subject follows the verb. The words *there* and *here* never function as the subject of a sentence.

EXAMPLES

SINGULAR Here **comes** the **bus.**
There **goes** your **friend.**

PLURAL Here **come** the **buses.**
There **go** your **friends.**

In questions an auxiliary verb usually comes before the subject. Look for the subject between the auxiliary verb and the main verb.

EXAMPLES

SINGULAR **Does** that **woman teach** English?

PLURAL **Do** those **women teach** English?

PRACTICE Agreement in Inverted Sentences

Most of the following sentences contain an error in Subject-Verb Agreement. For each sentence, write the incorrect verb and the correct verb. If a sentence is already correct, write C.

1. Do spring begin in March or April?
2. Across the meadow speeds the doe and her fawn.
3. Here are the missing papers.
4. Over the fence springs the rabbits.
5. With whom will Janice attends the spring dance?
6. There is the famous Mount Saint Helens.
7. Why does Toshiro like biology so much?
8. Under the arch and through the gate marches the preschoolers.

9. Here is Bill and his cousin Gene.

10. Do anyone prefer chocolate to strawberry?

| **PRACTICE** | **Subject-Verb Agreement with Special Subjects, in Inverted Sentences, and with Indefinite Pronouns** |

Write the subject of each sentence. Then write the correct verb from the choice in parentheses.

1. Today Paul's family (is packing, are packing) for their trip to Orlando.

2. The business news (is, are) not very good today.

3. These barber shears (is becoming, are becoming) dull.

4. Fifteen dollars (was, were) the price I paid for this scarf.

5. Three-fourths of the marchers (is, are) band members.

6. Doesn't anyone (know, knows) the password?

7. Some of my baseball cards (is, are) missing!

8. Under the canopy (stands, stand) Eric, unwilling to get his new jacket wet.

9. Oh, no! There (goes, go) my bus!

10. (Do, Does) the ninth-grade teachers meet in the gym?

6.7 AGREEMENT WITH SUBJECT, NOT PREDICATE NOMINATIVE

Don't be confused by a predicate nominative that is different in number from the subject. Only the subject affects the number of the linking verb.

EXAMPLE   The first **act was** jugglers. [**The singular verb *was* agrees with the singular subject, *act*, not with the plural predicate nominative, *jugglers*.**]

EXAMPLE   Airline **tickets were** the first prize. [**The plural verb *were* agrees with the plural subject, *tickets*, not with the singular predicate nominative, *prize*.**]

Write the subject of each sentence. Then write the correct verb from the choice in parentheses.

1. The last act in the show (was, were) the singers from Rome.
2. The competitive dancers (was, were) the first act on the program.
3. Five acrobatic skiers (is, are) our entertainment on the slopes today.
4. These gems (is, are) the property of Ms. Jenny Swanson.
5. The city's volunteers (is, are) the center of attention today.
6. On Monday, fresh peaches and cookies (was, were) our dessert.
7. Andy's favorite exhibit (was, were) the Van Gogh paintings.
8. Minerva's least favorite food (is, are) brussels sprouts.
9. Banjo players (was, were) the featured act at the carnival.
10. My mom's favorite television show (is, are) *Friends.*

PRACTICE Proofreading

Rewrite the following passage, correcting errors in spelling, capitalization, grammar, and usage. Add any missing punctuation. There are ten errors. Some sentences are correct.

Louise Erdrich

[1]A member of the Turtle Mountain Band of Chippewa and the granddaughter of the Tribal Chairman of the Turtle Mountain Reservation in North dakota are writer and scholar Louise Erdrich. [2]She attended

Dartmouth College for her undergraduate degree and the Writing Program at Johns Hopkins University for her Master of Arts degree. [3]She have written a memoir, books, stories, introductions and poems so far, as well as dozens of scholarly articles that have earned her international renown. [4]Video recordings and sound recordings are available in which she reads excerpts from her favorite pieces and discuss her life and work.

[5]Erdrich has finded a similarity between the fight to survive as a Native American and the struggle to write. [6]In both efforts, concentration is needed to block out the noise of the modern world so that she can listen to her inner voice. [7]Her work tends to be literary rather than commerical, but that doesn't mean its hard to read. [8]A review of her first children's book *Grandmother's Pigeon,* said, "Besides the sense of the unexpected that permeates every page is the freshness of the language. [9]The sentence structure is elegant, and since one quality of elegance is simplicity, the writing is never over children's heads." [10]Whether she is writing four children, for the general public, or for the scholarly community, Erdrich weaves her heritage and her experiences of the modern world together to tell stories that be rich and original.

POSTTEST Subject-Verb Agreement

Write the main word or words from the subject of each sentence. Then write the correct verb from the choice in parentheses.

1. What a great friend you (is, are)!
2. The spices in this curry (is, are) very hot!
3. Rain, along with heavy wind, (is, are) not good for traveling.
4. Neither Ed nor the Estevez brothers (goes, go) to Highland High School.
5. The freshman class (is, are) having their lunches early today.
6. "Politics (is, are) no career for the faint of heart," exclaimed Mr. Tucker.

7. Tuberculosis (is, are) making an unwelcome comeback today.
8. "Sixteen Tons" (is, are) an old song about the hardships of a coal miner's life.
9. The Philippines (is, are) an island country in the South Pacific Ocean.
10. Seventy percent of the Earth's surface (is covered, are covered) by water.
11. One thousand seven hundred sixty yards (equals, equal) one mile.
12. Eliza looked at the soup; enough (was, were) left for her to have one bowl.
13. Some students vote for Kit; others (is choosing, are choosing) Megan.
14. Across the wide ocean (sails, sail) the liner.
15. Jaime, here (comes, come) your bus!
16. (Has, Have) the teachers computed their students' grades?
17. Two classes of sophomore English (was, were) the responsibility of Mrs. Sanapaw.
18. One of the first games in the tournament (is, are) checkers.
19. Cream cheese and olives on sourdough bread (is, are) one of my favorite sandwiches.
20. Either the student council or the library aides (handles, handle) the crowds on Career Day.
21. The Committee for Creative Engineering (is, are) holding its annual meeting in Austin, Texas.
22. Snow and ice (covers, cover) most of the Northeast at this time of year.
23. Many a family home (was, were) lost during the Depression.
24. "Trees" (is, are) a poem by Joyce Kilmer.
25. Hives (is caused, are caused) by a virus.

Chapter 7

Using Pronouns Correctly

● ● ● ● ● ● ● ● ● ● ● ● ● ● ●

PRETEST   **Using Pronouns Correctly**

For each sentence, write the correct pronoun from the choice in parentheses.

1. Emele and (I, me) are ninth-graders at Shaw School.
2. Lien also goes to Shaw with (we, us).
3. Lien is the best hitter on our softball team; none of our other players are better than (she, her).
4. Did you know that the most populous country is China? (It's, Its) population is greater than one billion people!
5. The least populous country is Vatican City; (it's, its) a very small country, and (it's, its) population hovers around one thousand people.

6. Roger is good at many sports, so (he, his, him) disliking soccer doesn't matter to Coach Hawkins.

7. (We, Our, Us) preferring cauliflower to broccoli is just a matter of taste.

8. The only two students taking the make-up test were Felipe and (she, her).

9. The chairman of the bake sale met with her assistants, Mrs. Medford and (he, him).

10. Among the Parents' Guild officers, all hard workers, are Mrs. Connolly and (she, her).

11. (We, Us) newcomers to the neighborhood will learn a lot from the longtime residents.

12. The school chess team will help (we, us) beginners to learn the skills of the game.

13. At the picnic, Tracy seemed to relax more than (I, me).

14. Waiting in line annoys Carol as much as (he, him).

15. Yes, Alfredo understands music better than (we, us).

16. Jesse taught (hisself, himself) to dive off the high board.

17. Aleene will accompany (me, myself) to tonight's performance.

18. Did you find out (who, whom) Mateo saw at the supermarket?

19. Jo didn't know (who, whom) had sent her that birthday card.

20. Gary Soto writes (his, her, its) novels with humor and compassion.

21. In India, (people, you) welcome guests with bows and folded hands.

22. How do (people, they) travel in the Philippines?

23. None of us knows how (you, people) get from Sacramento to San Diego.

24. Everyone must hand in (his, her, his or her, their) term paper today.

25. How did the twins lose (his, her, his or her, their) way on the road from Tampa to Miami?

7.1 CASE OF PERSONAL PRONOUNS

Pronouns that refer to persons or things are called **personal** pronouns.

Personal pronouns have three **cases,** or forms. The three cases are called **nominative, objective,** and **possessive.** The case of a personal pronoun depends on the pronoun's function in a sentence—that is, whether it is a subject, a complement, an object of a preposition, or a replacement for a possessive noun.

Study the chart to see the different forms of personal pronouns.

PERSONAL PRONOUNS			
CASE	**SINGULAR PRONOUNS**	**PLURAL PRONOUNS**	**FUNCTION IN SENTENCE**
NOMINATIVE	I, you, she, he, it	we, you, they	subject or predicate nominative
OBJECTIVE	me, you, her, him, it	us, you, them	direct object, indirect object, or object of preposition
POSSESSIVE	my, mine, your, yours, her, hers, his, its	our, ours, your, yours, their, theirs	replacement for possessive noun(s)

Use these rules to avoid errors in the case of personal pronouns.

1. Use the nominative case for a personal pronoun in a compound subject.

EXAMPLE   Mindy and **I** play tennis.

EXAMPLE   **She** and **I** are equally matched.

2. Use the objective case for a personal pronoun in a compound object.

EXAMPLE   May my mom sit between you and **me?**

EXAMPLE   Ahmad spoke to Rick and **me.**

EXAMPLE   This is for you and **her.**

Hint: When you are choosing a pronoun for a sentence that has a compound subject or a compound object, try saying the sentence to yourself without the conjunction and the other subject or object.

EXAMPLE   The ball bounced toward **[Mindy and] me.**

Note: It is considered courteous to place the pronoun *I* or *me* last in a series.

EXAMPLE   **Lou, Sandy,** and **I** will be line judges. **[nominative case]**

EXAMPLE   He aimed his camera at **Julie** and **me. [objective case]**

3. Use the nominative case for a personal pronoun after a linking verb.

EXAMPLE   The best line judge is **he.**

EXAMPLE   Is it **I?**

EXAMPLE   The oldest guest is **she.**

This rule is changing. In informal speech, people often use the objective case after a linking verb; they say, *It's me, It was him.* Some authorities even recommend using the objective case in informal writing to avoid sounding artificial. To be strictly correct, however, use the nominative case after a linking verb, especially in formal writing.

4. Never spell possessive personal pronouns with apostrophes.

EXAMPLE   This wrist brace is **hers.**

EXAMPLE   The cooler is **theirs.**

EXAMPLE   That one is **yours.**

It's is a contraction for *it is* or *it has*. Don't confuse *it's* with the possessive pronoun *its*.

EXAMPLE **It's** too late to play tennis. Give me the racket and **its** case.

5. Use possessive pronouns before gerunds (*-ing* forms used as nouns).

EXAMPLE I don't like **his** calling the shots.

EXAMPLE **Our** objecting would do no good.

PRACTICE **Case of Personal Pronouns**

Write the correct personal pronoun from the choice in parentheses.

1. Gloria and (I, me) enjoy studying the ancient Greeks.
2. (She, Her) and (I, me) both like (there, their) colorful mosaics.
3. Would (you, your) like to study with (we, us)?
4. Paolo prefers the Romans; (they, them) dominated the Mediterranean world for centuries.
5. Yes, it was (I, me) who phoned (he, him) on Monday.
6. Do (you, your) appreciate (him, his) taking charge?
7. I lent my tennis racket and (it's, its) cover to Raja.
8. Don't you think (it's, its) a great racket?
9. Is this racket cover (you're, yours) or (him, his)?
10. Please send invitations to (he, him) and (I, me).

FRANK & ERNEST by ® Bob Thaves

7.2 PRONOUNS WITH AND AS APPOSITIVES

Use the nominative case for a pronoun that is an appositive to a subject or a predicate nominative.

EXAMPLE The producers, **Mrs. Singh** and **she,** have raised enough money. [*Producers* **is the subject of the sentence.**]

EXAMPLE The leads will be two sophomores, **Liam** and **she.** [*Sophomores* **is a predicate nominative.**]

Use the objective case for a pronoun that is an appositive to a direct object, an indirect object, or an object of a preposition.

EXAMPLE The director rehearsed the leads, **Liam** and **her.** [*Leads* **is a direct object.**]

EXAMPLE The prompter gave the minor actors, **Barbara** and **me,** our cues. [*Actors* **is an indirect object.**]

EXAMPLE Fancy costumes went to the dancers, **Keesha** and **him.** [*Dancers* **is the object of the preposition** *to.*]

It is considered courteous to place the pronoun *I* or *me* last in a pair or series of appositives.

EXAMPLE The lighting crew, **Rob, Luellen,** and **I,** are ready for the technical rehearsal. [**nominative case**]

EXAMPLE Our soundtrack was recorded by a local pair, **Rob** and **me.** [**objective case**]

When a pronoun is followed by an appositive, choose the case of the pronoun that would be correct if the appositive were omitted.

EXAMPLE **We beginners** hope to learn fast. [*We,* **which is in the nominative case, is correct because** *we* **is the subject of the sentence.**]

EXAMPLE The director has helped **us beginners.** [*Us,* **which is in the objective case, is correct because** *us* **is the direct object.**]

Hint: When you are choosing the correct pronoun, it is helpful to say the sentence to yourself leaving out the appositive.

EXAMPLE **We** hope to learn fast.

EXAMPLE The director has helped **us.**

PRACTICE **Pronouns with and as Appositives**

Write the correct pronoun from the choice in parentheses.

1. The scout leaders, Mr. Hackett and (he, him), will lead the troop on a hike tomorrow.
2. Two Eagle Scouts, their assistants, are Brian and (he, him).
3. Will they take along Billy and (he, him)?
4. New leaders-in-training, Barbara, Luisa, and (I, me), will help Mrs. Giaimo with the youngsters.
5. (We, Us) violinists have never played together.
6. The drummers have shown (we, us) beginners where to sit.
7. Why are (they, them), the drummers, allowed to stand in the back on risers?
8. Ms. Blake gave (they, them), the members of the woodwind section, the correct sheet music.
9. Next year I'll join the art club; maybe Shawna and (I, me), the newest artists, will exhibit some watercolors.
10. If I do well, the club moderator may choose (I, me), a beginning painter, as a permanent member.

7.3 PRONOUNS AFTER *THAN* AND *AS*

When words are left out of an adverb clause that begins with the word *than* or *as*, choose the case of the pronoun that you would use if the missing words were fully expressed.

EXAMPLE   You ride a skateboard more skillfully than **I. [That is, . . .** **than I ride a skateboard. The nominative pronoun I is the** **subject of the adverb clause than I ride a skateboard.]**

EXAMPLE   The loud thunder bothered Lindsay as much as **me.** **[That is, . . . as much as it bothered me. The objective pro-** **noun me is the direct object in the adverb clause as much as** **it bothered me.]**

In some sentences, the correct pronoun depends on the meaning intended by the speaker or writer.

EXAMPLE   Aliko liked Cadeo more than **I [liked Cadeo].**

EXAMPLE   Aliko liked Cadeo more than **[he liked] me.**

PRACTICE **Pronouns After *Than* and *As***

Rewrite each sentence, choosing the correct pronoun from the choice in parentheses and adding the necessary words to complete the incomplete comparison.

  1. Jessica is a year older than (I, me).
  2. Am I as good a pianist as (she, her)?
  3. Can Jason run faster than (he, him)?
  4. Allan gave Art and Patrick more time than (I, me).
  5. You sat closer to (they, them) than to (I, me).

6. I understand Raymond better than (she, her).

7. Did you send Josh as many postcards as (I, me)?

8. Can Ms. Fuentes tutor Ramón as well as (I, me)?

9. Carol's more familiar with Kim's dog than (I, mine).

10. Is Jamyce a better conversationalist than (he, him)?

7.4 REFLEXIVE AND INTENSIVE PRONOUNS

Observe the following rules when you use reflexive and intensive pronouns.

1. Don't use *hisself, theirself,* or *theirselves.* All three are incorrect forms. Use *himself* and *themselves.*

EXAMPLE   Pablo designed the sailboat **himself.**

EXAMPLE   My brothers **themselves** remodeled the basement.

2. Use a reflexive pronoun when a pronoun refers to the subject of a sentence.

EXAMPLES

INCORRECT	CORRECT
I bought me a book.	I bought **myself** a book.
He found him a chair.	He found **himself** a chair.

3. Don't use a reflexive pronoun unnecessarily. Remember that a reflexive pronoun must refer to the subject, but it must not take the place of the subject.

EXAMPLES

INCORRECT	CORRECT
Mama and myself are here.	Mama and **I** are here.
Ron and yourself are lucky.	Ron and **you** are lucky.

Most of the sentences below contain errors in pronoun use. Rewrite the incorrect sentences, correcting the errors by replacing the incorrect pronouns. If a sentence is already correct, write C.

1. Geraldo gave the gloves to Ilona and myself.
2. Did you carry all those materials to the house yourself?
3. The twins gave theirselves *A*'s on their practice tests.
4. Mr. Thompson hisself gave Freddie the extra homework.
5. Shani and Sue, please schedule yourselves for conferences tomorrow.
6. Mr. and Mrs. Garanzini assigned Room 205 to theirselves.
7. He did hisself a favor by studying hard last night.
8. Hurrah! I did all the work myself, and I hope I'll receive a good grade.
9. I'm sending these flowers to yourself and Mrs. Collins in gratitude for that delicious dinner.
10. Uh, oh! Now we've managed to get ourselves into big trouble!

7.5 *WHO* AND *WHOM* IN QUESTIONS AND SUBORDINATE CLAUSES

THE USES OF *WHO*

Use the nominative pronouns *who* and *whoever* for subjects.

EXAMPLE   **Whoever** made these cookies? [*Whoever* **is the subject of the verb** *made*.]

EXAMPLE   Ask them **who** will be home for dinner. [*Who* **is the subject of the noun clause** *who will be home for dinner*.]

In questions that have an interrupting expression (such as *did you say* or *do you think*), it often helps to drop the interrupting phrase to make it easier to decide whether to use *who* or *whom*.

EXAMPLE **Who** do you think will win the contest? [Think, **"Who** will win the contest?" **Who** is the subject of the verb *will win.*]

THE USES OF *WHOM*

Use the objective pronouns *whom* and *whomever* for the direct object or the indirect object of a verb or a verbal and for the object of a preposition.

EXAMPLE **Whomever** are you calling first? [**Whomever** is the direct object of the verb *are calling.* Think, "You are calling whomever first?"]

EXAMPLE They told her **whom** she could invite to the show. [**Whom** is the direct object of the verb *could invite* in the noun clause *whom she could invite to the show.* Think, "She could invite whom to the show?"]

EXAMPLE Picasso is a painter about **whom** I have read quite a bit. [**Whom** is the object of the preposition *about* in the adjective clause *about whom I have read quite a bit.* Think, "I have read quite a bit about whom?"]

EXAMPLE **Whom** did you say the new kitten likes best? [**Whom** is the direct object of the verb *likes.* Drop the interrupting phrase *did you say* and think, "The new kitten likes whom best?"]

In informal speech, many people generally use *who* in place of *whom* in sentences such as *Who did you call?* In writing and in formal speaking situations, however, make the distinctions between *who* and *whom*.

For each sentence, write the correct pronoun from the choice in parentheses.

1. Were you the one (who, whom) left the milk on the table all night?
2. (Whoever, Whomever) did you say you noticed at the movies yesterday?
3. (Who, Whom) should I ask, Mrs. Marcus or Mrs. Albertson?
4. (Who, Whom) do you think will be the new Cougar fullback?
5. Please let me know to (who, whom) you've sent the tickets.
6. Sally has no idea (who, whom) left her the birthday gift.
7. (Who, Whom) was it?
8. To (who, whom) did you send that note, Cheralyn?
9. The messenger (who, whom) was just here left you this package.
10. By (who, whom) was *Ivanhoe* written?

7.6 PRONOUN-ANTECEDENT AGREEMENT

An **antecedent** is the noun to which a pronoun refers or that a pronoun replaces. All pronouns must agree with their antecedents in number, gender, and person.

AGREEMENT IN NUMBER AND GENDER

A pronoun must agree with its antecedent in number (singular or plural) and gender (masculine, feminine, or neuter).

A pronoun's antecedent may be a noun, another pronoun, or a phrase or a clause acting as a noun. In the following examples, the pronouns appear in blue type and their antecedents appear in italic blue type. Notice that they agree in both number and gender.

EXAMPLE   *Octavio Paz* is one of the greatest poets of **his** era.
[singular masculine pronoun]

EXAMPLE   *Emily Dickinson* wrote **her** poems on scrap paper.
[singular feminine pronoun]

EXAMPLE   *Walt Whitman* and *Emily Dickinson* are famous for
their poetry. [plural pronoun]

EXAMPLE   This poetry *book,* despite **its** tattered cover, is valuable.
[singular neuter pronoun]

Traditionally, a masculine pronoun was used when the gender of an antecedent was not known or might be either masculine or feminine. When you are reading literature written before the 1970s, remember that *his* may mean *his*, it may mean *her*, or it may mean *his or her*.

EXAMPLE   An *author* must capture **his** readers' interest.

This usage has recently changed, however. Many people now feel that the use of masculine pronouns excludes half of humanity. Use gender-neutral language when the gender is unknown or could be either masculine or feminine. Here are three ways to avoid using a masculine pronoun when the antecedent may be feminine:

1. Use *his or her*, *he or she*, and so on.
2. Make the antecedent plural and use a plural pronoun.
3. Eliminate the pronoun.

EXAMPLE   An *author* must capture **his or her** readers' interest.

EXAMPLE   *Authors* must capture **their** readers' interest.

EXAMPLE   *Authors* must capture readers' interest. [no pronoun]

Rewrite each sentence in three different ways, using gender-neutral language.

1. A ship-to-shore telegraph operator must always be able to pinpoint his location on the ocean.
2. An editor is famous for his blue pencil.
3. A telephone saleswoman must have a very difficult job.
4. That computer technician never once consulted his user's manual.
5. A musician must play for herself as well as for her audience.

AGREEMENT WITH COLLECTIVE NOUNS

When the antecedent of a pronoun is a collective noun, the number of the pronoun depends on whether the collective noun is meant to be singular or plural.

EXAMPLE The *orchestra* played **its** last song of the concert. **[The collective noun *orchestra* conveys the singular sense of one unit. Therefore, the singular pronoun *its* is used.]**

EXAMPLE The *orchestra* carried **their** instruments off the stage. **[The collective noun *orchestra* conveys the plural sense of several people performing separate acts. Therefore, the plural pronoun *their* is used.]**

EXAMPLE The *team* tried on **their** new uniforms. **[The collective noun *team* conveys the plural sense of several people performing separate actions. Therefore, the plural pronoun *their* is used.]**

EXAMPLE The *team* heard **its** fans cheering as **it** ran onto the field. **[The collective noun *team* conveys the singular sense of one unit. Therefore, the singular pronouns *its* and *it* are used.]**

Write the correct pronoun from the choice in parentheses. Then write the collective noun that is the subject of each sentence, and tell whether it is singular or plural in the sentence.

1. The union addresses (its, their) demands to the corporation today.

2. The carnival committee are making wonderful progress in setting up (its, their) booths and coordinating the rides.

3. Our varsity cheerleading squad are being measured for (its, their) uniforms this afternoon.

4. This jury makes (its, their) decisions based on evidence and testimony, not on hearsay.

5. The swim team travels to (its, their) tournament sites by bus or train.

AGREEMENT IN PERSON

A pronoun must agree in person (first, second, or third person) with its antecedent.

Do not use *you*, a second-person pronoun, to refer to an antecedent in the third person. Either change *you* to an appropriate third-person pronoun or replace it with a suitable noun.

EXAMPLES

POOR   Suki and Jim are going to visit the Everglades, where **you** can see alligators.

BETTER   Suki and Jim are going to visit the Everglades, where **they** can see alligators.

BETTER   Suki and Jim are going to visit the Everglades, where **tourists** can see alligators.

When the antecedent of a pronoun is another pronoun, be sure the two pronouns agree in person. Avoid unnecessary shifts from *they* to *you, I* to *you,* or *one* to *you.*

GRAMMAR/USAGE/MECHANICS

EXAMPLES

POOR   **They** often visit the Centerville Fruit Farm, where **you** can pick **your** own strawberries.

BETTER   **They** often visit the Centerville Fruit Farm, where **they** can pick **their** own strawberries.

EXAMPLES

POOR   I hiked on trails that amazed **you** with their beauty.

BETTER   I hiked on trails that amazed **me** with their beauty.

EXAMPLES

POOR   When **one** travels by train, **you** can learn a lot.

BETTER   When **one** travels by train, **one** can learn a lot.

BETTER   When **you** travel by train, **you** can learn a lot.

PRACTICE   **Agreement in Person**

Rewrite each item, correcting the inappropriate use of you *by substituting a third-person pronoun or a suitable noun.*

1. Neighbors can be wonderful friends from whom you can borrow almost anything in an emergency.
2. Stopping is easy on a bike with hand brakes; you just grasp both brakes gently at the same time.
3. In some countries you can safely walk alone at night.
4. Art communicates directly to its viewers; you might not always understand the meaning of a painting, but you can usually grasp its mood immediately.
5. A fitness club is very convenient. You can exercise at any hour, as long as the building is open.

AGREEMENT WITH INDEFINITE PRONOUN ANTECEDENTS

In general, use a singular personal pronoun when the antecedent is a singular indefinite pronoun. Use a plural personal pronoun when the antecedent is a plural indefinite pronoun.

INDEFINITE PRONOUNS

ALWAYS SINGULAR	another	either	neither	other
	anybody	everybody	no one	somebody
	anyone	everyone	nobody	someone
	anything	everything	nothing	something
	each	much	one	

ALWAYS PLURAL	both	few	many	others	several

SINGULAR OR PLURAL	all	any	enough	most	none	some

EXAMPLE **Each** of the girls must bring **her** own toolbox.

EXAMPLE **One** of the boys has **his** own safety glasses.

EXAMPLE **Many** of the workers take **their** toolboxes home at night.

Note that the plural nouns in the prepositional phrases—*of the girls, of the boys*—do not affect the number of the personal pronouns. *Her* and *his* are singular because *each* and *one*, their antecedents, are singular.

When no gender is specified, use gender-neutral wording.

EXAMPLE **Everyone** must bring **his or her** own jacket.

If you find the previous sentence a bit awkward, the best solution may be to reword the sentence. You might use a plural indefinite pronoun or a suitable noun (such as *people*) to replace the singular indefinite pronoun. You might even eliminate the personal pronoun entirely.

EXAMPLE   *All* must bring **their** own jackets.

EXAMPLE   *People* must bring **their** own jackets.

EXAMPLE   *Everyone* must bring **a** jacket. **[no pronoun]**

PRACTICE   Gender-Neutral Agreement with Indefinite Pronoun Antecedents

Rewrite each item in three ways, using gender-neutral language.

1. Everyone must bring his own music stand to the theater.
2. Will someone please lend me his pen?
3. Each student has studied his lessons long enough.
4. Has everyone brought her notebook?
5. Each team member carries his own luggage.

7.7 CLEAR PRONOUN REFERENCE

Make sure that the antecedent of a pronoun is clearly stated. Make sure that a pronoun doesn't refer to more than one antecedent.

VAGUE PRONOUN REFERENCE

Don't use the pronoun *this, that, which, it, any,* or *one* without a clearly stated antecedent.

EXAMPLES   **VAGUE**   Seung is a wonderful magician, and **this** was evident in last night's show. **[What was evident? His magic skill was evident, but the word *skill* is not specifically mentioned.]**

CLEAR	Seung is a wonderful magician, and **his skill** was evident in last night's show.
VAGUE	The senator loved public speaking, and **that** greatly boosted his popularity. **[What boosted his popularity? His speeches did, but the word *speeches* is not specifically mentioned.]**
CLEAR	The senator loved public speaking, and **his speeches** greatly boosted his popularity.
VAGUE	Last week our garage burned, **which** started from a kerosene heater. **[What started from a kerosene heater? A fire started, but the word *fire* is not specifically mentioned.]**
CLEAR	Last week a fire, **which** started from a kerosene heater, burned our garage.
VAGUE	The Supreme Court is deliberating on the question of disability, and **it** will affect anti-discrimination lawsuits. **[What will affect lawsuits? The Supreme Court's decision will do so, but the word *decision* is not specifically mentioned.]**
CLEAR	The Supreme Court is deliberating on the question of disability, and **its decision** will affect anti-discrimination lawsuits.

PRACTICE Clear Pronoun Reference

Rewrite each item, replacing vague pronouns with specific words.

1. Luisa is a fine athlete, and this was obvious from her gymnastic performance.

2. I phoned George again and again, but it was always busy.

3. Although Johnna is a good baker, she seldom shares any with us.

4. Angelika and Jung were arguing, which started from a misunderstanding.

5. Derek writes all the time. I wonder when he'll ever show us one.

UNCLEAR AND INDEFINITE PRONOUN REFERENCE

If a pronoun seems to refer to more than one antecedent, either reword the sentence to make the antecedent clear or eliminate the pronoun.

EXAMPLES

UNCLEAR ANTECEDENT	After the tickets slipped between the reports, **they** were lost. **[Which word is the antecedent of *they*? Were the tickets or the reports lost?]**
CLEAR ANTECEDENT	The tickets were lost when **they** slipped between the reports.
NO PRONOUN	When the tickets slipped between the reports, **the tickets** were lost.

The pronouns *you* and *they* should not be used as if they were indefinite pronouns. Instead, you should name the performer of the action. In some cases, you may be able to reword the sentence in such a way that you do not name the performer of the action and you do not use a pronoun.

EXAMPLES

INDEFINITE	In Japan **you** bow after saying hello.
CLEAR	In Japan **people** bow after saying hello.
INDEFINITE	In some countries, **they** take naps after lunch.
CLEAR	In some countries, **people** take naps after lunch.
CLEAR	In some countries, **it is customary** to take a nap after lunch.

Rewrite each sentence, correcting any unclear or indefinite pronoun references.

1. In Europe they often dine about nine or ten o'clock in the evening.
2. In some places, they belch as a sign of appreciation for a delicious meal.
3. How do you answer the telephone in Italy?
4. At the table, you can sometimes wipe up a spill with a corner of your napkin.
5. In some countries, you wear white instead of black at funerals.

PRACTICE Proofreading

Rewrite the following passage, correcting errors in spelling, capitalization, grammar, and usage. Add any missing punctuation. There are ten errors. Some sentences are correct.

Guy de Maupassant

[1]High-school students are probably most familiar with author Guy de Maupassant as a short story writer. [2]De Maupassant was a good friend of the novelist Gustave Flaubert; in fact, his' writing style is like Flaubert's. [3]As a child, De Maupassant often observed the worst side of society and later he used that in his stories. [4]His short stories are memorable for their ironic endings in which the main character's beliefs are turned upside down. [5]In "the Necklace," for example, he describes a minor official and his wife what reduce theirselfs to poverty by repaying a debt. [6]After years of hardship, they learn that the debt was all together unnecessary. [7]De Maupassant's novels, like his stories, are simple realistic, and pessimistic. [8]In the novel *Bel-Ami,* for instance, the central character is an unethical journalist which succeeds despite his dishonesty. [9]De Maupassant allows hisself to feel compassion for only the poor and powerless. [10]The vain, foolish, or selfish he portrays with merciless clarity.

For each sentence, write the correct pronoun from the choice in parentheses.

1. Please don't call (I, me) during school hours; (I, me) can be reached after three o'clock.
2. How many of (we, us) are going to the lake?
3. (Who, Whom) is bringing the sandwiches?
4. Ask Leanne to make (they, them) for (we, us); no one makes better sandwiches than (she, her).
5. Did you know that (it's, its) five miles to Springfield?
6. Dave is such a good baseball player that the crowd was surprised at (he, him, his) striking out three times today.
7. Have Mr. and Mrs. Shapiro been asked about (we, our, us) staying with them this weekend?
8. The only new members of the drama club are Felipe and (she, her).
9. The principal asked to speak with Mr. Davis and (he, him).
10. Please have Simon and Hiroshi bring their violins with (they, them) when (they, them) attend the rehearsal.
11. (We, Us) amateur writers still have a lot to learn.
12. The newspaper advisor will help (we, us) reporters.
13. Aimee is more familiar with the Chicago area than (I, me).
14. On the other hand, (I, me) know the St. Louis area better than (she, her).
15. Waiting for online access annoys Edward as much as (I, me).
16. Arminda and (I, myself) volunteer at our local animal shelter on weekends.
17. (We, Us) find that very satisfying, although it pains (we, us) to see the animals in cages.

18. Did you find out (who, whom) Roy saw at the store on Friday?

19. (Who, Whom) do you want to address in the salutation of your letter?

20. Did you ever identify the student (who, whom) gave you the flowers on your birthday?

21. How do (people, you) get from Rio de Janeiro to Caracas?

22. What do (people, they) do at the Chinese New Year festival?

23. Does each member of the choir have (his, her, his or her, their) sheet music?

24. How do (you, people) say "hello" in Japanese?

25. Do (you, people) say "ciao," "adios," or "adieu" in Paris?

Using Modifiers Correctly

• • • • • • • • • • • • • • •

PRETEST   **Using Modifiers Correctly**

Write each sentence, choosing the correct word or words in parentheses.

1. Mary's cats are (fat, fatter, fattest) than mine.

2. *A Wrinkle in Time* is (an inventive, a more inventive, the most inventive) science-fiction novel.

3. Shelley thinks *A Swiftly Tilting Planet* is even (good, better, best) than *A Wrinkle in Time.*

4. Madeleine L'Engle has written (many, more, most) books for both children and adults.

5. A family nearby live (simply, more simply, most simply) than we do.

6. They eat (many, more, most) vegetables and (little, less, least) meat than our family does.

7. They use (few, fewer, fewest) disposable items than we do.

8. Of all our classmates, Hilda seems (informed, more informed, the most informed) about Alaska.

9. Her report was (well, better, more better, best) researched than mine.

10. The (high, more higher, highest) point in Alaska is Mount McKinley, soaring (much, more, most) than twenty thousand feet.

11. Hilda's report was so (well, better, best) done that I felt (bad, badly) about the quality of my own.

12. Tisa wasn't (good, well) this morning, and she stayed at home.

13. Later, Tisa realized that she had drunk some (bad, badly) milk without knowing it.

14. The milk had tasted (good, well), but it had been standing at room temperature for too long.

15. Her stomach had hurt (bad, badly) at first, but now she is (good, well).

PRETEST Double and Incomplete Comparisons, Double Negatives, Misplaced and Dangling Modifiers

Rewrite each sentence, correcting any errors.

16. A cheetah's speed is greater than an ostrich.

17. My dad is a better problem-solver than anyone.

18. Some fish can see colors better than sea creatures can.

19. The camper photographed a bear in his pajamas.

20. Marisa doesn't hardly ever eat brussels sprouts.

21. Lilly climbed the rope easily, but Sam can't hardly do it.

22. We spotted a leopard using our binoculars.

23. Reaching the supermarket, the week's groceries were bought.

24. Mike only missed the last test question.

25. Having located Springfield, the remaining fifty miles were soon covered.

26. Ms. Gaspar, our history teacher, is a better public speaker than the teachers.

27. We don't scarcely serve beef sandwiches anymore.

28. Requesting more vegetarian sandwiches, healthful food is eaten much more often now.

29. Hearing is more vital to bats than animals.

30. Sailing wildly in the breeze, Mr. Jeffries finally caught his baseball cap.

8.1 THE THREE DEGREES OF COMPARISON

Most adjectives and adverbs have three degrees: the positive, or base, form; the comparative form; and the superlative form.

The **positive** form of a modifier cannot be used to make a comparison. (This form appears as the entry word in a dictionary.)

The **comparative** form of a modifier shows two things being compared.

The **superlative** form of a modifier shows three or more things being compared.

EXAMPLES

POSITIVE	My dog is **small.**
	The cat ran **swiftly.**
COMPARATIVE	Kim's dog is **smaller** than my dog.
	My dog ran **more swiftly** than the cat.
SUPERLATIVE	Of the three dogs, Ray's dog is the **smallest** one.
	The squirrel ran **most swiftly** of all.

In general, for one-syllable modifiers add *–er* to form the comparative and *–est* to form the superlative.

green, green**er,** green**est**

The neighbor's grass always looks **greener** than ours.

loud, loud**er,** loud**est**

That sonic boom was the **loudest** one I've ever heard.

fast, fast**er,** fast**est**

Her hair grows **faster** than mine.

In some cases, adding *–er* and *–est* requires spelling changes.

big, bi**gger,** bi**ggest**

true, tru**er,** tru**est**

dry, dri**er,** dri**est**

With some one-syllable modifiers, it may sound more natural to use *more* and *most* instead of *–er* and *–est*.

just, **more** just, **most** just

Of the three, that judge's ruling was the **most just** decision.

For most two-syllable adjectives, add *–er* to form the comparative and *–est* to form the superlative.

ugly, ugl**ier,** ugl**iest**

Your mask is **uglier** than mine.

That is the **ugliest** mask I've ever seen.

If *–er* and *–est* sound awkward with a two-syllable adjective, use *more* and *most* instead.

afraid, **more** afraid, **most** afraid

No one is **more afraid** of wasps than I am.

Of all of us, I was the **most afraid.**

Chapter 8 Using Modifiers Correctly   **257**

In general, for adverbs ending in *–ly*, use *more* and *most* to form the comparative and superlative degrees. For some *–ly* adverbs, add *–er* and *–est*. Consult a dictionary if necessary.

GRAMMAR/USAGE/MECHANICS

EXAMPLES clearly, **more** clearly, **most** clearly

Tom gives directions **more clearly** than most people.

That candidate explains her position **most clearly** of all.

but

early, earli**er,** earli**est**

They arrived **earlier** than we did.

You must have arrived **earliest** of all.

For modifiers of three or more syllables, always use *more* and *most* to form the comparative and superlative degrees.

EXAMPLES attractive, **more** attractive, **most** attractive

Green looks **more attractive** on you than it does on me.

That oil painting is the **most attractive** one in the exhibit.

Less and *least,* the opposite of *more* and *most,* can also be used with most modifiers to show negative comparison.

EXAMPLES Are cooked vegetables **less nutritious** than raw vegetables?

Spinach is my **least favorite** green vegetable.

Less and *least* are used before modifiers that have any number of syllables.

Rewrite each sentence to correct the error in comparison. If the sentence is already correct, write C.

1. Of all the flying insects, I am afraidest of wasps.
2. Jennifer was very hungry, and she ate greedilier than the rest of us.
3. Of the southern states, I like Texas the goodest.
4. That grass is the most green I ever saw!
5. Today, Mom was more happy than I have ever seen her.
6. Parrots may be the conspicuousest of all the wild birds.
7. Lorienda's family gives generously to charities that rescue abused and abandoned animals.
8. This dog is definitely more tiny than that one.
9. All of Jefferson's cats purr happily.
10. Janet was dressed appropriatelier for the interview than Alyssa was.

8.2 IRREGULAR COMPARISONS

A few modifiers form their comparative and superlative degrees irregularly. It is helpful to memorize their forms.

MODIFIERS WITH IRREGULAR FORMS OF COMPARISON		
good	better	best
well	better	best
bad	worse	worst
badly	worse	worst
ill	worse	worst
far (distance)	farther	farthest
far (degree, time)	further	furthest
little (amount)	less	least
many	more	most
much	more	most

Write the correct modifier from the choice given in parentheses.

1. Washington University is (far, farther, farthest) from my house than St. Louis University is.

2. Sam has been suffering from (ill, worse, worst) health lately.

3. Of all the legislators, Senator Glenn wanted the trip to space (much, more, the most).

4. You may wish to explore the subject (far, farther, further) than you have explored it up to now.

5. Hector likes the poetry of E. E. Cummings (good, better, best) than that of Emily Dickinson.

6. Of all the foods he's tasted so far in the United States, Chung Sook likes spaghetti (good, better, best).

7. I'm sorry the interview went (badly, worse, worst), Marian; maybe the next one will be (good, better, best).

8. Doque ate (little, less, the least) ice cream of all.

9. The sulfur stench from the paper mill is just about the (bad, worse, worst) odor I've ever encountered.

10. Of all of us, Yukio is (little, less, least) satisfied with his situation.

8.3 CORRECTING DOUBLE COMPARISONS

Don't use both *–er* and *more*. Don't use both *–est* and *most*. To do so would be an error called a **double comparison.**

EXAMPLES

INCORRECT A redwood grows more taller than an oak.

CORRECT A redwood grows **taller** than an oak.

INCORRECT Aunt Ellie is my most kindest aunt.

CORRECT Aunt Ellie is my **kindest** aunt.

INCORRECT They will write to us more oftener after school starts.

CORRECT They will write to us **more often** after school starts.

PRACTICE **Correcting Double Comparisons**

Rewrite each sentence to correct the error in comparison. If the sentence is already correct, write C.

1. This is the most widest mobile home I've ever seen!

2. That tuna smells more fishier than the scrod.

3. Is vermicelli more thinner than regular spaghetti?

4. I'm pretty sure that linguini is more wider than both vermicelli and spaghetti.

5. After the test, Velma left the room more quickly than anyone else.

6. Sam always says that his life is just a little more solitarier than a hermit's.

7. When she pounced on the soap bubble and it disappeared, the kitten was the surprisedest thing in the world.

8. "This is the most long letter I've ever received," said Lee.

9. A hummingbird's nest is just a bit tinier than a tennis ball.

10. After dieting and daily exercise, I should become much more healthier and agiler than I am now.

8.4 CORRECTING INCOMPLETE COMPARISONS

Don't make an incomplete or unclear comparison by omitting the word *other* or the word *else* when you compare a person or thing with its group.

UNCLEAR	Mercury is closer to the sun than any planet. [*Any planet* includes Mercury.]
CLEAR	Mercury is closer to the sun than any **other** planet.
UNCLEAR	Aunt Elizabeth has more pets than anyone I know. [*Anyone I know* includes the aunt.]
CLEAR	Aunt Elizabeth has more pets than anyone **else** I know.

Be sure your comparisons are between like things—that is, similar things.

UNCLEAR	The grace of a basketball player is more obvious than a baseball player. [The grace of a basketball player is being compared illogically with everything about a baseball player.]
CLEAR	The grace of a basketball player is more obvious than **that of a baseball player.**
CLEAR	The grace of a basketball player is more obvious than **the grace of a baseball player.**
CLEAR	The grace of a basketball player is more obvious than **a baseball player's.**
UNCLEAR	The claws of a lion are larger than a house cat. [The claws of a lion are being compared illogically with everything about a house cat.]
CLEAR	The claws of a lion are larger than **those of a house cat.**
CLEAR	The claws of a lion are larger than **the claws of a house cat.**
CLEAR	The claws of a lion are larger than **a house cat's.**

GRAMMAR/USAGE/MECHANICS

Rewrite each sentence, correcting the error in comparison. If a sentence is already correct, write C.

1. Archie's test results are better than Andy.
2. Isn't Seaside Park cleaner than any park?
3. Sean is more organized than anyone.
4. Other than Maribeth, Sheila is the best swimmer.
5. Is banana ice cream really better than any flavor?
6. The speed of racing cars is greater than ordinary cars.
7. Eloise's artwork is better than anyone else's.
8. Was Michelangelo's art better than Leonardo da Vinci?
9. Shani thinks that yams are tastier than any vegetable.
10. Jeannie's voice is lower than Pat.

PRACTICE Irregular, Double, and Incomplete Comparisons

Rewrite each sentence, correcting the error in comparison. If a sentence is already correct, write C.

1. Cutting the sugar in one's diet may be even gooder than cutting the fat.
2. Does the Zambezi River flow quicklier than the Nile?
3. Is Emily Dickinson or Robert Frost the better poet?
4. Was Jesse Owens or Bob Mathias the swiftest runner?
5. Your little brother Donnie is least irritable than Jamie.
6. Do you wish to explore this topic farther in your paper?
7. Diego has the goodest costume of all.
8. Ange is more taller than Rick but more shorter than I.
9. Kele admires Dr. Martin Luther King Jr. more than anyone.
10. My boxer dog's bark is deeper and louder than other dogs.

8.5 *GOOD* OR *WELL*; *BAD* OR *BADLY*

Always use *good* as an adjective. *Well* may be used as an adverb of manner telling how ably or how adequately something is done. *Well* may also be used as an adjective meaning "in good health."

EXAMPLE   Red is a **good** color for you. **[adjective]**

EXAMPLE   You look **good** in red. **[adjective after a linking verb]**

EXAMPLE   I feel **good** when I hear our song. **[adjective after a linking verb]**

EXAMPLE   You dress **well.** **[adverb of manner]**

EXAMPLE   Aren't you feeling **well?** **[adjective meaning "in good health"]**

Always use *bad* as an adjective. Use *badly* as an adverb.

EXAMPLE   That's a **bad** idea. **[adjective]**

EXAMPLE   That milk tastes **bad.** **[adjective after a linking verb]**

EXAMPLE   I feel **bad** about your moving away. **[adjective after a linking verb]**

EXAMPLE   The porch swing is squeaking **badly.** **[adverb after an action verb]**

Calvin and Hobbes

by Bill Watterson

Write each sentence, choosing the correct word from those in parentheses. In one item, either word could be correct.

1. That television show was (bad, badly).
2. We wanted to go on a picnic, but the weather looked (bad, badly).
3. That scarf looks (good, well) on you.
4. I'll rewrite these invitations because someone wrote them (bad, badly).
5. French toast tastes (good, well) with homemade applesauce.
6. Beth thought she was catching a cold, but she feels (good, well) now.
7. Luc's trumpet solo sounded flat, but yours sounded (good, well).
8. This stuffy cabin smells (bad, badly); let's open the windows.
9. Sam felt (bad, badly) about forgetting to drive Lou home after her appointment.
10. Our science teacher said our project was done (good, well).

PRACTICE **Regular and Irregular Comparisons**

Give the comparative and superlative forms of each modifier. Consult a dictionary if necessary.

1. lonely
2. swiftly
3. well
4. light
5. little

Chapter 8 Using Modifiers Correctly **265**

6. afraid

7. much

8. ill

9. blue

10. nutritious

8.6 CORRECTING DOUBLE NEGATIVES

Don't use two or more negative words to express the same idea. To do so is an error, a **double negative.** Use only one negative word to express a negative idea.

EXAMPLES

INCORRECT	I don't have no stereo equipment.
CORRECT	I do**n't** have **any** stereo equipment.
CORRECT	I have **no** stereo equipment.
INCORRECT	We haven't seen no concerts this year.
CORRECT	We have**n't** seen **any** concerts this year.
CORRECT	We have seen **no** concerts this year.
INCORRECT	My parrot never says nothing.
CORRECT	My parrot **never** says **anything.**
CORRECT	My parrot says **nothing.**

The words *hardly* and *scarcely* are negative words. Don't use them with other negative words, such as *not.*

EXAMPLES

INCORRECT	I haven't hardly finished.
	He can't scarcely never be on time.
CORRECT	I **have hardly** finished.
	He **can scarcely ever** be on time.

GRAMMAR/USAGE/MECHANICS

Rewrite each sentence, correcting the double negative. If a sentence is already correct, write C.

1. Giuliana is a very quiet girl; she never says nothing.
2. I haven't hardly got no energy left to write.
3. Since I hurt my wrist, I can't hardly never throw foul shots as well as I used to.
4. We haven't seen no UFOs, and even if we had, we wouldn't have said nothing to nobody.
5. Liam isn't feeling no better; yet, if he were, he still wouldn't say nothing.
6. I hadn't scarcely finished my dinner when the doorbell rang, but nobody wasn't there.
7. Nobody didn't tell me nothing about the pep rally yesterday.
8. I asked the police officer what was new in the case, but she told me that officially nothing was.
9. Margaret hasn't scarcely ever had a loud voice, but now that she has tonsillitis, I can't never hear a word she says.
10. Mark and Kiyoshi had never planned to have their own band, but now they scarcely have time for anything else.

8.7 CORRECTING MISPLACED AND DANGLING MODIFIERS

Misplaced modifiers modify the wrong word, or they seem to modify more than one word in a sentence.

Place modifiers as close as possible to the words they modify in order to make the meaning of the sentence clear.

MISPLACED	**Soaring over the edge of the cliff,** the photographer captured an image of the eagle. **[participial phrase incorrectly modifying *photographer*]**
CLEAR	The photographer captured an image of the eagle **soaring over the edge of the cliff.** **[participial phrase correctly modifying *eagle*]**
MISPLACED	He easily spotted the eagle **with his high-powered binoculars.** **[prepositional phrase incorrectly modifying *eagle*]**
CORRECT	**With his high-powered binoculars,** he easily spotted the eagle. **[prepositional phrase correctly modifying *he*]**

Place the adverb *only* immediately before the word or group of words that it modifies.

If *only* is not positioned correctly in a sentence, the meaning of the sentence may be unclear.

EXAMPLES

UNCLEAR	Dan **only** has art class on Monday. **[Does Dan have only one class on Monday, or does he have art class on no other day than Monday, or is Dan the only person (in a group) who has one class on Monday?]**
CLEAR	Dan has **only** art class on Monday. **[He has no other class that day.]**
CLEAR	Dan has art class **only** on Monday. **[He does not have art class on any other day.]**
CLEAR	**Only** Dan has art class on Monday. **[No one else has art class on Monday.]**

GRAMMAR/USAGE/MECHANICS

Dangling modifiers seem logically to modify no word at all. To correct a sentence that has a dangling modifier, you must supply a word that the dangling modifier can sensibly modify.

EXAMPLES

DANGLING	**Working all night long,** the fire was extinguished. **[participial phrase logically modifying no word in the sentence]**
CLEAR	**Working all night long,** the firefighters extinguished the fire. **[participial phrase modifying *firefighters*]**
DANGLING	**Sleeping soundly,** my dream was interrupted by the alarm. **[participial phrase logically modifying no word in the sentence]**
CLEAR	**Sleeping soundly,** I had my dream interrupted by the alarm. **[participial phrase modifying *I*]**

GRAMMAR/USAGE/MECHANICS

PRACTICE **Correcting Misplaced and Dangling Modifiers**

Rewrite each sentence to make the writer's intended meaning clear.

1. Floating through the air, I watched my kite.
2. Thanking the operator, my call was made correctly.
3. Janine only had to tell her dad the problem once.
4. Filled with straw, the children played with the handmade dolls.
5. Lost on the country road, it was too dark to see the sign.
6. The United States Capitol came into view landing at Ronald Reagan Washington National Airport.

7. Mr. Atkinson watched the waves sitting quietly on the beach.

8. Rana anxiously watched the moose in the distance wearing his green plaid robe.

9. Running to catch the bus, the flour fell in the street.

10. Reaching into the bushes, the snake nearly bit me.

PRACTICE Proofreading

Rewrite the following passage, correcting errors in spelling, capitalization, grammar, and usage. Add any missing punctuation. There are ten errors. Some sentences are correct.

James Thurber

[1]Short story master James Thurber was a wonderful writer; no one's imagination was wackyer. [2]No reader could hope to find men dejecteder or women domineeringer than the ones in his stories. [3]They are characters whom you'd only meet in books like *The Middle-Aged Man on the Flying Trapeze*. [4]In one of his most popular short stories, The Secret Life of Walter Mitty, Thurber describes a meek little man who, through fantastic daydreams, becomes a superhero for a few minutes at a time. [5]In "The Unicorn in the garden," a mild-mannered man takes inspired revenge on his disagreeable wife. [6]Thurber himself drew the illustrations for his poems and stories, and the men and women he drew look like people who would naturally say the lines he wrote for them. [7]Many of his readers have wondered if his usual way of portraying husbands and wives was based on any of the author's personal relationships. [8]Thurber's most silly, most unbelievable, and most rollickingest story, however, is "The Night the Bed Fell." [9]That story tells about one memorable night in the Thurber home in Columbus, Ohio. [10]Using no fictional characters at all, Thurber nevertheless manages to leave his readers weak with laughter. [11]Fictional or not, Thurber's tales can warm his readers hearts on even the chillyest nights.

Write each sentence, choosing the correct word or words in parentheses.

1. There's no (smart, smarter, most smartest) person than my aunt Jane.

2. The school band is certainly playing its (loud, more louder, loudest).

3. Have you read A. E. Housman's (thought-provoking, more thought-provoking, most thought-provoking) poem, "To an Athlete Dying Young"?

4. Lorenzo thinks that equipment manager is the (rewarding, less rewarding, least rewarding) job on the football team.

5. We traveled (far, farther, more farther, farthest) than this on our last hike.

6. Do you still feel (well, bad, badly) about not being elected class president? I think you'll feel (good, better, more better, best) in a few days.

7. Aside from a good night's sleep, there's nothing (relaxing, more relaxing, most relaxing) than a warm bath.

8. No one feels (badly, more badly, bad, badder, worse, more worse, worst) than I do about your moving to Toledo.

9. I think I accidentally ate some (bad, badly) fruit this morning.

10. Kerry thinks that Eleanor dresses (good, well), but that she has a (poor, poorer, poorest) sense of color.

11. My little sister always smiles (bright, brightly, brighter, most brightest) when a visitor comes to the door.

12. I need the (recent, recenter, more recent, recentest, most recent) revision of your feature story for the school newspaper.

GRAMMAR/USAGE/MECHANICS

13. Is this your (late, later, most latest, latest) address?

14. Johanna is (tall, more taller, taller, tallest) than any of her other sisters.

15. After two weeks at home with the measles, Bobbi is finally (good, well) again.

POSTTEST **Double and Incomplete Comparisons, Double Negatives, Misplaced and Dangling Modifiers**

Rewrite each sentence, correcting any errors.

16. Enrico found someone's wallet walking down the road.

17. Raging all night, José was glad the storm was finally over.

18. We hadn't scarcely been aware of the storm until it started to rain.

19. I only want to help you reach your full potential.

20. Are a chef's hand movements more precise than a bricklayer?

21. My mom is more intelligent than anyone I know.

22. Practicing his yoga exercises, the elk surprised Roger in the woods.

23. I never did see nobody at Leslie's house yesterday.

24. Charlie only sings when he has an audience.

25. Ringing shrilly, I was late for school.

26. Stacking sandbags along the river's edge, the flood was diverted from Ames.

27. The light from these flashbulbs is brighter than a candle.

28. Ed hadn't hardly begun the test when his pencil point broke.

29. Typing quietly, the alligator surprised Grandma on the porch.

30. Renée, the class president, lives closer to the school than any student.

Chapter 9

Diagraming
Sentences

● ● ● ● ● ● ● ● ● ● ● ● ● ● ●

PRETEST **Diagraming Sentences**

Diagram each sentence.

1. Tonya left.
2. Wait!
3. Tonya and Shawna study and work.
4. Both girls spoke quite reasonably.
5. The school counselors have helped me.
6. Friends give me advice too.
7. The Parthenon is an ancient Greek temple.
8. The Athenian acropolis, an important city center, included many kinds of buildings.
9. Hoping for her help, builders erected a temple in honor of Athena.
10. Visiting the temple was a way of asking for favors.
11. To change one's course of study requires time for thinking.

12. Pang changed his course, but he asked for help first.
13. The counselor who advised him set him on the right track.
14. Because Pang likes his new courses, he studies quite hard.
15. Whoever wins the 500-meter event will certainly be champion.
16. Can you tell me where the coach's office is located?
17. I learned that his office is in the gym.
18. Coach Devin gives advice to whoever needs it.
19. Alyssa likes football, and she wants to play it someday.
20. These shoes, which I found on sale, match my dress perfectly.

9.1 DIAGRAMING SIMPLE AND COMPOUND SENTENCES

A **sentence diagram** shows how the various words and parts of a sentence function in the sentence and relate to the sentence as a whole.

It's vital to know the parts of a sentence before you begin diagraming. Diagraming just gives you a visual picture of how these parts relate to one another.

When writing a sentence in a diagram, retain the capitalization but leave out the punctuation.

SUBJECTS AND VERBS

Start your diagram with a horizontal line, called a baseline, intersected by a vertical line. Find the simple subject of the sentence and place it to the left of the vertical line; then place the simple predicate to the right of the vertical line.

EXAMPLE   Senators are meeting.

Senators | are meeting

EXAMPLE   Are senators meeting?

senators | Are meeting

A sentence with an understood subject is diagramed with the understood subject placed in parentheses.

EXAMPLE   Stop!

(you) | Stop

PRACTICE   Subjects and Verbs

Diagram each sentence.

1. Mom is working.
2. Does Dad cook?
3. Has Mindy telephoned?
4. Children have been playing.
5. Hide!

COMPOUND SUBJECTS AND COMPOUND VERBS

To diagram compound subjects and compound verbs, follow the example diagram. If a pair of correlative conjunctions, such as *both . . . and,* is used, place the conjunctions to the right and left of the dotted line.

EXAMPLE   Both staffers and senators meet and debate.

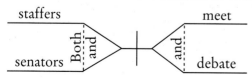

PRACTICE Compound Subjects and Compound Verbs

Diagram each sentence.

1. Maurice and Mandy harmonize.
2. Observers watch and wait.
3. Both diet and exercise tone and trim.
4. Alberto tries yet fails.
5. Either dancers or singers will perform.

ADJECTIVES AND ADVERBS

Both adjectives and adverbs are placed on slanted lines leading from the modified words. An adverb that modifies another modifier is placed on a slanted line parallel to the modifier and is connected to it with a straight line.

EXAMPLE   The older senators speak more frequently.

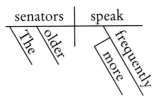

PRACTICE Adjectives and Adverbs

Diagram each sentence.

1. Alessandra is quietly waiting downstairs.
2. My best friend almost always skates very well.
3. Who is singing so loudly?
4. Listen carefully and learn.
5. Either the talented dancers or the skillful singers will perform professionally tonight.

DIRECT OBJECTS AND INDIRECT OBJECTS

A direct object appears on the baseline to the right of the verb. The verb and the direct object are separated by a vertical line that does not cross the baseline.

EXAMPLE   Experts have given advice.

Experts | have given | advice

Indirect objects are placed on a horizontal line below the baseline and are linked to the verb by a slanted line.

EXAMPLE   Experts have given senators advice.

Experts | have given | advice
\ senators

PRACTICE   **Direct Objects and Indirect Objects**

Diagram each sentence.

1. What inspired your last science project?
2. That incident taught me a lesson.
3. Has Hana hidden the harmonica?
4. Tell us your first name.
5. The baby cries and throws his food.

SUBJECT COMPLEMENTS AND OBJECT COMPLEMENTS

Subject complements—that is, **predicate nominatives** and **predicate adjectives**—are placed on the baseline to the right of the verb. They are separated from the verb by a slanted line that does not cross the baseline.

EXAMPLE   Senators are legislators.

Senators | are \ legislators

EXAMPLE   That senator is angry.

senator | is \ angry
That

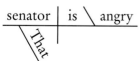

Object complements are diagramed the same way subject complements are, but a direct object comes between the verb and the object complement.

EXAMPLE   Everyone considers senators important.

| Everyone | considers | senators \ important |

PRACTICE   **Subject Complements and Object Complements**

Diagram each sentence.

1. My best friend is Chiang.
2. Jani seems quite impatient.
3. Everyone calls Guadalupe "Lupe."
4. Neither the cat nor the dog considers you its master.
5. The freshman class elected José president.

APPOSITIVES AND APPOSITIVE PHRASES

To diagram an appositive, simply place the word in parentheses beside the noun or pronoun it identifies. To diagram an appositive phrase, place the appositive phrase in parentheses and place any modifying words on slanted lines directly beneath the appositive.

EXAMPLE   Washington, the nation's capital, houses Congress.

| Washington (capital) | houses | Congress |

the   nation's

PRACTICE   **Appositives and Appositive Phrases**

Diagram each sentence.

1. My cousin Judy has only one brother.
2. The newspaper printed Iola's poem "Sentinel."

3. "Birches," a nostalgic poem, contains some wonderful imagery.

4. Sarah's cousin Harrison Hathaway is a corporate lawyer.

5. That building, the former county courthouse, is quite old.

PREPOSITIONAL PHRASES

To diagram prepositional phrases, follow the example diagram.

EXAMPLE During campaigns, senators of today address people through television advertisements.

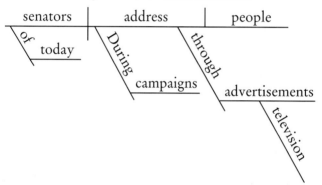

PRACTICE **Prepositional Phrases**

Diagram each sentence.

1. Who took my book from the hall table?

2. Darla planted daffodils along the walkway.

3. Our leaders sent messages of sympathy to the French government.

4. Seven candles on the table provided a bright glow.

5. The president of the company opened the meeting with a short film about environmental responsibility.

PARTICIPLES AND PARTICIPIAL PHRASES

To diagram participles and participial phrases, follow the example diagram.

EXAMPLE Bedraggled, the quarterback rose to his feet.

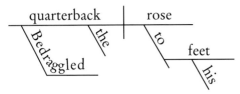

EXAMPLE Hopefully casting his ballot, the senator wanted a victory.

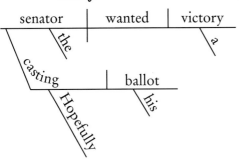

PRACTICE **Participles and Participial Phrases**

Diagram each sentence.

1. Exhausted, the hikers stopped for a short rest.
2. Opening his book, Ricardo began the French lesson.
3. Two children playing in the yard watched their neighbor weeding his rose garden.
4. The workers repairing the wall first removed the loosened bricks.
5. Elated by their victory, the cheering team carried their coach through the gym.

GERUNDS AND GERUND PHRASES

To diagram gerunds and gerund phrases, follow the example diagram.

EXAMPLE   Voting is a way of voicing your opinion.

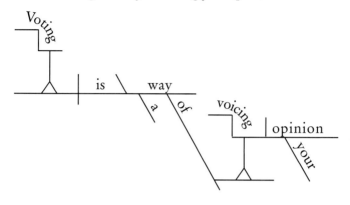

PRACTICE   **Gerunds and Gerund Phrases**

Diagram each sentence.

1. Finding the right path proved difficult.
2. The new lesson on diagraming gerund phrases was not a problem.
3. The class's last exercise was running laps.
4. For some reason nobody likes my singing.
5. Completing the project was the dean's main concern.

INFINITIVES AND INFINITIVE PHRASES

If an infinitive or an infinitive phrase functions as an adverb or an adjective, diagram it as you would diagram a prepositional phrase.

EXAMPLE   The place to vote is determined by your residence.

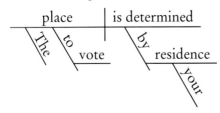

Infinitives and infinitive phrases functioning as nouns are also diagramed like prepositional phrases. However, they are placed on stilts.

EXAMPLE   To win an election is to know satisfaction.

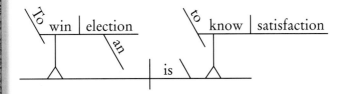

"THIS IS DR. GRUMBACHER, PROFESSOR EMERITUS OF COMPARATIVE PHILOLOGY. PERHAPS HE COULD TELL YOU THE DIFFERENCE BETWEEN AN ADVERB AND AN ADJECTIVE."

Diagram each sentence.

1. To train his dog was Raja's next goal.
2. Artemisia loves to hunt for shells on the beach.
3. I am too busy to cook dinner now.
4. Do you want to come to the mall with me?
5. Gerry's plan was to practice diligently for the race.

COMPOUND SENTENCES

A **compound sentence** is two or more simple sentences joined by either a comma and a conjunction or by a semicolon.

Diagram each main clause of a compound sentence separately. If the clauses are connected by a semicolon, use a dotted line to connect the verbs of each main clause. If the main clauses are connected by a conjunction, place the conjunction on a solid horizontal line, and connect it to the verbs of each main clause by dotted lines.

EXAMPLE   Voting is a privilege; you must be a citizen.

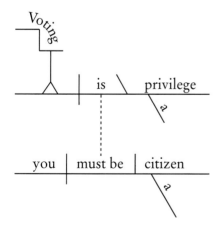

EXAMPLE To vote you must register in advance, and you need to bring current identification to the polling place.

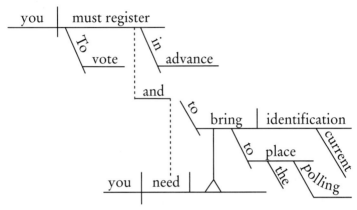

PRACTICE **Compound Sentences**

Diagram each sentence.

1. Senator Menendez is a married man, and he is also the father of twins.

2. Playing volleyball is allowed, but swimming is prohibited.

3. Have you finished your homework, or will you do it tomorrow?

4. The children are becoming fidgety; will you read to them?

5. Type your letters and then distribute these flyers.

9.2 DIAGRAMING COMPLEX AND COMPOUND-COMPLEX SENTENCES

A **complex sentence** has one main clause and one or more subordinate clauses.

ADJECTIVE CLAUSES

To diagram a complex sentence containing an adjective clause, place the main clause in one diagram and the adjective clause in another diagram beneath it. Use a dotted line to connect the introductory word of the clause to the modified noun or pronoun in the main clause.

EXAMPLE   The carpenter whom you hired fixed the shelves that were uneven.

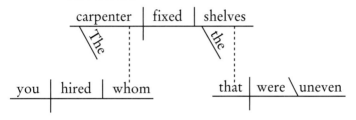

PRACTICE Adjective Clauses

Diagram each sentence.

1. The student who lent you her pen has left for the day.
2. Marilee, who is a new student, made friends easily.
3. The homework that I finished was the wrong assignment.
4. Is this the book that you borrowed from Leslie?
5. This recipe, which makes four servings, can really feed six people.

ADVERB CLAUSES

To diagram a complex sentence containing an adverb clause, place the adverb clause in a separate diagram beneath the main clause. Use a dotted line to connect the verb in the adverb clause to the modified word in the main clause. Write the subordinating conjunction on the dotted line.

EXAMPLE Before carpenters cut the wood, they make a design.

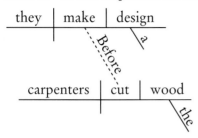

PRACTICE Adverb Clauses

Diagram each sentence.

1. Ignacio works in the student bakery as often as he can.

2. Since Alanna has arrived from Springfield, we should go inside.

3. Until the customers return, you may sit here.

4. Kelly may have the posters unless Lois wants them.

5. Do you know if the weather will be good tomorrow?

NOUN CLAUSES

Diagram the main clause and place the noun clause on a stilt in its appropriate position. The stilt that attaches the noun clause to the sentence may be connected to any point on the noun clause's baseline. You must identify the function of the introductory word of the noun clause. It can be the subject, an object, a predicate nominative, or an adverb in the noun clause; or it might simply connect the noun clause to the main clause. If the latter is the case, place the introductory word on a line of its own above the verb in the noun clause, connecting it to the verb with a dotted vertical line. If it has a function within the clause, diagram it appropriately.

Noun Clause as Subject

EXAMPLE What the carpenter builds is especially sturdy.

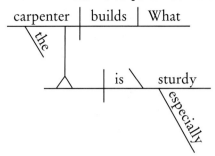

PRACTICE **Noun Clause as Subject**

Diagram each sentence.

1. Whatever she does will go wrong.
2. Whoever built these houses did a good job.
3. What nobody knows is Eleanora's real name.
4. How the roses grew here is a matter of speculation.
5. Where the hurricane will strike next is important.

GRAMMAR/USAGE/MECHANICS

Noun Clause as Direct Object

EXAMPLE We know that the mechanic works long hours.

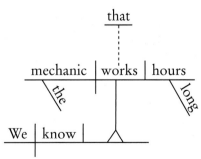

Diagram each sentence.

1. Graciela learned that her friend Genevieve would arrive at noon.
2. My parents give me whatever I need for school.
3. Joanie asked where the birds had gone.
4. Who knew that the builders would leave rubbish in the front yard?
5. I realize what the consequences are.

Noun Clause as Object of a Preposition

EXAMPLE   The carpenter builds cabinets for whoever requests them.

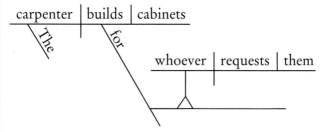

Diagram each sentence.

1. This is a summary of what I said at the meeting.
2. Alyson is worried about who would help her in an emergency.
3. Tranh is certain about where he would go in a storm.
4. Janeice will arrive by whichever route is best.
5. Haruo writes under whichever name he likes.

COMPOUND-COMPLEX SENTENCES

> A **compound-complex sentence** has two or more main clauses and at least one subordinate clause.

Diagram a compound-complex sentence as you would diagram a compound sentence.

EXAMPLE   Carpenters who do quality work are usually busy, and they often receive higher pay.

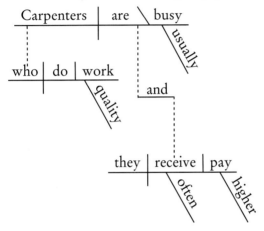

PRACTICE   Compound-Complex Sentences

Diagram each sentence.

1. The piano that Mom bought me is perfect, and I will never want another one.
2. Stories that warm the heart bring joy, but violent stories breed violence.
3. People who can accept others without reserve are admirable, and I would like to be one.
4. The apples that grow on our trees are delicious, and I will bring you some at our next meeting.
5. The child whose mother is buying groceries wants some candy, but sugar-free gum is better for her.

Diagram each sentence.

1. Jamal laughed.

2. Hurry!

3. Mr. Talbot and Mrs. Talbot cook and clean.

4. They live very happily.

5. Mr. Talbot has a beautifully flowering garden.

6. He gives his wife botanical information.

7. Now she knows much about plants.

8. The garden, an outdoor retreat, blooms lavishly in summer.

9. Jumping high, Lawanda easily made the three-point shot.

10. The class, voting together, elected Harv Bennett president.

11. To succeed in life is a common goal.

12. You work diligently, but you also need a plan.

13. The teacher who helped Lawanda stressed scholarship and physical exercise.

14. Painting the kitchen will give the room much more light.

15. Whichever college Giorgio chooses will probably accept him.

16. Can you tell me when the plane leaves for Atlanta?

17. I know that I will be there early.

18. The college sends bulletins to whoever wants them.

19. Angelica, who made the dean's list in her first semester, feels confident.

20. Literature that captures the imagination is perceptive, but it is also instructive.

Chapter 10

Capitalizing

● ● ● ● ● ● ● ● ● ● ● ● ● ● ● ●

PRETEST Capitalizing

Rewrite any incorrect sentences, correcting errors in capitalization. If a sentence is correct, write C.

1. Derek sullivan lives on first avenue in Swampscott, Massachusetts.

2. The first part of Liane's outline reads as follows:
   I. William shakespeare
      a. plays
         1. comedies
         2. tragedies

3. linus ended his letter with the words "sincerely yours, Linus Carpenter."

4. My Cousin was graduated from saint louis university with the degree of bachelor of arts.

5. After the uss *yorktown* was bombed during World war II, a new Ship with the Same name was built.

6. John f. Kennedy was one of the Nation's most beloved presidents.

7. hannah looked up at the big dipper and located the star Polaris.

8. Deepak was born in benares, a city holy to the Hindus of india.

9. "Dad," asked Tomás, "why doesn't julio's dad ever come to our baseball games?"

10. Linda's mother, who lived in florida at the time, witnessed the explosion of the *challenger* spacecraft.

11. Bob traded in his ford taurus for a 1998 dodge caravan.

12. Thanksgiving day always falls on a thursday.

13. Dylan Thomas was a Welsh poet.

14. Nanci decided that it was Time for her to leave.

15. In A.D. 79 the resort town of pompeii, Italy, was destroyed during an Eruption of Mount Vesuvius.

16. The american poet Oliver wendell holmes wrote "The chambered nautilus," one of his Most Famous Poems.

17. After he delivered the gettysburg Address, Lincoln felt that his historic Speech had been a Failure.

18. Angelo asked, "What time does Santa Claus reach our house?"

19. The Raleigh *News and Observer* is read by Thousands of subscribers in eastern North carolina.

20. Have you ever climbed to the top of the washington monument?

21. Jenny swanson was born in småland, sweden.

22. The United states constitution declares, "all men are created Equal."

23. Arlene chose *farewell to Manzanar* as her optional novel for the spring semester.

24. Tyler is a strong supporter of Friends of Animals.

25. Which Planets do we study besides venus, mars, and pluto?

10.1 CAPITALIZING SENTENCES AND QUOTATIONS

The use of capitalization across the English-speaking world varies. In business writing particularly, people capitalize terms according to company style, which may vary from the rules in this chapter. However, mastering these rules for your own writing will enable you to express yourself clearly in any situation.

Rule 1 Capitalize the pronoun *I* and the first word of a sentence.

EXAMPLE   Pets need love and attention.

EXAMPLE   Can you watch my dog while **I** am gone?

Rule 2 Capitalize the first word of a sentence in parentheses that stands by itself. Don't capitalize a sentence within parentheses that is contained within another sentence.

EXAMPLE   Games can be tools for learning about computers. (Many games require more computer knowledge than basic use requires.)

EXAMPLE   They were looking for software (they hoped to buy no more than two programs) that they could use for writing reports.

Rule 3 Capitalize the first word of a complete sentence that follows a colon. Lowercase the first word of a sentence fragment that follows a colon.

EXAMPLE   The poet's love letter was too well written: It intimidated the girl.

EXAMPLE   The poet's love letter was passionate, heartwarming, and one thing more: intimidating.

Rule 4 Capitalize the first word of a direct quotation that is a complete sentence.

A **direct quotation** gives the speaker's exact words.

EXAMPLE   My little brother asked, "Why can't I go too?"

Unless it begins a sentence, don't capitalize the first word of a direct quotation that cannot stand as a complete sentence.

EXAMPLE   Her boss described her as "energetic and intelligent."

Rule 5 Do not capitalize an indirect quotation.

An **indirect quotation** does not repeat a speaker's exact words and should not be enclosed in quotation marks.

EXAMPLE   My brother asked why he couldn't go.

An indirect quotation is often introduced with the word *that.*

EXAMPLE   She said that she wanted to leave early.

Rule 6 In a traditional poem, the first word of each line is capitalized.

EXAMPLE   Let us go then, you and I,
When the evening is spread out against the sky
Like a patient etherized upon a table; . . .
—from "The Love Song of J. Alfred Prufrock" by T. S. Eliot

| PRACTICE   Capitalizing Sentences and Quotations |

Copy the sentences, correcting any errors in capitalization. If a sentence is correctly capitalized, write C.

1. Jeannie said, "i don't know whether to add or subtract."
2. Pepper and Mint are known as Spice Kitties.

3. In her evaluation, Ms. Ching described Luisa as "Capable and responsible."

4. John Updike wrote the poem "Ex-Basketball Player" (Which has sometimes been compared to A. E. Housman's "To an Athlete Dying Young").

5. Larry groaned, "how will I ever finish this essay before Tomorrow morning?"

6. Ralph sighed and put his pencil down, wondering Why he had ever volunteered for the project.

7. Emelie asked, "Why did you come back?" although she thought She already knew the answer.

8. after the recital, Terry and her mother started for home.

9. "Not I!" roared Mr. Firth when asked who had broken Mom's favorite vase.

10. They planted tomatoes in a plot behind the house. (they wanted corn, too, but they didn't have room for it.)

10.2 CAPITALIZING LETTER PARTS AND OUTLINES

Rule 1 Capitalize the first word in the salutation and the closing of a letter. Capitalize the title and the name of the person addressed.

EXAMPLES

Dear Ms. Romano,   Dear Sir or Madam: Dear General Motors:

With love,   Yours truly,   Sincerely yours,

Rule 2 In a topic outline, capitalize the Roman numerals that label main topics and the letters that label subtopics. Do not capitalize letters that label subdivisions of a subtopic. Capitalize the first word in each heading and subheading.

EXAMPLE   **I.** **M**ain topic

    A. **S**ubtopic

        1. **D**ivision of a subtopic

           a. **S**ubdivision of a subtopic

           b. **S**ubdivision of a subtopic

  II. **M**ain topic

PRACTICE   **Capitalizing Letter Parts**

Write the letter of the correctly capitalized line in each pair.

1. **a.** sincerely,
   b. Sincerely,

2. **a.** Dear Mrs. Gore:
   b. dear Mrs. Gore:

3. **a.** gratefully,
   b. Gratefully,

4. **a.** Dear Mr. President:
   b. Dear mr. president:

5. **a.** Regretfully,
   b. regretfully,

PRACTICE   **Capitalizing Outlines**

Rewrite the partial outline, correcting any errors in capitalization.

  I. English Before Modern english

    A. Old English

      1. influence of Old Norse

      2. Influence of Latin

        A. Classical Latin

        b. Spoken Latin

    b. Middle English

      1. Influence of Old English

      2. influence of French

  II. Modern English

    A. British English

    B. American English

10.3 CAPITALIZING PROPER NOUNS AND PROPER ADJECTIVES

A **proper noun** names a particular person, place, thing, or idea.
Proper adjectives are formed from proper nouns.

Rule 1 Capitalize proper nouns and proper adjectives.

EXAMPLES **PROPER NOUNS**   **PROPER ADJECTIVES**

China   Chinese food

Islam   Islamic country

In proper nouns and adjectives made up of more than one word, capitalize all words except articles, coordinating conjunctions, or prepositions of fewer than five letters.

EXAMPLES

PROPER NOUNS	University of Nebraska
	American Society for the Prevention of Cruelty to Animals
PROPER ADJECTIVES	University of Nebraska students
	United States ambassadors

Note: Many proper nouns do not change form when used as adjectives.

Rule 2 Capitalize the names of people and pets and the initials that stand for their names.

EXAMPLES   Connie Chung   Spot and Puff
                Eric Cartman   Franklin D. Roosevelt   W. B. Yeats

Foreign names are often compounded with an article, a preposition, or a word meaning "son of" or "father of." These names often follow different rules of capitalization. The capitalization also depends on whether you are using the full name or just the surname, so be sure to look up the names in a reference source for proper capitalization.

EXAMPLES	FULL NAME	SURNAME ALONE
	Alfred de Musset	Musset
	Manuel de Falla	de Falla
	Aziz ibn Saud	Ibn Saud

Capitalize nicknames.

EXAMPLES   Shaq   Babe Ruth   the Sun King

Enclose nicknames in quotation marks when they are used with a person's full name.

EXAMPLE   Louis "Satchmo" Armstrong

Rule 3 Capitalize adjectives formed from people's names.

EXAMPLE   Shakespeare   Shakespearean sonnet

Napoléon   Napoléonic attire

Rule 4 Capitalize a title or an abbreviation of a title used before a person's name.

EXAMPLES

Mr. Jones	Ms. McGee	Mother Teresa
Dr. Greene	Secretary of State Albright	Chief Sitting Bull

Capitalize a title used in direct address.

EXAMPLE   How is she doing, Doctor?
              General, the troops are retreating.

Don't capitalize a title that follows a person's name.

EXAMPLE   Madeleine Albright, secretary of state, cancelled her visit.

Don't capitalize a title that is simply being used as a common noun.

EXAMPLE   Spiro Agnew was vice president in the 1960s.
              I didn't care whom she nominated for treasurer of the club.

Rule 5 Capitalize the names and abbreviations of academic degrees that follow a person's name. Capitalize *Jr.* and *Sr.*

EXAMPLE   Terrence Odlin, Doctor of Philosophy

EXAMPLE   Paula Martinéz, **B.A.**

EXAMPLE   Joe Wallace **J**r.

Rule 6 Capitalize a word showing family relationship when it is used either before a proper name or in place of a proper name.

EXAMPLE   Will **A**unt Fern visit this summer?

EXAMPLE   May I go to the movies, **M**om?

Don't capitalize a word showing family relationship if it is preceded by a possessive noun or pronoun.

EXAMPLE   Pilar's **a**unt will visit this summer.

EXAMPLE   Your **m**om said you may go.

Rule 7 Capitalize the names of ethnic groups, nationalities, and languages.

EXAMPLES

ETHNIC GROUPS	**N**ative **A**merican, **C**aucasian, **H**ispanic
NATIONALITIES	**I**talian, **B**razilian, **S**outh **A**frican
LANGUAGES	**R**ussian, **S**wahili, **H**indi, **M**andarin

Rule 8 Capitalize the names of organizations, institutions, political parties and their members, government bodies, business firms, and teams.

EXAMPLES

ORGANIZATIONS	**L**eague of **W**omen **V**oters
	American **M**edical **A**ssociation
	People for the **E**thical **T**reatment of **A**nimals
INSTITUTIONS	**O**hio **S**tate **U**niversity
	Mayo **C**linic
	Metropolitan **M**useum of **A**rt

POLITICAL PARTIES AND MEMBERS	Libertarian Party/Libertarian Democratic Party/Democrat Socialist Party/Socialist
GOVERNMENT BODIES	House of Commons Senate Federal Bureau of Investigation
BUSINESS FIRMS	American Electric Power Glencoe Working Assets Long Distance
TEAMS	Cincinnati Reds New York Knicks Seattle Seahawks

Note: Don't capitalize words such as *court* and *university* unless they are part of a proper noun.

EXAMPLE   I will attend a university next year.

EXAMPLE   I will attend New York University next year.

Note: When referring to a specific political party or party member, words such as *democrat* and *republican* should be capitalized. However, when used to describe a way of thought or an ideal, such words should be lowercase.

EXAMPLE   They are members of the Democratic Party (*or* party).

EXAMPLE   She supported a democratic government.

EXAMPLE   The Communist Party (*or* party) was powerful in the twentieth century.

EXAMPLE   Marx wrote about communist theories.

Note: Capitalize brand names of products but not the nouns following them.

EXAMPLES   Kornee corn dogs   Land Shark motorcycles

Rule 9 Capitalize the names of roads, parks, towns, cities, counties, townships, provinces, states, regions, countries, continents, other land forms and features, and bodies of water.

Fifth Avenue	Hocking Hills	Kansas City
Franklin County	State Park	the Pacific
Guatemala	New York	Northwest
Rocky Mountains	Africa	Mojave Desert
Mediterranean	Long Island	Lake Pontchartrain
Sea	Pacific Ocean	Platte River

Note: Capitalize words such as *city, island,* and *mountains* only when they are part of a proper name.

Capitalize compass points, such as *north, south, east,* and *west,* when they refer to a specific region or when they are part of a proper name. Don't capitalize them when they indicate direction.

EXAMPLES

REGIONS/PROPER NAMES	DIRECTIONS
the South	driving south
East Lansing	eastern Kentucky

Capitalize *northern, southern, eastern,* and *western* when they refer to hemispheres and cultures.

EXAMPLES   Northern Hemisphere   Eastern culture

Capitalize adjectives that are formed from place names.

EXAMPLES   Chinese cuisine   Roman statues   Saharan winds

Rule 10 Capitalize the names of planets and other astronomical bodies.

EXAMPLES

Jupiter	Venus	Uranus
Milky Way	Alpha Centauri	Little Dipper

Rule 11 Capitalize the names of monuments, buildings, bridges, and other structures.

EXAMPLES

Tomb of the Unknowns	Golden Gate Bridge
Empire State Building	Grand Coulee Dam
Taj Mahal	Westminster Abbey

GRAMMAR/USAGE/MECHANICS

Rule 12 Capitalize the names of ships, planes, trains, and spacecraft. Note that these names are italicized, but the abbreviations before them are not.

EXAMPLES *Air Force One*   *Columbia*   SS *United States*

Rule 13 Capitalize the names of historical events, special events, and holidays and other calendar items.

EXAMPLES Texas State Fair   Memorial Day Olympics

Parent-Teacher Book Fair Wednesday   December

Historical events require capitalization, as do some historical periods. However, most historical periods are not capitalized. It is best to check a dictionary or other reference source for the proper capitalization of historical periods.

EXAMPLES

HISTORICAL EVENTS   Boston Tea Party, Battle of Gettysburg, French Revolution

HISTORICAL PERIODS   Roaring Twenties, Age of Reason, Dark Ages

eighteenth century, the twenties, baroque period

Note: Historical periods using numerical designations are lowercase unless they are part of a proper name.

Note: Do not capitalize names of the seasons—*spring, summer, fall, winter.*

Rule 14 Capitalize the names of deities and words referring to deities, words referring to a revered being, religions and their followers, religious books, and holy days and events.

NAMES OF AND WORDS REFERRING TO DEITIES	Allah	Brahma	God
WORDS REFERRING TO A REVERED BEING	the Prophet	the Baptist	
RELIGIONS	Hinduism	Sikhism	Buddhism
FOLLOWERS	Christian	Muslim	Mormon
RELIGIOUS BOOKS	Koran	I Ching	Talmud
RELIGIOUS HOLY DAYS AND EVENTS	Good Friday	Yom Kippur	Ramadan

Note: When you're referring to ancient Greek or Roman deities, don't capitalize the words *god, gods, goddess,* and *goddesses.*

Rule 15 Capitalize only those school courses that name a language, are followed by a number, or name a specific course. Don't capitalize the name of a general subject.

EXAMPLES

Japanese	foreign language
Economics 101	economics
Advanced Calculus	calculus

Rule 16 Capitalize the first word and the last word in the titles of books, chapters, plays, short stories, poems, essays, articles, movies, television series and programs, songs, magazines, newspapers, cartoons, and comic strips. Capitalize all other words except articles, coordinating conjunctions, and prepositions of fewer than five letters.

EXAMPLES

The Mists of Avalon	*Romeo and Juliet*	*Sports Illustrated*
the *New York Times*	"A Room of One's Own"	"Home on the Range"

Note: It is common practice not to capitalize or italicize articles preceding the title of a newspaper or a periodical.

Rule 17 Capitalize the names of documents, awards, and laws.

EXAMPLES

Constitution of the United States   Treaty of Versailles

Pulitzer Prize   New Economic Policy

North American Free Trade Agreement   Nobel Prize

PRACTICE **Capitalizing Proper Nouns and Proper Adjectives**

Copy the sentences, correcting any errors in capitalization. If a sentence is correctly capitalized, write C.

1. Pakistan is an islamic country, whereas india is Hindu.
2. Leona attended Duquesne university for the first two years of her college career.
3. The humane society of the United States wages a constant war against animal abuse.
4. Attorney general Janet Reno testified at the senate hearings.
5. Ursula and her mom attended a special seminar on preserving the brazilian rain forest.
6. "I need a ride to band practice, dad," said Jeremy. "can you help me out?"
7. Maria Tallchief was a famous native american ballerina.

8. Former President Lyndon Johnson is also referred to as lbj.

9. new england is noted for its emphasis on education, industry, and the arts.

10. Some anthropologists believe that the three major egyptian pyramids were sited to imitate the positions of the three stars in the "belt" of the constellation orion.

11. The saint louis arch is also known as the gateway arch; its formal name is the jefferson national expansion memorial.

12. Mario read that tanzania's lake tanganyika is part of a rift valley that runs north and south through eastern africa.

13. Do you know Who the current goalie for the montreal canadiens is?

14. Because the soldiers did not know that the war had ended a month earlier, the last battle of the civil war was fought on may 13, 1865, at palmito hill, texas.

15. The united states secret service is one of the bureaus of the department of the treasury.

16. Years ago, many tourists bought deeds to the brooklyn bridge before they realized they had been swindled.

17. osceola county in florida is named for a great seminole chief.

18. osiris, according to this book, was the egyptian god of the underworld.

19. new guinea is the second-largest island in the world; only greenland is larger.

20. Kirk remembered that australia is considered a continent, not an island.

Rewrite each item, correcting any errors in capitalization. If an item is already correct, write C.

1. Consuelo announced, "today I'm going to be chosen to be the female lead in *my Fair Lady,* our school show."

2. "Sure," raúl said, "and I'm going to play hamlet in london."

3. gentlemen:

     please delete my name from your internet list service. I have no time to read the constant stream of messages.

                                   sincerely,
                                   kathryn kramer

4. Arlene wisely decided that she would keep her mouth shut.

5. Susan signed the letter with her initials, sjs.

6. I. major cities of connecticut
     a. central cities
        1. hartford
        2. windsor
     b. cities on long island sound
        1. new haven
        2. bridgeport
   II. state government

7. Marilee read an italian sonnet today in english class.

8. Luis saw the *spirit of st. louis* at the smithsonian institution in washington, d.c.

9. mrs. Nesbitt asked, "for what are king arthur and the round table remembered?"

10. do you know which book won the newbery medal this year?

SUMMARY OF CAPITALIZATION RULES

NAMES AND TITLES OF PEOPLE

CAPITALIZE	DO NOT CAPITALIZE
M. L. King **J**r.	a **l**eader
Miss **J**ody **P**acella	a **n**eighbor
General **S**chwarzkopf	a **g**eneral
Uncle **K**arl	my **u**ncle
Dr. **G**reene	a **d**octor

ETHNIC GROUPS, NATIONALITIES, AND LANGUAGES

Maori	an **e**thnic **g**roup
French	a **n**ationality
Yiddish	a **l**anguage

ORGANIZATIONS, INSTITUTIONS, POLITICAL PARTIES AND THEIR MEMBERS, GOVERNMENT BODIES, BUSINESS FIRMS, AND TEAMS

Girl **S**couts of **A**merica	an **o**rganization
Smithsonian **I**nstitution	an **i**nstitution
Democratic **P**arty / **D**emocrat	**d**emocratic theories
Parliament	a **g**overning **b**ody
General **M**otors	an automobile **m**anufacturer
Cleveland **I**ndians	a baseball **t**eam

NAMES OF PLACES

Third **S**treet	a **s**treet
Portland, **O**regon, **U.S.A.**	a **c**ity, **s**tate, or **c**ountry
Galapagos **I**slands	**i**slands
New **E**ngland	a **r**egion
Pacific **O**cean	an **o**cean

Summary of Capitalization rules, *continued*

PLANETS AND OTHER ASTRONOMICAL BODIES	
CAPITALIZE	DO NOT CAPITALIZE
Jupiter	a planet
Big Dipper	a constellation

MONUMENTS, BUILDINGS, BRIDGES, AND OTHER STRUCTURES	
Washington Monument	a monument
Sears Tower	a skyscraper
JFK Bridge	a bridge
Eiffel Tower	a structure

SHIPS, PLANES, TRAINS, AND SPACECRAFT	
USS Constitution	a ship
Enola Gay	a plane
Apollo 13	a spacecraft

HISTORICAL EVENTS, SPECIAL EVENTS, AND CALENDAR ITEMS	
the Civil War	a war
Kentucky Derby	a race
Inauguration Day	a holiday
July, December	summer, winter
Monday	a day of the week

RELIGIOUS TERMS	
Allah	a deity
Our Lady	a revered being
Catholicism / Catholic	a religion / a religious follower
Koran	a religious book
Passover	a holy day

Summary of Capitalization rules, continued

SCHOOL COURSES	
CAPITALIZE	DO NOT CAPITALIZE
French	a foreign language
Advanced Calculus	calculus
History 152	a history course
TITLES OF WORKS	
Fools of Fortune	a book
"A Rose for Emily"	a short story
National Geographic	a magazine
the *Daily News*	a newspaper
DOCUMENTS, AWARDS, AND LAWS	
the Magna Carta	a document
Distinguished Flying Cross	an award
Atomic Energy Act	a law

PRACTICE Proofreading

Rewrite the following passage, correcting errors in spelling, capitalization, grammar, and usage. Add any missing punctuation. There are ten errors. Some sentences are correct.

"Through the Tunnel" by Doris Lessing

[1]"Through the Tunnel" is Doris Lessing's story of Jerry, an english boy visiting a mediterranean beach resort with his Mother. [2]The mother, a single parent, tries hard not to treat her son like a little boy. [3]However, she worries obsessively about him whenever he was away from her side. [4]Anxious to be excepted by the local boys at the beach, Jerry tries to

imitate their daring underwater tricks. [5]They have one particular activity, that terrifies and yet fascinates Jerry. [6]The local boys dive into a rocky cove and swim underwater for several minutes through a scary, dark twisting rock tunnel. [7]Jerry believes if he can perform this dive and long underwater swim just once before the vacation ends, he will have proved his courage to himself. [8]Jerry secretly practices holding his breath over longer and longer periods. [9]He also practices swimming underwater until his fears subside. [10]jerry at last do manage to swim through the undersea passage, and his mother manages to relax a bit when he is out of her sight. [11]At the end of the story, both charactars have successfully faced down their fears.

POSTTEST Capitalizing

Rewrite any incorrect sentences, correcting errors in capitalization. If a sentence is correct, write C.

1. Wilfrid Cadrain was named for sir wilfrid laurier, a former prime minister of Canada.
2. The first part of Harriet's outline read as follows:
   I. famous caves
      A. Blue grotto, Capri, italy
      b. carlsbad caverns, New mexico
      c. lascaux Cave, France
   II. how caves are formed
3. "dear mrs. fuentes," was the salutation of Andrea's friendly letter.
4. Leslie delaney attended four universities: the University of north carolina, ohio State university, the university of southern California at berkeley, and yale university.
5. The panama canal links the atlantic Ocean and the pacific Ocean.
6. Franklin D. Roosevelt helped bring the United States out of the Depression.
7. Ursa major is the name of a constellation that includes the well-known big dipper.

8. Frogner park in Oslo, norway, is the site of an outdoor Exhibit of statues by gustav vigeland, the Country's greatest sculptor.
9. Constitution day is a National holiday in Norway.
10. canada's Provincial parliament Buildings are located in Toronto, the Capital of Ontario.
11. Josh, which do you like better, the Mitsubishi Galant or the Honda Accord?
12. In 1998, Canadians celebrated victoria day on may 18; in the United states, Thanksgiving day fell on november 26.
13. "The masque of the red Death" was written by edgar allan poe, an american.
14. By eleven o'clock, Roberto and Paulo had both decided that They had better leave the party.
15. King Louis xiv of France was a powerful ruler.
16. The year 1789 marked the beginning of the french revolution.
17. Cape fear, North carolina, was hit hard by Hurricane Bonnie in 1998.
18. matthew arnold, the british essayist and poet, wrote the melancholy Poem "Dover beach."
19. Rachel asked, "Where does the president go when he goes on vacation?"
20. The Canton *repository* is a local paper in eastern ohio.
21. Aimée has seen the eiffel tower in Paris and the statue of Liberty in the United states.
22. King harald V heads norway's Evangelical lutheran church.
23. The largest lake in the british isles is lough neagh.
24. The initials *ASPCA* identify the American society for the Prevention of cruelty to animals.
25. Who wrote *A Bridge to terebithia?*

Chapter 11

Punctuation, Abbreviations, and Numbers

● ● ● ● ● ● ● ● ● ● ● ● ● ● ●

PRETEST Punctuation

Rewrite each sentence, correcting any errors in punctuation.

1. Please hand me that yellow towel?
2. Yikes. That pan is hot:
3. Who said that you could come with us.

4. Please bring these items with you, a hammer, finishing nails, and an awl;

5. Roberto is our star quarterback: he is also a straight-A student.

6. Three of the rivers that flow into the Mississippi are as follows; the Missouri, which rises in Montana, the Ohio, which rises in Pennsylvania, and the Red, which rises in Texas?

7. To select a candidate for the job, try this? ask questions. check references. and request a demonstration of skills.

8. Pounding on the door she screamed but no one heard.

9. The tall man, in the red suit, was never seen again by any of us.

10. After a while she was transferred to Texas: her work however remains with us.

11. After a day in the far North John had learned the importance of wearing warm lightweight clothing.

12. Say Frankie youve ridden a horse before havent you

13. The lark's song a lilting deep throated warble stayed with me all day.

14. Despite her mothers advice wear a warm coat Laurel left the house with only a thin jacket over her dress.

15. Harris' answer was "No; his wife though knew that he secretly agreed with her?

16. Do you have a model of the starship Enterprise or the space habitat Babylon 5!

17. Edna works in Boston during the week; but she lives in Waltham.

18. Have you ever visited Taos New Mexico, or Flint Michigan.

19. The state motto of Michigan is If you seek a beautiful peninsula, look around.

20. Please dont ask me any more questions about the wedding Im exhausted?

Rewrite each item, correcting any errors in the use of abbreviations and numbers.

21. Alexis addressed her envelope this way: Mrs J R Morosoff, P O Box 55, Vernon, N J 07462.

22. Do you support the policies of Senator Elaine Greene or Representative Scott Lynley?

23. The secret ingredient of my blackberry pie is one-fourth of a tsp. of ground cloves.

24. It isn't hard to plan a trip in terms of km instead of mi.

25. Did the envelope say "Hilo, H.I" or "Portland, M.E"?

26. Riley's play is scheduled to begin at exactly three fifteen in the afternoon.

27. How many animals has the A S P C A helped?

28. C L Grimes left at AM ten o'clock with $12 in his pocket.

29. The 1990's were technologically explosive, but I preferred the lively 1980's.

30. During its first year, the company lost five million dollars.

11.1 THE PERIOD

Use a period at the end of a declarative sentence—a statement—and at the end of an imperative sentence—a polite command or a request.

EXAMPLES **DECLARATIVE SENTENCE** Track practice starts soon.

IMPERATIVE SENTENCE Please sign up for two events.

11.2 THE EXCLAMATION POINT

Use an exclamation point to show strong feeling and to indicate a forceful command.

EXAMPLE What a beautiful day this is!

EXAMPLE Look out!

Use an exclamation point after an interjection that expresses a strong feeling.

EXAMPLES   Yikes!   Hurray!   Ow!   Good heavens!

11.3 THE QUESTION MARK

Use a question mark at the end of a direct question.

EXAMPLE   Who would like a part-time job for the summer?

EXAMPLE   Which call should I answer first?

Don't use a question mark after an indirect question (one that has been reworded so that it is part of a declarative sentence).

EXAMPLE   He asked whether I needed a work permit.

EXAMPLE   I wondered how much the job would pay.

PRACTICE   End Marks

Rewrite each item, adding the correct end punctuation.

1. What did you say Mark's last name is
2. Wow I just got an A on my report
3. Please hand me the hedge clippers, Alison
4. Where did you get that beautiful vest
5. Meerkats are small burrowing animals that live in open, dry regions of Africa
6. Ow That hurt
7. Kwam asked me why I was wearing a hat
8. Don't leave yet, class; I still have to collect your homework
9. Lydia, has anyone inquired about your Lost-and-Found ad
10. Tryouts for the track team will be held at three o'clock

11.4 THE COLON

COLONS TO INTRODUCE

Use a colon to introduce lists, especially after statements that use such words as *these*, *namely*, *the following*, or *as follows*.

EXAMPLE Friday's test will cover **these** areas: the circulatory, the digestive, and the nervous systems.

EXAMPLE He requested **the following:** a screwdriver, a level, and wood screws.

Don't use a colon to introduce a list if the list immediately follows a verb or a preposition. That is, be sure the words preceding the colon form a sentence.

EXAMPLE The best nonanimal sources of protein **are** soybeans, wheat germ, brewer's yeast, nuts, seeds, and whole grains. **[The list follows the verb *are* and acts as the sentence's predicate nominative. Don't use a colon.]**

EXAMPLE My sister likes to decorate her hamburgers **with** lettuce, tomato, mustard, ketchup, and relish. **[The list follows the preposition *with* and acts as the object of the preposition. Don't use a colon.]**

Use a colon to introduce material that illustrates, explains, or restates the preceding material.

EXAMPLE I often wish my parents had had more than one child: they worry too much about me.

EXAMPLE The epidemic grew ever more serious: now children as well as adults were being affected.

A complete sentence following a colon is capitalized.

EXAMPLE Caution: **D**o not enter until car has come to a complete stop.

Use a colon to introduce a long or a formal quotation. A formal quotation is often preceded by such words as *this*, *these*, *the following*, or *as follows*.

EXAMPLE Mrs. Hoskins asked us to write an essay on **the following** African saying: "It is the rainy season that gives wealth."

Poetry quotations of more than one line and prose quotations of more than four or five lines are generally written below the introductory statement and are indented on the page.

EXAMPLE In his long poem *The Other Pioneers*, Roberto Félix Salazar describes some of the early settlers of the United States:

> Now I must write
> Of those of mine who rode these plains
> Long years before the Saxon and the Irish came.

OTHER USES OF COLONS

- Use a colon between the hour and the minute of the precise time.
- Use a colon between the chapter and the verse in biblical references.
- Use a colon after the salutation of a business letter.

EXAMPLES 12:30 A.M.   Genesis 7:20–24   Sir:

4:00 P.M.   Ruth 1:16–18   Dear Ms. Davis:

PRACTICE   Colons

Rewrite each item below, correcting any errors in the use of colons and other punctuation.

1. I have only one thing: to say to you, Brett; either attend the practice sessions or leave the team.
2. Yes, Narciso; class begins at 2 10: P.M. sharp.

3. Emily Dickinson: wrote the following

We never know how high we are
  Till we are called to rise;
And then, if we are true to plan,
  Our statures touch the skies.

4. Have you read Isaiah: 9;1-6?

5. Actually: I have many reasons to be glad I live in an apartment there is no lawn to mow, a bus stop is nearby, and I babysit for four families without going outside.

6. Our assignment was to write a brief essay: on these lines from Robert Frost "Nature's first green is gold,/Her hardest hue to hold."

7. The primary colors are: red, yellow, and blue.

8. Dear: Sir

9. Nadine puts peanut butter on: bananas, apples, and grapes.

10. These are Takara's favorite flowers. daffodils, lilacs, and sunflowers.

11.5 THE SEMICOLON

SEMICOLONS TO SEPARATE MAIN CLAUSES

Use a semicolon to separate main clauses that are not joined by a comma and a coordinating conjunction (*and, but, or, nor, so, yet,* or *for*).

EXAMPLE Paul Robeson was a talented singer and actor, **and** he was also a famous football player.

EXAMPLE Paul Robeson was a talented singer and actor; he was also a famous football player.

Use a semicolon to separate main clauses that are joined by a conjunctive adverb (such as *however, therefore, nevertheless, moreover, furthermore,* and *subsequently*) or by an expression such as *for example* or *that is*.

In general, a conjunctive adverb or an expression such as *for example* is followed by a comma.

EXAMPLE Robeson appeared in many plays and musicals; **for example,** he starred in *Othello* and *Porgy and Bess*.

EXAMPLE Robeson appeared in *Show Boat* in 1928; **subsequently,** he acted in the films *Jericho* and *Song of Freedom*.

SEMICOLONS AND COMMAS

Use a semicolon to separate the items in a series when one or more of the items already contain commas.

EXAMPLE Some of the powerful African kingdoms that flourished before the sixteenth century were Kush, which dominated the eastern Sudan; Karanga, which was located around Zimbabwe in southern Africa; Ghana, Mali, and Songhai, which successively controlled the Niger River in West Africa; and Benin, which had its center in what is now Nigeria.

Use a semicolon to separate two main clauses joined by a coordinating conjunction when one or both of the clauses already contain several commas.

EXAMPLE The rule of Mansa Musa, the Moslem emperor of the African kingdom of Mali from 1312 to 1337, is remembered for military success, trade expansion, and Moslem scholarship; but this period is probably most noteworthy as a golden age of peace and prosperity.

Rewrite each item below, correcting any errors in the use of semicolons and other punctuation.

1. Two excellent collections of Inuit art are found in Manitoba, one is housed in the Eskimo Museum in Churchill; and the other can be seen at the Winnipeg Art Gallery.

2. A land region that covers almost half of Manitoba; is the Canadian Shield thanks to ancient glaciers, the region is rich in lakes, streams, and forests.

3. A large breeding ground for polar bears lies south of Hudson Bay near Churchill as a result; Churchill is nick-named *Polar Bear Capital of the World.*

4. Mrs. Stebbins recently learned that Chun has a beautiful bass voice, moreover; he's a great clog dancer.

5. Frank and Lillian Gilbreth, a husband and wife team, were well-known engineers, Frank Gilbreth founded a management consulting firm in 1911; and Lillian Gilbreth, who held a Ph.D. in industrial engineering, ran the business after her husband's death.

11.6 THE COMMA

As you study the rules for comma usage, keep in mind that to *separate* elements means to place a comma between two equal elements. To *set off* an element means to put a comma before it and a comma after it. Of course, you never place a comma at the beginning or the end of a sentence.

COMMAS IN A SERIES

Use commas to separate three or more words, phrases, or clauses in a series.

EXAMPLE A chair, a table, a lamp, and a sofa were the room's only furnishings.

EXAMPLE The cat ran into the room, across the floor, and up the curtain.

EXAMPLE Skim the section titles, study the picture captions, and make a note of any boldface terms.

Note: The comma before the *and* is called the serial comma. Some authorities do not recommend it. However, many sentences may be confusing without it. We recommend that you always insert the serial comma for clarity.

EXAMPLES UNCLEAR Bob, Joe and Tim are ready. [might be telling Bob that two people are ready]

CLEAR Bob, Joe, and Tim are ready. [clearly says that three people are ready]

When all the items in a series are connected by conjunctions, no commas are necessary.

EXAMPLE It was a hot and sunny and humid day in July.

EXAMPLE I want red or black or orange or purple.

Nouns that are used in pairs to express one idea *(thunder and lightning, table and chairs, bread and butter)* are usually considered single units and should not be separated by commas. If such pairs appear with other nouns or groups of nouns in a series, however, they must be set off from the other items in the series.

EXAMPLE My favorite breakfast is toast, bacon and eggs, and tomato juice.

EXAMPLE Spread out your wet shoes and socks, hat, and jacket on the register.

COMMAS AND COORDINATE ADJECTIVES

Place a comma between coordinate adjectives that precede a noun.

Coordinate adjectives modify a noun equally. To determine whether adjectives are coordinate, try to reverse their order or put the word *and* between them. If the sentence still sounds natural, the adjectives are coordinate.

EXAMPLE Popeye is a playful, affectionate, intelligent cat.

Don't use a comma between adjectives preceding a noun if the adjectives sound unnatural with their order reversed or with *and* between them. In general, adjectives that describe size, shape, age, and material do not need to be separated by commas.

EXAMPLE Jelani grew up in a small white frame house.

Commas may be needed between some of the adjectives before a noun and not between others.

EXAMPLE I like to read in our bright, cozy family room.

In the preceding sentence, *and* would sound natural between *bright* and *cozy*, but it would not sound natural between *cozy* and *family*.

COMMAS AND COMPOUND SENTENCES

Use a comma between the main clauses in a compound sentence.

Place a comma before a coordinating conjunction *(and, but, or, nor, for, so,* or *yet)* that joins two main clauses.

EXAMPLE I am not going to the concert, **for** I am too busy.

EXAMPLE Many prospectors searched for years, **but** others found gold at once.

EXAMPLE Lindy wanted her own guitar, **so** she started saving all of her paper-route income.

322 *Grammar, Usage, and Mechanics*

Commas in a Series, Commas with Coordinate Adjectives, and Commas in Compound Sentences

Rewrite each item below, correcting any errors in the use of commas and other punctuation.

1. Pepper is a good obedient gentle, dog.
2. Jeanne wore a plaid, wrap skirt, today and Tisa wore a beige print, skirt.
3. I like squash, corn and green beans.
4. Ricardo washed, and dried the dishes, fed the canary and cleaned his room.
5. This was a wonderful, and productive, and exhausting day.

COMMAS AND NONESSENTIAL ELEMENTS

Use commas to set off participles, infinitives, and their phrases if they are not essential to the meaning of the sentence. These nonessential elements are also known as non-restrictive elements.

EXAMPLE She watched, **puzzled,** as the man in the yellow convertible drove away.

EXAMPLE A customer, **complaining loudly,** stepped up to the counter.

EXAMPLE I have no idea, **to be honest,** what you would like for a graduation present.

FRANK AND ERNEST reprinted by permission of
Newspaper Enterprise Association, Inc.

Don't set off participles, infinitives, and their phrases if they are essential to the meaning of the sentence. Such essential elements are also known as restrictive elements.

EXAMPLE   The man **standing by the door** is my dad.

EXAMPLE   My mother's car is the one **parked in the driveway.**

EXAMPLE   She went to medical school **to become a doctor.**

EXAMPLE   **To become a doctor** had been her goal for years.

EXAMPLE   I wanted **to go home.**

Use commas to set off a nonessential adjective clause.

A nonessential clause can be considered an extra clause because it gives optional information about a noun. Because it is an extra clause that is not necessary, it is set off by commas.

EXAMPLE   Atlanta, **which is the capital of Georgia,** is the transportation center of the Southeast. [**The adjective clause** *which is the capital of Georgia* **is nonessential.**]

Don't set off an essential adjective clause. Because an essential adjective clause gives necessary information about a noun, it is needed to convey the exact meaning of the sentence.

EXAMPLE   People **who are afraid of heights** don't like to look down from balconies or terraces. [**The adjective clause** *who are afraid of heights* **is essential. It tells** *which* **people.**]

EXAMPLE   The paramedics first attended the victims, **who were badly hurt. [This clearly states that all the victims were badly hurt.]**

EXAMPLE   The paramedics first attended the victims **who were badly hurt. [This clearly states that the paramedics first decided which victims urgently needed help and which victims could wait.]**

Use commas to set off an appositive if it is not essential to the meaning of a sentence.

A nonessential appositive can be considered interesting but optional, extra information; it calls for commas.

EXAMPLE   Nelson Mandela, **the president of South Africa,** was freed from a South African prison in 1990.

EXAMPLE   My mother lives in Escondido, **a town near San Diego.**

A nonessential appositive is sometimes placed before the noun or pronoun to which it refers.

EXAMPLE   **An insurance executive,** Charles Ives wrote music in his spare time. [The appositive, *an insurance executive,* precedes the noun it identifies, *Charles Ives.*]

An essential appositive gives necessary information about a noun and is not set off with commas.

EXAMPLE   The word *fiesta* came into English from Spanish. [The appositive, *fiesta,* is needed to identify *word.*]

PRACTICE   **Commas and Nonessential Elements**

Rewrite each item below, correcting any errors in the use of commas and other punctuation.

1. Cathy lost the cardigan sweater, that she had worn to the game.
2. Edwin Arlington Robinson an American poet, wrote the simple yet frightening, poem "Richard Cory."
3. My friend, Jeralyn had always wanted, to be an artist.
4. These sunglasses, which Ross took with him only at the last minute, did come in handy, at the seashore.
5. Crying hysterically the little girl told us, that she was lost.

COMMAS WITH INTERJECTIONS, PARENTHETICAL EXPRESSIONS, CONJUNCTIVE ADVERBS, AND ANTITHETICAL PHRASES

Use commas to set off the following:

- interjections (such as *oh, well, alas,* and *good grief*)

- parenthetical expressions (such as *in fact, on the other hand, for example, on the contrary, by the way, to be exact,* and *after all*)

- conjunctive adverbs (such as *however, moreover, therefore,* and *consequently*)

EXAMPLE   **Well,** we'd better hit the road.

EXAMPLE   **Oh,** I don't know.

EXAMPLE   We have to leave**, unfortunately.**

EXAMPLE   Last night**, on the other hand,** we could have stayed longer.

EXAMPLE   We said we'd be home early**; therefore,** we'd better leave now.

EXAMPLE   You might want to come with us**, however.**

Use commas to set off an antithetical phrase.

An **antithetical phrase** uses a word such as *not* or *unlike* to qualify what precedes it.

EXAMPLE   You**, not I,** deserve this honor.

EXAMPLE   Bicycles**, unlike cars,** produce no pollution.

Rewrite each item below, correcting any errors in the use of commas.

1. Jared had promised to be home on time; to make it though he had to run two blocks, climb a fence, and jump over a hedge.
2. Unlike Laura Rick was obsessively neat.
3. Drat I forgot my house, key.
4. Reynaldo left for band practice after school; however he didn't know that the session had been canceled.
5. "We're happy to see you this morning, Susan," said Miss Sullivan, "and by the way please, be on time from now on."

COMMAS WITH OTHER ELEMENTS

Set off two or more introductory prepositional phrases or a single long one.

EXAMPLE **On the afternoon of the day of the game,** we made a banner. **[three prepositional phrases—*On the afternoon, of the day,* and *of the game*]**

EXAMPLE **Because of the rather frightening and extremely unusual circumstances,** the king and his ministers conferred till dawn. **[one long prepositional phrase—*Because of the rather frightening and extremely unusual circumstances*]**

You need not set off a single short introductory prepositional phrase, but it's not wrong to do so.

EXAMPLE In 1789 John Jay became Chief Justice of the Supreme Court of the United States of America. **[one short introductory prepositional phrase—*In 1789*]**

or

In 1789, John Jay became Chief Justice of the Supreme Court of the United States of America.

Don't use a comma if the introductory prepositional phrase is immediately followed by a verb.

EXAMPLE Over the mantelpiece hung a pair of crossed swords.

EXAMPLE On the stone above the front door of the building was inscribed the date.

Use commas to set off introductory participles and participial phrases.

EXAMPLE **Purring,** the kitten curled up in my lap. **[introductory participle]**

EXAMPLE **Sitting in a tree,** my little sister called down to us. **[introductory participial phrase]**

Use commas after all introductory adverbs and adverb clauses.

EXAMPLE **Surprisingly,** no one objected to the new curfew.

EXAMPLE **Hopefully,** Tom and Becky climbed toward the ray of sunlight.

EXAMPLE **Although I like country music,** I did not want to hear his entire collection just then.

EXAMPLE **Until she arrived,** I thought no one else was coming.

Also use commas to set off internal adverb clauses that interrupt the flow of a sentence.

EXAMPLE Evan, **after he had thought about it awhile,** agreed with our conclusion.

In general, don't set off an adverb clause at the end of a sentence unless the clause is parenthetical or the sentence would be misread without the comma.

EXAMPLE   Evan agreed with our conclusion after he had thought about it awhile. **[no comma needed]**

EXAMPLE   Those voting against were nine of the twenty councillors, **if you must know. [parenthetical adverb clause needs comma]**

EXAMPLE   We were just rehearsing the timing for my scream, **when the bomb exploded. [comma needed to prevent misreading]**

PRACTICE   Commas with Other Elements

Rewrite each item below, correcting any errors in the use of commas and other punctuation.

1. From, under a corner, of the blanket Peppermint peeked out at Luisa.
2. In the middle, of the story John stopped suddenly and looked down at his audience.
3. Next to the photograph, of stern old Uncle David, stood a silver vase holding two delicate white roses.
4. With any luck the snow, will hold off until the weekend.
5. Whenever Terry and the dogs come to visit the house is a wreck, for a full week afterward.

ADDITIONAL USES OF COMMAS

Use commas to set off a title when it follows a person's name.

EXAMPLE   Alicia Wong, **M.D.,** will speak after Jorge Gonzalez, **Ph. D.,** has spoken.

Set off the name of a state or a country when it's used after the name of a city. Set off the name of a city when it's used after a street address. Don't use a comma after the state if it's followed by a ZIP code.

EXAMPLE   Anaheim, California, is the home of Disneyland.

EXAMPLE   Her address is 9 Lee Road, Nome, AK 99762.

In a date, set off the year when it's used with both the month and the day. Don't use a comma if only the month and the year are given.

EXAMPLE   March 17, 2000, was the day I got my driver's license.

EXAMPLE   We moved to Dallas in September 1999.

Use commas to set off the parts of a reference that direct the reader to the exact source.

EXAMPLE   Odysseus becomes reunited with his son, Telemachus, in the *Odyssey*, Book 16, lines 177-219.

Use commas to set off words or names in direct address.

EXAMPLE   **Nathaniel,** do you know where Katie is?

EXAMPLE   I can order the book for you, **sir,** if you like.

Use commas to set off tag questions.

A tag question (such as *shouldn't I?* or *have you?*) suggests an answer to the question that precedes it.

EXAMPLE   You've already seen this movie, **haven't you?**

EXAMPLE   We're not going to be ready on time, **are we?**

Place a comma after the salutation of an informal letter. Place a comma after the closing of all letters. In the inside address, place a comma between the city and state and between the day and year.

EXAMPLE

90 Sherwood Road
New Bedford, MA 02745
July 7, 2000

Dear Dolores,

Very truly yours,

PRACTICE Additional Uses of Commas

Rewrite each item below, correcting any errors in the use of commas and other punctuation.

1. Sherrie was born on August, 13 1989.
2. George Silver D.V.M., is a respected veterinarian.
3. Christie where is Max?
4. There isn't enough milk left to make pudding is there?
5. Dear, Tyrone

With best, wishes

Chapter 11 Punctuation, Abbreviations, and Numbers **331**

MISUSE OF COMMAS

In general, don't use a comma before a conjunction that connects a compound predicate or compound subject.

EXAMPLES	**INCORRECT**	She started the car, and drove down the hill. **[compound predicate]**
	CORRECT	She started the car and drove down the hill.
	INCORRECT	The adults playing softball, and the children playing soccer argued in the field. **[compound subject]**
	CORRECT	The adults playing softball and the children playing soccer argued in the field.

Don't use only a comma to join two main clauses unless they are part of a series of clauses. Such a sentence punctuated with a comma alone is called a *run-on sentence* (or a *comma splice* or a *comma fault*). To join two clauses correctly, use a coordinating conjunction with the comma, or use a semicolon.

EXAMPLES	**INCORRECT**	John Wayne worked in Hollywood for almost fifty years, he made more than 175 films.
	CORRECT	John Wayne worked in Hollywood for almost fifty years, **and** he made more than 175 films.
	CORRECT	John Wayne worked in Hollywood for almost fifty years; he made more than 175 films.

Don't use a comma between a subject and its verb or between a verb and its complement.

EXAMPLES	**INCORRECT**	What you do, is your business.
	CORRECT	What you do is your business.
	INCORRECT	You will need, a sleeping bag, a towel, soap, and a toothbrush.

| CORRECT | You will need a sleeping bag, a towel, soap, and a toothbrush. |

PRACTICE Misuse of Commas

Rewrite each item below, correcting any errors in the use of commas and other punctuation.

1. Eliseo put on the parking brake, but didn't get out of the car.
2. Neither Alani, nor Kimiko, could ever have imagined what happened next.
3. "The Celebrated Jumping Frog of Calaveras County" was written by Mark Twain, it was published in the New York *Saturday Press* in 1865.
4. The girls at the sleepover, watched MTV and VH-1 until midnight.
5. If you go to the Dallas game, please buy, an extra Cowboys t-shirt for me.

PRACTICE Commas

Rewrite each item below, correcting any errors in the use of commas and other punctuation.

1. To test his speed and agility, Lee ran, across the field jumped over, three fences and climbed the ladder, in the barn.
2. I can't study, with you tonight Carmela but, maybe we can get together tomorrow.
3. Smiling Lydia watched her brother, pedal nearly a half block on his first, two-wheeler bike ride.
4. Janice's father an insurance agent works, with Mr. Hakim who owns Consolidated Protection, Inc.
5. "Oh, darn" said Terrye, "I've forgotten my English book again however I think, I have time to go back for it."

6. Among the papers, in the top drawer, of the desk, was the contract, Mrs. Johansen had hoped she'd find.
7. In 1945, World War II came to a close.
8. Eating, a peanut butter and jelly sandwich Molly, looked up at her mother and asked, "When can I learn to drive the car?"
9. After the road race is over will you give me an interview?
10. Both Tim and Patrick, left Helena standing on the sidewalk, neither returned to explain what she'd done wrong.

11.7 THE DASH

On a typewriter, indicate the dash with two hyphens (--). If you are using a computer, you may make a dash with a certain combination of keystrokes. Refer to the manual of your word-processing program for instructions.

Don't place a comma, a semicolon, a colon, or a period before or after a dash.

DASHES TO SIGNAL CHANGE

Use a dash to indicate an abrupt break or change in thought within a sentence.

EXAMPLE

A small stand sells sugar loaves—the gift to bring when invited to dinner—sugar for the mint tea and for the sweet pastry, so flaky and light, that they bake.

—Anaïs Nin

DASHES TO EMPHASIZE

Use a dash to set off and emphasize extra information or parenthetical comments.

EXAMPLE   It was a shiny new car—the first he had ever owned.

EXAMPLE   A shiny new car—the first he had ever owned—sat in the driveway.

Don't overuse dashes in your writing. Dashes are most often found in informal or personal letters. In formal writing situations, use subordinating conjunctions (such as *after, until, because,* and *unless*) or conjunctive adverbs (such as *however, nonetheless,* and *furthermore*), along with the correct punctuation, to show the relationships between ideas.

PRACTICE Dashes

Rewrite each item, correcting errors in the use of the dash and other punctuation.

   1. The kit two pencils—a ballpoint pen, and an—eraser was placed on the desk.
   2. There it sat—, in all its glory.
   3. Sara's little sister, —only two years old, —sat in the pool and splashed.
   4. It was a medal:—the only medal he'd ever won—and it was his at last.
   5. Myron stopped the line of children at the corner,—the corner of Concord Street and Dante Place—and counted them again.

11.8 PARENTHESES

PARENTHESES TO SET OFF SUPPLEMENTAL MATERIAL

Use parentheses to set off supplemental, or extra, material.

Commas and dashes as well as parentheses can be used to set off supplemental material; the difference between the three marks of punctuation is one of degree. Use commas to set off supplemental material that is closely related to the rest of the sentence. Use parentheses to set off supplemental material that is not important enough to be considered part of the main statement. Use dashes to set off and emphasize any material that interrupts the main statement.

EXAMPLE   Many contemporary women's fashions (business suits and low heels) show the influence of Gabrielle "Coco" Chanel.

A complete sentence within parentheses is not capitalized and needs no period if it is contained within another sentence. If a sentence within parentheses is not contained within another sentence—that is, if it stands by itself—both a capital letter and end punctuation are needed.

EXAMPLE   The unisex trend (it still seems to be popular) was started by Chanel, who often wore a man's trench coat.

EXAMPLE   Chanel introduced the world's most famous perfume, Chanel No. 5. (This scent is still in great demand.)

PARENTHESES WITH OTHER MARKS OF PUNCTUATION

Place a comma, a semicolon, or a colon *after* the closing parentheses.

EXAMPLE   Despite the simple clothes that Chanel designed and wore (the little black dress became her uniform), she became wealthy.

EXAMPLE   In the early 1950s, women wore high heels and long skirts with cinched waists (the Dior look); Chanel helped change that.

Place a question mark or an exclamation point *inside* the parentheses if it is part of the parenthetical expression.

EXAMPLE   Chanel believed that simplicity and practicality were more important than obviously expensive, complicated-looking clothes (who would not agree today?).

EXAMPLE   Chanel exerted only a little influence on fashion during World War II (1939–1945), but she reopened her fashion house in 1954 (when she was seventy!).

Place a period, a question mark, or an exclamation point *outside* the parentheses if it is part of the entire sentence.

EXAMPLE   Did you know that Chanel introduced many of today's fashion classics (sweaters, costume jewelry, sling-back shoes)?

EXAMPLE   How astounded I was to find out it was Chanel who made suntans fashionable (in the 1930s)!

PRACTICE Parentheses

Rewrite each item, correcting errors in the use of parentheses, other punctuation, and capitalization.

1. Robert Frost (He is one of my favorite poets) read his poem "The Gift Outright" at President Kennedy's inauguration.
2. The child (she seemed to be about five years old,) looked as if she were lost.
3. No one on our block (I took her to every house,) knew who she was.

4. Eating more fruit, vegetables, and grains may help people who have frequent heartburn and upset stomachs (although they should avoid tomatoes, wheat and corn products, and citrus fruits.)
5. Fritz was overly polite (Do you know what I mean)? and he annoyed quite a few people.

11.9 QUOTATION MARKS

QUOTATION MARKS WITH DIRECT QUOTATIONS

Use quotation marks to enclose a direct quotation.

Place quotation marks around the quotation only, not around purely introductory or explanatory remarks. Generally separate such remarks from the actual quotation with a comma. (For the use of colons to introduce quotations, see page 317.)

EXAMPLE A famous poster asks, "What if they gave a war and nobody came?"

EXAMPLE A Pawnee poem reminds us of "the sacredness of things."

Don't use a comma after a quotation that ends with an exclamation point or a question mark.

EXAMPLE "What is the question?" Gertrude Stein asked.

When a quotation is interrupted by explanatory words such as *he said* or *she wrote*, use two sets of quotation marks.

Separate each part of the quotation from the interrupting phrase with marks of punctuation before and after the phrase. If the second part of the quotation is a complete sentence, begin it with a capital letter and use a period, not a comma, after the interrupting phrase.

"A thing of beauty," wrote John Keats, "is a joy forever."

EXAMPLE "It wasn't just that he [Babe Ruth] hit more home runs than anybody else," said Red Smith. "He hit them better, higher, farther. . . ."

Do not use quotation marks in an indirect quotation.

EXAMPLE	**ORIGINAL QUOTATION**	"Dance is life at its most glorious moment," said Pearl Lang.
	INDIRECT QUOTATION	Pearl Lang has said that dance is life at its most glorious moment.

Use single quotation marks around a quotation within a quotation.

EXAMPLE President John F. Kennedy said, "I am one person who can truthfully say, 'I got my job through the *New York Times*.'"

In writing dialogue, begin a new paragraph and use a new set of quotation marks every time the speaker changes.

EXAMPLE He looked at me proudly. "Was it so hard to do, Daughter?"

"Not so hard as I thought." I pinned the brooch on my dress. "I'll wear it always," I said. "I'll keep it forever."
—Kathryn Forbes

QUOTATION MARKS WITH OTHER MARKS OF PUNCTUATION

Always place a comma or a period *inside* closing quotation marks.

EXAMPLE   "The frog does not drink up the pond in which it lives,"
           states a Native American proverb.

EXAMPLE   Henry David Thoreau humorously advises, "Beware of
           all enterprises that require new clothes."

Always place a semicolon or a colon *outside* closing
quotation marks.

EXAMPLE   Her father said, "We cannot go"; her mother said,
           "Perhaps we can go next summer"; her elder brother
           just shrugged.

EXAMPLE   This is what I think of Lady Ōtomo's poem "My Heart,
           Thinking": it is romantic and powerful.

Place the question mark or the exclamation point
inside the closing quotation marks when it is part of
the quotation.

EXAMPLE   A famous sonnet by Shakespeare begins with these
           words: "Shall I compare thee to a summer's day?"

EXAMPLE   She cried, "I never want to see you again!"

Place the question mark or the exclamation point
outside the closing quotation marks when it is part of
the entire sentence.

EXAMPLE   I've finally memorized all of "Paul Revere's Ride"!

EXAMPLE   Why do you keep saying, "I'm sorry"?

If both the sentence and the quotation at the end of the
sentence need a question mark (or an exclamation point),
use only one punctuation mark, and place it *inside* the
closing quotation marks.

EXAMPLE   When did he ask, "Why do you want to know?"

EXAMPLE   What a surprise it was to hear them shout, "Yahoo!"

Don't use a comma after a quotation that ends with a question mark or an exclamation point.

EXAMPLE   "That's incredible!" my father said yet again.

QUOTATION MARKS WITH TITLES, UNUSUAL EXPRESSIONS, AND DEFINITIONS

Use quotation marks to enclose titles of short works, such as short stories, short poems, essays, newspaper articles, magazine articles, book chapters, songs, and single episodes of a television series.

EXAMPLES

"The Legend of Sleepy Hollow" [short story]

"The Raven" [short poem]

"On the Duty of Civil Disobedience" [essay]

"Steven Spielberg's Newest Film" [newspaper article]

"The 1990s in Mexico" [book chapter]

"If I Had a Hammer" [song]

"Division of the Spoils" [episode in a television series]

(For the use of italics with longer titles, see page 343.)

Use quotation marks to enclose unfamiliar slang and other unusual or original expressions.

EXAMPLE   My cousin uses the expression "the cat's meow" to describe things she likes.

EXAMPLE   The 1920s were known as the "Roaring Twenties."

Be careful not to overuse quotation marks with unusual expressions. Generally, use quotation marks only the first time you use the unusual expression in a piece of writing.

Use quotation marks to enclose a definition that is stated directly.

EXAMPLE   The German noun *Weltanschauung* means "world view" or "philosophy of life."

EXAMPLE   In Japanese the word *ikebana* means "living flowers"; ikebana is the art of arranging cut flowers with other natural objects.

PRACTICE Quotation Marks

Rewrite each item, correcting errors in the use of quotation marks and other punctuation.

1. "Happiness is getting a bill you've already paid," someone once said, "It means you can sit down and write a nasty letter".

2. The word *autobiography* comes from the Greek *auto,* meaning self, *bios,* meaning life, and *graph,* meaning write.

3. Lokelani said, "I just can't deal with that now;" then she turned and walked away.

4. "What is Diane up to?," asked Jerol.

5. "I have no idea", said Ann, "but I saw ribbon and wrapping paper before she shut the door".

6. Robert Frost once said "that poetry makes you remember what you didn't know you knew."

7. After the birth of his son, Caleb walked out of the hospital, stopped at the top of the steps, and shouted "Hooray"!

8. "A no-brainer," is Paulo's description of any problem less complicated than one involving atomic physics.

9. Why did Wordsworth write "My Heart Leaps Up?"

10. "I don't believe you said that"! Jean exclaimed.

11.10 ITALICS (UNDERLINING)

Italic type is a special slanted type that is used in printing. *(This sentence is printed in italics.)* Indicate italics on a typewriter or with handwriting by underlining. (<u>This sentence is underlined</u>.) When you are using a computer, learn the special keystrokes for italics by referring to your software manual.

ITALICS WITH TITLES

Italicize (underline) the following: titles of books, long poems, plays, films, television series, paintings, sculptures, and long musical compositions. Also italicize (underline) the names of newspapers, magazines, ships, airplanes, and spacecraft.

A "long poem" or a "long musical composition" is any poem or musical composition published under its own title as a separate work.

EXAMPLES

Great Expectations [book]

Snow-Bound [long poem]

Romeo and Juliet [play]

Gone with the Wind [film]

Nova [television series]

Starry Night [painting]

The Thinker [sculpture]

Grand Canyon Suite [musical work]

the *Oakland Tribune* [newspaper]

Sports Illustrated [magazine]

USS *Enterprise** [ship]

Spirit of St. Louis [airplane]

Columbia [spacecraft]

*Don't italicize abbreviations such as USS in the name of a ship.

Italicize (underline) and capitalize articles (*a, an, the*) written at the beginning of a title only when they are a part of the title itself. It is common practice not to italicize (underline) the article preceding the title of a newspaper or a magazine. Do not italicize the word *magazine* unless it is a part of the title of a periodical.

EXAMPLES *The Red Badge of Courage*
A Light in the Attic

but

a *National Geographic* magazine
the *Chicago Tribune*

ITALICS WITH FOREIGN WORDS

Italicize (underline) foreign words and expressions that are not used frequently in English.

EXAMPLE The motto of the U.S. Marine Corps is **semper fidelis** ("always faithful").

Don't italicize (underline) a foreign word or expression that is commonly used in English. Consult a dictionary; if a foreign word or expression is a dictionary entry word, don't italicize (underline) it.

EXAMPLE I had **croissants** for breakfast.

ITALICS WITH WORDS AND OTHER ITEMS USED TO REPRESENT THEMSELVES

Italicize (underline) words, letters, and numerals used to represent themselves—that is, words used as words, letters used as letters, and numerals used as numerals.

For instance, if you were to say, "Don't start a sentence with *and*," you would pronounce the *and* in that sentence much differently than the *and* in the phrase "oranges and lemons." Your voice would make it clear that *and* was being used to represent itself. When you are writing, you don't have your voice to help, so you can use italic type to indicate a word that is being used as a word.

EXAMPLE   Do not start a sentence with **and** or **but.**

EXAMPLE   Replace all the number signs (#s) with the word **number.**

EXAMPLE   In your report about Robert Finnegan, you have spelled his last name with an extra **n**.

PRACTICE   Italics (Underlining)

Rewrite each item, correcting errors in the use of italics (underlining) and other punctuation.

1. When I last saw Reynaldo, he was reading Shakespeare's a *Midsummer Night's Dream*.
2. *The New York Times* crossword puzzle is really tough today!
3. Please add an "and" to the title; it should read *Lisa and the Talking Turtle*.
4. Michelangelo's "David" is one of the most recognizable sculptures in the world.
5. The state motto of Connecticut is Qui Transtulit Sustinet ("He who transplanted still sustains").

PEANUTS reprinted by permission of United
Feature Syndicate, Inc.

11.11 THE APOSTROPHE

APOSTROPHES TO SHOW POSSESSION

Use an apostrophe and *–s* for the possessive form of a singular indefinite pronoun.

Do not use an apostrophe with other possessive pronouns.

EXAMPLES

everybody**'s** problem   *but*   **its** owner

each other**'s** parents   **whose** talents

one**'s** record   The bikes are **theirs.**

The prize is **yours.**

The plan is **ours.**

Use an apostrophe and *–s* to form the possessive of a singular noun, even one that ends in *s*.

EXAMPLES

the woman**'s** briefcase   San Francisco**'s** earthquake

the class**'s** election   Robert Burns**'s** poetry

There are some exceptions to this rule, however. To form the possessive of ancient proper nouns that end in *es* or *is*, the name *Jesus*, and expressions with words that end in an "ess" sound, such as *conscience* and *appearance*, just add an apostrophe.

EXAMPLES

Isis**'** temple   Jesus**'** teachings

Moses**'** brother   for appearance**'** sake

Euripides**'** plays   his conscience**'** prodding

Use an apostrophe alone to form the possessive of a plural noun that ends in *s*.

the two countries' treaty   the Joneses' picnic
the trees' leaves   the Greens' barbecue

> Use an apostrophe and –*s* to form the possessive of a plural noun that does not end in *s*.

women's clubs   children's videos
Women's Bar Association   oxen's harness
men's course   mice's tunnels

> Put only the last word of a compound noun in the possessive form.

my sister-in-law's office   an attorney general's job
the court-martial's officers   the chief of staff's order

> If two or more persons (or partners in a company) possess something jointly, use the possessive form for the last person named.

Barbara and Andy's children
Johnson and Johnson's baby-care products
Abbott and Costello's routines

> If two or more persons (or companies) possess an item (or items) individually, put each one's name in the possessive form.

Tina Turner's and the Rolling Stones' songs
Chrysler's and the American Motor Company's cars

> Use a possessive form to express amounts of money or time that modify a noun.

The modifier can also be expressed as a hyphenated adjective. In that case, no possessive form is used.

EXAMPLES		
one dollar's increase	*but*	a one-dollar increase
five minutes' drive		a five-minute drive
ten days' wait		a ten-day wait

APOSTROPHES IN CONTRACTIONS

> Use an apostrophe in place of letters that are omitted in contractions.

A **contraction** is a single word made up of two words that have been combined by omitting letters. Common contractions combine a subject and a verb or a verb and the word *not*.

EXAMPLES		
you'd	*is formed from*	you had, you would
you're		you are
who's		who is, who has
it's		it is, it has
won't		will not
I'm		I am
doesn't		does not

> Use an apostrophe in place of the omitted numerals of a year.

EXAMPLES	
the class of '99	the '96 presidential campaign

Rewrite each item, correcting errors in the use of the apostrophe and other punctuation.

1. That was one of Jerry Lewis' films, wasnt it?
2. This pen is mine; that one is your's.
3. The visitors from Jamaica were able to attend one of Congress' sessions.
4. Were you invited to the Harrises's New Years' Eve party?
5. Thats one of my mother-in-laws' hats.
6. "I Am a Rock" is one of Simon's and Garfunkel's songs.
7. Robert faced ten day's anxiety when he planted the pumpkin seeds.
8. Matts birthday is almost a year after Jans', but they both belong to the class of 0'0.
9. These children were all winner's in the national childrens' art contest.
10. Id have thought you'd be glad wer'e all going to the mall with you.

11.12 THE HYPHEN

HYPHENS WITH PREFIXES

A hyphen is not ordinarily used to join a prefix to a word. There are a few exceptions, however. If you are in doubt about using a hyphen, consult a dictionary. Also keep in mind the following guidelines:

Use a hyphen after any prefix joined to a proper noun or a proper adjective. Use a hyphen after the prefixes *all-*, *ex-* (meaning "former"), and *self-* joined to any noun or adjective.

mid-Atlantic	post-Elizabethan
pre-Renaissance	all-city
trans-Pacific	ex-coach
all-American	self-confidence

Use a hyphen after the prefix *anti-* when it joins a word beginning with *i*. Also use a hyphen after the prefix *vice-*, except in *vice president*.

EXAMPLES anti-icing
vice-mayor
but vice president

Use a hyphen to avoid confusion between words beginning with *re-* that look alike but are different in meaning and pronunciation.

EXAMPLES re-cover the couch
re-store the supplies
re-lease the apartment

but

recover the ball at the ten-yard line
restore one's confidence
release the brake

HYPHENS WITH COMPOUNDS AND NUMBERS

Use a hyphen in a compound adjective that precedes a noun.

In general, a compound adjective that follows a noun is not hyphenated.

EXAMPLES

dark-green eyes	*but*	Her eyes are dark green.
a fifteen-year-old aunt		Her aunt is fifteen years old.
a well-liked reporter		That reporter is well liked.

Don't hyphenate an expression made up of an adverb that ends in *–ly* and an adjective.

EXAMPLES a nicely behaved dog   a fairly close race
         a slightly rusted exterior   a hastily written report

Hyphenate any spelled-out cardinal number (such as *twenty-one*) or ordinal number (such as *twenty-first*) up to *ninety-nine* or *ninety-ninth*.

EXAMPLES   sixty-four   **Sixty-four** tickets were sold.

           sixty-fourth   I was the **sixty-fourth** person to
                             buy a ticket.

           eighty-two   There were **eighty-two** in the
                             marching band.

           eighty-second   This is the **eighty-second** year of
                             the annual parade.

Hyphenate a fraction that is expressed in words.

EXAMPLE   one-eighth teaspoon

EXAMPLE   one-quarter cup

EXAMPLE   one-half of a pound

Hyphenate two numerals to indicate a span.

EXAMPLE   pages 30–56

EXAMPLE   1986–1996

When you use the word *from* before a span, use *to* rather than a hyphen. When you use *between* before a span, use *and* rather than a hyphen.

EXAMPLE   **from** 1986 **to** 1996

EXAMPLE   **between** 2:00 **and** 3:30 P.M.

HYPHENS TO DIVIDE WORDS AT THE END OF A LINE

Words are generally divided between syllables or pronounceable parts. Because it is often difficult to decide where a word should be divided, consult a dictionary.

In general, if a word contains two consonants occurring between two vowels or if it contains double consonants, divide the word between the two consonants.

EXAMPLES   mar-gin   prog-ress
                    lin-ger   sup-per
                    profes-sor   tomor-row

If a suffix has been added to a complete word that ends in two consonants, divide the word after the two consonants. Remember, the object is to make the hyphenated word easy to read and understand.

EXAMPLES   pull-ing   spelunk-er
                    harsh-ness   strong-est

PRACTICE Hyphens

Rewrite each item, correcting errors in the use of hyphens and other punctuation. Then make a list of all the italicized words, showing where each would be divided if it had to be broken at the end of a line.

1. Well, Jeremy, the Parthenon is a preRenaissance building, but the Eiffel Tower is definitely a postRenaissance *structure.*
2. My aunt Hana, a well respected member of our town, was chosen last night as Teacher of the Month.
3. Some Native American peoples in preColumbian America believed that the *Fountain* of Youth existed, but it was never found.

4. Hanh, it's *pointless* to sit here in silence when we could be having a *meaningful* conversation about the TransAlaska Pipeline.

5. Please recollect all the *yellow* ticket stubs, Angela.

11.13 ABBREVIATIONS

Abbreviations are shortened forms of words.

Abbreviations save space and time and prevent unnecessary wordiness. For instance, *M.D.* is more concise and easier to write than *Medical Doctor*. Most abbreviations have periods. If you are unsure of how to write an abbreviation, consult a dictionary.

Use only one period, not two, if an abbreviation that has a period occurs at the end of a sentence that would ordinarily take a period of its own.

If an abbreviation that has a period occurs at the end of a sentence that ends with a question mark or an exclamation point, use the abbreviation's period *and* the question mark or the exclamation point.

EXAMPLE   Gerry left at 8:00 A.M.

EXAMPLE   Did she really leave at 8:00 A.M.?

CAPITALIZING ABBREVIATIONS

Capitalize abbreviations of proper nouns.

EXAMPLES   37688 Lancaster **Blvd.**   **Rev.** Oral Roberts
           N. Michigan **Ave.**   **U.S.** Congress

Abbreviations of organizations and government agencies are often formed from the initial letters of the complete name. Such abbreviations, whether pronounced letter by letter or as words, don't have periods and are written with capital letters. Exceptions are *U.S.*, *U.S.A.*, and *Washington, D.C.*, which do have periods.

YWCA   **NAACP**   **IRS**   **CBS**   **NASA**   **UNICEF**

When abbreviating a person's first and middle names, leave a space after each initial.

E. B. White   **A. E.** Housman   **J.** Alfred Prufrock

Capitalize the following abbreviations related to dates and times.

A.D. (*anno Domini*, "in the year of the Lord" [since the birth of Christ]); place before the date: A.D. 5

B.C. (before Christ); place after the date: 1000 B.C.

B.C.E. (before the common era, equivalent to *B.C.*); place after the date: 164 B.C.E.

C.E. (common era; equivalent to *A.D.*); place after the date: 66 C.E.

A.M. (*ante meridiem*, "before noon"); place after exact times: 7:45 A.M.

P.M. (*post meridiem*, "after noon"); place after exact times: 2:30 P.M.

POSTAL ABBREVIATIONS

In ordinary prose, spell out state names. On envelopes, however, abbreviate state names using the two-letter abbreviations approved by the U. S. Postal Service.

A complete list of these abbreviations can be found in the Ready Reference section on pages 86–87.

Alaska   **AK**

Hawaii   **HI**

Maine   **ME**

Texas   **TX**

The postal abbreviation for the District of Columbia, for use on envelopes only, is **DC**. In ordinary prose, however, use periods to write **Washington, D.C.**

We moved from **Washington, D.C.,** to Baltimore.

ABBREVIATIONS OF TITLES AND UNITS OF MEASURE

Use abbreviations for some personal titles.

Titles such as *Mrs., Mr., Ms., Sr.,* and *Jr.* and those indicating professions and academic degrees *(Dr., Ph.D., M.A., B.S.)* are almost always abbreviated. Titles of government and military officials and members of the clergy are frequently abbreviated when used before a full name.

EXAMPLES **Mrs.** Roosevelt   **Sen.** Jesse Helms
          Harry Connick **Jr.**   **Gen.** Robert E. Lee
          Rosalyn Ying, **Ph.D.**   Myron Greene, **D.D.S.**

Abbreviate units of measure used with numerals in technical or scientific writing. Don't abbreviate them in ordinary prose.

The abbreviations that follow stand for both singular and plural units. Notice that the first list of abbreviations uses periods but the second does not.

EXAMPLES

U.S. SYSTEM		METRIC SYSTEM	
ft.	foot	cg	centigram
gal.	gallon	cl	centiliter
in.	inch	cm	centimeter
lb.	pound	g	gram
mi.	mile	kg	kilogram
oz.	ounce	km	kilometer
pt.	pint	l	liter
qt.	quart	m	meter
tbsp.	tablespoon	mg	milligram
tsp.	teaspoon	ml	milliliter
yd.	yard	mm	millimeter

Rewrite each item, correcting errors in the use of abbreviations and punctuation.

1. The envelope read as follows:
      W.H. Cadrain
      104 Concord St
      Hamden, C.T. 06514

2. Please be here by 6:15 AM.

3. What happened in 313 A.D?

4. The Greek civilization reached its height between B.C 500 and 400 BC.

5. Major Harmon moved from Goldsboro, N.C., to Washington, DC. in 1998.

6. The label on the medicine read, "Take 200 m.g. of this antibiotic three times a day."

7. The last sentence in Kumar's lab report said, "The experiment produced three-fourths lb, or slightly more than one-third k.g., of water."

8. I addressed the envelope to
      The Nature Conservancy
      1815 N. Lynn St
      Arlington, Va. 22209

9. C.B.S. stands for "Columbia Broadcasting System."

10. W.C. Fields was a popular comedian in early films.

For more information on abbreviations, see pages 82–89 in the Ready Reference.

11.14 NUMBERS AND NUMERALS

In nontechnical writing, some numbers are spelled out, and some are expressed in figures. Numbers expressed in figures are called *numerals*.

NUMBERS SPELLED OUT

In general, spell out cardinal numbers (such as *twenty*) and ordinal numbers (such as *twentieth*) that can be written in one or two words.

EXAMPLE   New Hampshire is one of the original **thirteen** colonies.

EXAMPLE   There are **fifteen hundred** students in the school.

EXAMPLE   Alaska was the **forty-ninth** state to join the Union.

Spell out any number that occurs at the beginning of a sentence. (Sometimes, it is better to revise the sentence to move the spelled-out number.)

EXAMPLE   **Sixteen hundred seventy** delegates attended the conference.

BETTER   The conference was attended by 1670 delegates.

NUMERALS

In general, use numerals to express numbers that would be written in more than two words.

EXAMPLE   Mount Mitchell, the highest mountain in the eastern United States, is **6,684** feet high.

EXAMPLE   In 1790 the total population of the United States (according to the first census) was **3,929,214.**

EXAMPLE   In 1984 Joe W. Kittinger covered **3,535** miles in eighty-three hours and fifty-three minutes, setting a new record for balloon flight.

Very large numbers are often written as a numeral followed by the word *million* or *billion*.

EXAMPLE   The surface area of the earth is close to **197 million** square miles.

If related numbers appear in the same sentence and some can be written out while others should appear as numerals, use all numerals.

EXAMPLE   Edgar ranked **5th** in the class; his brother ranked **119th.**

EXAMPLE   They ordered **38** dollhouses and **112** toy robots.

Use numerals to express amounts of money, decimals, and percentages. Spell out the word *percent*, however.

EXAMPLES   **$897** million   **1.2** kilograms   **5** percent

Amounts of money that can be expressed in one or two words, however, should be spelled out.

EXAMPLE   **forty-five** cents   a **thousand** dollars

Use numerals to express the year and day in a date and to express the precise time with the abbreviations A.M. and P.M.

EXAMPLE   The USSR launched *Sputnik I* on October **4, 1957.**

EXAMPLE   She reached the doctor's office at **4:15** P.M.

Spell out expressions of time that do not use A.M. or P.M.

EXAMPLE   She set her alarm clock for **five** o'clock.

To express a century when the word *century* is used, spell out the number. Likewise, to express a decade when the century is clear from the context, spell out the number.

EXAMPLE   The **twentieth** century saw great technological advances.

EXAMPLE   The Great Depression of the **thirties** was an economic crisis.

When a decade is identified by its century, use numerals followed by an *–s.*

1980s   the **1940s** and **1950s**

Use numerals for numbered streets and avenues above ninety-nine and for all house, apartment, and room numbers. Spell out numbered streets and avenues of ninety-nine and below.

EXAMPLE   **1654** West **347th** Street

EXAMPLE   **4** North **Ninety-ninth** Street

EXAMPLE   Apartment **8C**

EXAMPLE   **20 Second** Avenue

PRACTICE   Numbers and Numerals

Rewrite each item, correcting errors in the use of numbers, numerals, and punctuation.

1. In 1996 Portland, Oregon, had a population of about four hundred eighty-one thousand people.
2. At that time Portland was the 27th largest city in the United States.
3. What is 5% of 60?
4. Richard Brinsley Sheridan was an acclaimed dramatist whose best-known works were produced after seventeen hundred seventy-five.
5. A biography of Vincent Van Gogh can be found on pages 63–sixty-five in your textbook.
6. South Dakota has a total land area of about seventy-seven thousand square miles.
7. That publishing house is located at Seven hundred fifty-seven 3rd Avenue in New York City.
8. 4,700 Elks attended the convention in Pittsburgh.

9. The International Monetary Fund loaned $16,000,000,000 dollars to the new government.

10. The 21st century began with both fear and celebration.

PRACTICE Proofreading

Rewrite the following passage, correcting errors in spelling, capitalization, grammar, and usage. Add any missing punctuation. There are ten errors. Some sentences are correct.

Edgar Allan Poe

[1]Edgar Allan Poe was born in Boston Massachusetts in eighteen hundred nine. [2]Orphaned when he was three years old, he was adopted by John Allan, a tobacco exporter. [3]Although Mr Allan wanted him to study law. [4]The boy was determined to have a literary career. [5]Throughout his life, however, Poe always used his full middle name, Allan, as a token of gratitude to his adoptive father. [6]His first book; "Tamerlane and Other Poems," was published in 1827. [7]He worked as a journalist in Richmond, Virginia, and then moved to Philadelphia, where his work appeared in literary journals. [8]In 1841 he published "The Murders in the Rue Morgue," which is now celebrated as the first detective story. [9]In 1844 he moved to New York City, and imediately became famous for his poem "The Raven." [10]His style used classical themes mixed with a flair for dramatic horror, passionate suspense and grotesque justice. [11]Poe received so little money for his work, however, that often he and his young wife went without food. [12]By 1845 Poe had begun to be recognized as a major American author, yet he was nearly penniless. [13]When his wife died in 1847 Poe began a downhill spiral that ended in his own death in 1849.

POSTTEST Punctuation

Rewrite each sentence, correcting any errors in punctuation.

1. Jamal, please ask Annette to see me before she goes home?

2. Ouch. How many pots and pans just fell on me.

3. No one knew that "Jimmy was hiding in the closet"

4. You,ll need the following supplies for the standardized test, two pencils with erasers, a compass and a protractor.

5. Salvador is a great swimmer, he also runs in the two-hundred(meter track event.

6. The highest mountains in the world are as follows; Everest, a mountain in the Himalayas, K2 also known as Godwin-Austen in the Karakoram range in Kashmir. and Kanchenjunga in the Himalayas of Nepal and India?

7. Its hard enough to move a piano once, removing the same piano is too much!

8. Settled in his bed at last Kyutaro tried to relax.

9. The actor in the gorilla suit climbed a tree but he couldnt get down again.

10. Well you have to have lunch, still if you eat a healthful salad for lunch every day youl'l eventually fit into your good jeans again.

11. In the north corner of the attic Johanna found the dusty wooden trunk that had once belonged to her grandmother.

12. That was nice climbing Judy! Next time youll take the shingles up there with you (right)?

13. The bear it was a small black bear uttered a growl that I interpreted as a warning.

14. Dons sister I mean his little sister filled the freezer with snowballs she wanted to have a snowball fight on july fourth.

15. Tomás said "Yes Ill go with you; Pedro on the other hand refused to make the commitment.

16. What has happened to the USS "Ohio?"

17. One of John Donne's songs begins *Go, and catch a falling star.*

18. Yes it was Julius Caesar who said Veni, Vidi, Vici.

GRAMMAR/USAGE/MECHANICS

19. You need an "and" in that sentence Susan or it wont' make sense.

20. There was a two days wait at the motor vehicle bureau for a chauffeurs license.

POSTTEST Abbreviations and Numbers

Rewrite each item, correcting any errors in the use of abbreviations and numbers.

21. The founder of the Ringling Brothers and Barnum & Bailey Circus was PT Barnum.

22. What happened in bc 44?

23. Does Alaska or Alabama use the postal abbreviation al?

24. Did the package label read 5 gal or 19 l.?

25. The total land area of Portugal is eighty-eight thousand nine hundred forty-one sq k.m. or thirty-four thousand three hundred forty sq mi.

26. As the one thousand nine hundred ninety-second customer at First Bank in 1992, Mr Carlson won one thousand nine hundred ninety-two dollars.

27. What happened on nov 22 1963?

28. When did the 21st century begin?

29. Yes, Kara lives at 326 e 65 st.

30. Please read pages thirty-five through forty-eight tonight and be ready to discuss the material tomorrow.

Chapter 12

Sentence Combining

● ● ● ● ● ● ● ● ● ● ● ● ● ● ● ●

PRETEST   **Sentence Combining**

Read each group of sentences below. Combine the sentences in the way that seems best to you.

1. Jacob isn't in school today. He has the flu.
2. Have you heard? Antwan was in Florida.
3. I heard Kazuo's Jeep. It was bumping along the logging road.
4. That spider is huge. It's on the ceiling.
5. Jaime went to Six Flags Over Mid-America. He is a roller-coaster nut. He rode the coaster seven times.
6. I can't help you, Helen. I'm not very good at math.
7. Have you paid the bill? I ordered a Steelers sweatshirt. I ordered it last month.

8. Where is my book? I was reading it. It was the book for my literature class.

9. Janene enjoyed her seafood dinner. It was a prize. It was an all-you-can-eat meal.

10. I visited my grandmother. She's in a convalescent hospital. It was one of the hardest things I've ever done.

11. This is the pen I use for writing. It has a very fine point. I use it for drawing, too.

12. I wander down this path in good weather. Sandy walks with me. We cross the bridge. Then we go into the forest beyond.

13. The rabbit scampered away. It disappeared at the edge of the lake. It disappeared into the tall grass.

14. That's a strange costume. I've never seen one like it.

15. Where did Paul go? He left football practice early.

16. I'll finish the dinner. Judi, you may set the table.

17. Silk-screened posters are not difficult to make. You just need some practice.

18. Where's my dress, Mom? I wore it to the spring dance.

19. I've saved some money. Maybe I can afford a car. I saw a used Mustang in Martindale.

20. Earlier Cardiff's was very busy. Now no one is here.

12.1 TIPS FOR SENTENCE COMBINING

A distinctive writing style is one way of communicating your personality. Developing a clear, expressive writing style requires practice, of course. By writing regularly in your journal and by trying out different kinds of writing—poems, essays, stories, letters to the editor—you practice a range of skills. Another excellent approach for developing style is sentence combining.

The process of combining short sentences into more complex ones is the focus of this chapter. Your goal, though, is not to make long sentences, but to make good ones. Sometimes you'll find that longer, complex sentences let you express your ideas clearly and precisely. At other times, shorter is better.

Sentence combining is easy and fun. Here are some suggestions that have worked for other high school students—suggestions you might try as you explore your style.

1. **Whisper sentences to yourself.** This is faster than writing, and it helps you decide on the best sentence to write down.
2. **Work with a partner.** By trying out sentences on a partner and hearing your partner's ideas, you often discover new, interesting ways to solve specific challenges. Feel free to borrow ideas.
3. **Use context when choosing sentences for a paragraph.** Each paragraph has an emerging context: the sentences you have already combined. Reading this context aloud helps you decide on the best next sentence.
4. **Compare your sentences with those of other students.** Seeing how others have solved combining tasks broadens your awareness of sentence options. Keep asking yourself, "Which do I prefer?"
5. **Look for stylistic patterns in your writing.** Calculate the average number of words per sentence; study your sentence openers; listen to rhythms in your style. Try new patterns to stretch yourself.
6. **Take risks.** It makes good sense to take risks and make mistakes as you combine sentences. Mistakes provide feedback. As you learn from them, you develop a personal style, a voice. You come to know yourself as a writer.

The point of sentence combining is to improve your revising and editing skills. Practice in combining sentences helps you see that sentences are flexible tools for thought, not rigid structures cast in concrete. The simple fact that you feel confident in moving sentence parts around increases your control of revising and editing. To acquire this sense of self-confidence—based on your real competence in combining and revising sentences—try strategies like these:

1. **Vary the length of your sentences.** Work for a rhythmic, interesting balance of long and short sentences, remembering that short sentences can be dramatic.
2. **Vary the structure of your sentences.** By using sentence openers occasionally and by sometimes tucking information into the middle of a sentence, you can create stylistic interest.
3. **Use parallelism for emphasis.** Experiment with repeated items in a series—words, phrases, clauses.
4. **Use interruption for emphasis.** Commas, colons, semicolons, dashes, parentheses—all of these are useful in your stylistic toolkit.
5. **Use unusual patterns for emphasis.** That you might sometimes reverse normal sentence patterns may never have occurred to you, but it can strengthen your writing.

You'll use these four main strategies when you combine sentences:

- deleting repeated words
- adding connecting words
- rearranging words
- changing the form of words

12.2 COMBINING SENTENCES BY INSERTING WORDS

When two sentences talk about the same idea, sometimes you can effectively combine them simply by taking a word from one sentence and inserting it into the other sentence. Occasionally the word or words you are inserting must change form.

ORIGINAL VERSION	COMBINED VERSION
The breeze brought the fragrance of spring flowers. The breeze was light. The fragrance was welcome.	The **light** breeze brought the **welcome** fragrance of spring flowers. [**no change in form**]
A gas log burned in the fireplace. Its burning was cheerful.	A gas log burned **cheerfully** in the fireplace. [**The adjective** *cheerful* **changes to the adverb** *cheerfully*.]

GRAMMAR/USAGE/MECHANICS

PRACTICE Combining Sentences by Inserting Words

Read each group of sentences below. Combine the sentences by inserting a word or words.

1. The day started out. It was bright. It was sunshiny.
2. The stew was thick. It was flavorful.
3. Would you like to take this class? It's a cooking class.
4. The cat sniffed at my boots. The cat was curious.
5. Mara's dress was red and black. The dress was new.
6. The team members slapped their good-luck symbol before they loped onto the field. They slapped it one by one.
7. Do you think the Bears will do well this season? Why?
8. The teenagers danced to the new song. Their dancing was energetic.
9. The daffodils looked delicate. They bobbed on long stems.
10. The pizza was ready to be cut. The pizza was colorful. The pizza was sputtering.

12.3 COMBINING SENTENCES BY INSERTING PHRASES

Another way to combine sentences is to insert a phrase from one sentence into another sentence. Sometimes you can use the phrase unchanged; at other times, you must turn the words into a phrase. The most useful phrases for this purpose are prepositional phrases, appositive phrases, and participial phrases.

GRAMMAR/USAGE/MECHANICS

PREPOSITIONAL PHRASES

ORIGINAL VERSION	COMBINED VERSION
Left behind was a single shoe. It was under the bed.	Left behind **under the bed** was a single shoe. [no change]
The job applicant answered the interviewer's questions. Her smile was nervous.	**With a nervous smile,** the job applicant answered the interviewer's questions. [The second sentence is changed into a prepositional phrase.]

NOTE: For more information on prepositional phrases, see pages 147–148.

PRACTICE **Combining Sentences by Inserting Prepositional Phrases**

Read each group of sentences below. Combine the sentences by inserting phrases.

1. The float is nearly ready. It's for this year's homecoming parade.
2. Against the mirror was the letter that Ruby was expecting. It was from her father.

3. Mom made a full breakfast in ten minutes. She was in a frenzy of activity.

4. Odell caught the pass and made the touchdown. He did it with a surprising burst of speed.

5. Marcel looked out the window. It was at the break of dawn.

6. The child opened the box. Her fingers were trembling.

7. Inside was a small gold locket. It had a delicate golden chain.

8. Asunción kissed her mother for the last time. She did it in sorrow.

9. The day was clear and bright. There was a touch of spring in the air.

10. Mark read *Farewell to Manzanar.* He did it with a tremendous sense of guilt. His guilt was on behalf of his country.

APPOSITIVE PHRASES
● ● ● ● ● ● ● ● ● ● ● ● ● ● ● ● ● ●

ORIGINAL VERSION	COMBINED VERSION
Zora Neale Hurston's best-known novel is about an independent African American woman. It is called *Their Eyes Were Watching God.*	Zora Neale Hurston's best-known novel, ***Their Eyes Were Watching God,*** is about an independent African American woman.
	or
	Their Eyes Were Watching God, **Zora Neale Hurston's best-known novel,** is about an independent African American woman.

NOTE: For more information on appositive phrases, see pages 149–150.

Read each group of sentences below. Combine the sentences by inserting appositive phrases.

1. The light fell on Toni's upturned face. The light was clear and bright.
2. I find one of Keats's poems especially beautiful. It is "Ode on a Grecian Urn."
3. Aunt Grace turned and looked at Tom. She was thin and pale.
4. This new book seems to offer some hope for curing Grandma's arthritis. It is *The New Arthritis Breakthrough.*
5. Dan breezed into the classroom. He seemed confident and eager.
6. Mr. Hanamoto is the featured speaker at our technology seminar. He is Saburo's father.
7. The antique clock had been tucked away for years in the attic. It was dusty and worn.
8. Have you met my aunt? Her name is Hilda Lorenson.
9. Which elective do you think you'll take next semester? Will you choose French or Spanish?
10. Soledad accepted the honor with humility and poise. She is the new student body president.

PARTICIPIAL PHRASES

ORIGINAL VERSION	COMBINED VERSION
Moriah was doing a lazy sidestroke toward the raft. She felt her worries slip away.	**Doing a lazy sidestroke toward the raft,** Moriah felt her worries slip away.

or

	Moriah, **doing a lazy side-stroke toward the raft,** felt her worries slip away.
Small whitecaps were formed by the rising wind. The whitecaps glinted in the sun.	**Formed by the rising wind,** small whitecaps glinted in the sun.
	or
	Small whitecaps **formed by the rising wind** glinted in the sun.

NOTE: For more information on participial phrases, see pages 151–152.

see pages 151–152.

PRACTICE **Combining Sentences by Inserting Participial Phrases**

Read each group of sentences below. Using participial phrases, combine the sentences.

1. Megan rushed to help the victims. She had witnessed the auto accident only moments before.
2. Chung Sook watched his sister. She was walking away.
3. The salesperson glared at Sandra. He was tapping his foot.
4. Trenell looked at Marvella. His face was etched with concern.
5. Edgar Allan Poe died penniless. He had been poorly paid for his writing.
6. The eight-year-olds danced around their fort. It was made of hard-packed snow.
7. Sally reached into her purse. She was looking for her sunglasses.
8. Natasha wandered along the seashore. She found a cowrie shell that had washed up on the sand.

9. The Creek chief was impressed by his son's bravery. He declared him a warrior.
10. Iowa is known as the Corn State. It is one of the leading producers of corn in the United States.

12.4 COMBINING SENTENCES USING COORDINATION

To combine sentences that have equally important ideas, you can form compound sentence parts such as compound subjects, compound predicates, or compound objects by using a coordinating conjunction *(and, but, or, so, nor, for, yet)*. To form compound sentences, you can use one of those conjunctions or a pair of correlative conjunctions *(both . . . and, just as . . . so, not only . . . but (also), either . . . or, neither . . . nor, whether . . . or)*. As an alternative to using conjunctions to join the independent clauses, you could use a semicolon with or without a conjunctive adverb, such as *however, consequently,* and *furthermore.*

ORIGINAL VERSION	COMBINED VERSION
I need to fix our lunches. I also need to collect my homework.	I need to fix our lunches **and** collect my homework.
He wants to learn how to dance the tango. If not the tango, then he wants to learn to dance the rumba.	He wants to learn to dance the tango **or** the rumba.
Carla is only ten years old. She is a terrific chess player, however.	Carla is only ten years old, **but** she is a terrific chess player.
Painting the house is not all we will do. We will also repair the gutters and downspouts.	We will **not only** paint the house **but also** repair the gutters and downspouts.
The coat that I want costs more than I have. I will put it in layaway and pay ten dollars a week.	The coat that I want costs more than I have**; therefore,** I will put it in layaway and pay ten dollars a week.

NOTE: For more information on coordinating ideas, see pages 133–134 and page 173.

PRACTICE **Combining Sentences Using Coordination**

Read each group of sentences below. Combine the sentences using compound sentence parts or compound sentences.

1. Enrico enjoys hiking. He likes camping, too.
2. I sent a birthday card to Bob. However, he never got it.
3. Has your address changed? Is the card lost in the mail?
4. Dad and I may paint the house this summer. Dad may have aluminum siding put on the house instead.
5. Angela has just moved to this school district. She is not eligible for the varsity team yet.
6. Richard likes salted peanuts on chocolate sundaes. He also likes to eat potato chips with a chocolate milkshake.
7. Marc is just learning to skate. He can't turn yet. He can't stop, either.
8. Shawna likes science a lot. She can't stand math.
9. I'm worried about Tomás. He won't eat right. He won't take his medicine.
10. Darlene is petite. She's a great volleyball player, though.

12.5 COMBINING SENTENCES USING SUBORDINATION

Sometimes the ideas in two sentences are not equally important. Instead, one idea is more important than the other. You can combine these kinds of sentences by making the less important idea into a subordinate clause.

ADVERB CLAUSES

One kind of subordinate clause is an adverb clause, a clause that is introduced by a subordinating conjunction. An adverb clause modifies a verb, an adjective, or another adverb in the main clause. Following are some subordinating conjunctions you might use to show the relationship between the two clauses.

SUBORDINATING CONJUNCTIONS	
FOR EXPRESSING TIME RELATIONSHIPS	after, as, as soon as, before, since, so long as, until, when, whenever, while
FOR EXPRESSING PLACE RELATIONSHIPS	as far as, where, wherever
FOR EXPRESSING CAUSE-AND-EFFECT RELATIONSHIPS	as, because, since, so (that)
FOR EXPRESSING CONDITIONAL RELATIONSHIPS	although, as if, as long as, as though, considering (that), if, inasmuch as, in order that, provided (that), since, so (that), than, though, unless, whereas

In the following examples, some of the techniques you have already seen are used along with subordinating conjunctions to combine several sentences into one. Study the examples to see how the techniques can be used together.

ORIGINAL VERSION	COMBINED VERSION
Rain began to fall in drops. The drops were fat. Trees swayed like dancers. Trees jerked like dancers. The dancers were frantic.	**As** rain began to fall in fat drops, trees swayed and jerked like frantic dancers.
She had made her decision. Her decision was not to see him again. His apologies had been weak. His apologies had been pathetic.	She had made her decision not to see him again **because** his apologies had been weak and pathetic.

Suntans may suggest good health. They seriously damage your skin. They destroy its elastic fibers.	**Although** suntans may suggest good health, they seriously damage your skin by destroying its elastic fibers.

NOTE: For more information on using subordinating conjunctions in adverb clauses, see pages 168–169.

PRACTICE **Combining Sentences Using Subordination: Adverb Clauses**

Read each group of sentences below. Using adverb clauses, combine the sentences.

1. You have to finish your homework, Reynaldo. Then you may call Danielle.
2. Steve forgot to study. He may have failed the geometry test.
3. Jamyce has the wrong information. Coretta is right.
4. You may move. I will always be your friend.
5. You may go out with Dan. You must be back by eleven o'clock.
6. Mom has to work. I cook dinner.
7. I like the works of most American authors. I don't like Faulkner's at all.
8. Donna is moving away. I don't care.
9. Isabel has three cats. She must love animals.
10. You're here. Let's work on our project.

ADJECTIVE CLAUSES

An adjective clause is a subordinate clause that modifies a noun or a pronoun in the main clause. To combine ideas using an adjective clause, replace the subject of one sentence with the word *who, whose, which,* or *that.*

ORIGINAL VERSION	COMBINED VERSION
Octavio Paz was a diplomat, a teacher, an author, and a poet. He stood at the top of Mexican literature throughout the twentieth century.	Octavio Paz, **who stood at the top of Mexican literature throughout the twentieth century,** was a diplomat, a teacher, an author, and a poet.
	or
	Octavio Paz, **who was a diplomat, a teacher, an author, and a poet,** stood at the top of Mexican literature throughout the twentieth century.
Paz taught at Texas, Harvard, and Cambridge universities. His *Collected Poems* was published in 1987.	Paz, **whose *Collected Poems* was published in 1987,** taught at Texas, Harvard, and Cambridge universities.
Paz's *Collected Poems* offers a unique view of a poet's mind. I read the book of poems last summer.	Paz's *Collected Poems*, **which I read last summer,** offers a unique view of a poet's mind.
	or
	Last summer I read Paz's *Collected Poems*, **which offers a unique view of a poet's mind.**

NOTE: For more information on adjective clauses, see pages 167–168.

PRACTICE **Combining Sentences Using Subordination: Adjective Clauses**

Read each group of sentences below. Using adjective clauses, combine the sentences.

1. Eastern North Carolina gets its share of hurricanes. It's not the place to be during August and September.

2. The state is on the Atlantic seaboard. It is prone to thunderstorms and lightning.

3. The skateboard looks well used. I donated the skateboard to the neighborhood recreation center.
4. I gave Patwin a memory box for his birthday. It is made of maple.
5. Gates of the Arctic National Park is in north-central Alaska. The park features a mountain range, tundra, winding rivers, broad valleys, and glacial lakes.
6. The gift is for Kamla. Its bow has sequins and glitter.
7. Edvard Grieg wrote the *Peer Gynt Suite.* He was a native of Bergen, Norway.
8. Grieg's quaint house can still be seen near Bergen. It is a monument to his simple life and his love of Norwegian folklore.
9. The name *England* means "Land of the Angles." England has been inhabited since well before Roman times.
10. The British empire reached its height during the Victorian Age. It is smaller now but still strong.

NOUN CLAUSES

A noun clause is a subordinate clause used as a noun. To combine ideas using a noun clause, begin one sentence with one of the words in the following chart. (It will probably be necessary to change some other words in the sentence.) Then put the noun clause you have made into another sentence.

WORDS THAT CAN INTRODUCE NOUN CLAUSES

how	whatever	which	whoever
that	when	whichever	whose
what	where	who, whom	why

ORIGINAL VERSION	COMBINED VERSION
He never learned something. He can't change the oil in his car.	He never learned **how to change the oil in his car.** [noun clause acting as direct object]
They want to hang rings from their noses. The reason for this is a mystery to their elders.	**Why they want to hang rings from their noses** is a mystery to their elders. [noun clause acting as subject]
Someone hires lifeguards. Send your application to him or her.	Send your application to **whoever hires lifeguards.** [noun clause acting as object of the preposition *to*]

NOTE: For more information on noun clauses, see pages 169–170.

PRACTICE **Combining Sentences Using Subordination: Noun Clauses**

Read each group of sentences below. Using noun clauses, combine the sentences.

1. Someone deserves a prize. It's the person who wrote that essay.
2. What made Edward sick? Let's try to find out.
3. Wesley can write exquisite poetry. It is a source of satisfaction to him.
4. The Sage Award goes to a senior. He or she must be the student showing the most improvement over four years.
5. The students still remember Eugene Sage. The award is named for him.
6. You know something about the incident. It should be shared with the principal.

7. Rafael sent the certificate to a freshman. Are you that person?

8. Where did Elijah go? He left after math class. It's a mystery.

9. Who will the class scholar be? It's always the person with the highest average.

10. When will the award be presented? No one knows.

PRACTICE **Combining Sentences Using Subordination**

Read each group of sentences below. Combine the sentences using adverb clauses, adjective clauses, or noun clauses.

1. Scientists once thought the dawn redwood was extinct. Several specimens were found in China.

2. Ellen wants to be a veterinarian. Her cat just had eight kittens.

3. Josephine's mother is the best cook in Minneapolis. I'm not surprised at that.

4. Spotted Tail was a nineteenth-century leader of the Sioux. He supported peaceful relations between the Sioux and the settlers.

5. The present-day Sioux in South Dakota named their community college after Spotted Tail. They used his Sioux name, *Sinte Gleska.*

6. Who chose Stuttgart as the capital of Baden-Württemberg, Germany? He or she did the entire region a favor.

7. The New Palace served as a residence of several dukes and kings of Württemberg. It is built in the baroque and rococo styles.

8. Why is Paulo late? I don't know.

9. William is fine. That's all I know.

10. Please bring me a cold drink. You're already up.

The following passages are about the writers Maya Angelou and Anton Chekhov. Rewrite each passage, combining sentences that are closely related in meaning.

Maya Angelou

Maya Angelou was born in 1928. She was born in St. Louis, Missouri. Angelou has been a successful singer. She has been a successful dancer. She has been a successful activist for African American rights. She has been a successful author. Angelou toured in the Gershwin musical *Porgy and Bess*. The tour took place in Europe and in Africa. She was editor of *African Review* for several years. That was in Ghana. In 1970 she published the first volume of her autobiography. Her autobiography's first volume is called *I Know Why the Caged Bird Sings*.

Anton Chekhov

Anton Chekhov was born in 1860. He was born in Taganrog, Ukraine. As a young man, he studied in Moscow to be a doctor. At the age of twenty-six, he published his first book of short stories. At that time, he was still a medical student. The book of short stories was successful. He soon began to think of himself as a writer rather than a medical student. All his life, he wrote brilliant short stories. Indeed, even today Chekhov is regarded as a master of the short story genre. He next tried to write full-length plays. However, it took him a long time to master playwrighting. *The Seagull* was his first successful play. *The Seagull* was written when he was thirty-six. Three more theatrical masterpieces followed in the next eight years. The masterpieces were *Uncle Vanya, The Three Sisters,* and *The Cherry Orchard. The Cherry Orchard* was published in 1904. That was the year he died of tuberculosis.

Read each group of sentences. Combine the sentences in the way that seems best to you.

1. We have the day off. I'm going swimming.
2. This is a souvenir. I bought it in Mexico.
3. You'll be on your way home. We need eggs, milk, and hamburger buns.
4. Here's the poster. It's for the spring dance. It's silk-screened.
5. Leonora plays the lead in our drama. She's an excellent actress.
6. I'm not much of a mechanic, Sal. I'll look at your car anyway. Maybe I can fix it.
7. Has anyone seen my tennis shoes? They're new.
8. The members of the Polar Bears Club swim in the ocean on New Year's Day. It's beyond me.
9. You all know Mr. Atkinson's work. He designed our new gymnasium.
10. I used to swim. I swam in Long Island Sound. It was so much fun!
11. I'll call you. I'll be leaving the office.
12. Who will be the athlete of the month? It's a member of the football team. He made the most touchdowns.
13. The stew bubbled on the stove. It foamed. Then it boiled over.
14. I loved that coat. It was the one you bought for me. Now it's lost.
15. How has Amy been? She came down with the measles last week.
16. Please cook the rice, Eleanor. I'll prepare the curry.
17. You'll learn to play the clarinet, Tomás. You'll have to practice every day.
18. I'll never understand it. Why do kids do such dangerous things?
19. Sheila works in the fast-food restaurant. She was fifteen when she started working there.
20. That Saint Bernard belongs to Max. He's a beautiful dog.

Chapter 13

Spelling and Vocabulary

● ● ● ● ● ● ● ● ● ● ● ● ● ● ●

13.1 SPELLING RULES

The following rules, examples, and exceptions will help you master the spelling of many words. However, not all words follow the rules. When you're not sure how to spell a word, the best thing to do is check a dictionary.

Spelling *ie* and *ei*

An easy way to learn when to use *ie* and when to use *ei* is to memorize a simple rhyming rule. Then learn the common exceptions to the rule.

RULE	EXAMPLES
"WRITE *I* BEFORE *E*	achieve, believe, brief, chief, die, field, friend, grief, lie, niece, piece, pier, quiet, retrieve, sieve, tie, tier, yield
EXCEPT AFTER *C*	ceiling, conceit, conceive, deceit, deceive, receipt, receive
OR WHEN SOUNDED LIKE *A*, AS IN *NEIGHBOR* AND *WEIGH*."	eight, eighth, eighty, freight, neigh, reign, sleigh, veil, vein, weigh, weight

Some exceptions: *either, caffeine, foreign, forfeit, height, heir, leisure, neither, protein, seize, species, their, weird*; words ending in *cient (ancient)* and *cience (conscience)*; plurals of nouns ending in *cy (democracies)*; the third-person singular form of verbs ending in *cy (fancies)*; words in which *i* and *e* follow *c* but represent separate sounds *(science, society)*

Words Ending in *cede, ceed,* and *sede*

The only English word ending in *sede* is *supersede.* Three words end in *ceed: proceed, exceed,* and *succeed.* You can remember these three words by thinking of the following sentence:

If you **proceed** to **exceed** the speed limit, you will **succeed** in getting a ticket.

All other words ending with the "seed" sound are spelled with *cede: concede, intercede, precede, recede, secede.*

Spelling Unstressed Vowels

Listen to the vowel sound in the second syllable of the word *or-i-gin.* This is an unstressed vowel sound. Unstressed vowel sounds can be spelled in many ways. Dictionary respellings use the schwa (ə) to indicate an unstressed vowel sound.

To spell a word that has an unstressed vowel sound, think of a related word in which the syllable containing the vowel sound is stressed.

The word *original*, for example, should help you spell the word *origin*. The chart shows some other examples.

SPELLING UNSTRESSED VOWELS

UNKNOWN SPELLING	RELATED WORD	WORD SPELLED CORRECTLY
leg_l	le**gal**ity	legal
fant_sy	fan**tas**tic	fantasy
host_le	hos**til**ity	hostile
opp_site	op**pose**	opposite
def_nite	de**fine**	definite

Adding Prefixes

To add prefixes, keep the spelling of the root word and add the prefix. If the last letter of the prefix is the same as the first letter of the word, keep both letters.

un- + happy = unhappy

dis- + appear = disappear

re- + enlist = reenlist

mis- + spell = misspell

co- + operate = cooperate

il- + legal = illegal

un- + natural = unnatural

im- + migrate = immigrate

Adding Suffixes

When you add a suffix beginning with a vowel, double the final consonant if the word ends in a **single consonant preceded by a single vowel** *and*

- the word has one syllable

mud + -y = muddy   sad + -er = sadder

put + -ing = putting   stop + -ed = stopped

- the word is stressed on the last syllable and the stress remains on the same syllable after the suffix is added

occur + -ence = occurrence

regret + -able = regrettable

begin + -ing = beginning

repel + -ent = repellent

commit + -ed = committed

refer + -al = referral

Don't double the final consonant if the word is not stressed on the last syllable or if the stress shifts when the suffix is added.

murmur + -ed = murmured

refer + -ence = reference

Don't double the final letter if the word ends in *s, w, x,* or *y: gases, rowing, waxy, employer.*

Don't double the final consonant before the suffix *-ist* if the word has more than one syllable: *druggist* but *violinist, guitarist.*

Adding suffixes to words that end in *y* can cause spelling problems. Study the following rules and note the exceptions.

When a word ends in **a vowel and *y,*** keep the *y.*

---

play + -s = plays   joy + -ous = joyous

obey + -ed = obeyed   annoy + -ance = annoyance

buy + -ing = buying   enjoy + -ment = enjoyment

employ + -er = employer	enjoy + -able = enjoyable
joy + -ful = joyful	boy + -ish = boyish
joy + -less = joyless	coy + -ly = coyly

SOME EXCEPTIONS: gay + -ly = gaily, day + -ly = daily, pay + -d = paid, lay + -d = laid, say + -d = said

When a word ends in **a consonant and y,** change the y to *i* before any suffix that doesn't begin with *i.* Keep the *y* before suffixes that begin with *i.*

carry + -es = carries	deny + -al = denial
dry + -ed = dried	rely + -able = reliable
easy + -er = easier	mercy + -less = merciless
merry + -ly = merrily	likely + -hood = likelihood
happy + -ness = happiness	accompany + -ment =
beauty + -ful = beautiful	accompaniment
fury + -ous = furious	carry + -ing = carrying
defy + -ant = defiant	baby + -ish = babyish
vary + -ation = variation	lobby + -ist = lobbyist

SOME EXCEPTIONS: shy + -ly = shyly, dry + -ly = dryly, shy + -ness = shyness, dry + -ness = dryness, biology + -ist = biologist, economy + -ist = economist, baby + -hood = babyhood

Usually a **final silent e** is dropped before a suffix, but sometimes it's kept. The following chart shows the basic rules for adding suffixes to words that end in silent e.

RULE	EXAMPLES
Drop the *e* before suffixes that begin with a vowel.	care + -ed = cared dine + -ing = dining move + -er = mover type + -ist = typist blue + -ish = bluish arrive + -al = arrival desire + -able = desirable accuse + -ation = accusation noise + -y = noisy
Some exceptions	mile + -age = mileage dye + -ing = dyeing
Drop the *e* and change *i* to *y* before the suffix *–ing* if the word ends in *ie*.	die + -ing = dying lie + -ing = lying tie + -ing = tying
Keep the *e* before suffixes that begin with *a* and *o* if the word ends in *ce* or *ge*.	dance + -able = danceable change + -able = changeable courage + -ous = courageous
Keep the *e* before suffixes that begin with a vowel if the word ends in *ee* or *oe*.	see + -ing = seeing agree + -able = agreeable canoe + -ing = canoeing hoe + -ing = hoeing
Some exceptions (There can never be three of the same letter in a row.)	free + -er = freer free + -est = freest
Keep the *e* before suffixes that begin with a consonant.	grace + -ful = graceful state + -hood = statehood like + -ness = likeness encourage + -ment = encouragement care + -less = careless sincere + -ly = sincerely

See next page for some exceptions

GRAMMAR/USAGE/MECHANICS

RULE	EXAMPLES
Some exceptions	awe + -ful = awful argue + -ment = argument true + -ly = truly due + -ly = duly whole + -ly = wholly
Drop *le* before the suffix *–ly* when the word ends with a consonant and *le*.	possible + -ly = possibly sniffle + -ly = sniffly sparkle + -ly = sparkly gentle + -ly = gently

Don't drop any letters when you add *–ly* to a word that ends in a single *l*. When a word ends in *ll*, drop one *l* when you add the suffix *–ly*.

real + -ly = really   chill + -ly = chilly
cool + -ly = coolly   full + -ly = fully

Don't drop any letters when you add the suffix *-ness* to a word that ends in *n*.

stubborn + -ness = stubbornness
mean + -ness = meanness

Compound Words

Keep the original spelling of both parts of a compound word.

Remember that some compounds are one word, some are two words, and some are hyphenated. Check a dictionary when in doubt.

foot + lights = footlights   fish + hook = fishhook
busy + body = busybody   with + hold = withhold
book + case = bookcase   book + keeper = bookkeeper
light + house = lighthouse   heart + throb = heartthrob

Spelling Plurals

A singular noun names one person, place, thing, or idea. A plural noun names more than one. To form the plural of most nouns, you simply add –s. Remember, however, that simple plural nouns never use apostrophes.

The following chart shows other basic rules.

GENERAL RULES FOR PLURALS		
NOUNS ENDING IN	**TO FORM PLURAL**	**EXAMPLES**
ch, s, sh, x, z	Add –es.	lunch → lunches bus → buses dish → dishes box → boxes buzz → buzzes
a vowel and *y*	Add –s.	boy → boys turkey → turkeys
a consonant and *y*	Change *y* to *i* and add –es.	baby → babies penny → pennies
a vowel and *o*	Add –s.	radio → radios rodeo → rodeos
a consonant and *o*	Usually add –es.	potato → potatoes tomato → tomatoes hero → heroes echo → echoes
	Sometimes add –s.	zero → zeros photo → photos piano → pianos

NOUNS ENDING IN	TO FORM PLURAL	EXAMPLES
f or *fe*	Usually change *f* to *v* and add –*s* or –*es*.	wife → wives knife → knives life → lives leaf → leaves half → halves shelf → shelves wolf → wolves thief → thieves
	Sometimes add –*s*.	roof → roofs chief → chiefs cliff → cliffs giraffe → giraffes

The plurals of **proper names** are formed by adding –*es* to names that end in *ch, s, sh, x,* or *z.*

EXAMPLE The **Woodriches** live on Elm Street.

EXAMPLE There are two **Jonases** in our class.

Just add –*s* to form the plural of all other proper names, including those that end in *y.* Remember that the rule of changing *y* to *i* and adding –*es* doesn't apply to proper names.

EXAMPLE The **Kennedys** are a famous American family.

EXAMPLE I know three **Marys.**

EXAMPLE The last two **Januarys** have been especially cold.

To form the plural of a **compound noun written as one word,** follow the general rules for plurals. To form the plural of **hyphenated compound nouns** or **compound nouns of more than one word,** usually make the most important word plural.

GRAMMAR/USAGE/MECHANICS

EXAMPLE The two women's **fathers-in-law** have never met.

EXAMPLE The three **post offices** are made of brick.

EXAMPLE There have been three **surgeons general** in this decade.

EXAMPLE The list of **poets laureate** in Great Britain is short.

EXAMPLE The general presided over two **courts martial** today.

Some nouns have **irregular plural forms** that don't follow any rules.

man → men

woman → women

child → children

foot → feet

tooth → teeth

mouse → mice

goose → geese

ox → oxen

Some nouns have the same singular and plural forms. Most of these are the names of animals, and some of the plural forms may be spelled in more than one way.

deer → deer

sheep → sheep

head (of cattle) → head

Sioux → Sioux

series → series

species → species

fish → fish *or* fishes

antelope → antelope *or* antelopes

buffalo → buffalo *or* buffaloes *or* buffalos

Learning to Spell New Words

You can improve your spelling by improving your study method. Try the following method to learn to spell new words. You can also improve your spelling by thoroughly learning certain common but frequently misspelled words.

1. Say It
Look at the printed word and say it aloud. Then say it again, pronouncing each syllable correctly.

2. Visualize It
Picture the word in your mind. Avoid looking at the printed word on the page. Try to visualize the word letter by letter.

3. Write It
Look at the printed word again, and write it two or three times. Then write the word without looking at the printed spelling.

4. Check It
Check your spelling. Did you spell the word correctly? If not, repeat each step until you can spell the word easily.

How Do You Find a Word in the Dictionary If You Can't Spell It?

Write down letters and letter combinations that could stand for the sound you hear at the beginning of the word. Try these possible spellings as you look for the word in a dictionary.

Using a Computer to Check Spelling

A spelling checker is a useful computer tool. If you have misspelled any words, a spelling checker can find them for you. Not only will it save you time, but it will also show you words you need to learn to spell.

Although spelling checkers are handy, they can't do the whole job. When a spelling checker finds a misspelled word, it searches the computer's dictionary for words spelled in a similar way. *You* must choose the correct word from the options the computer gives you.

Furthermore, a spelling checker can't check for sense. If you type *right* instead of *write*, the spelling checker won't highlight the error because both *right* and *write* are correctly spelled words. You still need to know correct spellings.

PRACTICE **Spelling Rules**

Find the misspelled word in each group and write it correctly.

1. biege, conceit, thief
2. exceed, supercede, accede
3. definite, editor, abdumen
4. enjoiment, daily, marriage
5. truly, arguement, probably
6. disappoint, reenter, unoticed
7. puting, preference, forgotten
8. withhold, newstand, roommate
9. birthdays, beliefs, daisys
10. deers, men, teeth

13.2 SPELLING DIFFICULT WORDS

Some words are more difficult to spell than others, and not all words follow basic spelling rules. Each person has an individual list of "problem" words. One useful strategy for learning difficult words is to develop a list of words that you frequently misspell and study them often.

A list of frequently misspelled words follows. Use it for quick reference.

FREQUENTLY MISSPELLED WORDS

abdomen
absence
abundant
academically
accelerator
accept
accessible
accidentally
acclimated
accommodate
accompaniment
accomplishment
acknowledge
acknowledgment
acquaintance
adequately
admission
admittance
adolescent
advantageous
advertisement
adviser
aerate
aerial
against
alcohol
allegiance
alliance
allot
allotting
all right
anonymous
answer
apologetically

apparatus
apparent
arctic
arousing
arrangement
atheistic
attendant
ballet
bankruptcy
beautiful
beginning
behavior
bibliography
biscuit
blasphemy
boulevard
buffet
bureau
bureaucrat
burial
business
cafeteria
calendar
camouflage
canceled
canoe
capitalism
carburetor
caricature
cataclysm
catastrophe
cemetery
changeable
chassis

choir
circumstantial
colleague
colonel
coliseum
coming
commercial
competition
complexion
concede
conceivable
connoisseur
conscience
conscientious
conscious
consciousness
consistency
controlling
controversy
convenient
cruelty
curriculum
decadent
decathlon
deceitful
deference
definite
deodorant
descend
descendant
descent
desirable
detrimental
devastation

develop
devise
dilemma
diligence
diphtheria
disastrous
disciple
discipline
discrimination
disease
diseased
dissatisfied
division
efficiency
eighth
elementary
eligible
embarrass
embarrassed
emperor
emphasize
endeavor
enormous
entertainment
entrance
environment
espionage
essential
exceed
except
exhibition
exhilaration
expensive
exuberant

familiarize
fascinating
fascism
February
feminine
financier
fission
foreign
forfeit
forty
fulfill
fundamentally
funeral
gaiety
galaxy
gauge
genius
government
grammatically
guarantee
guidance
harassment
height
hereditary
hindrance
hippopotamus
horizontal
hospital
humorous
hygiene
hypocrisy
hypocrite
ideally
idiomatic

immediate
incidentally
independent
inevitable
influential
ingenious
innocent
inoculate
institution
intellectual
interference
irresistible
jewelry
judgment
knowledge
knowledgeable
laboratory
larynx
legitimate
leisure
leisurely
library
license
livelihood
luxurious
magistrate
magnificence
maintenance
malicious
manageable
maneuver
marital
marriageable
martyrdom

mathematics	original	proceed
mediocre	outrageous	propaganda
melancholy	pageant	propagate
melodious	pamphlet	prophecy
metaphor	parallel	prophesy
miniature	paralysis	psychoanalysis
mischievous	parliament	questionnaire
misspell	pastime	realtor
molasses	peasant	rebellion
mortgage	pedestal	receipt
mosquito	perceive	receive
municipal	permanent	recognize
muscle	permissible	recommend
naive	personnel	recommendation
necessary	perspiration	reference
necessity	persuade	referred
negligence	pharmacy	rehearsal
negotiable	physical	reminiscent
neighborhood	physician	remittance
neurotic	picnic	repetitive
newsstand	picnicking	representative
niece	pilot	responsibility
nucleus	playwright	restaurant
nuisance	pneumonia	reveal
nutritious	politician	rhythm
occasion	possessed	rhythmical
occasionally	precede	ridiculous
occur	preferable	salable
occurrence	presence	schedule
occurring	prestige	seize
omission	presumption	separate
omitting	prevalent	separation
opportunity	privilege	sergeant
orchestra	procedure	significance

Frequently Misspelled Words, continued

sincerely	symmetrical	undoubtedly
souvenir	synonymous	unmistakable
specimen	technique	unnecessary
sponsor	technology	unscrupulous
statistics	temperament	usually
strategic	tendency	vaccine
stubbornness	theory	vacuum
succeed	tolerance	valedictory
succession	tortoise	variety
sufficient	traffic	vaudeville
superintendent	tragedy	vehicle
supersede	transparent	vengeance
suppress	truly	versatile
surprise	twelfth	villain
susceptible	unanimous	Wednesday

GRAMMAR/USAGE/MECHANICS

PRACTICE Spelling Difficult Words

Find each misspelled word and write it correctly.

1. Were you conshus while the surgeon operated on your abdoman?
2. Here is an interesting pamplet about the habits of the hippopatamus.
3. Did you see this advertizement from the neighborhood pharmasy?
4. I was looking at the library for some elementry books about artic glaciers.
5. Studying ballet is a fasinating passtime.
6. Was there suficient food on the buffay table to accommodate all the guests?
7. Juanita is a concientious worker, but her effishency may excede our requirements.

8. Will you conceed that your bureau drawers are a catastrophy?

9. We asked Kumo to preceed us during our desent of the mountain so that we could observe his technique.

10. The villian in the play had a pale complection, a mischievous leer, a definite accent, and a rediculous costume.

13.3 EXPANDING YOUR VOCABULARY

Increasing your vocabulary improves your reading and writing skills and your chances of scoring well on standardized tests. The following tips suggest ways to expand your vocabulary and remember new words you encounter.

1. **Notice** new words when you're reading or listening. Write the words and their meanings in a notebook.

2. **Check** the meaning and pronunciation of a new word in a dictionary. Use the original context—surrounding words that are familiar—to understand the word's meaning and use.

3. **Relate** the new word to words you already know. Associate its spelling or meaning with a familiar word that will make the new word easier to remember.

4. **Verify** your understanding of the new word with someone else. A teacher, a parent, or a friend may be able to tell you if you correctly understand the meaning of the word.

5. **Practice** using the new word in your writing and conversation. Try to use the new word at least once a day for a week. Using a word repeatedly is the best way to remember it.

LEARNING FROM CONTEXT

You can often figure out the meaning of an unfamiliar word by looking for clues in the surrounding words and sentences, called the context.

A Fork in the Road

GRAMMAR/USAGE/MECHANICS

USING SPECIFIC CONTEXT CLUES

The following chart shows five types of specific context clues. It also lists clue words to look for. Finally, the chart gives examples of sentences with unfamiliar words whose meanings you should be able to figure out from the context. In the examples, the clue words are in bold type. The unfamiliar words and the helpful context are in italic type.

INTERPRETING CLUE WORDS IN CONTEXT

TYPE OF CONTEXT CLUE	CLUE WORDS	EXAMPLES
Definition The meaning of the unfamiliar word is stated in the sentence.	also known as in other words or that is which is which means	The course emphasized *demography,* **which is** *the study of human populations.* The lecturer was *verbose;* **that is,** he was *wordy.*

GRAMMAR/USAGE/MECHANICS

Example The meaning of the unfamiliar word is explained through familiar examples.	for example for instance including like such as	Osbert served as the old duke's *amanuensis;* **for example,** *he took dictation and copied manuscripts.* *Miscreants* of all kinds, **including** *pickpockets, thieves, and vandals,* roamed the streets of Victorian England.
Comparison The unfamiliar word is similar to a familiar word or phrase.	also identical like likewise resembling same similarly too	Joan's friend testified to her *veracity.* Her teacher, **too,** said Joan's *truthfulness* was evident to all who knew her. Consuela suffered from *acrophobia;* her father **also** had a *fear of heights*.
Contrast The unfamiliar word is the opposite of a familiar word or phrase.	although but however on the contrary on the other hand though unlike	**Unlike** his *despondent* opponent, Kwami appeared *hopeful, happy,* and *sure* he would win. Martin always *grouses* about doing his chores, **but** his sister does her work *without complaining*.
Cause and Effect The unfamiliar word is explained as part of a cause-and-effect relationship.	as a result because consequently therefore thus	Maria felt the stranger was being *intrusive* **because** he *asked too many personal questions*. Otis has a *loquacious* nature; **consequently,** the teacher is constantly telling him to stop talking.

USING GENERAL CONTEXT

Sometimes there are no special clue words to help you understand an unfamiliar word. However, you can still use the general context. That is, you can use the details in the words or sentences around the unfamiliar word. Read the following sentence:

EXAMPLE Ramon was in a *jocund* mood, laughing and joking with his friends.

Even if you don't know the meaning of *jocund,* you do know that it must be an adjective describing *mood.* From other details in the sentence (*laughing and joking*), you may guess correctly that *jocund* means "merry, cheerful, carefree."

PEANUTS reprinted by permission of United Feature Syndicate, Inc.

PRACTICE **Using Context Clues**

Use context clues to figure out the meaning of the italicized word. Write the meaning. Then write definition, example, comparison, contrast, cause and effect, *or* general *to tell what type of context clue you used to define the word.*

1. Our biology teacher told us to rely only on *empirical* evidence, that is, evidence obtained through observation and experimentation.
2. The World Trade Center and the Empire State Building are examples of New York City's tallest *edifices.*
3. The army's store of food was almost *depleted;* likewise, the troops had used up all their ammunition.

4. Countries with *contiguous* borders, such as the United States and Mexico, usually have border patrols.

5. Unlike the preceding day, the *ensuing* one was clear and sunny.

6. Do you believe that everyone has a *doppelganger,* in other words, a double or look-alike?

7. Herman has a *volatile* temper; consequently, we never know what his mood will be.

8. Eduardo is an *immaculate* housekeeper, but his twin sister, Mercedes, has a dusty and untidy apartment.

9. Monica was, like her pleasant and friendly brother, an *affable* young woman.

10. His *somnambulance* worried us. We were afraid he might come to harm while walking in his sleep.

13.4 ROOTS, PREFIXES, AND SUFFIXES

You can often figure out the meaning of an unfamiliar word by analyzing its parts. The main part of a word is its root. When the root is a complete word, it's sometimes called a base word. A root or base word can be thought of as the "spine" of a word. It gives the word its backbone of meaning.

A root is often combined with a prefix (a word part added to the beginning of a word), a suffix (a word part added to the end of a word), or another root. Prefixes and suffixes change a word's meaning or its part of speech.

Although the English language borrows words from many other languages, a large number of words we use have their origins in Latin and Greek roots. Knowing some of these Latin and Greek roots will help you analyze many unfamiliar words and determine their meanings.

encryption

Prefix	The prefix *en-* means "to put into."

Root	The root *crypt* means "hidden" or "secret." The word *encrypt,* therefore, means "to put into a hidden or secret form."

Suffix	The suffix *–ion* changes *encrypt* from a verb to a noun meaning "the state of being encrypted."

The word *encryption,* then, means "something that has been put into a secret code," in other words, "a coded message." Although this word's parts add up to its meaning in a fairly clear way, sometimes an analysis of a word's parts doesn't yield the word's meaning so readily. Use a dictionary to check your analysis.

ROOTS

When you're trying to determine the meaning of an unfamiliar word, think of words that might share a root with it. The meanings of these other words might give you clues to the meaning of the unfamiliar word. The following chart lists some common roots and some words that share them. Keep in mind that one or more letters in a root may change when the root is combined with other word parts.

GRAMMAR/USAGE/MECHANICS

GRAMMAR/USAGE/MECHANICS

ROOTS	WORDS	MEANINGS
ac or *ag* means "do"	action	act or process of doing
	agenda	list of things to do
agri or *agro* means "field"	agriculture	science of cultivating the soil
	agronomy	study of crop production and soil management
am means "love" or "friend"	amicable	friendly
	amorous	relating to love
anima means "life" or "mind"	animate	having life
	unanimous	being of one mind
anthrop means "human beings"	anthropology	study of human beings
	misanthrope	one who hates or distrusts human beings
aqua means "water"	aquarium	tank of water in which living animals are kept
	aqueduct	structure for moving water
arch means "rule" or "government"	anarchy	absence of government
	archives	government records
astr or *astro* means "star"	astronaut	traveler among the stars
	astronomy	study of stars
audio means "hear"	audience	group that hears a performance
	audiometer	device for measuring hearing
aut or *auto* means "self"	autistic	absorbed in the self
	autobiography	story of a person's life written by that person

ROOTS	WORDS	MEANINGS
bene means "good"	beneficial	good, helpful
	benevolent	inclined to do good
bibli or *biblio* means "book"	bibliography	list of books related to a particular subject
	bibliophile	lover of books
bio means "life"	autobiography	story of a person's life written by that person
	biology	study of living things
brev means "short" or "brief"	abbreviate	shorten a word or phrase
	brevity	shortness of expression
cand means "shine" or "glow"	candle	molded mass of wax that may be burned to give light
	incandescent	bright, glowing
capit means "head"	capital	place where the head of government sits
	decapitate	remove the head
ced means "go"	proceed	go forward
	recede	go back
cent means "hundred"	centimeter	one hundredth of a meter
	century	one hundred years
chron or *chrono* means "time"	chronological	arranged in time order
	synchronize	cause to happen at the same time
cid or *cide* means "kill"	germicide	agent that destroys germs
	homicide	killing of one human being by another

GRAMMAR/USAGE/MECHANICS

ROOTS	WORDS	MEANINGS
circ means "circle"	circumference	distance around a circle
	circus	entertainment usually held in a circular area
cis means "cut"	incision	surgical cut
	incisor	tooth adapted for cutting
cline means "bend," "lean," or "slope"	decline	slope downward
	incline	lean forward
cogn means "know"	cognition	knowledge; awareness
	recognize	know someone or something
corp means "body"	corps	body of military troops
	corpse	dead body
cracy means "government"	democracy	government by the people
	technocracy	government by technical experts
cred means "believe" or "trust"	credible	believable
	incredible	unbelievable
crypt or *crypto* means "hidden" or "secret"	cryptic	having a hidden meaning
	cryptogram	communication in secret code
culp means "blame" or "guilt"	culpable	guilty
	culprit	one who is guilty
cur or *curs* means "run"	current	water running in a stream or electricity running through a wire
	cursory	rapidly performed or produced

GRAMMAR/USAGE/MECHANICS

ROOTS	WORDS	MEANINGS
cycl means "circle" or "wheel"	bicycle	two-wheeled vehicle
	cyclone	storm that rotates in a circle
dec or *deca* means "ten"	decade	ten years
	decathlon	athletic contest consisting of ten events
dem or *demo* means "people"	democracy	rule by the people
	epidemic	affecting many people
di means "two"	dichotomy	division into two groups
	dichromatic	having two colors
dict means "say"	contradict	say the opposite of
	dictate	speak for another to record
duc or *duct* means "lead" or "draw"	conductor	one who leads
	deduct	take away from a total
ectomy means "surgical removal"	appendectomy	surgical removal of the appendix
	mastoidectomy	surgical removal of part of the mastoid bone or process
equi means "equal"	equilateral	having sides of equal length
	equitable	dealing equally with all
err means "wander" or "err"	aberration	result of straying from the normal way
	erratic	inconsistent, irregular
eu means "good" or "well"	eulogize	praise
	euphoria	feeling of well-being
exo means "outside" or "outer"	exoskeleton	outer supportive covering of an animal, as an insect or mollusk
	exotic	outside the ordinary

GRAMMAR/USAGE/MECHANICS

ROOTS	WORDS	MEANINGS
fac or *fec* means "make" or "do"	effective factory	done well place where things are made
ferous means "bearing" or "producing"	coniferous somniferous	bearing cones, as a pine tree producing sleep
fid means "faith" or "trust"	confidant fidelity	person one trusts faithfulness
fin means "end" or "limit"	define infinite	limit the meaning of having no end
fix means "fasten"	fixate fixative	fasten one's attention intently substance that fastens or sets
frac or *frag* means "break"	fracture fragile	break easily broken
fus means "pour" or "melt"	effusive fusion	demonstrating an excessive pouring out of talk or affection joining by melting
gen means "class," "kind," "descent," or "birth"	general generate	affecting a whole class start or originate
geo means "earth," "ground," or "soil"	geocentric geology	measured from the center of the earth study of the earth
grad or *gress* means "step" or "go"	egress gradual	way to go out proceeding by steps or degrees
gram or *graph* means "writing"	autograph telegram	written signature written message sent over a distance

ROOTS	WORDS	MEANINGS
grat means "pleasing" or "thanks"	congratulate	express sympathetic pleasure
	gratuity	something given voluntarily to show thanks for service
hetero means "different"	heterogeneous	made up of different kinds of things
	heteronym	word spelled like another word but different in meaning and pronunciation, for example, *bow*
homo means "same"	homogeneous	made up of the same kinds of things
	homophone	word pronounced like another word but different in meaning and spelling, for example, *to, too,* or *two*
hydr or *hydro* means "water"	dehydrate	remove water
	hydrant	large pipe used to draw water
ject means "throw"	eject	throw out
	trajectory	path of something thrown
jud means "judge"	judicious	using good judgment
	prejudice	judgment formed without sufficient knowledge
junct means "join"	conjunction	word that joins other words
	junction	place where two things join

GRAMMAR/USAGE/MECHANICS

ROOTS	WORDS	MEANINGS
jur or *jus* means "law"	jurisprudence	system of law
	justice	determination of rights according to the law
lect or *leg* means "read"	lectern	stand used to support a book or paper for reading
	legible	capable of being read
like means "resembling"	businesslike	resembling the conduct of a business
	childlike	resembling the behavior of a child
loc means "place"	local	relating to a place
	location	position, site, or place
locut or *loqu* means "speak" or "speech"	locution	style of speaking
	loquacious	talkative
log or *logo* means "word," "thought," or "speech"	dialogue	speech between two people
	monologue	speech by a single person
logy means "science" or "study"	biology	science of living things
	genealogy	study of ancestors
	mineralogy	study of minerals
	pathology	study of disease
luc means "light"	lucid	suffused with light; clear
	translucent	permitting the passage of light
macro means "large"	macrocosm	world; universe
	macroscopic	large enough to be observed with the naked eye

ROOTS	WORDS	MEANINGS
magn means "large" or "great"	magnificent magnify	large and grand make larger
mal means "bad" or "badly"	maladjusted malice	badly adjusted desire to see another suffer
man means "hand"	manual manuscript	done by hand document written by hand or typed
meter or *metr* means "measure"	metric thermometer	relating to meter instrument for measuring heat
micr or *micro* means "small"	micrometer microwave	device for measuring very small distances a short electromagnetic wave
milli means "thousand"	millimeter million	one thousandth of a meter one thousand times one thousand
mis or *mit* means "send"	remiss transmit	failing to respond send across a distance
mon means "warn"	admonish premonition	express warning or disapproval in a gentle way forewarning
mon or *mono* means "one"	monarchy monochromatic	rule by one person having one color
morph or *morpho* means "form"	metamorphosis morphology	change in physical form study of the form and structure of animals and plants

Chapter 13 Spelling and Vocabulary **411**

ROOTS	WORDS	MEANINGS
mort means "death"	mortal	subject to death
	mortician	one who prepares the dead for burial
neo means "new"	neologism	new word, usage, or expression
	neonatal	affecting the newborn
nym means "name"	anonymous	not named or identified
	pseudonym	fictitious or pen name
octa or *octo* means "eight"	octagon	figure with eight sides
	octopus	creature with eight limbs
omni means "all"	omniscient	knowing all
	omnivorous	eating both animal and vegetable matter
oper means "work"	opera	musical and dramatic work
	operative	working
pan means "all" or "whole"	panacea	remedy for all problems
	Pan-American	relating to the whole of North and South America
path or *pathy* means "feeling" or "suffering"	pathology	study of disease
	sympathy	inclination to feel like another
ped means "child" or "foot"	pediatrician	physician who cares for children
	quadruped	animal having four feet
pend or *pens* means "hang" or "weigh"	pendant	something hanging or suspended
	suspense	feeling that leaves one hanging or unsure of an outcome

ROOTS	WORDS	MEANINGS
phil or *phile* means "loving" or "fondness"	bibliophile	lover of books
	philanthropist	one who loves human beings
phobia means "fear"	acrophobia	fear of heights
	hydrophobia	fear of water
phon or *phono* means "sound," "voice," or "speech"	phonics	method of teaching relationships between sounds and letters
	phonograph	instrument for playing recorded sound
physi or *physio* means "nature" or "physical"	physiognomy	natural features of the face believed to show temperament and character
	physiotherapy	physical therapy
poly means "many"	polyglot	composed of numerous language groups
	polygon	a many-sided figure
pon or *pos* means "place" or "put"	exponent	symbol placed above and to the right of a mathematical expression
	position	place where something is situated
port means "carry"	portable	capable of being carried
	porter	one who carries
prehend means "seize" or "grasp"	apprehend	arrest by seizing
	comprehend	grasp the meaning of
prim means "first"	primary	first in order of time or development

GRAMMAR/USAGE/MECHANICS

ROOTS	WORDS	MEANINGS
prim, continued	primitive	characteristic of an early stage of development
prot or *proto* means "first" or "beginning"	proton prototype	elementary particle original model
pseudo means "false"	pseudoclassic pseudonym	pretending to be classic fictitious or pen name
psych or *psycho* means "mind"	psychology psychotherapy	study of the mind therapy for the mind
punctus means "point"	punctual puncture	on time hole or wound made by a pointed instrument
quadr or *quadri* means "four"	quadrangle quadrilateral	four-sided enclosure having four sides
rect means "right" or "straight"	rectangle rectitude	figure with four right angles quality of being correct in judgment or procedure
reg means "rule" or "direct"	regular regulate	according to rule direct according to rule
rupt means "break"	interrupt rupture	stop or hinder by breaking in break
sang means "blood"	consanguinity sanguine	blood relationship marked by high color and cheerfulness; confident; optimistic
sci means "know"	omniscient science	knowing all things knowledge about the natural world

GRAMMAR/USAGE/MECHANICS

ROOTS	WORDS	MEANINGS
scope means "a means for viewing"	microscope	a means for viewing small things
	telescope	a means for viewing things at a distance
scrib or *script* means "write"	prescribe	write an order for medicine
	prescription	written order for medicine
secu or *sequ* means "follow"	sequel	installment that follows a previous one
	sequence	series in which one item follows another
sens or *sent* means "feel" or "sense"	sensation	feeling
	sentence	group of words that makes sense
sol or *solv* means "dissolve" or "solve"	solution	that which solves a problem
	solvent	that which dissolves
son means "sound"	resonant	continuing to sound
	sonorous	full of sound
soph means "wise" or "clever"	sophisticated	having wise and clever knowledge of the ways of the world
	sophomore	student in the second year of high school or college (a combination of wise and foolish)
spec or *spect* means "look" or "watch"	perspective	way of looking at something
	spectator	one who watches an event

ROOTS	WORDS	MEANINGS
spir means "breath" or "breathe"	inspire respiration	exert an influence on breathing
strict or *string* means "bind"	constrict stringent	draw together strict; severe
tact or *tang* means "touch"	contact tangible	touching of two things or people capable of being touched
tele means "far off" or "distant"	telephone television	instrument for hearing sound at a distance instrument for viewing pictures at a distance
terr means "earth"	extraterrestrial terrain	being from beyond earth physical features of a tract of land
therm or *thermo* means "heat"	thermal thermometer	relating to heat instrument for measuring heat
trac means "draw" or "pull"	extract traction	pull out friction caused by pulling across a surface; pulling force
tri means "three"	triangle triathlon	figure with three angles athletic contest consisting of three events
vac means "empty"	evacuation vacant	process of emptying out empty

GRAMMAR/USAGE/MECHANICS

ROOTS	WORDS	MEANINGS
ven or *vent* means "come"	intervene	come between
	venue	place related to a particular event
verb means "word"	verbal	having to do with words
	verbose	wordy
vers or *vert* means "turn"	avert	turn away
	reverse	turn back
vid or *vis* means "see"	evident	plain to see
	visible	capable of being seen
viv means "live" or "alive"	revive	bring back to life
	vivacious	full of life; lively
vit means "life"	vital	necessary to the maintenance of life
	vitamin	substance necessary for the regulation of life processes
voc or *vok* means "call" or "call forth"	evoke	call forth
	vocation	job a person feels called to do
vol or *volv* means "roll"	evolve	develop
	revolution	rotation

PREFIXES

Prefixes are word parts added to the beginning of a root or a base word to change its meaning. They are important tools for understanding and learning new words. The following chart shows common prefixes and their meanings. Notice that some prefixes have more than one meaning and that some prefixes convey the same meaning as others.

PREFIXES	WORDS	MEANINGS
a- means "without" or "not"; it can also mean "on," "in," or "at"	amoral atypical aboard abloom	without morals not typical on board in bloom
ant- or *anti-* means "against" or "opposing"	antacid antiwar	agent that works against acidity opposing war
ante- means "before"	antecedent antediluvian	going before before the biblical flood
be- means "cause to be"	befriend belittle	act as a friend to cause to seem little or less
bi- means "two"	bimonthly bisect	once every two months *or* twice a month divide into two equal parts
cat- or *cata-* means "down"	catacomb catastrophe	subterranean cemetery final stage of a tragedy
circum- means "around" or "about"	circumference circumstance circumvent	distance around a circle surrounding condition avoid by going around
co- means "with" or "together"	coworker cowrite	person one works with write together
col-, com-, con-, or *cor-* means "together" or "with"	collaborate companion confer	work with others one who accompanies another consult with others

PREFIXES	WORDS	MEANINGS
col-, com-, con-, or *cor-,* continued	correspond	exchange letters with another
contra- means "against"	contradict contrary	speak against opposite
counter- means "opposite" or "opposing"	counterbalance counterclockwise	oppose with an equal weight or force opposite of clockwise
de- means "do the opposite of," "remove," or "reduce"	de-emphasize defrost devalue	do the opposite of emphasize remove frost reduce the value of
dia- means "through" or "across"	diameter diaphragm	length through the center of a circle a membrane stretching across an area
dis- means "not" or "absence of"	dishonest distrust	not honest absence of trust
e- or *ex-* means "out"; *ex-* also means "former"	eject exceed ex-president	throw out go beyond former president
en- means "cause to be" or "put into"	enlarge enthrall	cause to be made large put into thrall
extra- means "outside" or "beyond"	extralegal extraordinary	outside of legal means beyond the ordinary
for- means "so as to involve prohibition or exclusion"	forgive forgo	give up feelings of resentment give up pleasure or advantage
hemi- means "half"	hemicycle hemisphere	structure consisting of half a circle half a sphere

GRAMMAR/USAGE/MECHANICS

PREFIXES	WORDS	MEANINGS
hyper- means "excessive" or "excessively"	hyperbole hypersensitive	excessive exaggeration excessively sensitive

il-, im-, in-, or *ir-* means "not" or "into"	illegal
	illuminate
	immature
	immigrant
	
	inconvenient
	insight
	
	irregular
	irrigate
		not legal
		bring light into
		not mature
		one who comes into
		    a country
		not convenient
		power of seeing into
		    a situation
		not regular
		bring water into

inter- means "among" or "between"	international interscholastic	among nations between schools
intra- means "within"	intramural intrastate	within the walls (of a school) within a state
intro- means "in" or "into"	introspection introvert	looking within oneself one who is turned inward
mis- means "bad," "badly," "wrong," or "wrongly"	misspell mistreat	spell wrong treat badly
non- means "not"	nonallergenic nonconformist	not causing allergies one who does not conform

over- means "exceed," "surpass," or "excessive"	overeat
	overqualified
		eat to excess
		qualified beyond
		    the normal
		    requirements

GRAMMAR/USAGE/MECHANICS

PREFIXES	WORDS	MEANINGS
para- means "beside" or "beyond"	paramedic	one who works beside a physician
	paranormal	beyond the normal
peri- means "around"	perimeter	distance around a plane figure
	periscope	instrument for looking around
post- means "after"	postgame	after the game
	postwar	after the war
pre- means "before"	precede	go before
	premonition	advance warning
pro- means "in favor of," "forward," "before," or "in place of"	pro-American	in favor of America
	proceed	go forward
	prologue	introduction before the main text
	pronoun	word that takes the place of a noun
re- means "again" or "back"	recall	call back
	replay	play again
retro- means "back," "backward," or "behind"	retroactive	effective as of a prior date
	retrogress	move backward
semi- means "half" or "partly"	semicircle	half a circle
	semisweet	partly sweet
sub- means "under" or "less than"	subhuman	less than human
	submarine	underwater
super- means "over and above"	superabundant	having more than an abundance
	superhuman	over and above what is normal for a human being

GRAMMAR/USAGE/MECHANICS

PREFIXES	WORDS	MEANINGS
sym- or *syn-* means "with" or "together"	symbiosis	living together of two dissimilar organisms
	synchronize	make happen at the same time
trans- means "across"	transmit	send across
	transport	carry across
un- means "not" or "do the opposite of"	unhappy	not happy
	untie	do the opposite of tie
uni- means "one"	unicycle	one-wheeled vehicle
	unified	joined into one

PEANUTS reprinted by permission of United Feature Syndicate, Inc.

SUFFIXES

Suffixes are word parts added to the end of a root or a base word to change its meaning and sometimes its part of speech. The following chart shows common suffixes and their meanings. Notice that some suffixes have more than one meaning and that some suffixes convey the same meaning as others. Notice also that the spelling of a root often changes when a suffix is added. Furthermore, more than one suffix may be added to many words.

SUFFIXES	WORDS	MEANINGS
-able or *-ible* means "capable of," "fit for," or "tending to"	agreeable	tending to agree *or* able to be agreed with
	breakable	capable of being broken
	collectible	fit for collecting
-age means "action," "process," or "result"	breakage	action or process of breaking
	marriage	action, process, or result of marrying
	wreckage	result of wrecking
-al means "relating to" or "characterized by"; it can also mean "action," "process," or "result"	fictional	relating to fiction
	rehearsal	action or process of rehearsing
-an or *-ian* means "one who is of or from"; it can also mean "relating to"	Bostonian	one who lives in Boston
	Elizabethan	relating to the reign of Queen Elizabeth I
-ance, -ancy, -ence, or *-ency* means "action," "process," "quality," or "state"	dependency	state of being dependent
	performance	action or process of performing
	persistence	quality of persisting
	vacancy	state of being vacant
-ant means "one who or that which"; it can also mean "being"	contestant	one who participates in a contest
	observant	being observing
-ar means "relating to" or "resembling"; it can also mean "one who"	liar	one who lies
	molecular	relating to molecules
	spectacular	resembling a spectacle

GRAMMAR/USAGE/MECHANICS

SUFFIXES	WORDS	MEANINGS
-ard or *-art* means "one who"	braggart dullard	one who brags one who is dull
-ary means "person or thing belonging to or connected with"; it can also mean "relating to or connected with"	complimentary functionary	relating to a compliment person who serves a particular function
-ate means "of," "relating to," or "having"; it can also mean "cause to be"	activate collegiate	cause to be active relating to college
-cy means "state," "quality," "condition," or "fact of being"	accuracy bankruptcy infancy	quality of being accurate condition of being bankrupt state of being an infant
-dom means "state of being"	boredom freedom	state of being bored state of being free
-ee means "receiver of action" or "one who"	escapee trainee	one who escapes receiver of training
-eer means "one who"	auctioneer engineer	one who runs an auction one who is concerned with engines
-en means "made of or resembling"; it can also mean "cause to be or become"	golden strengthen	made of or resembling gold cause to be strong
-ent means "one who"	resident superintendent	one who resides in a place one who superintends

GRAMMAR/USAGE/MECHANICS

SUFFIXES	WORDS	MEANINGS
-er means "one who" or "native or resident of"; it can also mean "more"	New Yorker reporter sooner stronger	resident of New York one who reports more soon more strong
-ery or *-ry* means "character," "art or practice," "place," or "collection"	bakery cookery jewelry snobbery	place for baking art of cooking collection of jewels character of being a snob
-ese means "originating in a certain place," "resident of," or "language of"	Japanese	originating in Japan; resident of Japan; language of Japan
-esque means "in the manner or style of" or "like"	picturesque statuesque	in the manner or style of a picture like a statue
-et or *-ette* means "small" or "group"	islet kitchenette quartet	small island small kitchen group of four
-fold means "multiplied by"	fourfold	multiplied by four
-ful means "full of" or "tending to"; it can also mean "amount that fills"	fearful forgetful spoonful	full of fear tending to forget amount that fills a spoon
-fy or *-ify* means "make or form into," "make similar to," or "become"	fortify glorify solidify	make similar to a fort make glorious become solid
-hood means "state," "condition," "quality," or "character"	childhood likelihood statehood	state of being a child quality of being likely condition of being a state

GRAMMAR/USAGE/MECHANICS

Chapter 13 Spelling and Vocabulary **425**

GRAMMAR/USAGE/MECHANICS

SUFFIXES	WORDS	MEANINGS
-ic or *-ical* means "having the qualities of," "being," "like," "consisting of," or "relating to"	angelic	like an angel
	athletic	having the qualities of an athlete
	atomic	consisting of atoms
	historical	relating to history
-ile means "tending to" or "capable of"	contractile	capable of contracting
	infantile	tending to be like an infant
-ine means "of," "like," or "relating to"	Alpine	relating to the Alps
	crystalline	like crystal
	marine	of the sea
-ion or *-ation* means "act or process," "result," or "state or condition"	pollution	result of polluting
	selection	process of selecting
	sensation	state or condition of feeling something
-ish means "like," "inclined to," "somewhat," or "having the approximate age of"	bookish	inclined to be interested in books
	foolish	like a fool
	reddish	somewhat red
	thirtyish	about thirty
-ism means "act, practice, or process," "prejudice," "state or condition," "doctrine or belief," or "conduct or behavior"	criticism	act of criticizing
	heroism	conduct or behavior of a hero
	Mormonism	belief in the doctrines of the Mormon faith
	parallelism	state of being parallel
	racism	prejudice against a race of people
-ist means "one who"	violinist	one who plays a violin
	finalist	one who takes part in the final playoff
-ite means "native or resident of"	Brooklynite	native or resident of Brooklyn

SUFFIXES	WORDS	MEANINGS
-ity means "quality," "state," or "condition"	humanity	condition of being human
	purity	quality of being pure
	sanity	state of being sane
-ive means "performing or tending toward"	active	tending toward action
	excessive	tending toward excess
-ize means "cause to be," "become," or "make"	Americanize	become American
	modernize	make modern
	sterilize	cause to be sterile
-less means "without"	hopeless	without hope
-ly means "like"; it can also mean "in a manner" or "to a degree"	easily	in an easy manner
	friendly	like a friend
	partly	to a partial degree
-ment means "result," "action," or "condition"	amazement	condition of being amazed
	astonishment	result of being astonished
	development	act of developing
-ness means "state," "condition," or "quality"	darkness	condition of being dark
	goodness	state of being good
	heaviness	quality of being heavy
-or means "one who or that which"	elevator	that which raises people or goods to a higher level
	inventor	one who invents
-ory means "place of or for"; it can also mean "relating to" or "characterized by"	contradictory	characterized by contradiction
	observatory	place for observing
	sensory	relating to the senses
-ose means "full of" or "having"	grandiose	having grand ideas
	verbose	full of words; wordy

Chapter 13 Spelling and Vocabulary **427**

SUFFIXES	WORDS	MEANINGS
-ous means "full of," "having," or "characterized by"	courageous	characterized by courage
	gracious	having grace
	joyous	full of joy
-ship means "state, condition, or quality," "office, dignity, or profession," or "art or skill"	ambassadorship	office of an ambassador
	friendship	state of being a friend
	horsemanship	art or skill of horseback riding
-some means "characterized by"; it can also mean "group of"	foursome	group of four
	troublesome	characterized by trouble
-th or *-eth* is used to form ordinal numbers	seventh	ordinal for *seven*
	twentieth	ordinal for *twenty*
-ty means "quality," "condition," or "state"	novelty	quality or condition of being novel
	safety	state of being safe
-ure means "act," "process," "state," or "result"	composure	state of being composed
	erasure	result of erasing
	exposure	act of exposing
-ward means "toward" or "in a certain direction"	afterward	at a later time
	homeward	toward home
-y means "characterized by or full of," "like," or "tending or inclined to"; it can also mean "state, condition, or quality" or "instance of an action"	chatty	tending or inclined to chat
	homey	like home
	inquiry	instance of inquiring
	jealousy	state, condition, or quality of being jealous
	juicy	full of juice
	waxy	characterized by wax

Use the following roots, prefixes, and suffixes to make a list of ten words you know or combinations you think might be words. Use at least one root, prefix, or suffix from the chart in each word you write. Check your words in a dictionary.

PREFIXES	ROOTS	SUFFIXES
co-, col-, com-, con-, cor-	bene	-able, -ible
de-	chron, chrono	-age
dis-	dict	-ary
hyper-	geo	-er
il-, im-, in-, ir-	ject	-ful
mis-	neo	-ic, -ical
pro-	nym	-ize
re-	oper	-less
super-	port	-ship
un-	vers, vert	-ty

GRAMMAR/USAGE/MECHANICS

Part Three

● ● ● ● ● ● ● ● ● ● ●

Composition

Chapter 14

The Writing Process

• • • • • • • • • • • • • • •

Writing is a process done in different stages: prewriting, drafting, revising/editing, and publishing/presenting. These stages are recursive, that is, they do not necessarily follow one another in order; you can go back and forth among steps, repeating those that you need to until you end up with the result you want.

The Writing Process

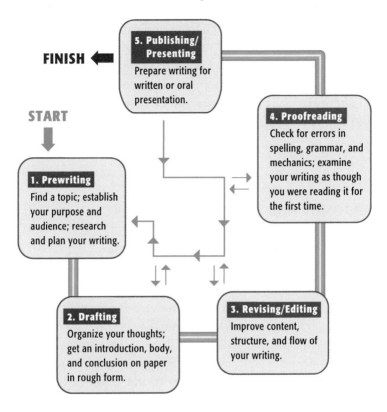

5. Publishing/Presenting
Prepare writing for written or oral presentation.

FINISH

START

1. Prewriting
Find a topic; establish your purpose and audience; research and plan your writing.

4. Proofreading
Check for errors in spelling, grammar, and mechanics; examine your writing as though you were reading it for the first time.

2. Drafting
Organize your thoughts; get an introduction, body, and conclusion on paper in rough form.

3. Revising/Editing
Improve content, structure, and flow of your writing.

STAGE 1: PREWRITING

During Prewriting, you decide what you want to write about by exploring ideas, feelings, and memories. Prewriting is the stage in which you not only decide what your topic is, but

- you refine, focus, and explore your topic
- you gather information about your topic
- you make notes about what you want to say about it
- you also think about your audience and your purpose

Your audience is whoever will read your work. Your purpose is what you hope to accomplish through your writing.

After you've decided on a topic and explored it, making notes about what you will include, you will need to arrange and organize your ideas. This is also done during the Prewriting stage, before you actually draft your paper.

There are many techniques you can use to generate ideas and define and explore your topic.

CHOOSING AND EXPLORING YOUR TOPIC

Keeping a Journal

Many writing ideas come to us as we go about our daily lives. A journal, or log, can help you record your thoughts from day to day. You can then refer to this record when you're searching for a writing topic. Every day you can write in your journal your experiences, observations, thoughts, feelings, and opinions. Keep newspaper and magazine clippings, photos, songs, poems, and anything else that catches your interest. They might later suggest questions that lead to writing topics. Try to add to your journal every day. Use your imagination. Be creative and don't worry about grammar, spelling, or punctuation. This is your own personal record. It is for your benefit only, and no one else will read it.

Freewriting

Freewriting means just what it says: writing freely without worrying about grammar, punctuation, spelling, logic, or anything. You just write what comes to your mind. Choose a topic and a time limit and then just start writing ideas as they come to you. If you run out of ideas, repeat the same word over and over until a new idea occurs to you. When the time is up, review what you've written. The ideas that most interest you are likely to be the ones that will be most worth writing about. You can use your journal as a place for freewriting, or you can just take a piece of paper and start the process. The important thing is to allow your mind to follow its own path as you explore a topic. You'll be surprised where it might lead you.

FREEWRITING TIP

1. Let your thoughts flow. Write ideas, memories, anything that comes to mind.
2. Don't edit or judge your thoughts; just write them down. You can evaluate them later. In fact, evaluating your ideas at this point would probably dry up the flow. Accepting any idea that comes is the way to encourage more ideas.
3. Don't worry about spelling, punctuation, grammar, or even sense; just keep writing.

COMPOSITION

Brainstorming

Brainstorming is another free-association technique that you can use to generate ideas. It is often most effective to brainstorm with others because ideas can spark new ideas. Start with a key word or idea and list other ideas as they occur to you. Don't worry about the order; just let your ideas flow freely from one to the next.

1. Choose someone to list ideas as they are called out.
2. Start with a topic or a question.
3. Encourage everyone to join in freely.
4. Accept all ideas; do not evaluate them now.
5. Follow each idea as far as it goes.

Clustering

Write your topic in the middle of a piece of paper. As you think about the topic, briefly write down everything that comes to mind. Each time you write something, draw a circle around it and draw lines to connect those circles to the main idea in the center. Continue to think about the secondary ideas and add offshoots to them. Draw circles around those related ideas and connect them to the secondary ideas.

Clustering TIP

1. Start with a key word or phrase circled in the center of your paper.
2. Brainstorm to discover related ideas; circle each one and connect it to the central idea.
3. Branch out with new ideas that add details to existing ideas.
4. Review your chart, looking for ideas that interest you.

COMPOSITION

Clustering

Collecting Information

Whether you're deciding on your topic or exploring a topic you've already chosen, you need to discover as many facts as possible about your topic or possible topic.

Asking Questions To discover the facts you need, begin by writing a list of questions about your topic. Different questions serve different purposes, and knowing what kind of question to ask can be as important as knowing how to ask it clearly. The chart that follows will help you categorize your list of questions.

KINDS OF QUESTIONS	
PERSONAL QUESTIONS°	ask about your responses to a topic. They help you explore your experiences and tastes.
CREATIVE QUESTIONS	ask you to compare your subject to something else or to imagine observing your subject as someone else might. Such questions can expand your perspective on a subject.
ANALYTICAL QUESTIONS	ask about structure and function: How is this topic constructed? What is its purpose? Analytical questions help you evaluate and draw conclusions.
INFORMATIONAL QUESTIONS	ask for facts, statistics, or details.

Library Research If your topic requires information you do not already have, your school or public library is the best place to find it.

Library Research TIP

1. Search for books by title, author, and subject, using either the card catalog or the online computer system.
2. Use the subject heading for each listing as a cross-reference to related material.
3. Browse among other books in the section where you locate a useful book.
4. Jot down the author, title, and call number of each book you think you will use.
5. Record the titles of books that don't provide help (so you won't search for them again).
6. Examine each book's bibliography for related titles.
7. Try to be an independent researcher but ask a librarian for help if you cannot locate much information on your topic.

If you do your research on the Internet, evaluate your sources carefully and always find at least one more source to verify each point. The reliability of Internet information varies a great deal. Use print sources to verify information you find on the Internet, if that is possible.

Observing One good starting point for exploring a topic is simply to observe closely and list the details you see. After you've listed the details, arrange them into categories. The categories you choose depend on the details you observe and your writing goal. For example, you might want to organize your details using spatial order, chronological order, or order of importance.

Interviewing Get your information directly from the source; interview someone. You may choose someone whom you can interview in person, or you might investigate the possibility of an interview conducted over the telephone, through e-mail, or online. Follow these steps:

BEFORE THE INTERVIEW	Make the appointment.
	Research your topic and find out about your source.
	Prepare four or five basic questions.
DURING THE INTERVIEW	Ask informational questions (who, what, where, when, why, and how).
	Listen carefully.
	Ask follow-up questions.
	Take accurate notes (or tape-record with permission).
AFTER THE INTERVIEW	Write a more detailed account of the interview.
	Contact your source to clarify points or to double-check facts.

COMPOSITION

IDENTIFYING PURPOSE AND AUDIENCE

Purpose

Before you start to write, you must determine the primary purpose for your writing: to inform or explain, to explore or analyze, to persuade, to amuse or entertain, to narrate, or to describe. Sometimes you might want to accomplish more than one purpose, so you will have a primary purpose and a secondary purpose. To determine the primary purpose, answer these questions:

1. Do I want to tell a story?
2. Do I want to describe someone or something—a place, a person, a process, a relationship, an event, an impression?
3. Do I want to inform my readers about the topic or to explain something about it?
4. Do I want to persuade my readers to change their minds about something or take some action?
5. Do I want to amuse or entertain?
6. Do I want to explore or analyze a topic someone else has written about and perhaps argue with the conclusions he or she has drawn?

Audience

Your audience is anyone who will be reading your writing. Sometimes you write just for yourself. Most often, however, you write to share information with others. Your audience might include a few friends or family members, your classmates, the population at large, or just your teacher. As you write, consider these questions:

1. Who will my audience be? What do I want to say to them?
2. What do my readers already know about my topic?
3. What types of information will interest my audience?

ARRANGING AND ORGANIZING IDEAS

Once you have gathered your information and ideas, you can choose from many kinds of details—examples, facts, statistics, reasons, and concrete and sensory details—to support your main idea. As a writer, you need to organize these details and put them in order. Some possible patterns of organization include

- chronological order (by time)
- spatial order (relationships based on space, place, or setting)
- order of importance
- cause and effect (events described as reason and result, motive and reaction, stimulus and response)
- comparison and contrast (measuring items against one another to show similarities and differences)

The technique you choose to organize details might be as simple as making a list or an outline that shows how the details will be grouped under larger subtopics or headings. You can also organize details visually by making a chart or a diagram similar to the Clustering diagram on page 437. You might better be able to see a plan for organizing your paper when you see the relationships among the parts of your topic.

"It's plotted out. I just have to write it."

© The New Yorker Collection 1996 Charles Barsotti
from cartoonbank.com. All Rights Reserved.

COMPOSITION

STAGE 2: DRAFTING

When you write your draft, your goal is to organize the facts and details you have accumulated into unified paragraphs. Make sure each paragraph has a main idea and does not bring in unrelated information. The main idea must be stated in a topic sentence, and it must be supported by details that explain and clarify it. Details can be facts and statistics, examples or incidents, or sensory details.

Writing a draft, or turning your ideas into paragraphs, is a stage in the Writing Process and a tool in itself. During Prewriting, you started to organize your details. You will continue to do this as you write your draft because you might find links between ideas that give new meanings to your words and phrases. Continue to organize your details using one of the methods discussed in Prewriting.

To make your sentences interesting, be sure to vary the length of sentences. Don't use too many short, choppy sentences when you can incorporate some of your ideas in subordinate clauses or compound or complex sentences.

Writing Tip

Your composition should consist of three parts: the introduction, the body, and the conclusion (see the Outlining Tip on page 476). Begin your paper with an **introduction** that grabs the reader's interest and sets the tone. The introduction usually gives the reader a brief explanation of what your paper is about and often includes the **thesis.** The thesis states your paper's main idea or what you're trying to prove or support.

Each paragraph in the **body,** or main part, of your paper should have a topic sentence that states what the paragraph is about. The rest of the paragraph should include details that support the topic sentence. Similarly, each topic sentence should support the thesis, or main idea of the paper.

Writing Tip (continued)

End your paper with a good **conclusion** that gives a feeling of "completeness." You might conclude your paper in any of the following ways:

- Summarize what you've said in the body of your paper.
- Restate the main idea (using different words).
- Give a final example or idea.
- Make a comment on or give a personal reaction to the topic.
- End with a quotation that sums up or comments on the topic.
- Call for some action (especially in persuasive papers).

STAGE 3: REVISING/EDITING

The purposes of Revising are to make sure that your writing is clear and well organized, that it accomplishes your goals, and that it reaches your audience. The word *revision* means "seeing again." You need to look at your writing again, seeing it as another person might. You might read your paper very carefully, you might tape-record yourself reading your paper aloud, or you might share your writing with another student, a small group of students, or your teacher. After evaluating your work, you might want to move things around or change them completely. You might want to add or cut information. Mark these changes right on your draft and then incorporate them.

The revision stage is the point at which you can

- improve paragraphs
- implement self-evaluation and peer evaluation
- check content and structure
- make sure the language is specific, descriptive, and nonsexist
- check unity and coherence
- check style and tone

COMPOSITION

Writing Tip

When you are writing about people in general, people who may be either male or female, use nonsexist language. That is, use words that apply to all people, not specifically to males or females. For example, instead of *mailman,* which is gender-specific, you could use the term *mail carrier.*

Traditional nouns for males and females in the same occupation (for instance, *poet* and *poetess*) are no longer encouraged. The noun *poet* now refers to both males and females. Refer to the following list for other gender-neutral terms to use in your writing.

Use	Instead of
actor	actress
Briton	Englishman
businesspeople	businessman/woman
chairperson, chair, moderator	chairman/woman
a member of the clergy	clergyman
craftspeople	craftsmen
crewed space flight	manned space flight
fisher	fisherman
flight attendant	stewardess
Framers, Founders	Founding Fathers
handmade, synthetic, manufactured	manmade
homemaker	housewife
humanity, human beings, people	mankind
it/its (in reference to ships, countries)	she/her/hers, he/his
land of origin, homeland	mother country
letter carrier/mail carrier	mailman
police officer	policeman
representative	congressman/woman
server	waiter or waitress
supervisor	foreman
watch, guard	watchman
worker	workman
workforce	manpower

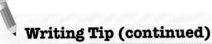

Writing Tip (continued)

Masculine pronouns (such as *he, him, his*) were once used to refer to mixed groups of people. Females were understood to be included. That is, a sentence like *A reporter must check his facts* was understood to apply to both male and female reporters. Now everyone is encouraged to use gender-neutral wording. Some gender-neutral possibilities for that sentence are *Reporters must check their facts, A reporter must check the facts,* and *A reporter must check his or her facts.* (See page 243.)

STAGE 4: PROOFREADING

The purposes of Proofreading are to make sure that you've spelled all words correctly and that your sentences are grammatically correct. Proofread your writing and correct mistakes in capitalization, punctuation, and spelling. Refer to the chart on the next page for Proofreading symbols to help you during this stage of the Writing Process.

FRANK & ERNEST® by Bob Thaves

FRANK AND ERNEST reprinted by permission of
Newspaper Enterprise Association, Inc.

COMPOSITION

Proofreading Marks		
Marks	**Meaning**	**Example**
∧	Insert	My gra**ᵈ**nmother is eighty-six years old.
ℰ	Delete	She grew up on a dairy farm.
# ∧	Insert space	She milked**#**cows every morning.
⌒	Close up space	She fed the chickens in the barn͜yard.
≡	Capitalize	times have changed.
/	Make lowercase	Machines now do the /Milking.
⌒ *sp*	Check spelling	Chickens are fed autommatically. *sp*
‿	Switch order	Modern farms are like more factories.
¶	New paragraph	¶Last year I returned to the farm.

STAGE 5: PUBLISHING/PRESENTING

This is the stage at which you share your work with others. You might read your work aloud in class, submit it to the school newspaper, or give it to a friend to read. You could illustrate a copy to send to a favorite relative or to hang on a school corkboard. You might find a web page on which to print it, or you might find an online chat room or bulletin board where its posting could spark comments. There are many avenues for Presenting your work.

COMPOSITION

Modes of Writing

● ● ● ● ● ● ● ● ● ● ● ● ● ● ● ●

15.1 DESCRIPTIVE WRITING

In descriptive writing, your goal is to help your reader experience the subject described. You will find descriptive writing in advertisements, stories, newspapers, travel guides, scientific journals, and many other places. It is important to appeal to as many senses as possible, allowing your audience to appreciate the subject fully.

BEFORE YOU WRITE

Before you begin to write a description, you must choose a topic, such as an object, a person, a place, or an event.

Observe and Take Notes If possible, spend some time directly observing your topic. As you observe, ask yourself

- What is the most striking thing about this subject?
- What colors do I see? What sounds do I hear? What do I smell? Taste? Feel?

- What should I include in the description so that my audience will see what I am seeing, feel as I am feeling?

As you observe, take detailed notes about the subject, recording your impressions.

Establish Your Vantage Point From your notes and observations, you will be able to establish your vantage point, or point from which you view the subject. You may choose a stationary vantage point, a fixed position from which you view your subject; or you may select a moving vantage point, which allows you to view your subject from different angles.

THE FAR SIDE By GARY LARSON

"Hold up, Niles. It says here, 'These little fish have been known to skeletonize a cow in less than two minutes.' ... Now *there's* a vivid thought."

Whichever vantage point you choose, remember that it limits the available details.

Establish Order Once you have chosen your vantage point, it will be easy to decide how to order your description. The following chart contains a few possibilities.

ORGANIZING DETAILS	
SPATIAL ORDER	Spatial order is often used when observing from a stationary vantage point. You can organize details from top to bottom, left to right, front to back, east to west, clockwise, or counterclockwise.
ORDER OF IMPORTANCE	When you organize details according to their importance, you may want to begin with the least important detail and build to the most important. This builds the description to a climax.
ORDER OF IMPRESSION	Using order of impression, you give the reader the feeling of being there. Relay the details of the things that you noticed first. Keep in mind that the first impression is not always right—you can build on this and construct a suspenseful mood.

Writing Tip

Use transitions to make your writing read smoothly and to make your description coherent. Some common transitional words include *next to, across from, behind, after, above all*, and *finally*.

WRITE A DESCRIPTIVE ESSAY

Now that you have observed your topic, taken detailed notes, and established your organization, you are ready to write your description.

Topic Sentence The first step to forming a coherent paragraph is to write a topic sentence to give each paragraph unity and to help your readers identify your purpose. You can place a topic sentence at the beginning, in the middle, or at the end of a paragraph.

Use Descriptive Language Support each topic sentence with vivid, precise details.

- Try to stay away from overused modifiers, such as *good, bad, really, so,* and *very.* Consider these modifiers instead: *completely, definitely, especially, exceptionally, largely, mostly, notably, oddly, particularly, strikingly, surprisingly, terribly, thoroughly, unusually.*
- Use precise verbs to capture the essence of actions.
- Think of words that appeal to sight, sound, taste, smell, and touch. For your reader to experience your topic in the same way you did, you must appeal to the senses.

Writing Tip

Descriptive language brings writing alive. When you revise your work, use a thesaurus to find varied words that appeal to the senses and replace repetitive language. Keep in mind, though, that synonyms are very seldom interchangeable. When you have selected a synonym, look in a dictionary for its meaning. For instance, *eager* and *anxious* aren't exact synonyms, although both mean "looking forward to a future event." *Eager* means "anticipating with pleasure," but *anxious* means "anticipating with dread."

Use Analogies An analogy is an extended comparison between two things that are usually considered unlike but that do share some common features. An analogy makes an extended comparison, supported point by point with examples and details. It can last through several paragraphs or an entire essay.

CREATING SUCCESSFUL ANALOGIES

1. Find at least three similarities between the ideas you are comparing.

2. Use specific details and examples to support your comparisons.

3. Write a topic sentence that establishes the basis of the comparison.

4. Decide on a logical order for the points of the analogy and use transitions such as *similarly* and *also* to link them clearly.

Possible analogies:

- Going on a school field trip is a lot like going on a family vacation.
- The new baby at our house reminds me of a very young puppy.
- Being in a group science-fair project is like running in a relay race.

Create a Mood With the descriptive language and the organization you choose, you will produce a certain mood, or overall feeling, for your descriptive writing. To achieve a suspenseful mood, you could organize your description by order of importance, leaving the surprise for the end. To express excitement, you may choose the same order but change the descriptive language you use.

GUIDELINES FOR DESCRIPTIVE WRITING

- Gather vivid details that will help you describe a person or re-create a scene or an experience for your readers.

- Decide which kind of organization will be more appropriate for your subject—spatial order, order of importance, or order of impression.

- Write a thesis sentence that presents your central idea.

- Use transitions to clarify the organization and relationships among ideas.

- Use descriptive language and analogies to make your writing vivid.

15.2 NARRATIVE WRITING

A narrative is a story of an event. Narrative writing can be **personal,** allowing the author to focus on important events in his or her life; **historical,** capturing a moment from the past and presenting it in a story format; or **fictional,** using imagination to produce a short story. Here are the basic elements of a narrative:

- **Plot** is the story's action and events. When you tell what happened, you are relating plot. Plots have a **conflict,** a problem basic to human experience, and a **resolution**, the outcome of the conflict.
- **Characters** are the people, animals, or main actors in the plot. Their actions and thoughts enable you to express the **theme,** or overall idea, of the narrative.
- **Setting** is the time and place in which the events of a narrative occur. The setting helps create the **mood,** or general feeling, of a narrative.

DEVELOP YOUR NARRATIVE

Most authors do not just sit down and write. Usually they follow several steps before getting the first draft onto paper. These steps allow for planning and organization, as well as character and plot development.

For Better or For Worse   by Lynn Johnston

© Lynn Johnson Productions Inc./Dist. By
United Feature Syndicate, Inc.

Find a Story Idea Your story should have a conflict, which can be external—a person struggling against another person, for example, or internal—such as a person torn between two ideals. You can search your everyday life for story ideas for a personal narrative, or you might try looking through newspapers and magazines for ideas. Talk about story ideas with friends.

After you have an idea for your narrative, evaluate it:

- Does the conflict concern a basic human experience, such as love, hate, loyalty, pain, survival, or death?
- Does the conflict matter deeply to the characters?
- Does the resolution grow directly out of the conflict?
- Is the resolution a result of the characters' efforts?
- Does the resolution provide a theme for the narrative?
- Do the characters grow or change by resolving the conflict?

Develop Character Your characters should be as lifelike as possible. Relate the characters' physical descriptions, thoughts, personality traits, actions, and reactions to one another. Include dialogue to let the reader witness the characters' conversations. Dialogue not only gives readers important information about the characters, but it also moves the plot along, foreshadows possible trouble, and produces a sense of time and place.

DIALOGUE GUIDELINES
• Use language that reflects the age, background, and personality of each character.
• Give your dialogue a purpose—to advance the action, to reveal a character's personality, to show relationships between characters, or to build the conflict.
• Enclose a quotation in quotation marks and begin it with a capital letter.
• Begin a new paragraph each time the speaker changes.

Set the Scene A setting includes information about time, place, weather, and historical period. Often the setting will affect the way your characters act. Setting also contributes heavily to mood. For instance, if the action of the narrative takes place in an old, abandoned house, the mood will most likely be suspenseful or scary. As you write, consider how each element of the setting can help advance your narrative.

Communicate a Theme The theme of a story is the insight into human life that the writer conveys through the narrative. One way to express the theme of your narrative is through your description of the setting. Ask yourself how you can create a mood and hint at the theme through scenery, props, color, and sound. Then use concrete words to describe these details.

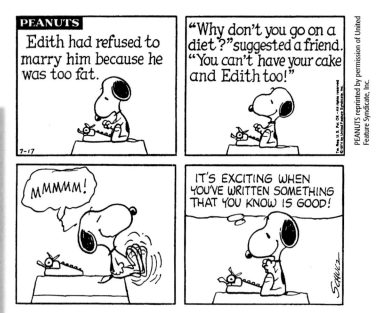

Choose a Point of View Once you have decided on the characters, plot, and setting, you must choose the point of view from which you will tell the story.

- **First-person point of view:** The narrator is a character in the story; he or she uses the pronoun *I*.

- **Third-person point of view:** The narrator is not a character in the story but an observer of it. Using this point of view, you may choose a **third-person limited narrator,** who sees the world through the eyes of one character and knows and relays the thoughts and actions of only this character. Alternatively, you may choose a **third-person omniscient narrator,** who knows and relays the thoughts and actions of all of the characters.

Remember that the point of view you choose significantly affects the story. It can give the story a bias, or it can limit what the audience knows until the very end. Think carefully about the point of view and how it will affect the development of the plot.

ORGANIZE YOUR NARRATIVE

When you begin to organize the information you have decided to include in your story, review the basic plot structure diagram that follows.

You don't have to follow this curve precisely in your narrative, but it gives you a basis to follow. You might want to use **flashbacks** in the rising action that take you back to a time before the story began. You might also consider opening with the climax and then giving the background that led up to it. As you are writing, try several ways of organization, then evaluate the flow of the narrative to see which organization is most successful.

Most Plots Develop in Five Stages.

- **Exposition** is background information about the characters and setting. This sets the scene for the conflict that follows.
- **Rising action** develops the conflict.
- **Climax** is the point of highest interest, conflict, or suspense in the story.
- **Falling action** shows what happens to the characters after the climax.
- **Resolution** shows how the conflict is resolved or the problem solved.

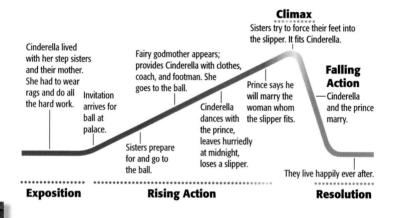

Climax
Sisters try to force their feet into the slipper. It fits Cinderella.

Falling Action
—Cinderella and the prince marry.

Cinderella lived with her step sisters and their mother. She had to wear rags and do all the hard work.

Invitation arrives for ball at palace.

Fairy godmother appears; provides Cinderella with clothes, coach, and footman. She goes to the ball.

Prince says he will marry the woman whom the slipper fits.

Sisters prepare for and go to the ball.

Cinderella dances with the prince, leaves hurriedly at midnight, loses a slipper.

They live happily ever after.

Exposition   **Rising Action**   **Resolution**

15.3 EXPOSITORY WRITING

Giving directions, explaining an idea or term, comparing one thing to another, and explaining how to do something are all forms of expository writing. The purpose of expository writing is to inform your audience or explain something to them. The chart on the next page describes several types of expository writing.

TYPES OF EXPOSITORY WRITING	
TYPE	EXPLANATION
EXPLAIN A PROCESS	Uses step-by-step organization to explain how something happens, works, or is done
CAUSE AND EFFECT	Finds the causes or effects or both of a system; examines the relationship between causes and effects
COMPARE AND CONTRAST	Examines similarities and differences to find relationships and draw conclusions
DEFINITION	Explains a term or concept by listing and examining its qualities and characteristics
PROBLEM AND SOLUTION	Examines aspects of a complex problem and explores or proposes possible solutions

Writing Tip

In expository writing, consider using graphs. Often expository writing includes so many statistics that it is hard to read. A visual element, such as a bar graph, a line graph, or a circle graph, will help your readers grasp your topic.

EXPLAIN A PROCESS

Before you begin to explain a process, you should do at least one of the following: go through the process yourself, watch someone go through the process, or research the process. Take detailed notes as you go.

Organization In most process explanations, you will use chronological order, or the order in which steps will occur. After you have placed the basic steps in order, elaborate on them, supplying necessary details to clarify your explanation.

EXPLAIN A CAUSE-AND-EFFECT RELATIONSHIP

Cause-and-effect relationships occur when one event produces another event, or outcome. Cause-and-effect writing gives explanations for events, conditions, and behavior. For this kind of expository writing, you can

- start with one cause and lead to one effect
- start with one cause and lead to several effects
- start with several causes and lead to one effect
- start with several causes and lead to several effects
- start with one cause that leads to an effect, which in turn becomes a cause that leads to another effect, and so on. The result is a chain of events.

Organization When you describe a cause-and-effect relationship, you can

- describe the effect first and then explain its cause, or you can
- describe the cause first and then explain how it leads to the effect.

Whichever organizational method you choose, make sure that your cause-and-effect relationship is valid—that is, be sure you have not assigned an effect to the wrong cause or causes.

COMPOSITION

COMPARE AND CONTRAST

When you compare two topics, you're discussing their similarities. When you contrast two topics, you're addressing ways in which they are different. In a compare-and-contrast essay, you must choose two topics that share both similarities and differences, and you must explain these.

Organization As you organize your two topics, you might consider using a Venn diagram such as the one that follows.

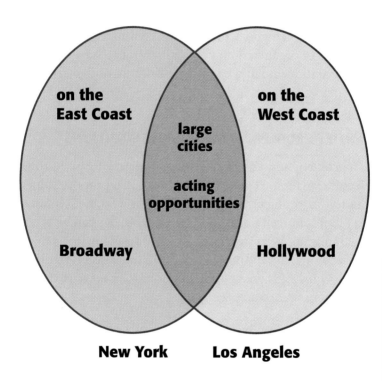

Once you have identified the similarities and differences of your topics, you can choose the most effective way to present the information—by subject or by similarities and differences.

EXPLAIN A DEFINITION

When you write to define a term or an idea, you can give a formal definition or a personal definition. If you are presenting a formal definition, you should provide specific qualities of the term you are explaining to help your audience understand. If you are presenting a personal definition, you might instead use real-life examples and vivid details to convey your personal feelings about the idea or term.

Organization Begin your research with a dictionary or other source. Once you have the basic definition or idea, you can add details. When you actually write your draft, try different orders of organization; you might want to start with the basic definition and move to a broader sense of the term or vice versa.

IDENTIFY PROBLEMS AND PROPOSE SOLUTIONS

In problem-and-solution writing, you investigate a problem and explain it to your readers. Then you propose solutions to that problem. As you think of the possible solutions, don't limit yourself to just one. Most problems can be solved in a number of ways, and by proposing many solutions you open up the possibility of finding a solution that actually works. Evaluate your solutions to make sure they aren't impossible to achieve.

Organization As you begin your research, consider the causes of the problem. You might want to include these in your writing to help your audience better understand the extent of the problem. You might also include different examples, such as personal anecdotes and statistics.

After you have thoroughly covered the problem, propose solutions. In your writing, you should address both the pros and the cons of the solutions you propose. Keep in mind that there is often no one solution that will fix the entire problem.

15.4 PERSUASIVE WRITING

Persuasive writing surrounds you in everyday life. You encounter persuasive writing in advertisements on television, radio, and billboards. Politicians give persuasive speeches during campaigns. Organizations persuade you to adopt their causes, encouraging you to donate time or money to them.

Persuasive writing is used to motivate readers—to change their minds about a topic, to convince them to buy a product, or to get them to vote for a certain candidate or issue. The main reason behind persuasive writing is to convince readers to take action, in whatever form that might be.

CHOOSE A TOPIC

When you write persuasively, make sure you choose a topic worth addressing. Consider the following when choosing a topic.

- **Are opinions concerning this topic varied?** In persuasive writing, you must argue a point and try to convince readers to support your opinion or somehow to take action. If your opinion is not disputed, it probably is not worth arguing. For example, it would be pointless to argue that pollution is bad because almost everyone would agree with you. However, you might argue for a certain antipollution law, such as mandatory carpooling, and try to convince your audience that such a law is necessary to battle pollution.

- **Will your audience be receptive to your argument?** Take into consideration your audience and their opinions and situations when you choose a topic. For instance, it would be pointless to argue for mandatory carpooling if your audience was too young to drive.
- **Does enough evidence exist to support your argument?** Briefly investigate the amount of supporting evidence for your argument. If little support for your opinion exists, you will be fighting a losing battle.

Writing Tip

Before you begin writing, you must also identify your purpose. Do you want to change the opinions of your audience? To motivate them to take action? Or simply to encourage them to recognize the validity of your opinion?

KNOW YOUR AUDIENCE

When you choose a topic, it is important to evaluate your audience—to know their concerns, their general opinions and beliefs, and their prior knowledge of or biases toward the subject. After all, your purpose is to influence their opinions and perhaps change their actions.

As you evaluate your audience, answer the following questions:

- Does the issue apply to my audience's lives? Will their action bring about positive change for them?
- What is the current attitude of my audience? Are they likely to agree or disagree?
- What do they already know about the issue? Do I need to provide background or clear up misconceptions?

- What types of evidence will have the strongest impact on my audience? Will facts and statistics alone be effective? Should I include emotional language to convey my point?

From your answers to these questions, you can evaluate the topic you have chosen. If the audience seems appropriate, your next step is to gather evidence to support your topic.

SUPPORT YOUR ARGUMENT

When you present an argument, you can appeal to emotion or to reason. To appeal to emotion, use words that elicit strong positive or negative reactions. Also, you might use real-life examples. For instance, if you were addressing the issue of homelessness, you might consider interviewing a homeless person to give your argument not only factual support but also emotional appeal. To appeal to reason, include facts, statistics, and expert opinions.

Use Evidence to Support Your Viewpoint Persuasive writing is more than just a statement of your opinion. You need to back up your opinion with evidence—facts and expert opinions that support your viewpoint.

Evaluate Your Evidence When gathering evidence, be careful to evaluate the type of support you include. Often opinions are presented as facts. Consider the following chart as you decide which information you will include in your persuasive writing.

RECOGNIZING FACTS AND OPINIONS	
FACTS	• are statements, statistics, observations, examples that can be verified, or experiments that can be repeated
OPINIONS	• are personal judgements • can be supported but not proven by facts • are often biased

Even though opinions are usually personal viewpoints, often they are influenced by supporting facts and statistics. When you evaluate opinions, including your own, make sure that enough supporting evidence exists. Expert opinions can be valuable in supporting your argument because an expert is likely to give an informed, reasoned opinion.

Use Inductive and Deductive Reasoning Either of two kinds of reasoning can support strong arguments. Both kinds of reasoning involve using facts to arrive at conclusions, but they work in opposite ways.

First, let's look at inductive reasoning. We rely on this kind of reasoning for much of our knowledge. When you use *inductive reasoning,* you follow these steps:

1. You begin with a series of facts you've observed.
2. You study the facts, looking for connections or patterns among them.
3. You draw a conclusion or a generalization.

Inductive reasoning proceeds logically from limited facts or observations to a general conclusion. An inductive argument will hold up only if the evidence is accurate and the conclusion follows reasonably from the evidence. Check your reasoning by asking whether any other conclusions can be drawn from the evidence.

EVALUATE INDUCTIVE REASONING

1. What are the specific facts or evidence from which the conclusion is drawn?

2. Is each fact or piece of evidence accurate?

3. Do the facts form a sufficiently large and representative sample?

4. Do all of the facts or the evidence lead to the conclusion?

5. Does the argument contain any logical fallacies?

The other kind of reasoning is called deductive. When you use *deductive reasoning*, you follow these steps:

1. You begin with a generalization.
2. You apply that generalization to a specific example.
3. You arrive at a conclusion.

Deductive reasoning may involve a **syllogism,** which consists of a *major premise,* which is a general statement; a *minor premise,* which is a related fact; and a *conclusion* based on the two.

SYLLOGISM	
STRUCTURE	**EXAMPLE**
Start with a generalization, a MAJOR PREMISE.	Multimedia computers require fast modems.
State a related fact, a MINOR PREMISE.	Lou is getting a multimedia computer.
Draw a CONCLUSION based on the two.	Therefore, Lou needs a fast modem.

NOTE: A syllogism is *valid* if it follows the rules of deductive reasoning. A syllogism is *true* if the statements are factually accurate. A perfectly valid syllogism, then, can be untrue. Here is an example:

Major premise: All voters are good citizens. [There is more to good citizenship than just voting.]

Minor premise: My parents are voters.

Conclusion: Therefore, my parents are good citizens. [This conclusion is valid according to the premises; however, it isn't necessarily true, because the major premise is flawed.]

EVALUATE DEDUCTIVE REASONING

1. What are the major premise, the minor premise, and the conclusion?

2. Is the major premise a universal statement?

3. Are both premises true?

4. Does the conclusion follow logically from the major and the minor premises?

5. Does the argument contain any logical fallacies?

Recognize Logical Fallacies Faulty reasoning involves errors called logical fallacies. Learning to recognize your own and others' logical fallacies will strengthen your skills in persuasive writing. Here are three of the most common types of flaws.

- A **red herring** statement diverts attention from the issue at hand. A senator who is attacked for irregular attendance might describe her charitable work to prove she is productive. However, she has not addressed the criticism about the missed meetings.

- **Circular reasoning** is an argument that apparently leads to a logical conclusion but actually takes you back to where you started. The statement "Frank Sinatra was a great singer because he had such a wonderful voice" sounds true, but the statement doesn't prove anything; it merely repeats the point in different words. There is nothing to prove or disprove.

- **Bandwagon reasoning** The term "jumping on the bandwagon" means doing or thinking something because everyone else is doing or thinking it. This type of reasoning provides no evidence to support a decision or a viewpoint.

Address the Opposition As you research supporting evidence, take time to address opposing evidence and opinions. If you do not argue against opposing viewpoints, your argument may seem weak.

ORGANIZE YOUR ARGUMENT

To be a successful persuasive writer, you must state your case well. As you organize your argument, take the following steps.

GUIDELINES FOR ORGANIZATION			
INTRODUCE THE ISSUE.	**STATE YOUR OPINION.**	**SUPPORT YOUR POSITION.**	**DRAW YOUR CONCLUSION.**
Describe the issue, supplying any background information needed.	Take your stand in a clear, direct thesis statement.	Present your evidence and show the flaws in opposing viewpoints.	Summarize your ideas and state your purpose.

Chapter 16

Research Paper Writing

• • • • • • • • • • • • • •

When you write a research paper, you collect information from several sources, analyze and organize this information, and present it to your readers in a clear and interesting way.

Calvin and Hobbes
by Bill Watterson

CALVIN AND HOBBES © Watterson. Reprinted with permission of UNIVERSAL PRESS SYNDICATE. All rights reserved.

To write a research paper, you need to

- choose a topic that interests you
- narrow the topic to fit your paper's length
- perform extensive research to gather information about the topic
- organize your research and write an outline
- form a thesis statement and support the thesis with the information you gathered in your research
- compile a list of your sources

16.1 PREWRITING

CHOOSE A TOPIC

One of your first decisions is what to write about. Try to find a topic that interests you. Researching and writing will be easier if you are curious about the topic you choose. Also consider how much information will be manageable given the length of your research paper. If the topic is very broad, you'll have too much information. If the topic is too narrow, you won't be able to uncover enough material. If you write about a topic either too broad or too narrow, your paper will probably lack substance.

Which of the following topics would be manageable in one composition?

TOO BROAD	NARROW	TOO NARROW
Art	Pablo Picasso	Picasso's painting *Les Demoiselles d'Avignon*
Tennis	The History of Wimbledon	1999 Wimbledon

Decide on a Central Idea

Once you have a topic, you need to decide on your paper's central idea. This idea will guide your thinking and your selection of research questions. Try to identify three to seven research questions, each question focusing on one aspect of the topic. Ask the *whats*, *whys*, and *hows* about your topic. As you begin to find answers, you'll come up with more sharply focused questions. Feel free to modify your central idea as you learn more about the topic.

Sample Questions for a Paper about Pablo Picasso
- How did Picasso learn to paint?
- What other art works, besides paintings, did he produce?
- Why is Picasso so famous?
- What inspired Picasso's art works?
- What is Cubism?

FIND INFORMATION ON YOUR TOPIC

Use two types of sources when you do your research—primary and secondary.

- A **primary source** is firsthand information that has not been evaluated or analyzed by someone else. If you are studying the painter Pablo Picasso, for example, a letter he wrote or a painting he created would be considered a primary source. Historical documents from the era you are researching and statistics are considered primary sources.

- A **secondary source** is information that has been organized and analyzed by someone else. An article analyzing

Picasso's paintings would be a secondary source. Most books and magazines are considered secondary sources.

Technology Tip

The Internet can be a valuable tool for finding both primary and secondary sources. Evaluate Internet sources carefully. Not all Internet sites contain accurate information. To make sure you are obtaining accurate data, find another source that contains the same information.

Take Notes

Once you have found some sources, you can begin taking notes and collecting information. Taking notes efficiently and accurately is one of the most important steps in writing a good research paper. You'll probably take many more notes than you'll use. It's better to have too much information than too little.

Prepare Note Cards Read your sources thoroughly for information, ideas, statements, and statistics that relate to your research topic and your main idea. When you find something you can use, write it on a three-by-five note card, with one piece of information per card, and record the number of that source's bibliography card (see Develop a Working Bibliography on p. 474). You can take notes in one of three ways:

- by quoting the sources directly. Use quotation marks to indicate direct quotations.
- by paraphrasing (writing the information in your own words)
- by summarizing (writing a brief summary of the information, highlighting the most important parts)

Types of Note Cards

EXAMPLE Direct Quotation Note Card

> Record **direct quotations** exactly as they appear, including punctuation. Put quotation marks around all quoted material.

An Introduction to Music and   Bib 8
Art in the Western World.

"Cubism was a style of twentieth-century
art that reduced nature to basic
geometric patterns.... Again, the artists
painted what they knew, not what they
saw. In pursuing this style, they
were concerned more with _how_ a work
was painted and less with _what_
was painted."
        (quotation)   page 307

EXAMPLE Paraphrase Note Card

> A **paraphase** is a restatement of someone else's original idea. In what other ways could you restate this information?

An Introduction to Music and   Bib 8
Art in the Western World

Cubists painted geometric patterns to
represent how they thought of a
subject, not what it looked like to
other people.

      (paraphrase)   page 307

COMPOSITION

EXAMPLE Summary Note Card

When you **summarize**, you put together key points and important details.

An Introduction to Music and   Bib-8
Art in the Western World

Cubists focused on the method of
painting, not on the painting's
subject.

        (summary)   page 307

The page number of the source is 307. Complete information about the source is on bibliography card #8.

Read Sources Critically As you read and research, evaluate your sources. A source may be biased; that is, the writer may be prejudiced toward one particular viewpoint. Using a biased source without recognizing it as such can hurt your argument. To detect bias, ask yourself, "Does this writer have a hidden purpose? Is she [*or* he] taking sides?"

When you take specific notes, pay attention to each idea's context, its relation to the ideas presented before and after it. Information out of its context may be misleading.

Avoid Plagiarism Presenting someone else's ideas or statements as your own is plagiarism. You must avoid even accidental plagiarism. Writers sometimes begin to paraphrase but instead present an idea almost as it was originally written and then take credit for it. Read your sources critically, keep complete and well-documented notes, and credit other writers when you should. If you have doubts about whether you may be plagiarizing, try rewriting the passage again in your own words, and then compare your new version with the source.

COMPOSITION

Develop a Working Bibliography

As you begin your research, assemble a record of the books, articles, Internet sites, and other sources you consult. This record is your working bibliography. When you find a useful source, record the publishing data on a three-by-five index card. This way you can easily find and use the information later. Complete bibliography cards will also help you write your list of works cited.

Different kinds of sources need different data on their bibliography cards. See the examples under A List of Works Cited on page 485 for more information about what you need to record on these cards.

Types of Bibliography Cards
EXAMPLE   Book

> 1
>
> Penrose, Roland. *Picasso.* London : Phaidon Press Ltd., 1991.

> 2
>
> "Picasso and Cubism." Designer: Denise Hall. 7 Nov. 1996. University of Texas. 15 July 1998
>
> <http://ccwf.cc.utexas.edu~/ifeh 750/index.html>,

CHOOSE A METHOD OF ORGANIZATION

How can you decide on the best way to arrange the ideas in your notes? You have a number of options, depending on the nature of your information.

- **Chronological:** arrange the information according to when it happened. This organization is often used in papers describing historical changes. The outline about Picasso's life and work is organized chronologically.

- **Cause and Effect:** arrange items in causal order to show how one idea or event directly determines another. This organization is often used in papers exploring why something happened.

- **Cumulative:** arrange items according to how important or how familiar to the reader each one is. This organization is often used in papers evaluating results.

Develop an Outline

An outline is a summary of the main points and the ideas that support them. As you take notes, look for ways to classify the facts and ideas you find and begin to group the note cards accordingly. As you make decisions about how to organize your cards, you are developing the information you need to write a working outline. You'll continue to write and revise this outline as you conduct your research. The following tips will help you write a working outline, which will eventually become the formal outline you will use when you write your first draft.

Outlining TIP

1. Look for similarities among notes; group note cards on similar topics together. Use each group as a main topic in your outline.

2. Within groups, cluster similar note cards into subgroups that elaborate on the larger and more general topic. Use these subgroups as the subheadings in your outline.

3. Arrange main topics to build on your central idea. Under each topic, arrange subheadings so they elaborate on the heading, or main topic, in a logical way.

4. As you continue your research and learn more, revise and elaborate on your outline. Subdivide information in subheadings into outline entries if necessary.

5. Set aside note cards that don't fit under any heading. Don't discard them.

6. Before you begin your first draft, prepare a formal outline.

> Title of Paper
> I. Introduction
>   Central idea (thesis statement)
> II. Heading (main topic)
>   A. Subheading (supporting detail)
>   1. sub/subheading
>   2.
>   B. Subheading (supporting detail)
>   1.
>   2.
> III. Heading (main topic)
> IV. Heading (main topic)
>   V. Conclusion

Body — (II through IV)

COMPOSITION

The Life and Work of Pablo Picasso

I. Introduction

Picasso was not content to paint in one style; instead he experimented with different styles and media and he changed the style of his art frequently over the course of his life.

II. Early life
A. Talented by age 10
B. Art school in Madrid
C. Trip to Paris
1. Influenced by other artists
2. Use of color

III. Blue period
A. Depression caused by friend's death
B. Subjects of blue period

IV. Rose period
A. Settles in Monmartre
1. Meets artists
2. Lighter mood
B. Inspirations and influences

V. Les Demoiselles d'Avignon
A. First work of Cubism
1. Reaction of contemporaries
2. Put away for twenty years
B. Description of painting
1. Motivation
2. Philosophy

VI. Cubism
A. Development
1. Georges Braque
2. Dates of Cubism
B. Definition
1. "Paint objects as I think them..."
2. Goals of Cubists
3. Influences

VII. Post-Cubist painting
A. Realistic style portraits
B. Political art
1. Guernica
2. History of Guernica
3. Description of painting
4. "Painting...instrument of war"

VIII. Other media
A. Scene and set design
B. Poetry and plays
C. Sculpture
D. Ceramics

IX. Conclusion

16.2 DRAFTING

DEVELOP A THESIS STATEMENT

So far, you have guided your research and your outline according to your central idea, or the basic question you've been exploring. You've probably rethought this idea as you have learned about the topic. Now it's time to turn that central idea into a **thesis statement**—that is, a concise idea that you try to prove, expand on, or illustrate in your writing. Your thesis statement will focus your writing from start to finish.

FOUR TYPES OF THESIS STATEMENTS		
TYPE	**DESCRIPTION**	**EXAMPLE**
Original	Used to demonstrate new information you have developed	My survey of students and teachers at Lincoln High School has uncovered a desire for more and better computers.
Evaluative	Used when stating your opinion on a topic	Solar power provides our best option for future energy needs, taking into account both economic and environmental concerns.
Summary	Used when your paper primarily reports the ideas of others	High-speed trains have revolutionized long-distance travel in both France and Japan.
Combination	Combines any two or all three of the above approaches	Interviews with music store salespeople and CD owners lead me to believe that the CD has replaced the record once and for all.

USE YOUR OUTLINE AND NOTES

Using the structure you have given your formal outline, you will be able to transform your piles of note cards into a first draft. Look at your outline again to be sure you're satisfied with the way each idea leads to the next. Then begin drafting.

1. Try to draft as smoothly and logically as possible without getting stalled on details. Don't worry about finding the "perfect" word or phrase; you can revise later.
2. Write at least one paragraph for each heading in your outline. Each paragraph should have a topic sentence and supporting details.
3. When you use data from a note card, write the number of that card near the data in the text to help you document the idea later.
4. Use your outline as a "map" to guide you in your writing. The outline should remind you of what comes before or after a particular idea.

Write the Introduction and Conclusion

A good introduction should grab your reader's attention and make him or her want to read on. Consider the following techniques for capturing your reader's attention:

1. Summarize by providing an overview of the main headings in your paper to make your reader comfortable with the topic.

COMPOSITION

2. Include an unusual anecdote or fact about your topic.

3. Pose a question that you plan to answer or explore in your paper.

4. Use a quotation.

Your conclusion should alert the reader that you are wrapping up. You might summarize your main points or mention any new questions your paper raises.

"Well, at last we have a volunteer to do the oral report on osmosis."

RESEARCH PAPER FORMAT

Use the following format for your research paper:

- At the top, bottom, and both sides of each page, leave margins of one inch.
- Double-space every line, including the title if it is more than one line long.

- Unless you are told to include a cover page, write your name, your teacher's name, the name of the course, and the date on four lines along the left margin at the start of page one.
- Center the title on the next line.
- Except for the first page, put the first line of type one inch from the top edge of the paper.
- For all pages except the cover page: Put your last name and the page number in the upper right corner of each page, one-half inch from the top and even with the right margin. Number all pages consecutively.
- Indent each paragraph's first line one-half inch from the left margin.
- If you use a set-off quotation, indent each line of it one inch from the left margin.
- At the end of your research paper, on a new page, begin your list of works cited. Center the title, *Works Cited*, an inch from the top of the page. Begin each entry even with the left margin. If an entry is more than one line long, indent the next line or lines one-half inch from the left margin.

16.3 CITING SOURCES

Document Information In a research paper, you need to be careful to indicate the sources of the information you present—including all ideas, statements, quotes, and statistics you have taken from your sources and that are not common knowledge. One reason for documenting your sources is to enable your reader to check the source personally and to judge how believable or important a piece of information is. Another reason is to avoid plagiarism.

What to Document What kinds of information need documentation? You should document your information

- whenever you use someone's exact words
- whenever you paraphrase a particular idea or series of ideas
- whenever you use information that is not generally known or found in most books on the subject

You do not need to document widely known proverbs, famous quotations, and simple definitions.

Parenthetical Documentation One way to cite sources is to insert the author's name and a page reference in parentheses after the information that requires citation. Place this documentation at the end of the sentence containing the information. The following chart explains how to document different sources in the body of your paper.

DOCUMENTING SOURCES WITHIN THE RESEARCH PAPER	
Kind of Source	**Example**
Author named in text Insert the page number in parentheses.	As Hughes points out, by the time of Picasso's death, millions of people around the world could recognize his work (72).
Work with two authors Insert both authors' last names in parentheses before the page number.	In 1937 Picasso's work changed dramatically, becoming for the first time political (Smith and Jones 15).
Work with three or more authors Give the last name of the first author listed, followed by *et al.* ("and others") and the page number.	In 1907 Picasso painted *Les Demoiselles d'Avignon*, "an early experiment" in the Cubist style (Wold et al. 307–308).

Kind of Source	Example
Work with no author or editor Use the title or a shortened version of the title, and give the page number.	The distortion, especially the "presentation of multiple perspectives," shows early signs of Cubism ("Picasso and Cubism" 1).
Source on a page with no page number Use *n. pag.* ("no pagination") in place of the page numbers.	"When I was a child, my mother said to me, 'If you become a soldier you'll be a general. If you become a monk you'll end up as the Pope.' Instead, I became a painter and wound up as Picasso" (Clark n. pag.).
More than one work by the same author Use the author's name, the title or a shortened version of the title, and the page number.	As long as he lived, Picasso regarded Spain as his homeland and the source of his creativity (Jaffé Picasso 14).
More than one source at a time Include both sources and their page numbers, separated by a semicolon.	Picasso rolled up the just-finished *Les Demoiselles d'Avignon* and stored it for over twenty years (Penrose 12; McCully 861).

Use Quotations

You may quote from a source in the following ways:

1. You may quote one word or part of a sentence, including it in a sentence of your own.

In 1907 Picasso painted *Les Demoiselles d'Avignon*, which was "an early experiment" with the Cubist style (Wold et al. 308).

2. You may quote one or more complete sentences, which you should introduce in your own words.

As Picasso once said about his work, "If you know exactly what you are going to do, what's the good of doing it? There's no interest in something you know already. It's much better to do something else" (Clark 24).

3. You may omit words or sentences from a quotation by using ellipses in place of the omitted words or sentences. Place brackets around words you have inserted in place of the omitted words or sentences. Be careful not to change the meaning of the original sentences.

Picasso's interest in the Iberian figures and other primitive sculpture "urged along . . . [his] tendency to simplification and greater objectivity of form, to suppression of detail" (Jaffé 22).

4. You may use a quotation of more than four lines by starting a new line and indenting the quote. In this case, do not use quotation marks.

Compile a List of Works Cited

From your bibliography cards, record the publishing information about the sources in the form of a Works Cited list. The list should be alphabetized by the authors' last names. If a work has no author, alphabetize it by the title. Include this list on a new page at the end of your report.

The following chart shows the proper bibliographic style for various sources, as recommended by the Modern Language Association of America (MLA). If your teacher asks you to use a different style to document your sources, you can still refer to this chart to be sure you have included everything necessary.

A LIST OF WORKS CITED	
TYPE OF CITATION	EXAMPLE
Book with Single Author	Penrose, Roland. <u>Picasso</u>. London: Phaidon Press Ltd., 1991.
Book with Two Authors	Robb, David M., and J. J. Garrison. <u>Art in the Western World</u>. New York: Harper & Row, 1963.
Book with Three or More Authors	Wold, Milo, et al. <u>An Introduction to Music and Art in the Western World</u>. Dubuque: Brown and Benchmark, 1996.
Magazine Article	Hughes, Robert. "The Artist: Pablo Picasso." <u>Time</u> 8 Jun. 1998: 72-77.
Newspaper Article	Bradley, Jeff. "Picasso's Genius as a Graphic Artist on Display at New Metro State Center." <u>Denver Post</u> 10 Jun. 1998: F1.
Encyclopedia Article	McCully, Marilyn. "Picasso." <u>The New Encyclopaedia Brittanica: Macropaedia</u>. 15th ed. 1998.
Internet Article	"Picasso and Cubism." Des. Denise Hall. 7 Nov. 1996. University of Texas. 15 July 1998 <http://ccwf.cc.utexas.edu/~ifeh750/ index.html>.

Not all sources fit the categories listed above. To cite such sources, check the *MLA Handbook for Writers of Research Papers,* and adapt one of the above entries, arranging the information in the following order:

Author information should appear at the beginning of the entry, with the author's last name first.

- If the source has two or more authors, reverse only the first author's name.

- If no author is listed, list the editor. If no editor is listed, begin with the title.
- If you use more than one work by the same author, you do not need to repeat the author's name for each entry; use a dash instead.

Title information follows any author information and lists the title of the article, essay, or other part of the book first if needed, then the title of the book.

Publication information follows the author and title, and as needed, lists the editor's name, edition number, volume number, and series name. Always list the city of publication, publisher's name, and the publication date.

Citing Online Sources

You won't need to include everything from the following list in a single citation; most sources don't require all the information in this list. If you cannot find all the information needed for a particular source, provide as much information as is available.

1. Author, editor, or compiler of the source
2. Title of the article, poem, or short work (in quotation marks); or title of a posting to a discussion line or forum followed by the phrase *Online posting.*
3. Title of the book (underlined)
4. Editor, compiler, or translator of the text (if not mentioned earlier)
5. Publication information for any print version of the text

6. Title of the scholarly project, database, periodical, or professional or personal site (underlined). If the professional or personal site has no title, add a description such as *Home page.*

7. Editor or director of the scholarly project or database

8. Version number of the source, or for a journal, the volume number, issue number, or other identifying number

9. Date of electronic publication, of the last update, or of the posting

10. Total number of pages (if they are numbered)

11. Name of the institution or organization sponsoring or associated with the Internet site

12. Date when you accessed the source

13. Electronic address of the source (in angle brackets)

Writing Tip

Page numbers in parenthetical documentation indicate the pages from which the information is taken. Page numbers in Works Cited entries are for the page span of the entire periodical or anthologized work.

16.4 REVISING/EDITING

When you revise your first draft, you can improve your choice of words, your transitions, and—most important—the way you present your ideas. Use the chart on the next page to help you revise your draft.

SOLVING REVISION PROBLEMS	
PROBLEM	SOLUTION
My first draft needs a clearer focus.	Review your thesis statement. Delete or rewrite anything in the paper that doesn't support it.
My argument should be easier to follow.	Add transitions. Rearrange and add ideas to make the paper more coherent. Delete irrelevant information.
My paragraphs don't flow smoothly from one to another.	Add or change transitions between paragraphs. Rearrange paragraphs to achieve a more logical order.
My introduction doesn't connect well with the rest of my paper.	Add transitions or rewrite the introduction to conform with the purpose and main idea.
My sentences sound repetitive.	Vary the sentence structure. Use precise, lively language. Find synonyms for repeated words.

16.5 PROOFREADING

After revising your draft, type or print a new copy of it with your corrections included. Then you can proofread your paper one final time, checking citations, grammar, spelling, punctuation, and word use. The following checklist can help you catch any remaining problems or errors.

Proofreading Checklist
1. Have I organized my ideas clearly?
2. Have I explained or defined any words that may be unfamiliar to the reader?
3. Have I discussed my topic completely?
4. Have I corrected all grammar and spelling errors?

5. Have I documented my sources properly?

6. Have I considered the meanings of the words I've used?

7. Have I capitalized everything correctly?

8. Is my final copy neat and easy to read?

16.6 PUBLISHING/PRESENTING YOUR RESEARCH PAPER

If your teacher requests it, include a cover sheet containing the title of the paper as well as your name and other identifying information. Your teacher may also ask you for other materials to check the extent of your research and the construction of your paper. For example, you may be asked to include a clean copy of your formal outline.

Your teacher may also ask you to include a summary statement. This is a brief restatement of your thesis statement, no more than two sentences long and inserted before your report.

SAMPLE RESEARCH PAPER

Lionel Washington

Ms. Kim

4th period English 10

May 7, 2001

The Life and Work of Pablo Picasso

In 1998 *Time* magazine confirmed what many already knew when it named Pablo Picasso the most influential artist of the twentieth century. Picasso, who lived from 1881 to 1973, was one of the first visual artists in history to achieve a mass audience in his own lifetime. By the time of his death at age ninety-one, millions of people around the world knew his name and had seen reproductions of his work (Hughes 72). What was it about Picasso that made him so famous? There were certainly many other talented and innovative artists in the twentieth century. One reason for Picasso's fame may be the fact that throughout his

> The thesis statement clearly states the main idea of the paper.

COMPOSITION

lifetime he constantly reinvented himself and his work. He distinguished himself as an adept painter from the time he was a child; his early paintings show his skill at what some would call the "traditional" art of copying objects and people exactly as they are. But Picasso was not content to simply continue painting in this style. As he once said about his work, "If you know exactly what you are going to do, what's the good of doing it? There's no interest in something you know already. It's much better to do something else" (Clark 24).

The son of a professor of art, Picasso was born in Spain. By the time he was ten, Picasso's talent as an artist was evident, and he soon surpassed his father in skill and technique. His family recognized his rare talents and promising future.

When I was a child, my mother said to me, "If you become a soldier you'll be a general. If you become a monk you'll end up as the Pope." Instead, I became a

COMPOSITION

painter and wound up as Picasso (Clark
n. pag.).

Picasso's family hoped that he would become a government-supported painter, so they sent Picasso to art school when he was fourteen and to another school in Madrid when he was sixteen. Unimpressed with the teaching at the school in Madrid, Picasso left to wander the streets and visit art galleries. When he was eighteen, he returned to his family in Barcelona and met a fellow artist named Carles Casagemas. After one of his paintings was accepted for an exhibit in Paris, Picasso, who was eager to see the city of artists, left for Paris with Casagemas. In Paris, Picasso discovered the bright colors used by such artists as Vincent Van Gogh and Paul Gaugin. He began to use these brilliant colors in his own paintings.

Picasso returned to Spain after two months in Paris. He became depressed after the death of his friend Casagemas in 1901, and he expressed this depression during his Blue Period, which lasted from 1901 until 1904. He abandoned the bright colors he'd begun using in France and instead painted works mostly in cold blue tones. During this time, Picasso moved back and forth between Barcelona and Paris and used street beggars and poor people in each city as his subjects. During the Blue Period, "allegories concerning poverty, blindness, love, death, and maternity were often in his thoughts" (Penrose 9).

In 1904 Picasso decided to settle permanently in Montmartre, Paris, where he met and befriended many artists and poets. His mood became lighter, and he replaced the cold blue tones of the Blue Period with the pinks and grays of his Rose Period (1904–1906). Picasso often took inspiration from the circus performers he saw around Paris. During this period, Picasso became interested in the Iberian sculptures he saw in the Louvre Museum in Paris (Penrose 10). These sculptures, dating from

COMPOSITION

before the Roman Empire, were simple depictions
of people whose figures were out of proportion.
Some of Picasso's portraits from this era depict
women with similarly distorted figures. According to
Hans L. C. Jaffé, Picasso's interest in the Iberian figures and other primitive sculpture "urged along . . .
[his] tendency to simplification and greater objectivity of form, to suppression of detail." These ten-
dencies would later lead Picasso to develop the
style of art for which he is most famous, Cubism
(22).

In 1907 Picasso painted *Les Demoiselles
d'Avignon,* which was "an early experiment" with
the Cubist style (Wold et al. 308). Instead of depicting beautiful women, Picasso painted what was
considered to be a violent depiction of women—
prostitutes with distorted figures and mask-like
faces. Picasso once again found inspiration for
these figures from sculpture, this time from African
art (McCully 861), and the distortion in this painting,

especially the "presentation of multiple perspectives," shows the early signs of Cubism ("Picasso and Cubism"). Picasso's contemporaries were outraged by this "violent" depiction of women, so he rolled up the painting and put it away for more than twenty years.

In 1909, for the only time in his life, Picasso began working closely with another painter, Georges Braque. Together, Picasso and Braque developed the style of painting that became known as Cubism. As a Cubist, Picasso said he began to "paint objects as I think them, not as I see them" (<u>Oxford</u> 514). His goal was no longer to copy what he saw; instead he and Braque abandoned what was known about perception and presented a new kind of reality, in which objects were often depicted from several different perspectives at the same time. When one is looking at some Cubist paintings, one seems to be looking at the same object from many different angles. Cubists "were more concerned with *how* a work was painted and less with *what* was painted" (Wold et al. 307).

Those who knew Picasso as a Cubist were surprised when he began once again to draw portraits in a realistic style in the late 1910s (Jaffé 31). Picasso, though, was never again to remain faithful to one style during his long life; he combined and developed different styles to create works that suited his purpose. During World War II, when he lived in German-occupied France, he painted one of the most famous political paintings of the twentieth century, *Guernica*. The Nazis bombed the Spanish city of Guernica in 1937, and in his painting, Picasso relates the violence and mutilation of the bombing, and of war in general, by depicting dismembered body parts and ferocious monsters. He added a new purpose to his art when he declared "No, painting is not interior decoration. It is an instrument of war, for attack and for defense against the enemy" (Jaffé 12).

> The topic sentence of each paragraph supports or explains the thesis statement; the rest of the paragraph supports or explains the topic sentence.

Picasso's contribution to art was not limited to his work as a painter. In 1917 he created the costumes and sets for the Russian Ballet's performance of *Parade*. In the 1930s, he published two works of poetry, and he wrote a play in 1941.

He was also an innovative sculptor who was among the first to use found objects in his sculptures, such as the bicycle saddle and handlebar he made into "Head of a Bull, Metamorphosis" (Bradley F1). He also made ceramics, coloring and deforming plates and bowls until they could no longer be used as containers.

He created more than fifty thousand works of art in his lifetime (McCully 863) and did not slow down his creative output even during his last years. By then, Picasso's reputation had risen to almost mythological status.

Picasso himself put into words the theme of his whole career when he angrily said to a publisher who had criticized his work, "What is sculpture?

What is painting? Everyone clings to old-fashioned ideas and outworn definitions, as if it were not precisely the role of the artist to provide new ones" (Clark 29).

Picasso gained and kept the admiration of people worldwide throughout his life and even afterward. As stated in the introduction, twenty-five years after his death *Time* magazine declared him the most influential artist of the twentieth century. Why? His innovative approach to art and his constantly changing definition of what art should be kept his appeal fresh.

> The conclusion might restate the thesis statement, summarize the main points, or mention new questions the paper raises.

Works Cited

Bradley, Jeff. "Picasso's Genius as a Graphic Artist on
Display at New Metro State Center." <u>Denver Post</u>
10 Jun. 1998: F1.

Clark, Hiro ed. <u>Picasso: In His Words</u>. San Francisco:
Collins Publishers, 1993.

Hughes, Robert. "The Artist: Pablo Picasso." <u>Time</u>
8 Jun. 1998: 72-77.

Jaffé, Hans L. C. <u>Pablo Picasso</u>. New York: Harry N.
Abrams, Inc., Publishers, 1983.

McCully, Marilyn. "Picasso." <u>The New Encyclopaedia
Brittanica: Macropaedia</u>. 15th ed. 1998.

"Pablo Picasso." <u>The Oxford Dictionary of
Quotations</u>. 4th ed. 1996.

Penrose, Roland. <u>Picasso</u>. London: Phaidon Press
Ltd., 1991.

"Picasso and Cubism." Des. Denise Hall. 7 Nov.
1996. University of Texas. 15 July 1998
<http://ccwf.cc.utexas.edu/~ifeh750/index.html>.

COMPOSITION

Wold, et al. <u>An Introduction to Music and Art in the Western World</u>. Dubuque: Brown and Benchmark, 1996.

Chapter 17

Business Writing

● ● ● ● ● ● ● ● ● ● ● ● ● ●

17.1 WRITING A LETTER OF COMPLAINT

Maybe your new sweatshirt shrank two sizes the first time you washed it, and now you can't even pull it over your head. Perhaps you ordered your favorite group's newest CD—but the company sent you a CD by a group you never heard before and don't care about. Maybe a waiter acted as if you and your friends didn't deserve good service. You might decide to write a letter of complaint to let your feelings be known.

TIPS ON WRITING A LETTER OF COMPLAINT

Here are some tips that will help you write an effective letter of complaint.

- Provide all the necessary information. Include the time and place the event occurred and the names and titles of the people involved. If you're complaining about a purchase, describe the exact item you bought or ordered, its stock number and price, and the date you bought or ordered it. If you called in your order and remember the clerk's name, include that, too.

- Objectively describe the problem. Vague, emotional words such as *awful* and *disgusting* won't help. Instead, calmly and clearly explain what happened, as a reporter would do. Remember that the person reading your letter needs clear information in order to help you.

- Request a specific, reasonable solution. Demanding that the recipient just "do something" about a problem isn't helpful. Instead, say what you would like to happen, such as having an item replaced or receiving a refund. Most companies will go out of their way to keep customers happy and will be glad to fulfill a reasonable request—if they just know what the customer wants.

- Be polite. Calling people names, insulting their intelligence, or making threats won't help the situation. Remember that everyone makes mistakes, and misunderstandings do happen. Even more to the point, in most cases the person who will read your letter is not the person who made the mistake. Don't make an enemy of the person who opens your letter.

- Keep a copy of your letter until your complaint has been resolved in some way. If you need to write a follow-up letter, attach copies of any previous correspondence.

COMPOSITION

159 West Street
Bethel, IO 89753
June 20, 1999

Karla Lessing
Manager, The Place
429 Carriage Drive
Bethel, IO 89753

Dear Ms. Lessing:

Today, June 20, two of my friends and I ate dinner at
your new restaurant. We arrived about 6:20 pm, and our
waiter's name was Lee.

After we were seated, we had to wait fifteen minutes
for Lee to bring us menus. Then we waited another twenty
minutes before Lee took our order. After ordering, we had
to wait forty-five minutes for our food.

We saw Lee a lot during this time, but he was always
helping someone else. He seemed to be ignoring us. When
our food finally arrived, it was not what we had ordered.
Lee brought my friend Tony chicken even though Tony
had asked for chili. My friend Erin never did get her
French fries, but Lee still put them on our bill.

All in all, we were very dissatisfied with the service
we received. We know the restaurant just opened and Lee
is new at his job, so we would like to try again. Please
send us a coupon or some kind of credit for the cost of
our meal, so we can give your restaurant another chance.
I am enclosing a copy of the receipt for our meals, which
totalled $22.50 for the three of us.

Sincerely,

Mel Adams

Mel Adams

BE POLITE

Avoid using the pronouns *you* and *your.* Using these two pronouns in negative situations can seem like a personal attack on the reader, blaming the reader personally for whatever went wrong. These examples show the difference.

ATTACKING THE READER	STATING THE FACTS
You sent me the wrong CD!	I did not receive the CD I had ordered.
Your waiters are incompetent!	Lee did not bring the food we had ordered.
I *know* you don't want me to tell all my family and friends how you treated us.	A new restaurant, trying to build good public relations, has to try to give each customer an enjoyable dining experience.

Readers who feel they are being attacked or blamed may stop reading. Yet if you simply state the facts, they probably will read your entire letter and try to solve your problem.

To avoid insulting someone, don't mail anything you wrote while you were angry or upset. Wait until you cool off to revise. Here are some words and phrases that indicate an angry—or perhaps a rude—writer:

WORDS AND PHRASES TO AVOID

I'm sure you don't realize	you must realize
irresponsible	you don't expect me to
mistaken	I expect you to
incompetent	you should know
failed	if you care
inexcusable	you forgot to
obnoxious	why do you people always
ignorant	you leave me no choice
insist	your complaint
refuse	you say

You have a right to make complaints, but you also have a responsibility to make them courteously, without trampling on the reader's right to be respected.

WILL YOUR LETTER BE DIRECT OR INDIRECT?

Letters can be **direct,** getting to the point right away, or **indirect,** explaining the situation before getting to the point. Letters that offer good news should be direct, stating the reason for writing in the first sentence or two. Getting to the point immediately gives a busy reader the information he or she needs right away.

If you write with a simple request, you are asking a reader to do something he or she won't mind doing, such as attending a meeting or filling an order. These letters should also be direct, making the request in the first or second sentence.

However, sometimes you write to ask readers to do something that they might not want to do. If you make your request in the first or second sentence, the reader will probably say no. In these situations, readers are more likely to say yes if you use the indirect approach, which is more persuasive. To do this, you explain the situation first and then make your request.

TWO APPROACHES TO BUSINESS LETTERS	
DIRECT	Give the main point first, then provide details.
INDIRECT	Explain the situation first, then make a request.

Reread Mel's letter of complaint. Do you see that he explained the situation before making his request? Think for a minute about how the restaurant manager might have responded if Mel had used a direct approach, starting right off by asking for a refund of $22.50. Without knowing the

COMPOSITION

situation, the manager might think Mel is unreasonable, decide not to grant his request, and stop reading. Yet because Mel first explained the situation politely and objectively, the manager will probably keep reading and send him a coupon for three free meals.

BE BUSINESSLIKE

Being businesslike means avoiding slang. Words such as *awesome* and *diss* have no place in business writing. Save them for letters—or e-mail—to your friends. Fortunately, however, being businesslike does *not* mean using really long sentences and words. Neither does it mean using old-fashioned words and phrases, such as *herewith* and *the aforementioned*. Today's business writing uses simple, straightforward language and avoids the stilted words and phrases that make letters boring and difficult to understand. Your letters, including your letters of complaint, will be much improved if you make these kinds of substitutions:

Instead of	*Write*
herewith	with this letter
aforementioned	previously mentioned
As per your request,	As you asked,
Enclosed please find	I am enclosing
At this point in time,	Now *or* Today
is in possession of	has
forward it to the undersigned	send it to me

Writing Tip
Write letters of complaint when the situation requires it—but write ones that will get good results!

17.2 WRITING A MEMO

When you become a working adult, you'll probably need
to know how to write a memo. People who work for the
same company often communicate with one another using
memos. Memos can be sent from a manager to an employee,
from an employee to a manager, or from an employee to
another employee. The word *memo* is short for *memoran-
dum,* which means "a written reminder." Memos help
employees coordinate projects or request others' help or
opinions. They also are used to introduce new staff members, announce meetings, explain recent decisions, describe
changes in procedures, and just to get things done.

Unclear, unorganized memos can force other employees
to guess what the writer is trying to communicate. Guessing
can result in wasted time, missed deadlines, poor decisions,
and expensive mistakes. Managers and supervisors often
consider an employee's ability to write a clear, well-
organized memo when they are contemplating a raise or
a promotion. In other words, your skill in writing memos
will probably be used as a measure of your competence on
the job.

UNDERSTANDING THE DIFFERENCE BETWEEN
A LETTER AND A MEMO

While you'll use memos to communicate with people
within your organization, you'll use letters when you write
to people outside it. Letters and memos are similar in many
ways. Both can be either long or short, depending on how
much the writer has to say. Both can be informal when they
are written to someone the writer knows well, or they can
be formal when they are sent to a stranger, a superior, or a
group of people. A writer might spend a few minutes jotting
down a letter or memo—or hours on either one if the situation is sensitive or complex.

Although letters go to people outside the organization, they aren't necessarily more important than memos. A memo to another employee can be just as important as a letter to a customer.

FORMATTING A MEMO

Although letters and memos are similar, they have different formats. That is, they look different on the page. A letter begins with a heading (the writer's address and the date) followed by the inside address and the salutation. A memo begins with a different kind of heading, as shown here. Notice that the first letters of the date, names, and subject all line up vertically.

Date: March 13, 2000
To: Louis Morgan
From: Melloni Pollanski *mp*
Subject: Changes in ordering office supplies

The order of the information in memo headings can vary, with the date placed last instead of first, for example. Some memos also have a line labeled "CC:" that lists the people who receive carbon copies. (Today the copies are usually xerographic, but "C:" or "CC:" is still the label.) Some traditional writers use the label "Re:" instead of "Subject:" to indicate the topic of the memo. *Re* is Latin for "in regard to the thing."

Many businesses use a special letterhead for memos. No addresses are necessary in the heading of a memo, as it is going to someone within the company. Memos usually have no closing or signature. Instead, writers put their initials beside their names in the heading to show that they wrote the memo and are responsible for its contents.

Though the paragraphs in letters can be indented, the paragraphs in memos are usually written in full block form, without any indentation. Insert two or three extra lines between the heading and the memo, and put an extra line between the paragraphs.

DILBERT reprinted by permission of United Feature Syndicate, Inc.

ORGANIZING A MEMO

These steps will help you organize an effective memo:

1. Determine your purpose for writing Think about your reason to write. What do you need to communicate or request? If you tell yourself, "I need to write to Joan about the Simpson order," you haven't identified your purpose clearly enough. Here are more specific reasons to write to Joan:

- to inform her about a change in the shipping schedule
- to ask her to check on a price for an item in the order
- to tell her that Mr. Simpson has canceled his order

A memo should have one main point or two or three closely related points.

2. Choose a direct or an indirect approach

In a **direct** approach, you get to the point in the first sentence or two of the memo. Use a direct approach if your purpose is

- to give the reader good news or information that is not controversial or potentially upsetting
- to make a request that the reader will probably be willing to grant

The following is part of a "good news" memo that uses the direct approach. Notice that the main point is stated immediately.

> The company is introducing a flex-time working schedule. Starting November 1, employees will be able to choose their own working hours, with their supervisor's approval, as long as they work eight hours a day. Application forms for schedule changes will be available from the Human Resources Department as of October 15.

In an **indirect** approach, you explain the situation before getting to the point. Use an indirect approach if your purpose is

- to give bad news
- to persuade the reader to do something he or she might not want to do

On the next page is part of a "bad news" memo, organized using the indirect approach. Notice that the writer explains the situation before offering the bad news. This approach prepares readers for the bad news and helps them understand why a difficult decision was made. That way, they will be more likely to accept the bad news without becoming angry or upset.

> For the past three months, the Human Resources Department has been studying the practicability of a flextime working schedule. Flextime would enable employees to customize their hours at work to accommodate changeable responsibilities such as sick children or elderly family members, school holidays, and even community volunteering projects. The company supports employee resposibility to family and community and hopes to be able to offer flextime in the near future. However, as you know, the Simpson project has required a great deal of overtime recently. Because of the tight deadlines, supervisors have not had time to give us their input on flexible scheduling. They have asked us to delay our decision until after the Simpson delivery date, which is six months away. For that reason, we will put flextime on the back burner until the third quarter. In the meantime, employees are invited to contact the Human Resources Department with comments and suggestions for the flextime policy that we will eventually adopt.

3. Decide what information to include in the memo Ask yourself these questions:

- What does the reader *already know* about this topic?
- What does he or she *need* to know?
- What does the reader *want* to know?

Don't bore readers by repeating what they already know, but do provide any background information or details that you think are necessary. Sometimes, however, readers need to be reminded about the facts of a situation even though they are familiar with it.

COMPOSITION

4. Write the memo Skip the subject line for now. Start by explaining your main point, if you chose a direct approach, or the situation, if you're using an indirect approach. If your memo is long, organize the information in a logical way. For example, you might explain a situation chronologically—that is, in the order in which it happened. Alternatively, you might put the information in order of importance.

5. Write an effective subject line If you have chosen the direct approach, the subject line in your heading should summarize the memo. It should be short and specific. If the memo is going to all employees or to several departments, the subject line should attract the attention of those employees most affected by the memo.

Here are some subject lines that are poor choices, followed by some that are better:

TOO WORDY	New cafeteria schedule for the month of May because of the kitchen remodeling
BETTER	New cafeteria hours for May
TOO VAGUE	Survey results
BETTER	Employees' cafeteria preferences

If you're using an indirect approach, don't put the bad news or the request in the subject line. Your reader may stop right there and become angry at the bad news or reject your request. Instead, just mention the topic in the subject line.

TOO DIRECT	Problems in meeting the deadline on the conversion project
BETTER	Conversion project status
TOO DIRECT	Mandatory overtime for June
BETTER	New June work schedule

COMPOSITION

MAKING MEMOS MORE READABLE

The way your memo looks on the page—its format—will help determine whether anyone reads it. Following these tips as you edit and revise will help you invite people to read your memos:

- Break your memo into paragraphs, with one main topic per paragraph. A solid page of words can discourage readers.
- Use lists and bullet points whenever appropriate to add interest to the page and further break it into smaller "chunks."
- Use words that your readers will understand. Unfamiliar terms and abbreviations will only frustrate readers. Remember, the purpose of a memo is to communicate, not to impress readers with your vocabulary or to teach them new words.
- When you're finished, proofread. If you're working on a computer, use your computer's spell-checker, if possible, but also read the memo yourself word for word. A spell-checker will catch spelling errors, but only your careful reading will catch missing words or the wrong forms of words, such as *here* for *hear* or *it's* for *its.* Reading the memo aloud may help you spot these mistakes. Putting it aside for several hours and then rereading it will also help you see exactly what's on the page, instead of what you intended to say.

Writing effective memos takes some practice, but if you can learn to write clear, well-organized memos, your co-workers—and your supervisors or managers—will be glad to see your initials on a memo from you, and your job will be easier, more pleasant, and more productive.

Calvin and Hobbes

by Bill Watterson

17.3 MAKING A PRESENTATION

Oral presentations aren't just schoolwork. Any time you've planned what to say to a parent or guardian, any time you've thought out beforehand how a discussion with a friend might go, you've prepared for an oral presentation. When you begin working, you might have to explain a project to people in another department or ask other employees to contribute to a worthy cause. Maybe you'll be part of a team that is trying to get your department's proposal accepted by upper management. All these will be opportunities for you to use the oral presentation skills that you are practicing now in school.

Many people, even businesspeople, dread giving oral presentations. They worry about "doing something stupid" or looking foolish. They're afraid they'll forget what they planned to say—or remember it but "bore everyone to death." They don't want everyone to see how nervous they are. They don't want to be the focus of everyone's attention.

These panicked people probably don't know how to plan an effective oral presentation. If they did, they would feel more confident and comfortable about it. This lesson will help you look forward to your next presentation. Here are the steps you'll learn:

- Consider Your Topic and Your Purpose
- Analyze Your Audience
- Choose the Form of Your Presentation
- Decide What to Say
- Organize Your Presentation
- Create Visuals for a Multimedia Presentation
- Practice Giving Your Presentation
- Look Professional and Speak Effectively

CONSIDER YOUR TOPIC AND YOUR PURPOSE

In school or at work, you might choose a topic or one might be assigned to you. First, make sure you understand what is expected from your presentation. Are you simply informing the audience about a noncontroversial topic? If so, you might need to narrow a topic that is too broad. You might have to think of an approach that will interest your audience. You definitely must find out what the audience needs to know about the topic.

Maybe you're expected to persuade the audience to think differently about the topic. Perhaps you're supposed to convince them to do something they might not want to do. Then you will need to devote some time to analyzing the audience's different needs and viewpoints so you can determine what will best motivate them to act.

Often your next step will be learning more about the topic. This may require some time at the library, on the Internet, or both. You might also interview experts over the phone, in person, or via e-mail. The more you know about the topic, the better you can decide what to say to your audience. Feeling confident and knowledgeable about your topic is the foundation of giving an effective presentation.

ANALYZE YOUR AUDIENCE

Consider how your audience might respond to your topic. With interest? With indifference? Even with hostility? If the audience is familiar with the topic, some listeners might already have strong opinions about it. You will need to respect these opinions, even if you intend to persuade the listeners to change their minds. If the audience has heard about this topic many times before, you will have to think of an interesting new approach.

If the topic is relatively new to this audience, find out what, if anything, they already know about it. Can you use technical terms or will you have to define them—or avoid them? What is the audience's educational level? What interests or experiences do they have that will help them understand this unfamiliar topic? How can you show them that the topic is important in their everyday lives?

In a work setting, you will also need to know whether your audience will be mostly co-workers, mostly management, or a combination of the two. Are your listeners the decision makers or the ones who carry out decisions? Will they accept your recommendations at face value, or will you have to support your conclusions with statistics and experts' opinions?

The answers to these questions will help you decide what your presentation should include to meet the audience's needs and to accomplish your own goals.

CHOOSE THE FORM OF YOUR PRESENTATION

Decide how much your audience will participate. Here are two possibilities, but your presentation may fall somewhere in between:

A traditional speech or lecture In this approach, you provide information on a topic and answer questions from the audience afterward. This approach is often used because it is a direct way to share information. However, it can be boring for the audience, who must spend most of their time merely sitting and listening.

An interactive presentation This approach is more like a conversation and works best with a smaller audience. You provide basic information and then ask the audience questions. Here are some possible goals for this type of presentation:

- to get the audience's feedback on an issue
- to convince the audience to act on an issue
- to help a group work together to solve a problem
- to encourage the audience to ask questions that explore the topic
- to guide the audience to see how they can apply a certain concept or technique in specific situations

For example, if you were trying to get the audience to volunteer to be tutors in the community's Right to Read program, you might begin by explaining what the program does. You might also introduce some of the current tutors.

Next, you could involve the audience by asking for reasons why some people decide not to be tutors. Someone might point out, for example, that young people don't know how to be teachers. Then you can ask the audience if they've ever taught anyone to do something. What was it? (Be ready with examples of your own, such as shooting a basket, braiding hair, accessing the Internet, or programming a VCR. You are reminding the audience that they do, indeed, know how to be teachers.) After they've participated in the presentation, your audience is more likely to participate in the program.

Interactive presentations get the audience more involved than a traditional speech or lecture does, but the presenter must be able to keep discussions on track and quickly adjust

the questions to meet the audience's needs and interests.
You don't want the meeting to disintegrate into an argument.

DECIDE WHAT TO SAY

Learning more about your topic and analyzing your
audience will help you decide what to include in your presentation. The amount of time allowed for your presentation will also help determine how much information you
can include. Instead of saying a little about many aspects of
the topic, focus on two or three main points that will be
meaningful to your audience. They won't remember lots of
facts and statistics, but they are likely to remember two or
three points if you offer interesting examples and solid evidence to support them.

Writing Tip

While planning your presentation, ask yourself these questions:
· What do I want the audience to learn?
· What do I want the audience to do after my presentation?

ORGANIZE YOUR PRESENTATION

Plan an opening that will grab the audience's attention
and introduce your topic. Here are some possibilities:

Tell a story It can be a true story about yourself or others, as
long as it won't embarrass anyone else. (You can embarrass
yourself if you want to.) Alternatively, it could be a story
you've made up that helps you introduce the topic of your
presentation. Here's one example: "I wanted to get a job
this year, because. . . ."

Ask a question Get the audience thinking about the topic. For example, you might ask, "Where would you be today if you didn't know how to read?"

Offer a surprising fact Get the audience's attention with a fact that challenges their opinions. Here's an example: "Did you know that one in five adults in the United States cannot read as well as the average fourth grader?"

Tell a joke Do this only if you're good at it. Choose a joke that relates to your topic, and make sure it does not insult any person or group of people. Most libraries have books of jokes compiled especially for public speakers. Try the joke on friends first to see if they think it's funny, doesn't insult anyone, and isn't too silly.

"THERE ARE ESSENTIALLY FOUR BASIC FORMS FOR A JOKE — THE CONCEALING OF KNOWLEDGE LATER REVEALED, THE SUBSTITUTION OF ONE CONCEPT FOR ANOTHER, AN UNEXPECTED CONCLUSION TO A LOGICAL PROGRESSION AND SLIPPING ON A BANANA PEEL."

COMPOSITION

After deciding how to begin your presentation, make an outline that organizes your main points into a logical order. Be sure to include examples, quotations, or statistics to back up each point. Following are some organizational patterns you might use:

CHRONOLOGICAL	Describe a series of events or steps in the order in which they occurred.
PRIORITY	Persuade your audience by arranging the reasons they should do something from least to most important.
PROBLEM/SOLUTION	Describe a problem, explain why it happened (or will happen), and offer a solution (which usually involves some action by the audience).
COMPARE AND CONTRAST	Show how two events, people, or objects are similar and different. This approach can help the audience understand an unfamiliar concept or convince them that one course of action is better than another. A variation is the pro/con pattern, in which you give both the advantages and the disadvantages of a course of action.
CATEGORIES	Divide the topic into categories and explain each one. You might use this approach to explain new services offered by your school or by a community agency.

The ending of your presentation is just as important as the beginning. Here are two effective endings:

- Summarize your main points and then go back to your opening statement. Finish your story, repeat your question, or refer to the fact or joke you used. Going back to the beginning gives the audience a sense of closure.
- Repeat your strongest point and then ask the audience to do something specific in response, such as filling out an application form or making a donation.

After you've outlined your presentation, write the main points on separate note cards. On each note card, include any important details you want to mention, along with any quotations or statistics you think will be effective. Use words and phrases, not complete sentences. You aren't going to read these cards aloud. You'll just use them during the presentation to remind yourself of what you planned to say. Number the cards so you can keep them in order during your presentation.

CREATE VISUALS FOR A MULTIMEDIA PRESENTATION

Multimedia simply means "involving several media or channels of communication." Speaking is one channel of communication, and visuals are another. Some people prefer the auditory channel and like to listen to new information, while others prefer the visual channel and would rather read or view new information. This second group will certainly appreciate your use of visuals.

Wes Lunker uses a visual aid to enhance his report on the planets.

Visuals help interest the audience and explain your points. A series of visuals can serve as an outline for your presentation and reduce the number of note cards you need. Visuals have other important benefits: they give the audience something to look at besides you, they provide something for you to do with your hands, and they make you look professional and well organized.

Visuals can be as simple as a list printed on poster board or as complex as animated computer graphics. Visuals can include charts, tables, graphs, maps, models, samples, videotapes, drawings, photographs, or diagrams. They can be created by hand or by computer and presented on handouts, poster board, or overhead slides or transparencies.

When designing visuals

- Explain only one point with each visual. Keep the visual simple so your audience can grasp your point right away. If necessary, explain a complicated point with a series of visuals or with several overlays on a basic transparency.
- Give every visual an informative title that stresses the point you want to make. For example, instead of "Food Preferences in the Cafeteria," you could use "Increasing Preferences for Low-Fat Food."
- Use large enough type to enable your audience to read labels and explanations easily. Do not use all upper case, or capital, letters. ALL CAPS ARE MUCH HARDER TO READ, AND THEY "SOUND" LIKE SHOUTING!
- Don't try to include every detail in the visuals, just the main points.
- Avoid clutter, such as too many typefaces, colors, clip art graphics, or borders. Two typefaces are enough, and three colors are plenty. Choose art that closely relates

to your topic. You might use the same border on all your visuals to tie them together.

- Don't forget to proofread. Otherwise, a transparency might display a misspelled word or other error in three-inch letters!

Keep it simple! Limit each visual to
- one idea
- no more than 5 to 7 lines of type
- no more than 6 to 8 words per line
- no more than 35 words in all

Using Computer Software

Many software packages are being developed to aid in school and business presentations. Several programs can create slides and transmit them directly from a computer to an overhead screen. This allows you to make words, paragraphs, or graphics appear and disappear from the slide. You can also add sound effects and fade the picture between slides. Using a chart or a graph, you can make lines or bars "grow," or you can separate one bar into several.

Most of these software programs can also create (with the help of a properly equipped film developer) 35-mm slides to use in a projector, make color or black-and-white overhead transparencies, and print handouts. In addition, you can write notes to use during your presentation, with the appropriate slide or overhead printed right on the page.

COMPOSITION

Prior to giving your presentation, you need to evaluate your visuals. Look at them from the audience's point of view. Are they
• easy to understand?
• interesting?
• relevant?
• neat and uncluttered?

Using Visuals

Before using the visual aids you've prepared, check your equipment. Check it one more time just before the presentation to make sure it works. A program that worked fine at home may not work in another setting. A power surge may have damaged the computer. The bulb on the overhead projector may have burnt out. Be ready with another way to share the information in case of disaster.

When using your visuals, face your audience and stand to one side of the visual. Do explain your visuals, but don't read them to the audience. Don't show a visual until you're ready to talk about it. Then leave it displayed until you are ready for the next visual. Turning equipment on and off can annoy an audience. Glaring white screens can also be distracting.

PRACTICE GIVING YOUR PRESENTATION

Rehearse your speech, using your visuals so that you will feel comfortable with them. After your opening, tell the audience the points you will cover so they know what to

COMPOSITION

expect. Practice making smooth transitions between your points so your presentation will flow well.

Ask a few friends or family members to listen and give you feedback on both the content of your presentation and your delivery. Perhaps you can videotape yourself and do your own critique. Watch for times when your words were difficult to understand or you didn't clearly explain a point. Were any points or examples a little dry and boring? If so, find more interesting examples to liven them up.

Check your timing and make adjustments if your presentation is too long or too short. (You might also find that you speak more quickly than usual in front of a larger audience.) Be careful not to practice so many times that you memorize your presentation. You want it to be fresh and interesting for both yourself and the audience.

FoxTrot

by Bill Amend

Chapter 17 Business Writing **525**

LOOK PROFESSIONAL AND SPEAK EFFECTIVELY

If you feel nervous before speaking to a group, you're just like most speakers. Still, that doesn't mean you won't do well. Admit to yourself that you're feeling a little jittery and use that energy to focus your attention and do your best.

Getting Ready

Get a good night's sleep and arrive at the location at least a half hour ahead of time so you don't have to rush. To prevent burping, avoid carbonated beverages for several hours before your presentation. Also, don't drink any more caffeine than you usually do.

To help yourself relax just before the presentation, take several slow, deep breaths. Next, tighten and relax your muscles, working from your toes to the top of your head. Then take a few more slow, deep breaths for good measure. Gather your note cards in your hand and take your place in front of the group where your visuals are waiting for you. Pause and smile at the audience. DON'T apologize for being nervous. Just greet your audience and begin.

Using Your Body Effectively

- Stand up straight, but in a relaxed way.
- Maintain eye contact with the audience. Pretend you are talking to just one person, but focus on a different person in a different area of the audience every minute or so. (According to several studies, audiences believe that speakers who make eye contact are better informed, more experienced, friendlier, and more sincere than speakers who don't.)
- Use gestures when they're appropriate. They help show your enthusiasm and interest in your topic.
- Move around. Unless you're standing on a stage or must stay close to a microphone, try walking among the audience members. It will bring you closer to them physically and emotionally.

Using Your Voice Effectively

- Speak clearly and slowly. Let your voice rise and fall naturally, as if you were having a conversation. Try not to rush.
- Speak loudly enough to reach people in the back of the room. However, if you're using a microphone, let it do the work. Don't shout.
- Show enthusiasm in your voice. Get excited about your topic. Your audience will catch your excitement. Enthusiasm is contagious.

PUTTING IT ALL TOGETHER

Now you know how to do well on your next presentation. If you still feel nervous about it, imagine the worst thing that could happen.

FEARS	REALITIES
You'll forget what you were going to say.	No, you won't. Your note cards and your visuals will keep you on track.
You'll mispronounce a word.	If a word is giving you problems while you rehearse, ask someone how to say it, or use another word.
Your presentation will be boring.	No, it won't, not after all the thought you've put into it. You know your audience and your topic well. You're going to start with an interesting story, and you've found good examples to support your main points. You've also created excellent visuals.

So when is your next presentation? It's not too early to start planning. You'll amaze everyone with your new skills.

Part Four

● ● ● ● ● ● ● ● ● ● ● ●

Resources

Knowledge is of two kinds: we know a
subject ourselves, or we know where we
can find information on it.

—Samuel Johnson

Chapter 18

The Library
or Media Center

• • • • • • • • • • • • •

Although you've probably been in a library, you might not realize all the resources the library has to offer or how to find them. This chapter will guide you through the library and help you understand how and where to find what you need.

CIRCULATION DESK

At the circulation desk, you'll find a librarian who can answer your questions and check out your books. In addition to a circulation desk, some libraries have computers you can use to check out your own books. Larger libraries might station additional librarians at many of the following locations.

CATALOG

A computer or card catalog will tell you which books are available in the library and where to find them. You'll learn more about using both kinds of catalogs on pages 533–539.

STACKS

The stacks, or rows of book shelves, are called the "adult section" in some libraries, but you don't have to be an adult to use these books. The stacks are usually divided into sections for fiction (novels and short stories that are works of the imagination) and nonfiction (books based on fact about subjects such as history and science).

YOUNG ADULT AND CHILDREN'S SECTION

Young readers, including high school students, can find excellent resources in the young adult and children's section. Fiction, nonfiction, and biographies are usually grouped separately, with picture books for very young readers in their own section. All of these books are listed in the library's computer or card catalog.

REFERENCE AREA

The reference area might include encyclopedias, dictionaries, almanacs, yearbooks, atlases, and other reference materials. Books in this area can be used only in the library. By not allowing people to check out these books, the library ensures that all reference materials will always be available for anyone who needs to consult them.

NEWSPAPERS AND PERIODICALS

In the newspaper and periodical section, you can read local newspapers as well as papers from major cities in the United States and perhaps from other countries. You can also browse through periodicals, which include magazines and journals. You probably cannot check out the currrent issues, but you can usually take older issues home to read. The young adult and children's section might have its own periodicals area. You'll learn more about finding specific articles in newspapers and periodicals on pages 545–547.

AUDIO-VISUAL MATERIALS

The audio-visual section of the library may stock software programs, audiocassettes and compact discs (CDs) of your favorite music, books on tape, videos, and slides for you to borrow and enjoy at home.

COMPUTER AREA

Many of today's libraries offer the use of personal computers for research on the Internet or for writing reports and papers. You may have to reserve a computer ahead of time, and the library might set a time limit, such as two hours, on your use of it. Many library computer areas also have software programs for you to use there, such as a résumé-writing program, an accounting program, or even a program to teach you how to type. For a small fee per page, you can usually print the articles you've located or the papers you've written.

STUDY AREAS

Many libraries now have desks or small rooms set aside for quiet study. You might need to reserve them ahead of time.

SPECIAL COLLECTIONS

Some libraries set aside a special room or section for collections of rare books, manuscripts, and items of local interest, including works by local students.

Chapter 19

Using Print Resources

● ● ● ● ● ● ● ● ● ● ● ● ● ● ● ●

Imagine how frustrating it would be if you had to walk up and down the stacks in a library, looking for a book that might—or might not—be anywhere on the shelves! To make life easier, libraries use cataloging systems to keep track of what's available and arrange books on the shelves according to their content.

19.1 UNDERSTANDING CATALOGING SYSTEMS

Whether you want information on a particular subject, books by a certain author, or a specific book, the catalog will help you find whatever you're looking for. Many libraries now use computerized catalogs, but some still rely on paper card catalogs. You should be able to use both kinds of tools. Then no matter what library you enter, its catalog will be at your service.

COMPUTER CATALOGS

Computer systems vary, so before you use one for the first time, read the instructions posted beside the computer or printed on the screen. Most catalog programs begin by asking whether you want to search by author, title, or subject. If you use the author's name, type the last name first, followed by a comma and the first name, as in *Johnson, Samuel.* (Some systems will allow you to type *Samuel Johnson* or even just *Johnson*, although in the latter case you'll have to search through a list of all the authors named Johnson to find the one you want.) If you search by title, enter the title but start with the first important word, ignoring *A, An,* and *The.* For a subject search, you'll use a **keyword,** a word or phrase that describes your topic. Whenever you search a computer database, including the Internet, to find books, articles, or other media, the keyword you choose will greatly affect the results you get.

Search TIP

1. **Be specific.** A general keyword, such as *animal,* will get you a long list of sources, sometimes called **matches** or **hits.** However, few of them will be helpful to you. If you use a more specific keyword, such as *dachshund,* you won't have to read screen after screen of possible sources, trying to find a few that might be helpful.

2. **Use Boolean search techniques,** which offer different ways to combine words. You can use these techniques to look for books in a computer catalog, to find articles in magazine databases (described later), or to locate information on the Internet (also described later).

Named for George Boole, an English mathematician who lived during the nineteenth century, Boolean techniques use the words *and, or, not,* and sometimes *near* or *adj.*

and:	If you combine two keywords with *and* (such as *wetlands and conservation*), the computer will list only sources that have both words. This kind of search results in far fewer hits, but many more of them will relate to your topic. (Some programs use + in place of *and: wetlands + conservation.*)
or:	If you want information on either one of two related topics, link them with *or,* as in *alligators or crocodiles.* The computer will conduct two searches at once.
not:	To eliminate a category of information from a search, use *not.* For example, if you want information about genetic disorders but not Down's Syndrome, you can enter *genetic and disorders not Down.*
near *or* adj:	Some computer programs allow you to use *near* or *adj* (adjacent) to locate sources, usually articles, that have two keywords used near each other. For example, you might use *wildlife near preservation* as your keywords. One program may list only those sources in which the keywords are within eight words of each other. Another program might allow the keywords to be fifteen words apart. This search technique has

> an advantage over linking words with
> *and,* which can generate a long list of
> articles in which both words appear but
> never in connection with each other.

Not all computer programs recognize Boolean techniques; some will treat *and, or, not, near,* or *adj* as part
of your keyword/phrase. For some other computer
programs, you must begin a Boolean search with *b/,* as
in *b/wildlife and preservation.*

3. **Use quotation marks.** Enclosing a phrase in quotation
   marks (for instance, *"preserving natural resources"*) tells
   the computer to find every book or article with exactly
   those words.

4. **Try truncating.** If you **truncate,** or shorten, your keyword by using an asterisk (*), the computer will search
   for all words that begin with the letters before the asterisk. For example, using *experiment** as a keyword will
   tell the computer to list books or articles containing such
   words as *experiment, experimental, experimented,
   experimenting,* and *experiments.* By truncating your
   keyword, you make sure the computer doesn't overlook
   various forms of the word.

   You can also truncate when you aren't sure how to
   spell a word. For example, you could use *Azer** as a keyword if you couldn't remember how to spell Azerbaijan,
   a country in southeastern Europe.

5. **Use a "wildcard"** by inserting a question mark (?) into
   certain words. For example, if you aren't sure whether to
   use *woman* or *women,* enter *wom?n.*

Now that you know how to choose keywords, here is an example of their use. To use a computer catalog, you type in the author's name, the book title, or a keyword or phrase, and the screen will list any related sources available at that library. Let's say you type the keywords *credit card safety*. The screen will then show you a list similar to the one below. If the catalog program is connected to a printer, you could print this list.

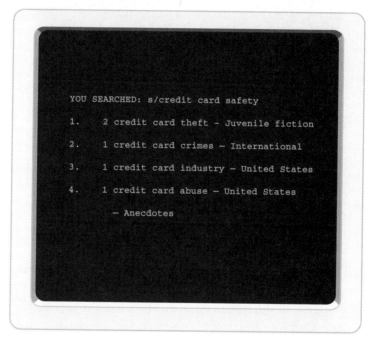

```
YOU SEARCHED: s/credit card safety

1.    2 credit card theft - Juvenile fiction

2.    1 credit card crimes — International

3.    1 credit card industry — United States

4.    1 credit card abuse — United States

        — Anecdotes
```

The first listing (1) tells you that the library has two books about credit card theft in the juvenile fiction category. Books listed in this category will be novels or collections of short stories that are appropriate for young readers. The second listing (2) tells you that the library has one book about international credit card crimes. This book isn't marked fiction, so it's nonfiction; it isn't marked juvenile, so it's for adults. To find out more about this book, enter the number of its listing, 2. The next screen might give you the following information.

```
CALL NO: 364.163 DAV

AUTHOR: Davisson, Judith

MAIN TITLE: Identities for Rent: how
international thieves can be you for a day
/ by Judith Davisson.

PUBLISHER: New York: Atheneum Books, c1995

LOCATION           STATUS          UNITS

1.   ADULT NON-FICTION  Available  364.163 DAV
```

The status column indicates that no one has checked out this book, so it should be filed on a shelf. To find it, you would write down its call number, shown at the top of the listing. (**Call numbers** are numbers and letters used to classify books. They are explained on pages 539–544.) Then you would go to the location listed (the adult non-fiction stacks), find the shelf with call numbers between 360 and 370, and look down the rows for the book marked 364.163 DAV. The books are in numerical and alphabetical order.

If someone had checked out this book, the status column would state the date when it was due back at the library. If the library had several copies of the book, the status of each copy would be stated. Some catalog entries also include the number of pages in the book; whether it has illustrations, an index, a glossary, or a bibliography; and what kind of medium it is, such as a book or videotape. Many entries list additional headings you could enter into the catalog as keywords to find more information about the same topic.

The computer instructions will tell you how to move forward and backward as you search through the library's listings. For example, you might enter *ns* (next screen) or *f* (forward) to see more of a listing. To go backward, you might enter *ps* (previous screen) or *b* (backward).

CARD CATALOGS

Card catalogs are stored in long, narrow drawers. The drawers hold two or three small cards for every book in the library, arranged alphabetically. Fiction books have two cards each, one listing the book by its author and one listing it by its title. Nonfiction books have three cards each, listing the book by its author, title, and subject.

The cards list the same information as the computer catalog, although they don't, of course, tell you whether someone has checked out the book. A library may divide its card catalog into two categories: subject cards and author/title cards. Often cards are cross-referenced, listing other available books on the same subject or a related topic. A card catalog might also have separate cross-reference cards, filed alphabetically and listing related topics.

19.2 LOCATING BOOKS

The purpose of call numbers is to help you locate books. Most school and community libraries use call numbers based on the Dewey decimal system, while many college

and university libraries use call numbers based on the
Library of Congress system.

DEWEY DECIMAL SYSTEM

The Dewey decimal system, created in 1876 by a librarian
named Melvil Dewey, divides nonfiction books into the ten
categories listed below.

DEWEY DECIMAL CATEGORIES OF NONFICTION

NUMBERS	CATEGORY	EXAMPLES OF SUBCATEGORIES
000-099	General Works	encyclopedias, bibliographies, newspapers, periodicals
100-199	Philosophy	ethics, psychology, personality
200-299	Religion	theology, mythology, bibles
300-399	Social Sciences	sociology, education, government, law, economics
400-499	Language	dictionaries, foreign languages, grammar guides
500-599	Sciences	chemistry, astronomy, biology, mathematics
600-699	Technology	medicine, engineering, business
700-799	Arts	painting, music, theater, sports
800-899	Literature	poetry, plays, essays
900-999	History	ancient history, biography, geography, travel

Let's say you wanted to know more about Samuel Johnson,
a seventeenth-century British author and dictionary writer.
You would begin by entering his name as a keyword in a
computer catalog or by looking under the *J*s in a card catalog.

The library might have many books about Johnson and his work, but the call numbers of these books could fall into different categories on the Dewey decimal chart, depending on their content. For example, one book listed by a computer catalog is *The Samuel Johnson Encyclopedia* by Pat Rogers. The 800 category, Literature, is broken down into subcategories; for example, 810 is American literature and 820 is English literature. Samuel Johnson was an English author, so this book has a call number of 820.

The more specific the topic, the more specific the call number. Some call numbers have decimals added to make them even more specific. We saw this earlier in *Identities for Rent*, which had a call number of 364.163 DAV.

Many libraries add the first three letters of the author's last name to the call number, in this case DAV for Davisson. Thus, in some libraries, the call number for *The Samuel Johnson Encyclopedia* would be 820 ROG (for Rogers).

Let's say our library also has a book titled *The Making of Johnson's Dictionary, 1746–1773* by Allen Reddick. Since this book is more about language than about Johnson, it's classified in the 400 category, Language, with a call number of 423. Another book is titled *Dr. Johnson's London*, by Dorothy Marshall. This historical account falls in the 900 category, History, so it has a call number of 942.1.

Research TIP

All libraries that use the Dewey decimal system use the same chart to assign call numbers to books. However, two librarians may put the same book into different categories. For this reason, the same book may have different call numbers in different libraries.

Biographies Our library has another book called *Everybody's Boswell: the Life of Samuel Johnson* by James Boswell. It has a call number of *B,* which stands for biography. Many libraries group their biographies together, with one biography section in the adult stacks and one in the young adult and children's department. Biographies are shelved alphabetically according to the last name of the subject of the book. *Everybody's Boswell: The Life of Samuel Johnson* will be in the *J* section of the biographies.

The library also has another biography of Johnson: *The Personal History of Samuel Johnson* by Christopher Hibbert. Two books about the same person will be shelved alphabetically by the author's last name. So Boswell's book will be before Hibbert's book in the *J* section of the biographies.

Fiction Most libraries that use the Dewey decimal system identify fiction with the call number *F* or *Fic.* The second line of the call number consists of the first three letters of the author's name or of the author's entire last name. Fiction is shelved alphabetically by the authors' last names. Books by the same author are shelved alphabetically by the first word in each title (not counting *A, An,* and *The*). Many public libraries have separate sections for some categories of fiction, such as mysteries or science fiction. In that case, usually a mark or label on the book's spine shows its inclusion on these special shelves. Within the mystery or science fiction section, books are shelved alphabetically by author's last name.

Reference Books Reference books, such as encyclopedias and current yearbooks, have an *R* or *Ref* preceding their call numbers. This will alert you that you cannot check out these sources and must use them in the library. An *OV* or another symbol added to a call number indicates that the book is oversized and kept in a section of the library with taller shelves. (Ask the librarian where this section is.)

LIBRARY OF CONGRESS SYSTEM

The Library of Congress system divides books into twenty-one categories, each represented by a letter as shown in the chart below. Like the Dewey decimal system, the Library of Congress system has subcategories identified by a second letter. For example, N is the category for fine arts. You would look under NA for books about architecture, NB for sculpture, ND for painting, and so on. Numbers added to the letter combinations identify more specific categories.

LIBRARY OF CONGRESS CATEGORIES

LETTER	CATEGORY	LETTER	CATEGORY
A	General Works	N	Fine Arts
B	Philosophy and Religion	P	Language and Literature
C–F	History	Q	Science
G	Geography and Anthropology	R	Medicine
H	Social Sciences	S	Agriculture
J	Political Science	T	Technology
K	Law	U	Military Science
L	Education	V	Naval Science
M	Music	Z	Bibliography and Library Science

In one library using the Library of Congress system, Pat Rogers' book, *The Samuel Johnson Encyclopedia,* has a call number of PR 3532.R64. *P* represents the general category of Literature, while *R* indicates a work by a British author.

The second *R* in the call number is from the author's name, Rogers.

Note that in the Library of Congress system, biographies are not filed separately but with the other books. Therefore, the call numbers of the biographies for Johnson begin with *PR*, indicating a British author.

FINDING INFORMATION IN NONFICTION BOOKS

Being familiar with the content and purpose of the parts of books will help you quickly determine whether a source will be useful to you. Not every book contains all the sections described below.

Information about a book

To find information about a book, check the following parts:

The **title page** contains the book title, author's name, and usually the publisher.

The **copyright page**, which is usually printed on the back of the title page, gives the publication or copyright date. Check the copyright date to determine how current the information is.

The **table of contents** lists the main topics covered to help you decide whether the book has the information you're seeking.

The **foreword, introduction,** or **preface,** which is written by the author or an expert in the same field, may explain the purpose of the book or the author's outlook on the subject.

Information in a book

To find information in a book, check the sections below:

The **index** lists alphabetically the people, places, events, and other significant topics mentioned in the book and gives the pages where you can find references to them.

The **glossary** lists terms in the book alphabetically and defines them, taking into account the intended readers. (Books for young children define basic terms; those for adults define terms that would be unfamiliar to most adult readers.)

The **bibliography** suggests additional research sources that are appropriate for the intended readers of the book. It may also include the sources of the information in the book.

The **appendix** contains additional information related to the book, such as maps, charts, illustrations, or graphs.

The **afterword** or **epilogue** is used by some authors to make a final statement about the book, discuss implications, or offer additional findings.

19.3 LOCATING ARTICLES IN NEWSPAPERS AND OTHER PERIODICALS

If you need current information from newspapers, magazines, or journals, the two tools described below may make your search easier.

COMPUTER DATABASES

Many libraries subscribe to databases holding collections of magazine, journal, and newspaper articles that you can access using the library computers. Most of these databases allow you to search by topic, by type of publication, or by specific publication. Some programs also allow you to select the years you want to search. You might choose to browse through all the magazines or all the newspapers in the database that cover a certain period of time, or you could narrow your search to a specific magazine or newspaper, such as the *New York Times.* Some databases allow you to review the table of contents of one issue of a magazine and read any of the articles that interest you.

If you enter a keyword that describes your topic, the database will list the title of each article on that topic along with the author, the publication, the date, and a short description of the article. You can select any titles that seem especially relevant and read either a short summary or the whole article on the computer screen. For a small fee, you can print a copy of articles that you want to take home with you.

What kinds of articles you will find depends on the database you use. If you search using the keywords *natural remedies,* for example, one database might list articles on this subject from publications such as *Prevention, Newsday, Rocky Mountain Press,* and *USA Today.* If you enter the same keywords in a more academically oriented database, you might find articles from the *Journal of the National Cancer Institute*, *Annual Review of Psychology,* and *Biological Bulletin.* Don't check just one database and assume you've seen all the articles that are available.

READERS' GUIDE TO PERIODICAL LITERATURE

Not every library can afford to subscribe to computer databases, but nearly every library stocks the paper edition of *Readers' Guide to Periodical Literature.* This guide includes the titles of articles from nearly two hundred magazines and journals, with both subjects and authors listed alphabetically and cross-referenced. It's also available on a compact disc that you can search using a computer.

An update of the paper index is published every two weeks, and information about all the articles for the year is reprinted in a hardbound book at the end of the year. One index provided the following listing under *credit card crimes.*

CREDIT CARD CRIMES
> *See also*
> Credit cards—Security measures
> Identity theft
Are your theft fears overblown? S. Medintz. il
   Money v27 no6 p137-9 Je '98

If the article "Are Your Theft Fears Overblown?" in *Money* sounds interesting, you must locate the June 1998 issue of this magazine and turn to page 137. (The *il* indicates that the article is illustrated.)

Libraries often keep issues for the current year in their newspapers and periodicals section. Issues from the previous one to five years may be stored in a different area, and older issues may be on **microfilm** (a roll or reel of film) or **microfiche** (a sheet of film). Both types of film must be inserted into special projectors that enlarge the images so you can read them. You can usually make photocopies of these articles to take home.

Not every book or article in the library or on its databases offers unbiased, valuable, reliable information. The following steps will help you avoid sources that offer irrelevant, outdated information or biased opinions.

1. **Evaluate the author of each source of information** and read any biographical information about him or her. Consider whether the author is an expert in a certain field or simply someone who has opinions about it.

2. **Evaluate the information itself,** starting with whether it is directly related to your topic. If it's only loosely related and you try to include it in your report, your work may seem unorganized and disjointed.

3. **Evaluate the author's reasoning.** Are the "facts" in a source actually unsupported opinions or exaggerations? Does the author seem to make too many assumptions? Does he or she overgeneralize from one situation to another?

4. **Check the publication date.** Are certain statistics now out of date? Is it likely that the findings have been contradicted by more recent research? Information on many topics, such as Mark Twain's childhood, may be the same whether it was published last week or twenty years ago. However, you must use up-to-date information when discussing topics that are still being researched or debated.

5. **Gather information** on the same topic from several sources. This way, you'll be more likely to become familiar with different opinions on the issue or topic. Then compare and contrast facts from each source. If three sources agree and one disagrees, the latter source may be mistaken—unless it's more current than the other sources.

19.4 USING OTHER REFERENCE SOURCES

GENERAL REFERENCE SOURCES

General reference sources are easy to locate and easy to use. They also provide detailed information on thousands of topics. Following are some excellent examples of these sources.

TYPE OF REFERENCE	EXAMPLES
General Encyclopedias These encyclopedias usually consist of many volumes. Subjects are arranged alphabetically, with an index and cross-referencing to help you find related topics. Many encyclopedia publishers offer yearly updates.	*World Book Encyclopedia* *Encyclopædia Britannica* *Collier's Encyclopedia* *Grolier Encyclopedia* *Encarta Encyclopedia* (Some encyclopedias are also available on compact discs; *Encarta Encyclopedia* is available only on a CD-ROM. CD-ROMs are described in Accessing Electronic Resources, page 567.)
Specialized Encyclopedias Each of these references focuses on a certain subject. Most provide specialized information, while some, such as *Books in Print,* tell you where to look for the information you seek. You might be surprised at the number of specialized encyclopedias that are available.	*Encyclopedia of World Art* *Van Nostrand's Scientific Encyclopedia* *Encyclopedia of World Crime* *Encyclopedia of the Opera* *Encyclopedia of the Third Reich* *Encyclopedia of Vitamins, Minerals, and Supplements* *Encyclopedia of Western Movies* *Encyclopedia of the Geological Sciences* *Books in Print*
Almanacs and Yearbooks These references are published frequently to provide up-to-date facts and statistics.	*Information Please Almanac* *World Almanac and Book of Facts* *Guinness Book of Records* *Statistical Abstract of the United States*
Atlases Atlases can be historical or current; they contain maps and statistics about countries and continents, climates, exports and imports, and the spread of world cultures, among other topics.	*Hammond World Atlas* *Cambridge Atlas of Astronomy* *Historical Atlas of the United States* *Goode's World Atlas* *National Geographic Atlas of the World* *Atlas of World Cultures*

RESOURCES

Literary and Other Biographical Works These references include brief histories of notable people, living or dead, and are usually organized by fields instead of by names.	*Contemporary Authors* *American Authors 1600–1900* *European Authors 1000–1900* *Cyclopedia of Literary Characters* *Webster's New Biographical Dictionary* *Dictionary of American Biography* *Current Biography* *Biographical Dictionary of World War I (and II)* *Biographical Dictionary of Scientists (by field)* *Biographical Dictionary of Artists*
Government Documents Some large libraries hold the federal government documents that are available to the public. These pamphlets, journals, and reports offer information on agriculture, population, economics, and other topics.	*Monthly Catalog of United States Government Publications* *United States Government Publications Catalog* (both also available on compact discs and online)
Books of Quotations The indexes of these references help you look up quotations by certain people and by subject. The quotation from Samuel Johnson at the beginning of Part Four was taken from *The Harper Book of Quotations*. It was included in the category titled "Knowledge."	Bartlett's *Familiar Quotations* *The Harper Book of Quotations* *The Oxford Dictionary of Quotations* *The International Thesaurus of Quotations*

PLANNING LIBRARY RESEARCH

1. Start early. If you wait, other students may have checked out the sources you want to use.
2. Begin with the general reference sources rather than those that deal with specific fields or topics. A general source will offer an overview of your topic. It may

RESOURCES

provide all the information you need, or it may guide you to additional sources.

3. List the sources you want to check and mark each one off your list after you've examined it so you won't check the same source twice.

4. Take careful notes and include the title, author, publisher, publication date, and page number of each source. (See page 471 for more information about compiling source cards.)

5. Talk with the librarian about your project, its purpose, its length, and the kinds of sources you have been asked to use. Describe what you've done so far and be ready with specific questions you'd like answered. Librarians can often suggest valuable references you haven't considered and perhaps help you locate them.

19.5 MAKING THE MOST OF WORD RESOURCES

When you're visiting a library's reference department, you want to be able to go right to the information you need. Hunting aimlessly through the shelves and finding only irrelevant information is a waste of your time, no matter how interesting the information might be. This section will show you the different reference books that are available and what they are good for.

KINDS OF DICTIONARIES

Maybe you never stopped to think about it, but there are many kinds of dictionaries. Most of the dictionaries you've seen at school and in public libraries are general dictionaries, each including words from general English for a general reader. Then there are specialized dictionaries that define only words used in a particular field or profession, art or craft.

General Dictionaries

General dictionaries fall into these three categories:

School dictionaries contain fewer than 90,000 entries. They focus on common words and offer easy-to-understand definitions.

College dictionaries have about 150,000 entries. These references are used in homes, schools, and businesses. They answer most questions about spelling and definitions.

Unabridged dictionaries contain more than 250,000 entries and often fill several volumes. They are generally located in libraries and include extensive definitions and word histories.

Specialized Dictionaries

Specialized dictionaries list words used in a particular field. Following are some examples of the many kinds of specialized dictionaries:

Dictionary of Sports Idioms
Dictionary of Inventions and Discoveries
Facts on File Dictionary of 20th-Century Allusions
Dictionary of Italian Literature
Dictionary of Occupational Titles
Dictionary of Medical Folklore
Dictionary of Historic Nicknames

WORD ENTRIES IN GENERAL DICTIONARIES

Any one page in a dictionary probably *contains* a few thousand words, but it probably *defines* only a few dozen. A word entry discusses the meanings and the various forms of the entry word or headword, which is the word in bold-faced type that begins the word entry. When you look up a word in a dictionary, you are looking for its word entry.

Finding Words

Words are listed alphabetically in dictionaries, usually with no regard to hyphenated words or open compounds, as in this example:

soften
soft-focus
soft pedal
softshell

Words beginning with the abbreviation *St.* are listed as if the abbreviation were spelled out. So *St. Louis encephalitis* comes before the word *saintly.*

As you search for a word, don't forget to use the guide words at the top of every page. Guide words are the first and last entry words on the page. If the word you seek doesn't fall between these words alphabetically, it won't be on that page.

Search TIP

When you can't find the word you're looking for, consider these possibilities:

1. The word might have silent consonants, such as the *k* in *knight,* the *b* in *doubt,* or the *gh* in *blight.*

2. A consonant in the word might have an unusual spelling. For example, the *k* sound can be spelled with a *k (kindness), c (contract, lecture), ck (mackerel),* or *ch (chrysanthemum, chrome).*

3. A vowel in the word might have an unusual spelling, such as the first vowel sound in *beautiful* and *eerie.*

4. Your dictionary might not be large enough. An unusual word might not be listed in a school dictionary, for example.

Understanding Word Entries

Let's analyze a sample word entry to see what kinds of information it offers.

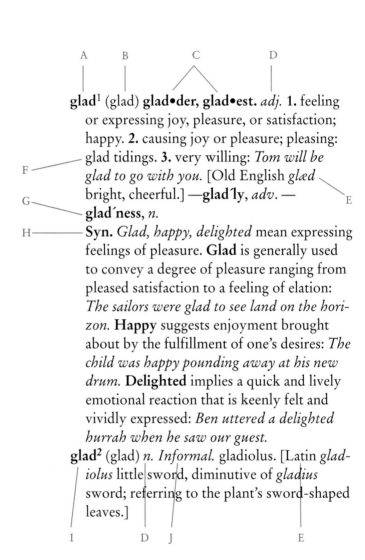

A   B   C   D

glad¹ (glad) **glad•der, glad•est.** *adj.* **1.** feeling or expressing joy, pleasure, or satisfaction; happy. **2.** causing joy or pleasure; pleasing: glad tidings. **3.** very willing: *Tom will be glad to go with you.* [Old English *glæd* bright, cheerful.] —**glad′ly,** *adv.* — **glad′ness,** *n.*

F   G   E

H — **Syn.** *Glad, happy, delighted* mean expressing feelings of pleasure. **Glad** is generally used to convey a degree of pleasure ranging from pleased satisfaction to a feeling of elation: *The sailors were glad to see land on the horizon.* **Happy** suggests enjoyment brought about by the fulfillment of one's desires: *The child was happy pounding away at his new drum.* **Delighted** implies a quick and lively emotional reaction that is keenly felt and vividly expressed: *Ben uttered a delighted hurrah when he saw our guest.*

glad² (glad) *n. Informal.* gladiolus. [Latin *gladiolus* little sword, diminutive of *gladius* sword; referring to the plant's sword-shaped leaves.]

I   D J   E

A. The Entry Word: The boldfaced word at the beginning of the entry is called the entry word. If this word can be divided at the end of a line, the divisions will be indicated by a raised dot. The word *explicate*, for example, is written ex•pli•cate. This means that you can divide the word after *ex* or after *expli.* In the sample word entry, *glad* cannot be divided; *gladder* and *gladdest,* however, can be divided. The entry word will also tell you when a compound word should be written as one word (as in *lighthouse*), when it should be hyphenated (as in *light-hearted*), and when it should be written as two words (as in *light meter*).

B. Pronunciation: The correct way to say the word is shown immediately after the entry word and indicated in three ways: accent marks, phonetic symbols, and diacritical marks. In entry words with more than one syllable, accent marks indicate which syllable should be stressed. To check the meaning of the other marks and symbols, look at the pronunciation key that is usually located at the bottom of the page.

C. Inflected Forms: Plural forms of nouns, adjective forms, and forms of verbs in other tenses are included in an entry. In this case, we see that the comparative and superlative forms of *glad* are *gladder* and *gladdest.*

When two spellings are connected with *or,* they are equally acceptable. However, when they are joined with *also,* the first spelling is preferred. For example, the dictionary shows the plural of *alga* as "**algae** *also* **algas.**"

D. Parts of Speech: Abbreviations in italics indicate the part of speech of the entry word and other forms of the word. At the beginning of this entry, we see that *glad* is usually used as an adjective, but later we learn that the same spelling can be used as a noun.

E. Etymology: Many entries include the history of the word, or etymology. The entry for *glad¹* indicates that this word is based on an Old English word. The entry for *glad²* shows this word comes from Latin.

F. Definitions: If an entry has more than one meaning, each meaning is numbered. Example sentences using the entry word are often included in definitions to make meanings clearer.

G. Derived words: A definition may end with a variation of the entry word, preceded by a dash and followed by its part of speech. In the example, the derived words *gladly* and *gladness* are shown. When the meaning of the variation is taken from the entry word, the variation is not defined. If the pronunciation changes, it is given for each variation.

H. Synonyms: Many entries list words with similar meanings along with examples so you'll know when to use each word. Understanding small differences in meaning will keep you from using words incorrectly. Some dictionaries also include antonyms in entries.

I. Homographs: Homographs are words that are spelled the same but have different meanings and histories. Homograph entries are listed separately and are followed by small numbers. *Glad* has two homographs pronounced the same. (When homographs vary in pronunciation, their entries make that clear.) As you can see, the homographs of *glad* have quite different definitions and completely different etymologies.

J. Usage Information: Some entries also provide information on how words are used in different contexts. The entry *glad²* is labeled *Informal*. The following chart describes some usage guidelines you might encounter in a dictionary entry.

TYPE OF INFORMATION	DESCRIPTION	EXAMPLE FROM AN ENTRY
Capitalization	indicates that a word should be capitalized under certain conditions	**pilgrim** . . . *n* . . . **3.** *cap:* one of the English colonists settling at Plymouth in 1620
Out-of-Date Usage	identifies meanings that are obsolete (no longer used) or used only in special contexts	**play**. . . *n* . . . **1.b** *archaic:* GAME, SPORT
Special Field Usage	uses a phrase or label to indicate a definition used only in a particular field	**break** . . . *n* . . . **5.d** *mining:* FAULT, DISLOCATION
Informal	advises that the word be avoided when speaking and writing formally	**bloom•ing** . . . *adj* . . . **3.** *Informal.* complete, utter: *a blooming idiot.*
Regional Usage	explains how a word is used in a certain geographical area	**pet•rol** . . . *n.* *British:* gasoline
Usage Note	offers general guidelines for using—or not using—a word in a certain situation; often preceded by a dash and by the abbreviation *usu.* for *usually* or the words *called also.*	**fire away** *vi* . . . — usu. used as an imperative. **hun•dred•weight** *n* . . . —called also *long hundredweight.*

OTHER KINDS OF INFORMATION IN GENERAL DICTIONARIES

When did Genghis Khan live? What does *omnia vincit amor* mean? You can find out by looking in the back of your dictionary.

Biographical Names

This section lists the spelling and pronunciation of the names of thousands of notable people. It also includes each person's birth and death dates, nationality, and field or title.

Geographical Names

In the geographical names section, you can find the correct spelling, pronunciation, and location of countries, regions, cities, mountains, rivers, and other geographical features.

Abbreviations and Symbols for Chemical Elements

Check this section if you can't remember the abbreviation for *kilometers per hour* (kmh or kmph), are confused by the abbreviation *PAT* (point after touchdown), or want to learn that *Fe* is the chemical symbol for iron.

Foreign Words and Phrases

The foreign words and phrases section defines unusual phrases, such as *Ars longa, vita brevis* (Art is long; life is short). Commonly used foreign phrases, such as *déjà vu,* are listed with the regular word entries.

Signs and Symbols

The signs and symbols section provides the symbols used in astronomy, business, math, medicine, weather forecasting, and other fields.

Style Handbook

Use the style section to check your punctuation or capitalization and for help with documentation of sources and ways to address people in certain positions, such as government officials.

THESAURUSES

A thesaurus, one kind of specialized dictionary, lists synonyms. The synonyms can be arranged categorically (traditional style) or alphabetically (dictionary style).

Traditional Style

To use a thesaurus arranged in the traditional style, begin by looking in the index for the word you want to change. For example, if you looked in the index under *require,* you might find these choices:

require entail 76.4
necessitate 637.9
lack 660.6
demand 751.4
oblige 754.5
charge 844.14
obligate 960.11

If none of these words seems exactly right, you could look in the front of the book under 751.4 for more choices. On the page with the guide numbers 748.16–751.7, you find that word 751 is *demand.* Under this word are numbered paragraphs, each with possible synonyms for *demand.* The most commonly used words are printed in boldface type. Because *demand* can be a noun or a verb, the synonyms are separated into those two categories. You locate paragraph 751.4:

VERBS **4. demand, ask,** make a demand; **call for,** call on *or* upon one for, come upon one for, appeal to for; cry for, clamor for; **require, exact,** require at the hands of; **requisition,** make *or* put in requisition, lay under contribution.

Some synonyms are marked *[coll.],* meaning "colloquial" or "informal." A page in the front or back of the thesaurus explains the other abbreviations that are used.

Dictionary Style

Looking up a word in a thesaurus organized alphabetically is just like looking up a word in a dictionary. Using the guide words at the top of the page, you locate the entry for the word *require:*

REQUIRE

Verb. **1.** [To need] want, feel the necessity for, have need for; see NEED. **2.** [To demand] exact, insist upon, expect; see ASK.

For more choices, you check *ask.*

ASK

Verb. request, query, question, interrogate, examine, cross-examine, demand, pose *or* raise *or* put a question, inquire, frame a question, order, command, challenge, pry into, scour, investigate, hunt for, quiz, grill, *needle, *sound out, *pump, *put through the third degree.

Antonym: see ANSWER, REFUTE, REJOIN.

Checking the front of the book, you learn that an asterisk (*) indicates that a term is colloquial or slang.

STYLE GUIDES

Should you capitalize a title when it follows a person's name? Should you write *87* or *eighty-seven?* You can find a number of style guides, such as *The Chicago Manual of Style*, that will answer these questions. Style guides are reference books with detailed indexes that allow you to look up specific questions. The index of one style guide, for example, devotes half a page to the uses of the comma. The answers in one style guide may contradict the answers in another guide, so everyone working on the same project should agree to use the same style guide. Perhaps some of your teachers have asked you to follow a certain style guide in your writing.

Chapter 20

Accessing Electronic Resources

● ● ● ● ● ● ● ● ● ● ● ● ● ● ● ●

The Internet is an increasingly important source of information for people of all ages worldwide, but CD-ROMs and other electronic resources not connected to the Internet also offer vast amounts of information.

20.1 USING THE INTERNET

The Internet is a computer-based, worldwide information network. The Internet uses telephone and cable lines and satellites to link personal computers worldwide. The World Wide Web, or WWW, is a set of programs and rules that determine how files are created and displayed on the Internet. To understand the difference, try this analogy: if the Internet were one computer, the WWW would be a program that runs on that computer. As you research a topic, the Internet and World Wide Web allow you to identify, retrieve, and study documents without leaving your home, school, or library. You can also use electronic mail, or e-mail, to communicate with others interested in a specific topic or with experts on that topic.

GAINING ACCESS

Your library computers can probably link you directly to the Internet at no cost to you. If you are using a computer at home, you'll need a **modem,** a device that connects your computer to a telephone or cable line. You must also subscribe to an **Internet service provider.** This service will connect you to the Internet for a fee.

UNDERSTANDING ADDRESSES

The information on the Internet is organized by locations, or sites, each with its own address. A Web address is also called a **Uniform Resource Locator,** or URL. Most addresses begin with *http://,* which stands for "hypertext transfer protocol" and identifies a way in which information is exchanged among computers connected by the Internet. The last part of an address, or its suffix, indicates the type of site it is. Here are some of the suffixes in use:

SUFFIX	TYPE OF SITE
.com	commercial
.edu	educational
.gov	government
.mil	military
.net	network organization or Internet service provider
.org	organization

USING BROWSERS

Each Internet service provider uses a specific **browser,** a program that locates and displays Web pages. Some browsers display only the text, or words, on a Web page;

most will display both text and **graphics** (pictures, photos, and diagrams). Browsers also allow you to print or download part or all of a Web site. (**Downloading** means copying information from Internet files onto a computer hard drive or a diskette.) Browsers permit you to move from page to page within a site or to jump from one site to a related site. Names of current browsers include Netscape Navigator and Internet Explorer.

ACCESSING WEB SITES

Let's say you are now connected to the Internet. If you want to see the information offered at a certain site, you can enter the site's address on the computer screen and be transferred there. You can also access specific reference sources this way, such as the *New York Times* or *Encyclopædia Britannica.* Some of these sources are free, but to gain access to others, you must subscribe and pay a fee in addition to the cost of the online service. A screen will explain any extra charges that are involved and let you choose whether to continue.

USING SEARCH ENGINES AND SUBJECT DIRECTORIES

If you don't have a specific address in mind, you can search by keyword with the help of a search engine or a subject directory.

Technology Tip

Be sure to read the Search Tip on pages 534–536, which provides information about using keywords. A keyword that is too general may generate hundreds of thousands of possible Web sites. It will take you a very long time to search them and find a few helpful sources.

Search Engines Search engines are a type of software that uses your keyword to compile lists of related Web sites. Internet service providers use certain search engines, but you can switch to a different one by entering its address. Many kinds of search engines are available, and they offer slightly different services. Some print the first sentence or two of the information offered at each Web site, while other search engines list only the site's title and address. Some search engines offer to list additional Web sites similar to those already on your screen.

Subject Directories Subject directories are a kind of software that provides an excellent place to start a search if you haven't selected a specific topic yet. A subject directory first lists general topics. After you choose one, the directory offers a list of possible subtopics from which to select. The directory then offers several more lists of subtopics for you to consider, allowing you to further narrow your topic. Finally, it provides a page of links to Web sites that are related to the specific topic you have now chosen.

For example, the search engine Yahoo! has a subject directory that offers fourteen general topics to choose from, such as Arts and Humanities. Then Yahoo! lists subtopics for you to choose from, helping you to narrow your search and define your topic until you reach a page of related Web sites.

MOVING AROUND WEB SITES

Often a word or phrase within the text of a Web page or at the end of the file will provide a link to a related Web site. These special words or phrases are called **hyperlinks.** They may be underlined or printed in a different color to make them easy to spot. When you click your mouse on a hyperlink, you'll immediately be transferred to another Web site. To get back, you can click on the back arrow or a similar symbol at the top of the computer screen.

EVALUATING TIP

Many Web sites are not checked for accuracy, so you must evaluate each site yourself. Begin by reviewing the Evaluating Tip on pages 547–548. This tip applies to Internet sources, too, especially the suggestions to use more than one source and to check for bias. Further suggestions follow.

1. Determine whether a Web site actually relates to your topic. A search engine will use every possible meaning of your keyword or phrase to compile a list of hundreds or thousands of sites. You may find that your keyword also happens to be the name of a computer game, a sports team, or even a cooking technique!

2. Pay particular attention to the source of the information in a Web site. (You may have to press the "move back" key several times to identify the organization sponsoring a site.) If a site is a personal Web page or if you cannot figure out its source or author, be sure to find another source to verify the information you find.

3. Evaluate the accuracy and fairness of the information. Is it based on more than one source? Are dissenting opinions included? After doing some of your own research elsewhere, are you aware of important information that was omitted from the site? Does the site include a bibliography and links to other sites? The answers to these questions can help you decide whether to use that source.

20.2 USING CD-ROMS AND DVDS

Technological advances create new research opportunities every day, so any discussion of the resources available quickly becomes out-of-date. Still, two resources are likely to be used for many years to come: CD-ROMs (Compact Disc-Read-Only Memory) and DVDs (Digital Video Discs). They can be used with a personal computer at home, at school, or at a library.

CD-ROM databases store both visual and audio information, such as photographs, maps, samples of different kinds of music, sound clips of famous speeches, and bird calls. Some CD-ROMs offer short videos of historical events and animated, narrated sequences that explain, for example, how acid rain forms or how airplanes fly.

One CD-ROM can store the same information as seven hundred diskettes; therefore, many dictionaries, encyclopedias, and other reference sources are now available as CD-ROMs. Many manufacturers offer yearly or monthly updates. To read a CD-ROM, your computer must have a CD-ROM drive. To broadcast sound effects, it must have speakers and a sound card.

Similar to a CD-ROM, a DVD has a larger storage capacity, enough space to store a full-length movie. DVDs require a DVD drive, which can also read CD-ROMs. (CD-ROM drives, however, cannot read DVDs.)

Library computer catalogs are another example of electronic resources that are not part of the Internet. Some of the databases available at the library are actually on CD-ROMs purchased by the library; other databases accessible from library computers are part of the Internet.

Knowledge often means knowing how to find information. Now you have knowledge. You can use it to find out more about the world and to take your place in it.

Answers

● ● ● ● ● ● ● ● ● ● ● ● ● ● ●

CHAPTER 1
PARTS OF SPEECH

PLURAL NOUNS, PAGE 94

1. stars
2. trout
3. halves
4. joys
5. waltzes
6. mysteries
7. flashes
8. teeth
9. boxes
10. onions

POSSESSIVE NOUNS, PAGE 95

1. the women's banquet
2. Shawna's talent
3. Chef Lorenson's recipe
4. the building's location
5. the books' titles
6. Mr. Sims's accident
7. Congress's schedule
8. the children's fever
9. Alfonso's job
10. the orange's seeds

COMMON, PROPER, CONCRETE, AND ABSTRACT NOUNS, PAGE 96

1. Homer's: proper; *Odyssey*: proper; poem: common, concrete
2. Steelers': proper; quarterback: common, concrete
3. Victoria: proper; Mrs. Ramos: proper
4. honesty: common, abstract; Andy's: proper; qualities: common, abstract
5. goal: common, abstract; health: common, abstract; glasses: common, concrete; water: common, concrete; day: common, concrete
6. Bessie Coleman: proper; pilot: common, concrete
7. explorer: common, concrete; astronauts: common, concrete; hope: common, abstract; world: common, concrete

8. Michiko: proper; song: common, concrete
9. vision: common, abstract; Chief Wilma Mankiller: proper; Cherokee Nation: proper; self-reliance: common, abstract
10. language: common, concrete; Old English: proper; Middle Ages: proper

COLLECTIVE NOUNS, PAGE 98

1. audience, P
2. class, S
3. union, S
4. association, S
5. corporation, S
6. Congress Party, P
7. family, S
8. orchestra, P
9. team, S
10. herd, P

PERSONAL PRONOUNS, PAGE 100

1. it, third person singular; his, third person singular possessive
2. their, third person plural possessive
3. her, third person singular possessive; they, third person plural; their, third person plural possessive

4. its, third person singular possessive
5. you, second person singular/plural; us, first person plural; I, first person singular; we, first person plural; our, first person plural possessive
6. her, third person singular possessive; it, third person singular
7. his, third person singular possessive; him, third person singular
8. her, third person singular possessive; theirs, third person plural possessive; her, third person singular
9. we, first person plural; you, second person singular/plural; me, first person singular
10. mine, first person singular possessive; you, second person singular; yours, second person singular possessive

REFLEXIVE, INTENSIVE, DEMONSTRATIVE, INTER-ROGATIVE, RELATIVE, AND INDEFINITE PRONOUNS, PAGE 105

1. none, indefinite; who, relative

2. Whoever, relative; those, demonstrative
3. Much, indefinite; few, indefinite
4. themselves, intensive; no one, indefinite
5. herself, reflexive; anyone, indefinite; who, relative
6. Whatever, interrogative; that, relative; most, indefinite
7. Whose, interrogative; this, demonstrative; that, relative
8. Those, demonstrative; whom, relative
9. neither, indefinite
10. himself, reflexive; whom, relative

TRANSITIVE AND INTRANSITIVE VERBS, PAGE 107

1. speaks, intransitive
2. saved, transitive, child
3. hid, transitive, gift
4. win, transitive, tournament
5. features, transitive, stripes; symbolizes, transitive, freedom; represents, transitive, people; signifies, transitive, wealth
6. spoke, intransitive
7. opened, intransitive

8. recruits, transitive, volunteers; repair, transitive, homes
9. recognized, transitive, brother
10. preserves, transitive, history

VERBS AND VERB PHRASES: TRANSITIVE, INTRANSITIVE, AND LINKING, PAGE 109

1. grew, linking; stepped, intransitive
2. has been, linking
3. will leave, transitive
4. fell, intransitive
5. may have forgotten, transitive
6. are cooking, transitive
7. is, linking
8. became, linking
9. have been, linking
10. stretches, intransitive

ADJECTIVES AND THE WORDS THEY MODIFY, PAGE 111

1. Five hundred fans; tired fans; four hours
2. No one; our class
3. aisle seat
4. that sandwich; peanut butter sandwich; my lunch

5. useful collection; four hundred guides; more guides
6. new president; PTA president; George's mother
7. this trip; long trip; some wood; petrified wood
8. his trip; Paris trip; some perfume; wonderful perfume; French perfume
9. enough juice; orange juice; Kia's friends
10. television networks; dizzying variety; drama programs; comedy programs [Alternative: *Drama* could be construed as a noun, not an adjective.]

COMPARATIVE AND SUPERLATIVE ADJECTIVES, PAGE 112
1. smoother
2. snowiest
3. larger; largest
4. best
5. most unpleasant
6. more qualified
7. happier; happiest
8. longer
9. tallest
10. worst

PROPER ADJECTIVES, PAGE 114
1. the Japanese embassy
2. Greek and Roman mythology
3. the Swiss Alps
4. the Welsh people
5. the Danish Vikings
6. the Dutch canals
7. the African veldt
8. the Chinese language
9. Icelandic winters
10. hot Thai spices

ADVERBS, PAGE 116
1. up, jumped, verb
2. never, have seen, verb
3. south, go, verb
4. suspiciously, sick, adjective
5. too, fast, adverb; fast, ran, verb; badly, hurt, verb
6. mightily, wrenched, verb
7. Soon, afterward, adverb; afterward, lay, verb; again, lay, verb
8. quietly, padded, verb; down, sat, verb; contentedly, sat, verb
9. particularly, smooth, adjective
10. quickly, keyed, verb; easily, found, verb; quite, useful, adjective; almost, too, adverb; too, many, adjective

ADVERBS THAT COMPARE, PAGE 118

1. more heartily, most heartily
2. sooner, soonest
3. more sadly, most sadly
4. worse, worst
5. less, least
6. more clearly, most clearly
7. better, best
8. more quickly, most quickly
9. more secretly, most secretly
10. faster, fastest

PREPOSITIONS, PAGE 120

1. <u>to</u> the emergency (call)
2. <u>for</u> the (picnic)
3. <u>From</u> the (porch), <u>to</u> the (river)
4. <u>at</u> the twins' (party), <u>except</u> (Anjelica)
5. <u>until</u> (midnight)
6. <u>In spite of</u> Emilio's (objections), <u>to</u> (Mexico)
7. <u>Prior to</u> Jorge's (arrival), <u>to</u> every (class)
8. <u>before</u> the huge (audience), <u>with</u> (confidence)
9. <u>of</u> (Washington), <u>of</u> (Montana)
10. <u>under</u> the (fence), <u>out of</u> the (yard), <u>for</u> a (moment), <u>by</u> the (brook)

CONJUNCTIONS, PAGE 122

1. both . . . and, correlative
2. Neither . . . nor, correlative
3. and, coordinating
4. either . . . or, correlative
5. or, coordinating
6. and, coordinating
7. Not only . . . but also, correlative
8. yet, coordinating
9. Just as . . . so, correlative
10. but, coordinating

SUBORDINATING CONJUNCTIONS, PAGE 123

1. wherever
2. as long as
3. Since
4. until
5. Although
6. whereas
7. After
8. if
9. While
10. unless

CONJUNCTIVE ADVERBS, PAGE 124

1. therefore CA
2. but CC
3. and CC, similarly CA
4. indeed CA
5. nor CC

6. for CC
7. consequently CA
8. however CA
9. also CA
10. nonetheless CA

INTERJECTIONS, PAGE 125

1. Oh, my goodness!
2. No kidding!
3. Uh-oh!
4. Hee, hee!
5. Ha!
6. Say
7. Well
8. Oh, rats!
9. Eeew,
10. Yuck!

PARTS OF SPEECH, PAGE 126

Answers will vary. Some suggested answers are given.

1. Aloysius has a (rash) on his arm. noun
   That was a (rash) thing to do. adjective
2. Form a (circle), girls! noun
   The officers will (circle) around to the front of the house. verb
3. The square dancers (bow) to their partners. verb
   The (bow) of the ship was painted red. noun

4. The young driver will (back) the car up the steep, curving driveway carefully. verb
   The kitten came (back) to the house right away. adverb
5. I like to sleep on a (down) pillow. adjective
   Climb (down) here at once! adverb
6. The children danced (around) the room. preposition
   Turn (around) and open your eyes. adverb
7. (Find) your places, students. verb
   This artifact was an important (find). noun
8. (Goodness)! It's a wonder you weren't hurt. interjection
   Sheila has the (goodness) of an angel. noun
9. (Which) way should we turn at the corner? adjective
   (Which) of these does Josh prefer? pronoun
10. Please open your (art) books, class. adjective
    Diplomacy is the (art) of saying no politely. noun

PROOFREADING, PAGE 127
Nikki Giovanni

1. no error
2. That's (contraction of *That is*)
3. stories (plural noun form)
4. American (capitalization of proper adjective)
5. *The 100 Best Colleges for African American Students* (italics for book titles)
6. present, (comma in a series)
7. courses (spelling); has (subject-verb agreement)
8. no error
9. no error
10. film, (comma before an appositive); won (irregular verb form)
11. 1997 (numeral instead of spelled-out number)

CHAPTER 2
PARTS OF THE SENTENCE

SIMPLE SUBJECTS AND SIMPLE PREDICATES, PAGE 131

1. days, <u>can make</u>
2. Charles Dickens, <u>used</u>
3. Tandra Sen, <u>will stand</u>
4. train, <u>goes</u>
5. Nobody, <u>told</u>
6. Nina, <u>listened</u>
7. You, <u>will sing</u>

8. everyone, <u>is</u>
9. squirrel, <u>is</u>
10. concert, <u>deserved</u>

COMPLETE SUBJECTS AND COMPLETE PREDICATES, PAGE 133

1. CS
2. CP
3. CS
4. CP
5. CP
6. CS
7. CP
8. CS
9. CP
10. CS

SIMPLE AND COMPOUND SUBJECTS AND PREDICATES, PAGE 135

1. CS; wheat, apples; are
2. CS; lakes, forests; make
3. CP; Noah Webster; wrote, simplified, campaigned
4. CS; Matthew Arnold, William Butler Yeats; are famous
5. CS; You or Mai; will go
6. CP; Waterfalls; plunge, merge
7. CP; Zambezi River; rises, follows
8. CS; Bill, Connie, Adam; sing

9. CP; You; have read, [have] memorized
10. CP; We; remember, honor

IDENTIFYING SIMPLE SUBJECTS AND PREDICATES IN SENTENCES WITH UNUSUAL ORDER, PAGE 137

1. [You], Have
2. anyone, Has seen
3. odor, drifted
4. list, is
5. Pittsburgh, is
6. twins, bounded
7. Marjorie, Does consider
8. [You], park
9. grapes, were
10. [You], tell

COMPLEMENTS, PAGE 141

1. delicious, PA
2. me, IO; card, DO
3. Tamara, DO; captain, OC
4. Philadelphia, DO; city, OC
5. sure, PA
6. spills, DO
7. place, PN
8. still, PA
9. family, IO; breakfast, DO
10. John F. Kennedy, DO; president, OC
11. sources, PN
12. dead, PA
13. posters, DO
14. volunteer, PN
15. me, IO; tickets, DO
16. close, PA
17. cause, PN
18. war, DO
19. one, PN
20. shelter, DO

PROOFREADING, PAGE 142
The Epic

1. An (capitalization of first word in sentence)
2. something (spelling); death. (end punctuation)
3. no error
4. or (spelling)
5. beings, but they or beings; they or beings. They (run-on sentence)
6. epic (spelling)
7. no error
8. enemy's (singular possessive noun)
9. are (subject-verb agreement); Hercules (capitalization of proper noun)
10. have (subject-verb agreement)
11. no error

CHAPTER 3
PHRASES

PREPOSITIONAL PHRASES, PAGE 149

1. of that chair, legs, *ADJ*
2. of summer, day, *ADJ*

3. in the attic, furniture, *ADJ;* for many years, has been stored, *ADV*

4. out of the oven, take, *ADV*

5. to the supermarket, went, *ADV;* for party supplies, went, *ADV*

6. of Mia's sorority, members, *ADJ;* at the neighborhood soup kitchen, work, *ADV;* on Saturdays, work, *ADV*

7. with fluency, writes, *ADV*

8. of Mr. Rasmussen's paintings, five, *ADJ;* to buyers, have been sold, *ADV;* across the country, buyers, *ADJ*

9. of Chicago, map, *ADJ*

10. in many Nantucket neighborhoods, streets, *ADJ;* with clamshells, are paved, *ADV*

APPOSITIVES AND APPOSITIVE PHRASES, PAGE 150

1. Our class's most accomplished musician, Minta

2. Jeanne, cousin

3. a poem of fourteen lines, sonnet

4. a Canadian province, Saskatchewan

5. a city in Iowa, Des Moines

6. a battered Ford sedan, car

7. a relief pitcher, Amedeo

8. her birthday, Valentine's Day

9. tuna salad on wheat bread, sandwich

10. A valuable vitamin, riboflavin

PARTICIPLES AND PARTICIPIAL PHRASES, PAGE 152

1. Purring loudly, kitten

2. flying low, plane

3. reported at 5:00, call

4. Completed a week early, report

5. blasting from the parked car, music; annoying, music

6. exhausted, girls

7. Realizing her luck, Yolanda; winning, ticket

8. Relieved, Deirdre

9. recovered, pet

10. pleased by the enthusiastic applause, band

GERUNDS AND GERUND PHRASES, PAGE 154

1. Finding a good parking space, subject

2. *Handling the Pain,* indirect object

3. working hard, object of a preposition

4. playing her flute, predicate nominative
5. keeping the babies in sight, direct object
6. playing flawlessly, appositive
7. Fighting back tears, subject
8. giving praise, object of a preposition
9. skating, direct object
10. losing one's keys, object of a preposition
11. Skipping rope, subject
12. fighting bravely, appositive
13. Hiking, subject
14. reading, direct object
15. forgiving Ryan, object of a preposition

INFINITIVES AND INFINITIVE PHRASES, PAGE 155

1. to sing in the shower, noun
2. to buy groceries, adverb
3. to disregard his fears, noun
4. to work faster, adjective
5. To have his artwork in the show, noun
6. to win, adverb
7. to choose in the election, adjective
8. to protect Mr. Williamson from harm, noun
9. to live, adjective
10. to continue their trip, noun

APPOSITIVES AND VERBALS, PAGE 155

1. *Rejoicing*, gerund
2. *to win*, infinitive
3. *swimming*, participle
4. *waiting*, participle
5. *her cousin Molly*, appositive
6. *Driving*, gerund
7. *changed*, participle
8. *to select*, infinitive
9. *singing*, gerund
10. *defeated*, participle

PHRASES, PAGE 156

1. *to do a good job*, infinitive phrase; *in Jake*, prepositional phrase
2. *moaning in the distance*, participial phrase
3. *Making silk-screen prints*, gerund phrase
4. *Entering the room*, participial phrase
5. *exhausted by their trip*, participial phrase
6. *to the tourist office*, prepositional phrase; *to plan our next vacation*, infinitive phrase
7. *Dorothy's cousins*, appositive phrase
8. *writing his letter*, gerund phrase; *at the clock*, prepositional phrase

9. *the peaceful city on the lake,* appositive phrase
10. *to play the trumpet,* infinitive phrase

PROOFREADING, PAGE 157
Mohandas Gandhi
1. no error
2. lawyer (no capitalization of common noun); people's (singular possessive noun); rights (word choice)
3. Deeply (adverb form); committed (spelling); nonviolence, (comma after participial phrase)
4. known (irregular verb form)
5. no error
6. soldiers (spelling); occupation (spelling)
7. in to (word choice)
8. no error
9. no error
10. no error

CHAPTER 4
CLAUSES AND SENTENCE STRUCTURE

SUBORDINATE CLAUSES, PAGE 166
1. Because she was late
2. while Seth looked for more information on the Internet

3. that they had already seen
4. who knows what she wants from life
5. If you aren't too busy
6. Whatever you decide
7. whose speech was very short
8. where the new shopping mall will be
9. unless someone will take his place
10. who has an office on the next street

MAIN AND SUBORDINATE CLAUSES, PAGE 166
1. <u>Unless Rachel goes with us</u>, <u>we won't know how to get there</u>.
2. <u>Whenever it snows</u>, <u>Alfonso and Max head for the slopes</u>.
3. <u>Alicia knows</u> <u>when the new merchandise arrives at the mall</u>.
4. <u>The band</u>, <u>which comes from England</u>, <u>will play at a local club Friday night</u>.
5. <u>We observed</u> <u>while the teacher dissected the frog</u>.
6. <u>Although Mai Lin later joined in</u>, <u>she did not begin singing with the rest of the choir</u>.

7. <u>Doing well in English is what is most important right now</u>.

8. Anyone <u>who is going to the movie</u> <u>should be at my house at seven o'clock</u>.

9. <u>Clare cleaned her room</u> before <u>she left for the party</u>.

10. Alex's project, <u>which was a demonstration of centrifugal force</u>, <u>won first prize</u>.

KINDS OF SUBORDINATE CLAUSES, PAGE 170

1. as long as we get home by eleven o'clock, ADV
2. which should arrive today, ADJ
3. Whichever dress you choose, N
4. when she is ready, ADV
5. why the error occurred in the first place, N
6. that she wants for her birthday, ADJ
7. Whoever gets there first, N
8. Whenever Luis prepares dinner, ADV
9. when she lost her dog, ADJ
10. who were most helpful, ADJ

KINDS OF SENTENCES, PAGE 172

1. IT
2. D
3. IM
4. E, D
5. D
6. IM
7. IT
8. E, D
9. D
10. IM

SIMPLE AND COMPOUND SENTENCES, PAGE 174

1. S
2. S
3. C
4. C
5. C
6. S
7. C
8. C
9. S
10. C

COMPLEX AND COMPOUND-COMPLEX SENTENCES, PAGE 175

1. CX who completed the marathon
2. CC Because she arrived first
3. CC when we would return

4. CC whatever is left from lunch
5. CX Although the lead actor had the flu
6. CX where we usually swim
7. CC Because he is a member of the school board
8. CX who starred in *Titanic*
9. CC which will be in the gym
10. CC Although Joey and Dawson are good friends

SIMPLE, COMPOUND, COMPLEX, AND COMPOUND-COMPLEX SENTENCES, PAGE 176

1. <u>Lauren and Jerome will set up for the meeting</u>, and <u>the rest of us will clean up later</u>. C
2. <u>Because our history class will be at the museum</u>, <u>I'll miss the Spanish quiz</u>, but <u>I'll take it after school</u>. CC
3. <u>In history class, our group is writing and presenting a report about the culture and history of Australia</u>. S
4. <u>Mr. Tananka helped us identify the person who could answer the questions correctly</u>. CX

5. <u>James's injury was</u> <u>why the coach took him out of the game</u>, but <u>he was able to play during the fourth quarter</u>. CC
6. <u>Anna and Luis will buy the tickets</u>, <u>which go on sale tomorrow</u>. CX
7. <u>Joe's brother has the lead in the musical</u> <u>because his voice best fits the part</u>. CX
8. <u>Will you read your report to the class</u>? S
9. <u>My dad taped *Silas Marner* last week</u>; <u>we can watch it in English class tomorrow</u>. C
10. <u>After we paint the scenery Saturday</u>, <u>we will set it up on the stage</u>, but <u>the cast won't rehearse onstage until Monday</u>. CC

FRAGMENTS AND RUN-ONS, PAGE 180

Answers will vary; below are suggested answers.

1. R Luis will play with the symphony orchestra next month, **and** his parents will be at the performance.
2. R Angela and Su Lin didn't bring the poster board**, and** they went back for it.

3. F **We** want to see a movie Friday night.

4. F The main concern of the committee **is the last part of the program.**

5. R Erica took the Scholastic Aptitude Test this spring; she will take it again in the fall.

6. F The team **will be practicing** before the play-offs.

7. R Tina was on the all-conference team last year, **but** she was on the all-district team this year.

8. R The Spanish Club meets once a month, and the Key Club meets every other week.

9. F **We decided to change the time of our study group** because Ms. Jameson postponed the test until Wednesday.

10. F **Sara** ran her fastest time in the citywide trials.

PROOFREADING, PAGE 180
Alice Walker

1. Walker was (no comma between subject and verb); Eatonville, (comma between city and state)

2. teacher, (comma in a series)

3. published (past participle verb form); movie. (end punctuation)

4. write (word choice)

5. no error

6. that (relative pronoun)

7. books (plural noun form)

8. no error

9. one (word choice); most famous (superlative adjective form)

10. no error

CHAPTER 5
VERB TENSES AND VOICE

PRINCIPAL PARTS OF VERBS, PAGE 188

1. cultivated
2. growing
3. swooped
4. hanging
5. painted
6. be
7. tasting, baked
8. suggested
9. regarded
10. reported

	Base Form	Past Form	Past Participle
1.	see	saw	seen
2.	fly	flew	flown
3.	gather	gathered	gathered
4.	bear	bore	borne
5.	choose	chose	chosen
6.	grow	grew	grown
7.	keep	kept	kept
8.	remember	remembered	remembered
9.	lie	lay	lain
10.	ring	rang	rung
11.	put	put	put
12.	climb	climbed	climbed
13.	write	wrote	written
14.	become	became	become
15.	tell	told	told
16.	let	let	let
17.	seek	sought	sought
18.	carry	carried	carried
19.	sit	sat	sat
20.	throw	threw	thrown
21.	rise	rose	risen
22.	believe	believed	believed
23.	hurry	hurried	hurried
24.	wear	wore	worn
25.	begin	began	begun

VERB FORMS, PAGE 195

1. drawn
2. was
3. hung
4. hanged
5. shone
6. chosen
7. shined
8. broke
9. written
10. saw

PRESENT TENSE, PAGE 197

Answers will vary. Possible answers are given.

1. Kai does fifteen push-ups every morning before breakfast.
2. Pamela brings her lunch to school almost every day.
3. On special occasions, the bell in the town hall rings from noon to one o'clock.
4. Pigs are very difficult to keep clean.
5. A lawyer, Deepak's father carries his cell phone everywhere.
6. Jenny hears the phone ringing and runs to answer it.
7. Fritz decides what to wear just before he puts it on.
8. Steam rises from the factory all day and all night.
9. Yellow is a common color for taxicabs in the United States.
10. Sherif always studies diligently.

FUTURE TENSE, PAGE 199

1. Seamus will run for the office of class president.
   Seamus is going to run for the office of class president.
   Seamus is about to run for the office of class president.
   Tomorrow Seamus runs for the office of class president.
2. Alison will congratulate Nancy Anderson on her award.
   Alison is going to congratulate Nancy Anderson on her award.
   Alison is about to congratulate Nancy Anderson on her award.
   This evening Alison congratulates Nancy Anderson on her award.
3. Mrs. Patterson will speak to Kenesha's teacher.

Mrs. Patterson is going to speak to Kenesha's teacher.

Mrs. Patterson is about to speak to Kenesha's teacher.

Next week Mrs. Patterson speaks to Kenesha's teacher.

4. The sophomores will find out who won the election.

The sophomores are going to find out who won the election.

The sophomores are about to find out who won the election.

In a few minutes the sophomores find out who won the election.

5. Emilio and Vicente will show the film to the class.

Emilio and Vicente are going to show the film to the class.

Emilio and Vicente are about to show the film to the class.

At ten o'clock Emilio and Vicente show the film to the class.

PRESENT, PAST, AND FUTURE TENSES, PAGE 199

1. future
2. past
3. future
4. present
5. past
6. present
7. future
8. past
9. present
10. past

PERFECT TENSES, PAGE 202

1. had varnished
2. have enjoyed
3. has worked
4. will have worked
5. had won
6. has explored
7. has agreed
8. will have claimed
9. had expected
10. has mentioned

ALL SIX TENSES, PAGE 204

1. present perfect
2. future perfect
3. past
4. present
5. past perfect
6. past perfect; past perfect; past
7. present
8. past
9. present perfect
10. future

PROGRESSIVE AND EMPHATIC FORMS, PAGE 205

1. future progressive
2. future perfect progressive
3. present emphatic
4. present perfect progressive
5. future progressive
6. past perfect progressive
7. present emphatic
8. present progressive
9. past emphatic
10. past progressive

CONSISTENCY OF TENSES, PAGE 207

1. cannot find
2. allow
3. floated
4. taught
5. were married
6. revolves
7. shall have
8. deposited
9. was
10. results

ACTIVE AND PASSIVE VOICE, PAGE 208

1. Each hippopotamus in the preserve eats up to 130 pounds of vegetable matter daily.
2. The last piece of cornbread was eaten by Ginger.
3. Leroy added the last piece of the puzzle.
4. The child's frantic cries were heard by the mail carrier.
5. The hippopotamus had crossed the river in about five minutes.
6. The birds ate Mr. Harris's entire stock of seed corn.
7. North Carolina farmers raise corn, soybeans, and cotton, among other things.
8. The gate was guarded by Sir Caraway and his servants.
9. The Petrillo family had already packed the luggage.
10. The Charleston Chargers had won the semifinal match.

PROOFREADING, PAGE 209
Chitra Banerjee Divakaruni

1. writer, (comma in a series); was born (passive voice verb form); two (word choice)
2. writes (subject-verb agreement)
3. women (irregular plural noun)

4. Divakaruni's (singular possessive proper noun); help (subject-verb agreement)
5. In (capitalization of first word of sentence)
6. no error
7. no error
8. no error
9. let (word choice)
10. She shows us the thoughts and hearts of new friends. (inappropriate passive voice)

CHAPTER 6 SUBJECT-VERB AGREEMENT

AGREEMENT OF SUBJECTS AND VERBS, PAGE 217

1. are
2. am
3. attend
4. are
5. has
6. has
7. are
8. carry
9. Do
10. watch

INTERVENING PHRASES, PAGE 218

1. snow becomes
2. Snowstorms keep
3. C
4. birds lull
5. C
6. feature is
7. C
8. water sounds
9. hunger suggests
10. rain hampers

AGREEMENT WITH COMPOUND SUBJECTS, PAGE 219

1. The *Iliad* and the *Odyssey* were composed
2. Both Athena and Poseidon have played
3. Writers and literature students prefer
4. *The Old Man and the Sea* and *The Secret Sharer* are
5. Both politics and the weather have influenced
6. Neither George nor the twins appreciate
7. Good looks and bad tempers are
8. Either Mr. Echevarria or Ms. Olivero is teaching
9. Do the juniors or the seniors read
10. Debra Johnson or Lillian and Tom Nash are scheduled

AGREEMENT WITH SPECIAL SUBJECTS, PAGE 222

1. are having
2. was deciding
3. is
4. seem
5. was
6. was abandoned
7. was
8. was
9. equals
10. is

INDEFINITE PRONOUNS AS SUBJECTS, PAGE 225

1. seems
2. has
3. are
4. Has
5. is
6. are
7. are
8. is
9. seems
10. have

INDEFINITE PRONOUNS AS SUBJECTS, PAGE 225

Sentences will vary. Possible sentences are given.

Singular subjects

1. <u>Is</u> anyone here?
2. Each of the students <u>does</u> his or her own laundry.
3. Nothing <u>was done</u> about the spilled paint.
4. Someone <u>knows</u> something about it, but no one <u>is talking</u>.
5. Talking of Mrs. Fujimori and Mr. Talbot, either <u>will be</u> a good coach.

Plural subjects

6. Several of the sophomores <u>are being considered</u> for the varsity football team.
7. Both of these jackets <u>look</u> alike.
8. All our students <u>are encouraged</u> to submit entries to the exhibition; many <u>have</u> already <u>done</u> so.
9. Some teenagers <u>are</u> very concerned about the safety of our environment; others <u>don</u>'t <u>care</u> at all.
10. Few sophomores ever <u>attend</u> the drama club tryouts.

Singular or Plural subjects

11. All of the doughnuts <u>are</u> gone.
12. All of the cooked squid <u>is</u> still on the serving dish.
13. Some of the term papers <u>have been completed</u>.

14. None of the pudding <u>is</u> left.
15. These paintings are all excellent; any of them <u>has</u> a chance to win first prize.

AGREEMENT IN INVERTED SENTENCES, PAGE 226

1. incorrect: Do begin; correct: Does begin
2. incorrect: speeds; correct: speed
3. C
4. incorrect: springs; correct: spring
5. incorrect: will attends; correct: will attend
6. C
7. C
8. incorrect: marches; correct: march
9. incorrect: is; correct: are
10. incorrect: Do prefer; correct: Does prefer

SUBJECT-VERB AGREE-MENT WITH SPECIAL SUBJECTS, IN INVERTED SENTENCES, AND WITH INDEFINITE PRONOUNS, PAGE 227

1. family are packing
2. news is
3. shears are becoming
4. dollars was
5. Three-fourths are

6. anyone Does know
7. Some are
8. Eric stands
9. bus goes
10. teachers Do meet

AGREEMENT WITH SUBJECT, NOT PREDICATE NOMINATIVE, PAGE 228

1. act was
2. dancers were
3. skiers are
4. gems are
5. volunteers are
6. peaches, cookies were
7. exhibit was
8. food is
9. players were
10. show is

PROOFREADING, PAGE 228
Louise Erdrich

1. Dakota (capitalization of proper noun); is (subject-verb agreement)
2. no error
3. has written (subject-verb agreement); introductions, (comma in a series)
4. discusses (subject-verb agreement)
5. has found (irregular verb form)
6. no error
7. it's (word choice)

8. book, (comma to set off an appositive)
9. no error
10. for (word choice); that are (irregular verb form)

CHAPTER 7
USING PRONOUNS CORRECTLY

CASE OF PERSONAL PRONOUNS, PAGE 235
1. I
2. She, I, their
3. you, us
4. they
5. I, him
6. you, his
7. its
8. it's
9. yours, his
10. him, me

PRONOUNS WITH AND AS APPOSITIVES, PAGE 237
1. he
2. he
3. him
4. I
5. We
6. us
7. they
8. them
9. I
10. me

PRONOUNS AFTER *THAN* AND *AS,* PAGE 238
1. Jessica is a year older than I am.
2. Am I as good a pianist as she is?
3. Can Jason run faster than he can?
4. Allan gave Art and Patrick more time than he gave me. *or* Allan gave Art and Patrick more time than I gave them.
5. You sat closer to them than you did to me.
6. I understand Raymond better than she does. *or* I understand Raymond better than I understand her.
7. Did you send Josh as many postcards as you sent me? *or* Did you send Josh as many postcards as I did?
8. Can Ms. Fuentes tutor Ramón as well as I can? *or* Can Ms. Fuentes tutor Ramón as well as she can tutor me?
9. Carol's more familiar with Kim's dog than she is with mine. *or* Carol's more familiar with Kim's dog than I am.
10. Is Jamyce a better conversationalist than he is?

REFLEXIVE AND INTENSIVE PRONOUNS, PAGE 240

1. Geraldo gave the gloves to Ilona and me.
2. C
3. The twins gave themselves *A*'s on their practice tests.
4. Mr. Thompson himself gave Freddie the extra homework.
5. C
6. Mr. and Mrs. Garanzini assigned Room 205 to themselves.
7. He did himself a favor by studying hard last night.
8. C
9. I'm sending these flowers to you and Mrs. Collins in gratitude for that delicious dinner.
10. C

WHO AND *WHOM* IN QUESTIONS AND SUBORDINATE CLAUSES, PAGE 242

1. who
2. Whomever
3. Whom
4. Who
5. whom
6. who
7. Who
8. whom
9. who
10. whom

GENDER-NEUTRAL PRONOUN-ANTECEDENT AGREEMENT, PAGE 244

Answers will vary. Possible answers are given.

1. A ship-to-shore telegraph operator must always be able to pinpoint his or her location on the ocean.
   Ship-to-shore telegraph operators must always be able to pinpoint the ship's location on the ocean.
   Ship-to-shore telegraph operators must always be able to pinpoint their location on the ocean.
2. Editors are famous for their blue pencils.
   An editor is famous for the blue pencil.
   Editors are famous for blue pencils.
3. A telephone salesperson must have a very difficult job.
   Telephone salespeople must have very difficult jobs.
   A telephone salesperson must find the job very difficult.

4. That computer technician never once consulted the user's manual.

That computer technician never once consulted a user's manual.

Those computer technicians never once consulted their user's manuals.

5. A musician must play for himself or herself as well as for the audience.

Musicians must play for themselves as well as for the audience.

Musicians must play for personal enjoyment as well as for the audience.

AGREEMENT WITH COLLECTIVE NOUNS, PAGE 245

1. its, union, singular
2. their, committee, plural
3. their, squad, plural
4. its, jury, singular
5. its, team, singular

AGREEMENT IN PERSON, PAGE 246

Answers will vary. Possible answers are given.

1. Neighbors can be wonderful friends from whom one can borrow almost anything in an emergency.

2. Stopping is easy on a bike with hand brakes; the rider just grasps both brakes gently at the same time.

3. In some countries tourists can safely walk alone at night.

4. Art communicates directly to its viewers; people might not always understand the meaning of a painting, but they can usually grasp its mood immediately.

5. A fitness club is very convenient. Members can exercise at any hour, as long as the building is open.

GENDER-NEUTRAL AGREEMENT WITH INDEFINITE PRONOUN ANTECEDENTS, PAGE 248

Answers will vary. Possible answers are given.

1. Everyone must bring his or her own music stand to the theater.

You must all bring your own music stands to the theater.

Each of you must bring a music stand to the theater.

2. Will someone please lend me his or her pen?
Will someone please lend me a pen?
Will someone please lend me something to write with?

3. Each student has studied the lessons long enough.
You have all studied your lessons long enough.
The students have studied their lessons long enough.

4. Has everyone brought his or her notebook?
Have you all brought your notebooks?
Has everyone brought a notebook?

5. Each team member carries his or her own luggage.
All team members carry their own luggage.
Each team member carries luggage.

CLEAR PRONOUN REFERENCE, PAGE 249

Answers will vary. Possible answers are given.

1. Luisa is a fine athlete, and her athletic ability was obvious from her gymnastic performance.

2. I phoned George again and again, but his phone was always busy.

3. Although Johnna is a good baker, she seldom shares any of her baked goods with us.

4. Angelika and Jung were having an argument, which started from a misunderstanding.

5. Derek writes all the time. I wonder when he'll ever show us one of his works.

CORRECTING UNCLEAR AND INDEFINITE PRONOUN REFERENCE, PAGE 251

Answers will vary. Possible answers are given.

1. In Europe people often dine about nine or ten o'clock in the evening.

2. In some places, it is considered polite to belch as a sign of appreciation for a delicious meal.

3. How do people answer the telephone in Italy?

4. At the table, one can sometimes wipe up a spill with the corner of a napkin.

5. In some countries, white instead of black is customarily worn at funerals.

PROOFREADING, PAGE 251
Guy de Maupassant
1. no error
2. Flaubert, (comma after an appositive); his (possessive personal pronoun form)
3. society, (comma in compound sentence)
4. no error
5. "The Necklace," (capitalization of first word of a title); that *or* who (relative pronoun); themselves (reflexive pronoun form)
6. altogether (word choice)
7. simple, (comma in a series)
8. who (relative pronoun)
9. himself (reflexive pronoun form)
10. no error

CHAPTER 8
USING MODIFIERS CORRECTLY

THE THREE DEGREES OF COMPARISON, PAGE 259
1. Of all the flying insects, I am most afraid of wasps.

2. Jennifer was very hungry, and she ate more greedily than the rest of us.
3. Of the southern states, I like Texas the best.
4. That grass is the greenest I ever saw!
5. Today, Mom was happier than I have ever seen her.
6. Parrots may be the most conspicuous of all the wild birds.
7. C
8. This dog is definitely tinier than that one.
9. C
10. Janet was dressed more appropriately for the interview than Alyssa was.

IRREGULAR COMPARISONS, PAGE 260
1. farther
2. ill
3. the most
4. further
5. better
6. best
7. badly, better
8. the least
9. worst
10. least

CORRECTING DOUBLE COMPARISONS, PAGE 261

1. This is the widest mobile home I've ever seen!
2. That tuna smells fishier than the scrod.
3. Is vermicelli thinner than regular spaghetti?
4. I'm pretty sure that linguini is wider than both vermicelli and spaghetti.
5. C
6. Sam always says that his life is just a little more solitary than a hermit's.
7. When she pounced on the soap bubble and it disappeared, the kitten was the most surprised thing in the world.
8. "This is the longest letter I've ever received," said Lee.
9. C
10. After dieting and daily exercise, I should become much healthier and more agile than I am now.

CORRECTING INCOMPLETE COMPARISONS, PAGE 263

Answers may vary. Possible answers are given.

1. Archie's test results are better than Andy's.
2. Isn't Seaside Park cleaner than any other park?
3. Sean is more organized than anyone else.
4. C
5. Is banana ice cream really better than any other flavor?
6. The speed of racing cars is greater than that of ordinary cars.
7. C
8. Was Michelangelo's art better than that of Leonardo da Vinci?
9. Shani thinks that yams are tastier than any other vegetable.
10. Jeannie's voice is lower than Pat's.

IRREGULAR, DOUBLE, AND INCOMPLETE COMPARISONS, PAGE 263

Answers may vary. Possible answers are given.

1. Cutting the sugar in one's diet may be even better than cutting the fat.
2. Does the Zambezi River flow more quickly than the Nile?
3. C
4. Was Jesse Owens or Bob Mathias the swifter runner?

5. Your little brother Donnie is less irritable than Jamie.
6. Do you wish to explore this topic further in your paper?
7. Diego has the best costume of all.
8. Ange is taller than Rick but shorter than I.
9. Kele admires Dr. Martin Luther King Jr. more than anyone else.
10. My boxer dog's bark is deeper and louder than that of other dogs.

GOOD OR *WELL*; *BAD* OR *BADLY*, PAGE 265

1. bad
2. bad
3. good
4. badly
5. good
6. good *or* well
7. good
8. bad
9. bad
10. well

REGULAR AND IRREGULAR COMPARISONS, PAGE 265

1. lonelier, loneliest
2. more swiftly, most swiftly
3. better, best
4. lighter, lightest
5. less, least
6. more afraid, most afraid
7. more, most
8. worse, worst
9. bluer, bluest
10. more nutritious, most nutritious

CORRECTING DOUBLE NEGATIVES, PAGE 267

Answers may vary. Possible answers are given.

1. Giuliana is a very quiet girl; she never says anything.
   Giuliana is a very quiet girl; she hardly ever says anything.
2. I have hardly got any energy left to write.
   I haven't got any energy left to write.
   I have got no energy left to write.
3. Since I hurt my wrist, I can hardly ever throw foul shots as well as I used to.
4. We haven't seen any UFOs, and even if we had, we wouldn't have said anything to anybody.
5. Liam is feeling no better; yet, if he were, he still wouldn't say anything.

Liam isn't feeling any better; yet, if he were, he still wouldn't say anything.

6. I had scarcely finished my dinner when the doorbell rang, but nobody was there.
   I hadn't finished my dinner yet when the doorbell rang, but nobody was there.

7. Nobody told me anything about the pep rally yesterday.

8. C

9. Margaret has never had a loud voice, but now that she has tonsillitis, I can't hear a word she says.
   Margaret has never had a loud voice, but now that she has tonsillitis, I can hardly ever hear a word she says.

10. C

CORRECTING MISPLACED AND DANGLING MODIFIERS, PAGE 269

Revised sentences will vary somewhat. Possible revisions are given.

1. I watched my kite floating through the air.

2. Thanking the operator, I made my call correctly.

3. Janine had to tell her dad the problem only once.

4. The children played with the handmade dolls, which were filled with straw.

5. Lost on the country road, we didn't see the sign in the dark.

6. Landing at Ronald Reagan Washington National Airport, we saw the United States Capitol come into view.

7. Sitting quietly on the beach, Mr. Atkinson watched the waves.

8. Wearing his green plaid robe, Rana anxiously watched the moose in the distance.

9. Running to catch the bus, I dropped the flour in the street.

10. The snake nearly bit me as I reached into the bushes.

PROOFREADING, PAGE 270
James Thurber

1. wackier (comparative adjective form)

2. more dejected (comparative adjective form); more domineering (comparative adjective form)

3. meet only (misplaced modifier)
4. "The Secret Life of Walter Mitty," (quotation marks around title of short story)
5. Garden (capitalization of important words in a title)
6. no error
7. no error
8. silliest (superlative adjective form); most rollicking (superlative adjective form)
9. no error
10. no error
11. readers' (plural possessive noun); chilliest (superlative adjective form)

CHAPTER 9
DIAGRAMING SENTENCES

Diagrams can be found in the Teacher's Guide.

CHAPTER 10
CAPITALIZING

CAPITALIZING SENTENCES AND QUOTATIONS, PAGE 294

1. Jeannie said, "I don't know whether to add or subtract."
2. C

3. In her evaluation, Ms. Ching described Luisa as "capable and responsible."
4. John Updike wrote the poem "Ex-Basketball Player" (which has sometimes been compared to A. E. Housman's "To an Athlete Dying Young").
5. Larry groaned, "How will I ever finish this essay before tomorrow morning?"
6. Ralph sighed and put his pencil down, wondering why he had ever volunteered for the project.
7. Emelie asked, "Why did you come back?" although she thought she already knew the answer.
8. After the recital, Terry and her mother started for home.
9. C
10. They planted tomatoes in a plot behind the house. (They wanted corn, too, but they didn't have room for it.)

CAPITALIZING LETTER PARTS, PAGE 296

1. b
2. a
3. b

Practice Answers   **597**

4. a

5. a

CAPITALIZING OUTLINES, PAGE 296

I. English Before Modern English
  A. Old English
    1. Influence of Old Norse
    2. Influence of Latin
      a. Classical Latin
      b. Spoken Latin
  B. Middle English
    1. Influence of Old English
    2. Influence of French
II. Modern English
  A. British English
  B. American English

CAPITALIZING PROPER NOUNS AND PROPER ADJECTIVES, PAGE 304

1. Pakistan is an Islamic country, whereas India is Hindu.

2. Leona attended Duquesne University for the first two years of her college career.

3. The Humane Society of the United States wages a constant war against animal abuse.

4. Attorney General Janet Reno testified at the Senate hearings.

5. Ursula and her mom attended a special seminar on preserving the Brazilian rain forest.

6. "I need a ride to band practice, Dad," said Jeremy. "Can you help me out?"

7. Maria Tallchief was a famous Native American ballerina.

8. Former president Lyndon Johnson is also referred to as LBJ.

9. New England is noted for its emphasis on education, industry, and the arts.

10. Some anthropologists believe that the three major Egyptian pyramids were sited to imitate the positions of the three stars in the "belt" of the constellation Orion.

11. The Saint Louis Arch is also known as the Gateway Arch; its formal name is the Jefferson National Expansion Memorial.

12. Mario read that Tanzania's Lake Tanganyika is part of a rift valley that runs north and south through eastern Africa.

13. Do you know who the current goalie for the Montreal Canadiens is?

14. Because the soldiers did not know that the war had ended a month earlier, the last battle of the Civil War was fought on May 13, 1865, at Palmito Hill, Texas.

15. The United States Secret Service is one of the bureaus of the Department of the Treasury.

16. Years ago, many tourists bought deeds to the Brooklyn Bridge before they realized they had been swindled.

17. Osceola County in Florida is named for a great Seminole chief.

18. Osiris, according to this book, was the Egyptian god of the underworld.

19. New Guinea is the second-largest island in the world; only Greenland is larger.

20. Kirk remembered that Australia is considered a continent, not an island.

CAPITALIZING, PAGE 306

1. Consuelo announced, "Today I'm going to be chosen to be the female lead in *My Fair Lady,* our school show."

2. "Sure," Raúl said, "and I'm going to play Hamlet in London."

3. Gentlemen:
   Please delete my name from your Internet list service. I have no time to read the constant stream of messages.
     Sincerely,
     Kathryn Kramer

4. C

5. Susan signed the letter with her initials, SJS.

6. I. Major Cities of Connecticut
     A. Central cities
      1. Hartford
      2. Windsor
     B. Cities on Long Island Sound
      1. New Haven
      2. Bridgeport
    II. State government

7. Marilee read an Italian sonnet today in English class.
8. Luis saw the *Spirit of St. Louis* at the Smithsonian Institution in Washington, D.C.
9. Mrs. Nesbitt asked, "For what are King Arthur and the Round Table remembered?"
10. Do you know which book won the Newbery Medal this year?

PROOFREADING, PAGE 309
"Through the Tunnel" by Doris Lessing
1. English (capitalization of proper adjective); Mediterranean (capitalization of proper adjective); mother (no capitalization of a word showing family relationship if it is preceded by a possessive pronoun)
2. no error
3. he is (consistency of tenses)
4. accepted (word choice)
5. activity that (no comma to set off essential adjective clause)
6. dark, (comma in a series)

7. no error
8. no error
9. no error
10. Jerry (capitalization of proper noun); does manage (subject-verb agreement with emphatic verb form)
11. characters (spelling)

CHAPTER 11 PUNCTUATION, ABBREVIATIONS, AND NUMBERS

END MARKS, PAGE 315
1. What did you say Mark's last name is?
2. Wow! I just got an A on my report! (*or* . . . report.)
3. Please hand me the hedge clippers, Alison.
4. Where did you get that beautiful vest?
5. Meerkats are small burrowing animals that live in open, dry regions of Africa.
6. Ow! That hurt!
7. Kwam asked me why I was wearing a hat.
8. Don't leave yet, class; I still have to collect your homework.
9. Lydia, has anyone inquired about your Lost-and-Found ad?

10. Tryouts for the track team will be held at three o'clock.

COLONS, PAGE 317

1. I have only one thing to say to you, Brett: either attend the practice sessions or leave the team.
2. Yes, Narciso; class begins at 2:10 P.M. sharp.
3. Emily Dickinson wrote the following: . . .
4. Have you read Isaiah 9:1-6?
5. Actually I have many reasons to be glad I live in an apartment: there is no lawn to mow, a bus stop is nearby, and I babysit for four families without going outside.
6. Our assignment was to write a brief essay on these lines from Robert Frost: "Nature's first green is gold,/Her hardest hue to hold."
7. The primary colors are red, yellow, and blue.
8. Dear Sir:
9. Nadine puts peanut butter on bananas, apples, and grapes.

10. These are Takara's favorite flowers: daffodils, lilacs, and sunflowers.

SEMICOLONS, PAGE 320

1. Two excellent collections of Inuit art are found in Manitoba; one is housed in the Eskimo Museum in Churchill, and the other can be seen at the Winnipeg Art Gallery.
2. A land region that covers almost half of Manitoba is the Canadian Shield; thanks to ancient glaciers, the region is rich in lakes, streams, and forests.
3. A large breeding ground for polar bears lies south of Hudson Bay near Churchill; as a result, Churchill is nicknamed *Polar Bear Capital of the World.*
4. Mrs. Stebbins recently learned that Chun has a beautiful bass voice; moreover, he's a great clog dancer.
5. Frank and Lillian Gilbreth, a husband and wife team, were well-known engineers; Frank Gilbreth founded a management

consulting firm in 1911, and Lillian Gilbreth, who held a Ph.D. in industrial engineering, ran the business after her husband's death.

COMMAS IN A SERIES, COMMAS WITH COORDINATE ADJECTIVES, AND COMMAS IN COMPOUND SENTENCES, PAGE 323

1. Pepper is a good, obedient, gentle dog.
2. Jeanne wore a plaid wrap skirt today, and Tisa wore a beige print skirt.
3. I like squash, corn, and green beans.
4. Ricardo washed and dried the dishes, fed the canary, and cleaned his room.
5. This was a wonderful and productive and exhausting day.

COMMAS AND NON-ESSENTIAL ELEMENTS, PAGE 325

1. Cathy lost the cardigan sweater that she had worn to the game.
2. Edwin Arlington Robinson, an American poet, wrote the simple yet frightening poem "Richard Cory."
3. My friend Jeralyn had always wanted to be an artist.
4. These sunglasses, which Ross took with him only at the last minute, did come in handy at the seashore.
5. Crying hysterically, the little girl told us that she was lost.

COMMAS WITH INTERJECTIONS, PARENTHETICAL EXPRESSIONS, CONJUNCTIVE ADVERBS, AND ANTITHETICAL PHRASES, PAGE 327

1. Jared had promised to be home on time; to make it, though, he had to run two blocks, climb a fence, and jump over a hedge.
2. Unlike Laura, Rick was obsessively neat.
3. Drat, I forgot my house key. *or* Drat! . . . key!
4. Reynaldo left for band practice after school; however, he didn't know that the session had been canceled.
5. "We're happy to see you this morning, Susan," said Miss Sullivan, "and by the way, please be on time from now on."

COMMAS WITH OTHER ELEMENTS, PAGE 329

1. From under a corner of the blanket, Peppermint peeked out at Luisa.
2. In the middle of the story, John stopped suddenly and looked down at his audience.
3. Next to the photograph of stern old Uncle David stood a silver vase holding two delicate white roses.
4. With any luck, the snow will hold off until the weekend.
5. Whenever Terry and the dogs come to visit, the house is a wreck for a full week afterward.

ADDITIONAL USES OF COMMAS, PAGE 331

1. Sherrie was born on August 13, 1989.
2. George Silver, D.V.M., is a respected veterinarian.
3. Christie, where is Max?
4. There isn't enough milk left to make pudding, is there?
5. Dear Tyrone,
   With best wishes,

MISUSE OF COMMAS, PAGE 333

1. Eliseo put on the parking brake but didn't get out of the car.
2. Neither Alani nor Kimiko could ever have imagined what happened next.
3. "The Celebrated Jumping Frog of Calaveras County" was written by Mark Twain; it was published in the New York *Saturday Press* in 1865.
4. The girls at the sleepover watched MTV and VH-1 until midnight.
5. If you go to the Dallas game, please buy an extra Cowboys t-shirt for me.

COMMAS, PAGE 333

1. To test his speed and agility, Lee ran across the field, jumped over three fences, and climbed the ladder in the barn.
2. I can't study with you tonight, Carmela, but maybe we can get together tomorrow.
3. Smiling, Lydia watched her brother pedal nearly a half block on his first two-wheeler bike ride.

4. Janice's father, an insurance agent, works with Mr. Hakim, who owns Consolidated Protection, Inc.

5. "Oh, darn," said Terrye, "I've forgotten my English book again; however, I think I have time to go back for it."

6. Among the papers in the top drawer of the desk was the contract Mrs. Johansen had hoped she'd find.

7. In 1945 World War II came to a close. *or* no error

8. Eating a peanut butter and jelly sandwich, Molly looked up at her mother and asked, "When can I learn to drive the car?"

9. After the road race is over, will you give me an interview?

10. Both Tim and Patrick left Helena standing on the sidewalk, and neither returned to explain what she'd done wrong. *or* . . . sidewalk; neither . . . *or* . . . sidewalk. Neither . . .

DASHES, PAGE 335

1. The kit—two pencils, a ballpoint pen, and an eraser—was placed on the desk.

2. There it sat—in all its glory.

3. Sara's little sister—only two years old—sat in the pool and splashed.

4. It was a medal—the only medal he'd ever won—and it was his at last.

5. Myron stopped the line of children at the corner—the corner of Concord Street and Dante Place—and counted them again.

PARENTHESES, PAGE 337

1. Robert Frost (he is one of my favorite poets) read his poem "The Gift Outright" at President Kennedy's inauguration.

2. The child (she seemed to be about five years old) looked as if she were lost.

3. No one on our block (I took her to every house) knew who she was.

4. Eating more fruit, vegetables, and grains may help people who have frequent heartburn and upset stomachs (although they should avoid tomatoes, wheat and corn products, and citrus fruits).

5. Fritz was overly polite (do you know what I mean?), and he annoyed quite a few people.

QUOTATION MARKS, PAGE 342

1. "Happiness is getting a bill you've already paid," someone once said. "It means you can sit down and write a nasty letter."

2. The word *autobiography* comes from the Greek *auto,* meaning "self," *bios,* meaning "life," and *graph,* meaning "write."

3. Lokelani said, "I just can't deal with that now"; then she turned and walked away.

4. "What is Diane up to?" asked Jerol.

5. "I have no idea," said Ann, "but I saw ribbon and wrapping paper before she shut the door."

6. Robert Frost once said that poetry makes you remember what you didn't know you knew.

7. After the birth of his son, Caleb walked out of the hospital, stopped at the top of the steps, and shouted "Hooray!"

8. "A no-brainer" is Paulo's description of any problem less complicated than one involving atomic physics.

9. Why did Wordsworth write "My Heart Leaps Up"?

10. "I don't believe you said that!" Jean exclaimed.

ITALICS (UNDERLINING), PAGE 345

1. When I last saw Reynaldo, he was reading Shakespeare's *A Midsummer Night's Dream.*

2. The *New York Times* crossword puzzle is really tough today!

3. Please add an *and* to the title; it should read *Lisa and the Talking Turtle.*

4. Michelangelo's *David* is one of the most recognizable sculptures in the world.

5. The state motto of Connecticut is *Qui Transtulit Sustinet* ("He who transplanted still sustains").

APOSTROPHES, PAGE 349

1. That was one of Jerry Lewis's films, wasn't it?

2. This pen is mine; that one is yours.
3. The visitors from Jamaica were able to attend one of Congress's sessions.
4. Were you invited to the Harrises' New Year's Eve party?
5. That's one of my mother-in-law's hats.
6. "I Am a Rock" is one of Simon and Garfunkel's songs.
7. Robert faced ten days' anxiety when he planted the pumpkin seeds.
8. Matt's birthday is almost a year after Jan's, but they both belong to the class of '00.
9. These children were all winners in the national children's art contest.
10. I'd have thought you'd be glad we're all going to the mall with you.

HYPHENS, PAGE 352

1. Well, Jeremy, the Parthenon is a pre-Renaissance building, but the Eiffel Tower is defi-nitely a post-Renaissance *structure.*
2. My aunt Hana, a well-respected member of our town, was chosen last night as Teacher of the Month.
3. Some Native American peoples in pre-Columbian America believed that the *Fountain* of Youth existed, but it was never found.
4. Hanh, it's *pointless* to sit here in silence when we could be having a *mean-ingful* conversation about the Trans-Alaska Pipeline.
5. Please re-collect all the *yellow* ticket stubs, Angela.
   struc-ture, foun-tain, point-less, meaning-ful, yel-low

ABBREVIATIONS, PAGE 356

1. The envelope read as follows:
   W. H. Cadrain
   104 Concord St.
   Hamden, CT 06514
2. Please be here by 6:15 A.M.
3. What happened in A.D. 313?
4. The Greek civilization reached its height between 500 B.C. and 400 B.C.
5. Major Harmon moved from Goldsboro, NC, to Washington, D.C., in 1998.

6. The label on the medicine read, "Take 200 mg of this antibiotic three times a day."

7. The last sentence in Kumar's lab report said, "The experiment produced three-fourths lb., or slightly more than one-third kg, of water."

8. I addressed the envelope to

> The Nature Conservancy
> 1815 N. Lynn St.
> Arlington, VA 22209

9. CBS stands for "Columbia Broadcasting System."

10. W. C. Fields was a popular comedian in early films.

NUMBERS AND NUMERALS, PAGE 359

1. In 1996 Portland, Oregon, had a population of about 481,000 people. *or* In 1996, ...

2. At that time Portland was the twenty-seventh largest city in the United States. *or* At that time, ...

3. What is five percent of sixty?

4. Richard Brinsley Sheridan was an acclaimed dramatist whose best-known works were produced after 1775.

5. A biography of Vincent Van Gogh can be found on pages 63–65 in your textbook.

6. South Dakota has a total land area of about 77,000 square miles.

7. That publishing house is located at 757 Third Avenue in New York City.

8. Four thousand seven hundred Elks attended the convention in Pittsburgh.

9. The International Monetary Fund loaned $16 billion to the new government.

10. The twenty-first century began with both fear and celebration.

PROOFREADING, PAGE 360
Edgar Allan Poe

1. Boston, Massachusetts, (commas to set off city and state); 1809 (numeral instead of spelled-out number)

2. no error

3–4. Mr. (period after abbreviation); law, the (sentence fragment)

5. no error

6. book, (comma to set off appositive); *Tamerlane and Other Poems,* (italics for book title)
7. no error
8. no error
9. City and (no comma between the parts of a compound predicate); immediately (spelling)
10. suspense, (comma in a series)
11. no error
12. no error
13. 1847, (comma to set off introductory adverb clause)

5. Mara's new dress was red and black.
6. The team members slapped their good-luck symbol one by one before they loped onto the field.
7. Why do you think the Bears will do well this season?
8. The teenagers danced energetically to the new song.
9. The delicate daffodils bobbed on long stems.
10. The colorful, sputtering pizza was ready to be cut.

CHAPTER 12
SENTENCE COMBINING

COMBINING SENTENCES BY INSERTING WORDS, PAGE 367

Answers will vary. Possible answers are given.

1. The day started out bright and sunshiny.
2. The thick stew was flavorful.
3. Would you like to take this cooking class?
4. The curious cat sniffed at my boots.

COMBINING SENTENCES BY INSERTING PREPOSITIONAL PHRASES, PAGE 368

Answers will vary. Possible answers are given.

1. The float for this year's homecoming parade is nearly ready.
2. Against the mirror was the letter that Ruby was expecting from her father.
3. In a frenzy of activity, Mom made a full breakfast in ten minutes.
4. With a surprising burst of speed, Odell caught the

pass and made the touchdown.

5. At the break of dawn, Marcel looked out the window.

6. With trembling fingers, the child opened the box.

7. Inside was a small gold locket on a delicate golden chain.

8. In sorrow, Asunción kissed her mother for the last time.

9. The day was clear and bright with a touch of spring in the air.

10. With a tremendous sense of guilt on behalf of his country, Mark read *Farewell to Manzanar.*

COMBINING SENTENCES BY INSERTING APPOSITIVE PHRASES, PAGE 370

Answers will vary. Possible answers are given.

1. The light, clear and bright, fell on Toni's upturned face.

2. I find one of Keats's poems, "Ode on a Grecian Urn," especially beautiful.

3. Aunt Grace, thin and pale, turned and looked at Tom.

4. This new book, *The New Arthritis Breakthrough,* seems to offer some hope for curing Grandma's arthritis.

5. Confident and eager, Dan breezed into the classroom.

6. Mr. Hanamoto, Saburo's father, is the featured speaker at our technology seminar.

7. The antique clock, dusty and worn, had been tucked away for years in the attic.

8. Have you met Hilda Lorenson, my aunt?

9. Which elective do you think you'll take next semester, French or Spanish?

10. Soledad, the new student body president, accepted the honor with humility and poise.

COMBINING SENTENCES BY INSERTING PARTICIPIAL PHRASES, PAGE 371

Answers will vary. Possible answers are given.

1. Having witnessed the accident only moments before, Megan rushed to help the victims.

2. Chung Sook watched his sister walking away.

3. The salesperson, tapping his foot, glared at Sandra.

4. Trenell looked at Marvella, his face etched with concern.

5. Poorly paid for his writing, Edgar Allan Poe died penniless.

6. The eight-year-olds danced around their fort made of hard-packed snow.

7. Looking for her sunglasses, Sally reached into her purse.

8. Wandering along the seashore, Natasha found a cowrie shell that had washed up on the sand.

9. Impressed by his son's bravery, the Creek chief declared him a warrior.

10. Known as the Corn State, Iowa is one of the leading producers of corn in the United States.

COMBINING SENTENCES USING COORDINATION, PAGE 373

Answers will vary. Possible answers are given.

1. Enrico enjoys both hiking and camping.

2. I sent a birthday card to Bob; however, he never got it.

3. Has your address changed, or is the card lost in the mail?

4. Either Dad and I will paint the house this summer or Dad will have aluminum siding put on the house.

5. Angela has just moved to this school district; therefore, she is not yet eligible for the varsity team.

6. Just as Richard likes salted peanuts on chocolate sundaes, he also likes to eat potato chips with a chocolate milkshake.

7. Marc is just learning to skate; he can't turn yet, nor can he stop.

8. Shawna likes science a lot, but she can't stand math.

9. I'm worried about Tomás; he won't eat right, and he won't take his medicine.

10. Darlene is petite, but she's a great volleyball player.

COMBINING SENTENCES USING SUBORDINATION: ADVERB CLAUSES, PAGE 375

Answers will vary. Possible answers are given.

1. As soon as you finish your homework, Reynaldo, you may call Danielle.
2. Because Steve forgot to study, he may have failed the geometry test.
3. Since Jamyce has the wrong information, Coretta is right.
4. Wherever you move, I will always be your friend.
5. You may go out with Dan provided that you are back by eleven o'clock.
6. Whenever Mom has to work, I cook dinner.
7. Although I like the works of most American authors, I don't like Faulkner's at all.
8. I don't care that Donna is moving away.
9. Since Isabel has three cats, she must love animals.
10. As long as you're here, let's work on our project.

COMBINING SENTENCES USING SUBORDINATION: ADJECTIVE CLAUSES, PAGE 376

Answers will vary. Possible answers are given.

1. Eastern North Carolina, which gets its share of hurricanes, is not the place to be during August and September.
2. The state, which is on the Atlantic seaboard, is prone to thunderstorms and lightning.
3. The skateboard that I donated to the neighborhood recreation center looks well used.
4. For his birthday I gave Patwin a memory box that is made of maple.
5. Gates of the Arctic National Park, which is in north-central Alaska, features a mountain range, tundra, winding rivers, broad valleys, and glacial lakes.
6. The gift whose bow has sequins and glitter is for Kamla.
7. Edvard Grieg, who was a native of Bergen, Norway, wrote the *Peer Gynt Suite.*
8. Grieg's quaint house, which is a monument to his simple life and his love of Norwegian folklore, can still be seen near Bergen.
9. England, whose name means "Land of the Angles," has been inhabited since well before Roman times.

10. The British empire, which reached its height during the Victorian Age, is smaller now but still strong.

9. The class scholar will be whoever has the highest average.
10. No one knows when the award will be presented.

COMBINING SENTENCES USING SUBORDINATION: NOUN CLAUSES, PAGE 378

Answers will vary. Possible answers are given.

1. Whoever wrote that essay deserves a prize.
2. Let's try to find out what made Edward sick.
3. That Wesley can write exquisite poetry is a source of satisfaction to him.
4. The Sage Award goes to whichever senior has shown the most improvement over four years.
5. The students still remember Eugene Sage, for whom the award is named.
6. Whatever you know about the incident should be shared with the principal.
7. Are you the freshman to whom Rafael sent the certificate?
8. Where Elijah went after math class is a mystery.

COMBINING SENTENCES USING SUBORDINATION, PAGE 379

Answers will vary. Possible answers are given.

1. Although scientists once thought the dawn redwood was extinct, several specimens were found in China.
2. Ellen, whose cat just had eight kittens, wants to be a veterinarian.
3. That Josephine's mother is the best cook in Minneapolis is no surprise to me.
4. Spotted Tail, who supported peaceful relations between the Sioux and the settlers, was a nineteenth-century leader of the Sioux.
5. When the present-day Sioux in South Dakota named their community college after Spotted Tail, they used his Sioux name, *Sinte Gleska.*

6. Whoever chose Stuttgart as the capital of Baden-Württemberg, Germany, did the entire region a favor.

7. The New Palace, which served as a residence for several dukes and kings of Württemberg, is built in the baroque and rococo styles.

8. I don't know why Paulo is late.

9. All I know is that William is fine.

10. As long as you're already up, please bring me a cold drink.

PROOFREADING, PAGE 380

Answers will vary. Check to be sure that you have combined only sentences that are closely related in meaning and that their combinations are logical. The following are possible sentence combinations.

Maya Angelou

1. Maya Angelou was born in 1928 in St. Louis, Missouri.

2. Angelou has been a successful singer, dancer, activist for African American rights, and author.

3. She toured in the Gershwin musical *Porgy and Bess* in Europe and in Africa.

4. She was editor of *African Review* for several years in Ghana.

5. In 1970 she published the first volume of her autobiography, *I Know Why the Caged Bird Sings*.

Anton Chekhov

1. Anton Chekhov was born in 1860 in Taganrog, Ukraine.

2. As a young man, he studied in Moscow to be a doctor. [no change]

3. At the age of twenty-six, while he was still a medical student, he published his first book of short stories.

4. It was successful, and he soon began to think of himself as a writer rather than a medical student.

5. All his life, he wrote brilliant short stories; indeed, even today Chekhov is regarded as a master of the short story genre.

6. He next tried to write full-length plays, but it took

him a long time to master playwrighting.

7. *The Seagull*, his first successful play, was written when he was thirty-six.

8. Three more theatrical masterpieces—*Uncle Vanya, The Three Sisters,* and *The Cherry Orchard*—followed in the next eight years.

9. *The Cherry Orchard* was published in 1904, the year he died of tuberculosis.

CHAPTER 13 SPELLING AND VOCABULARY

SPELLING RULES, PAGE 393

1. beige
2. supersede
3. abdomen
4. enjoyment
5. argument
6. unnoticed
7. putting
8. newsstand
9. daisies
10. deer

SPELLING DIFFICULT WORDS, PAGE 397

1. conscious, abdomen
2. pamphlet, hippopotamus
3. advertisement, pharmacy
4. elementary, arctic
5. fascinating, pastime
6. sufficient, buffet
7. conscientious, efficiency, exceed
8. concede, catastrophe
9. precede, descent
10. villain, complexion, ridiculous

USING CONTEXT CLUES, PAGE 401

1. obtained through observation and experimentation; definition
2. buildings; example
3. used up; comparison
4. touching, adjoining; example
5. following; contrast
6. a double or look-alike; definition
7. unpredictable, changeable; cause and effect
8. clean and tidy; contrast
9. pleasant and friendly; comparison
10. walking in one's sleep; general

ROOTS, PREFIXES, AND SUFFIXES, PAGE 429

Answers will vary. Students should be able to discuss the possible definitions of their words or pseudo-words by referring to the meanings of the prefixes, roots, and suffixes.

The following partial list includes only words formed using the ten given prefixes, roots, and suffixes.

convert, converter, convert-ible, cooperate, dejected, deport, disport, import, importer, indict, indictable, inject, injectable, inoperable, irreversible, operable, operate, porter, project, projectable, reject, reporter

Index

Months, abbreviations for, 82
Monuments, capitalizing names of, 301
Mood, creating, in descriptive writing, 451
Moral, morale, 65
Most, almost, 44
Multimedia presentation, creating visuals for, 521–524
Musical compositions, use of italics for titles of, 343
Must of, should of, would of, could of, might of, 54

Names
    capitalizing adjectives formed from people's, 298
    capitalizing for people, 297–298
    capitalizing of academic degrees, 299
Narrative writing, 452–456
    characters in, 452
    definition of, 452
    drafting in, 455–456
    fictional, 452
    historical, 452
    personal, 452
    plot in, 452
    prewriting in, 452–455
    setting in, 452
Nationalities, capitalizing names of, 299
Nauseated, nauseous, 65–66
Need, knead, 61
Negative comparison, 258
Negative words as adverbs, 116
Negatives, double, correcting, 266
Newspapers. *See also* Magazines; Periodicals
    italics for names of, 343
    locating articles in, 545–548

and periodicals in library, 531
    quotation marks to enclose article titles in, 341
Nicknames, enclosing in quotation marks, 298
Night, knight, 61
Nominative, predicate, **31,** 140, 227
    noun clauses as, 169–170
Nominative case, **8, 26,** 233
    for personal pronoun, 233, 234
Nonessential clauses, **26,** 168
Nonessential elements, use of commas to set off, 323–325
Nonfiction books, 539
    finding information in, 544–545
Nonrestrictive clauses,168
Nonsexist language, 444–445
Note cards, preparing, for research paper, 471–473
Notes
    in drafting research paper, 479–480
    taking, for prewriting, 447–448
    using, for research paper, 471–473
Noun clauses, **27,** 165, 169–170
    in combining sentences, 377–79
    diagraming, 286–287
    introductory words for, 377
Nouns, **26–27,** 93–97
    abstract, **4,** 95
    of amount and subject-verb agreement, 222
    collective, 97
        and subject-verb agreement, 220
    common, **10,** 96
    compound, 95
    concrete, **13,** 95
    definition of, 93
    gerund used as, 153
    infinitive used as, 154

Percentages, use of numerals to express amounts of, 358

Periodicals. *See also* Magazines; Newspapers
    locating articles in, 545–548

Periods, **29,** 314
    with abbreviations, 353–354
    as ellipses, 484
    to end declarative sentence, 171, 314
    to end imperative sentence, 171, 314
    with parentheses, 337
    with quotation marks, 339

Persecute, prosecute, 68

Personal, personnel, 68

Personal narrative, 452

Personal pronouns, **29–30,** 99–100, 233–238
    nominative case for, 233, 234, 238
    objective case for, 234, 238
    possessive case for, 233, 235

Personal questions, 438

Person in pronoun-antecedent agreement, 245–246

Personnel, personal, 68

Persuasive writing, 461–467
    definition of, 461
    drafting in, 463–467
    prewriting in, 461–463

Pets, capitalizing names of, 297

Phrases, **30,** 145–159
    adjective, 147–148
    adverb, **6,** 148
    appositive, **7,** 149–150
    combining sentences by inserting, 368–372
    definition of, 147
    gerund, **20,** 153
    infinitive, **22,** 155
    participial, **28,** 151–152
    prepositional, **31,** 118, 147–148
    verb, **40,** 108–109, 134

    verbal, **41,** 151

Piece, peace, 67–68

Plagiarism, avoiding, 473, 481

Plain, plane, 68

Planets, capitalizing names of, 301

Plays, use of italics for titles of, 343

Plot, constructing, in narrative writing, 452, 456

Plurals, spelling, 389–391

Poems
    capitalizing first word of each line in traditional, 294
    italics for titles of long, 343
    quotation marks to enclose titles of, 341

Point of view, choosing, in narrative writing, 455

Political parties, capitalizing names of, 299–300

Positive degree, **30,** 112, 117
    of modifiers, 256–258

Possession, apostrophes to show, 346–348

Possessive case, **8,** 233

Possessive nouns, 94
    as adjectives, 110

Possessive personal pronouns, 234–235

Possessive pronouns, **30,** 100
    as adjectives, 110

Postal abbreviations, 86–88, 354–355

Precede, proceed, 68

Precedence, precedents, 69

Predicate adjectives, **31,** 140
    diagraming, 277

Predicate nominative, **31,** 139–140
    diagraming, 277
    noun clause as, 169
    and subject-verb agreement, 227

Predicates, **30,** 131–134
    complete, 132
    compound, **12,** 134, 172
    definition of, 131

Teams, capitalizing names of, 299–300

Tear, 75

Television series
 italics for titles of, 343
 quotation marks to enclose titles of single episodes, 341

Tense, **39,** 195–203. *See under* Verbs
 future, **19,** 106, 198–199
 future perfect, **19,** 202
 past, **29,** 106, 198–201
 past perfect, **29,** 201
 present, **32,** 106, 195–197, 207
 present perfect, **31–32,** 200–201
 time line, 203

Than, pronouns after, 238

Than, then, 75–76

That, which, 168

That, which, who, 76

That there, this here, 76

Their, there, they're, 76

Theirs, there's, 76

Them, 76

Theme, communicating, in narrative writing, 452, 454

Then, than, 75–76

There, and subject-verb agreement, 226

There, they're, their, 76

There's, theirs, 76

Thesauruses, 560–561
 in descriptive writing, 450

These kinds, this kind, 77

Thesis statement, 442
 developing, in drafting research paper, 478–479

They, he, she, it, 59

They're, their, there, 76

Third-person limited narrator, 455

Third-person omniscient narrator, 455

Third-person point of view, 455

This here, that there, 76

This kind, these kinds, 77

Thorough, through, threw, 77

Threw, thorough, through, 77

Time
 abbreviations for, 83, 354
 numerals to express precise, 358
 use of colon between hour and minute of precise, 317

Titles
 of creative works
  capitalizing, 303–304
  italics for long, 343–344
  quotation marks for short, 341
  and subject-verb agreement, 222
 personal
  abbreviations for, 355
  capitalizing, 298
  commas to set off, 329

To, too, two, 77

Topics
 choosing
  for persuasive writing, 461–462
  for research paper, 469–470
 choosing and exploring as prewriting strategy, 434–439
 considering, in oral presentation, 515

Topic sentences, 442
 creating, for descriptive writing, 450

Toward, towards, 77

Towns, capitalizing names of, 300–301

Townships, capitalizing names of, 300–301

Trains, capitalizing names of, 302

Transitions, 449

Transitive verb, **39,** 106–107